Injury and the New World of Work

Edited by Terrence Sullivan

Injury and the New World of Work

UBCPress · Vancouver · Toronto

Printed in Canada on acid-free paper ∞

ISBN 0-7748-0747-4

Canadian Cataloguing in Publication Data

Main entry under title:

Injury and the new world of work

  Includes bibliographical references and index.
  ISBN 0-7748-0747-4

  1. Workers' compensation. 2. Occupational diseases. 3. Industrial accidents.
I. Sullivan, Terrence James, 1951-
HD7103.6I54 1999   368.41   C99-911018-7

UBC Press gratefully acknowledges the ongoing support to its publishing program from the Canada Council for the Arts and the British Columbia Arts Council. We also wish to acknowledge the financial support of the Government of Canada through the Book Publishing Industry Development Program (BPIDP) for our publishing activities.

Canada

Set in Stone by Val Speidel
Printed and bound in Canada by Friesens
Copy editor: Gail Copeland
Proofreader: Kate Baltais
Indexer: Patricia Buchanan

UBC Press
University of British Columbia
2029 West Mall
Vancouver, BC V6T 1Z2
(604) 822-5959
Fax: (604) 822-6083
E-mail: info@ubcpress.ubc.ca
www.ubcpress.ubc.ca

Contents

Figures and Tables

Tables

Acknowledgments

A number of the chapters in this collection began their life as submissions to the BC Royal Commission on Workers' Compensation in the spring of 1998. I would like to express my appreciation to the commission's Executive Director, Patrick Lewis; Research Director, Doug Hyatt; and the first Research Director, Dewey Evans, for their support and initiative in commissioning a number of the papers that were background for this volume. These papers have been substantially rewritten for the purposes of this collection. I would also like to thank the Ontario Workplace Safety and Insurance Board for their continued support for the work of the Institute for Work & Health. The Institute for Work & Health and its outstanding board, staff, and research associates have contributed much toward the original work injury research in this volume. I also acknowledge HEALNet, the Networks of Centres of Excellence in health research, which has supported the collaboration of a group of talented workplace investigators across Canada including a number in this volume. HEALNet supported the initial presentation and formulation of a number of ideas in the introductory chapter. Vincy Perri provided terrific administrative work in helping to chase down the materials, rendering chapters in a common format, and dealing with author redrafts and a range of important details with grace, humour, and exceptional competence. Emily Andrew, Camilla Jenkins, and two anonymous reviewers suggested numerous valuable improvements to the manuscript. My wife Cathy and children Megan, Jesse, Sarah, and Kate patiently helped me to maintain a balanced perspective on the changing world of disability and work.

Part 1: Introduction

1
Restating Disability or Disabling the State: Four Challenges

Terrence Sullivan and John Frank

> Of åll who follow the learned profession, those who are most exhausted
> by their studies are men who are preparing to publish an edition of their
> works and have set their hearts on winning immortal renown ... for very
> many are possessed by a mania for writing and hurry to publish stuff ...
> however, study is not so injurious to those who are satisfied with know-
> ing only what others have discovered and written (Ramazzini 1964, 385).

The disability concept owes its origins in the English tradition to the categories of the English poor laws and in the German tradition to the early
invalidity pensions of Bismarck (Stone 1984). Disability insurance programs have been intimately associated with the foundations and evolution
of the welfare state. As the administrative category has evolved in modern
states, the particular way each state defines and compensates for disability
embodies its distinct views of social justice. Every jurisdiction draws a precarious line between the expansion of needs-based justice and the preser-
vation of work-driven distribution of prosperity. In an era of globalization,
this line is more precarious than ever.

Ontario's Justice William Meredith is credited for his path-breaking
commission, which first established workers' compensation in Canada
(Meredith 1913). In his deliberations the key principles underlying workers' compensation schemes in Canada were laid out and largely endure to
this day. They encompassed the existing idea of compensation based on
work-relatedness rather than fault. Injured workers would be paid benefits
related to their earnings through an industry-financed scheme for as long
as the work-related disability endured. Such benefits would be in lieu of
any damages under the common law tort system. In short, this "historic
compromise" ensured that a worker would receive benefits, regardless of
fault, and an individual employer would be relieved of the responsibility to
pay benefits directly, regardless of fault. The fairness of the system was
such as to ensure "that an injured workman [sic] and his dependents shall
receive the compensation to which they are entitled and ... that the small
employer should not be ruined by having to pay compensation" (Meredith
1913, 3). Rather than relying on the individual employer obligations of the
British compensation law, Meredith was inspired more by the German
pooled social insurance model in the design of workers' compensation in
Canada, a scheme that resulted in the creation of a collective liability fund
for employers (Plumb and Cowell 1998).

Circumstances have changed significantly since Meredith and several factors compel some reconsideration of the foundation principles of workers' compensation. It is easy to be attached to a conservative view of policy change in the stormy world of workers' compensation – a historic policy innovation that combines fairness, insurance, tort principles, *realpolitik,* and medicine in one large, complex, articulated, and evolving administrative mechanism. Likewise one might be tempted to leap to bold and sometimes risky solutions to the challenges that face modern workers' compensation schemes, especially in an era that embraces the reduction of state and payroll regulatory burdens in order to sustain global investment appeal and competitiveness.

Workers' compensation sprang up as an institutional innovation to assist a society adjusting to the realities of the industrial revolution. The use of new forms of energy, hazardous forms of resource extraction and mass production, and new employment patterns and relationships placed workers in precarious situations regarding their health and livelihood. Today, we are in the midst of an industrial revolution no less dramatic than that at the turn of the last century. The present revolution is driven by the substitution of microchips and ingenuity for neurons and brawn. We are facing important changes in our labour force, driven by the forces of competitive globalization, by the kind of work we are all engaged in, by the new management practices and organizational arrangements in our places of work, by the pace and complexity of our work, and by the explosion of knowledge and technology.[1]

The original principles and administrative apparatus of workers' compensation in Canada, however appealing and sacrosanct they appear, may not serve us quite so well for another 100 years. We will argue that there are four fundamental challenges to the original formulation that warrant some deliberation in the evolution of workers' compensation policies in Canada.

The first challenge concerns the new world of work and labour market realities, which have changed dramatically since Meredith. The pervasive use of technology, new management and human resource practices, and the growth of knowledge-intensive and service industries have had substantial effects on the nature of compensable injuries. Indeed, they have had effects on all work-related health outcomes – what we will call here the industrial/epidemiological shift. Labour market changes also generate broader and pervasive effects on the overall health of populations as a function of wage polarization and distributive effects. From the perspective of the administration of workers' compensation, the growth of contingent, part-time, and non-standard employment has made more limited the regulatory sweep of prevention and the assignment of firm-level responsibility for injury and premiums.

The second challenge concerns the prevention of injury and disease, driven by our growing understanding of the social organization of health, injury, and disease.

New critical studies of various treatments' efficacy, and of the need for balance between clinical, workplace, and insurance approaches in treating and managing new forms of workplace injury constitute our third challenge: the timely treatment of injury and safe return to work.

We have long understood how work environments affect our health in the many disease-specific ways historically associated with workers' compensation (Barth 1998; Joseph 1983). Now we are facing the reality that work conditions affect health in a variety of pervasive and non-disease-specific ways, across a wide range of disease state outcomes (Johnson and Hall 1995; Karasek and Theorell 1990). This knowledge of generalized effects of work conditions, however, is emerging at a time of intense global pressures to deregulate and keep the domestic market attractive to investment, with predictable downward pressure on payroll costs and payroll financed benefits. Simply stated, our knowledge presses to enlarge entitlement while our economy acts to constrain it. Taken together, these factors create the fourth and final major challenge, a policy "trilemma": balancing the expanding scope of entitlement, relative fairness, and financial sustainability of compensation arrangements in an era of liberalized trade arrangements.

This introductory chapter explores these four challenges briefly and by so doing provides a thematic introduction to the thirteen essays that follow. Taken together, the essays in this volume explore these four challenges using some original labour force and injury data from British Columbia, Ontario, and Quebec. These local data help to place the Canadian issues squarely in a comparative North American and international frame of reference. The essays are authored by a group of talented Canadian researchers who have tackled these thematic problems of workers' compensation from a variety of disciplines.

The Industrial-Epidemiological Shift

Although sometimes overstated, significant changes are going on in the nature and quantity of work (Rifkin 1995). In Canada, the changes in our labour market have been significant. As have a number of western European countries, we too have struggled with chronically high levels of unemployment (Sullivan et al. 1998). The dynamics of the Canadian changes have been carefully summarized by others (Betcherman and Lowe 1997; Gunderson and Riddell 1996). These include the permanent change of greater participation of women in the labour force. Women's occupational health problems are poorly studied, they experience different exposure to injury and health problems, and they face different recovery challenges (Messing 1998). A number of these gender-specific challenges are well illustrated in the essay by Chung et al. in this volume. In their working life, women report more negative work characteristics than men, mainly because of differences in learning opportunities, and more monotonous work (Matthews et al. 1998).

In addition to the gender differences, there have been notable swings away from manufacturing and resource extraction toward service jobs in Canada. Changing workplace realities are also driven in part by new management practices that reduce the number of secure jobs to core business lines. The use of just-in-time and lean production methods, and contracting out non-core work has led to a rise in small business employment, contingent, and non-standard work. Indeed, these management changes have signalled some important societal-level changes in the employment "contract" between workers and employers (Betcherman and Lowe 1997).

The historical perspective of the resource-service swing in the Canadian economy is well illustrated in the chapter by Ostry on changes in British Columbia. This shift, and its associated injury patterns and costs, are projected into the future by Gunderson and Hyatt in this volume. Ostry notes in his chapter that for every four jobs in the forestry sector in British Columbia in the 1950s, there were three in the service sector. In the late 1990s, there are four service-sector jobs for each job in the forestry sector. The consequences for the kinds of work available and, therefore, the kinds of injury seen are dramatic. Many of the fatalities and serious injuries in British Columbia are in the forestry sector. A growing service sector and a shrinking forestry sector have produced a reduction in costly acute and sometimes fatal injuries, and a slow growth in soft tissue injuries (sprains and strains) associated with service work. This is exactly what Ostry found in his descriptive epidemiology of British Columbia using Workers' Compensation Board records over the last fifty years. As the labour force changes, so does the background composition of population health and injury against which workers' compensation is overlaid.

The productivity of an economy and the design of work environments affect the individual and aggregate health of workers in complex ways as illustrated in Figure 1.1. Figure 1.1 maps out areas of researchable levels and pathways by which work affects health.[2] These areas include the population level consequences of labour market experiences on health (labelled Labour market/Population effects), the effects of management and design processes at the workplace level (Workplace effects), and overall effects of rehabilitation process (Rehabilitation effects). In our view, the manner in which labour markets affect health status may be characterized in much greater detail than previously considered and is worthy of more extensive study (Lavis 1997; Sullivan et al. 1998). Regional trade blocs condition the regulatory frame for labour and health policy (Walters 1997). Likewise, the historical industrial base and gender mix in the workforce affect the nature of job exposures and vulnerability. The amount of work –

Figure 1.1

Conceptual map of how work affects health

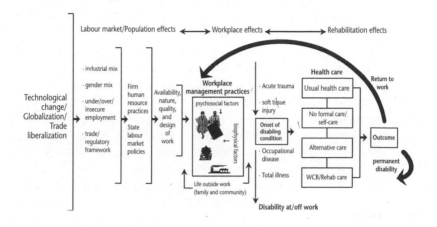

Source: IWH (1998).

over-, under-, or unemployed – and the community context all appear to have health impacts on the labour force. As well, organizational and management practices, job design, and process engineering affect worker health. Finally, the use and efficacy of different types of health care services and coordinated disability management practices all affect the health of workers and their eventual return to work.

The graded, stepwise manner in which overall health risks are distributed by occupational grouping and socio-economic status is fairly well documented (Blane et al. 1996). Those at the lower end of the occupational and income scale do more poorly on a host of health outcomes, including injury. Jobs low on the occupational hierarchy (production helpers, labourers, janitors, nursing orderlies, truckers, machine operators, freight handlers, construction helpers, food preparation workers) also experience the most injury and the most costly injury (Leigh and Miller 1997), and manual workers seem more vulnerable to the effects of job strain on heart disease (Hallqvist et al. 1998). Therefore, any serious focus on the health of workers needs to be both sensitive to the pervasive occupational gradient in health and concerned with the full range of factors affecting the health of the working population, as well as responsive to the concentration of risks at the lower end of the occupational hierarchy (Johnson and Hall 1995; Mustard 1999).

Outside of the workers' compensation system, there are important effects on workers' health associated with the increased polarization of labour markets and income distribution. It has long been understood that absolute levels of income affect the health of populations (Evans et al. 1994). Changes in the nutritional status and health of the workforce are important in explaining the sudden rise in prosperity and the longevity of the total population since the eighteenth century (Frank and Mustard 1994; Fogel 1993).

There is now growing evidence in advanced economies, albeit not without contention, that equitable income distribution in the population income levels is a driver of overall – not just mean or median – health status in the population (Wilkinson 1996; Sullivan 1998; Mustard 1999). Recently, Kaplan and colleagues showed a surprisingly strong association between the proportion of income earned by the bottom 50 percent of the population within all US states and a variety of state-level health and social indicators. They also found that the share of total income received by the 10 percent who were least well off was predictive of smaller mortality declines over the decade from 1980 to 1990 (Kaplan et al. 1996). Interestingly, a comparable American study using two other income inequality measures, the Robin Hood index and the Gini coefficient, found similar correlations between state-level income dispersion and health (Kennedy et al. 1996). This latter study also concluded that inequality in the distribution of income explained a significant portion of cross-state variance in a number of cause-specific mortality rates, independent of poverty and smoking, and that policies dealing with the growing inequities in US income dispersion may have considerable impact on the health of the population. This view has been echoed by others in the European jurisdiction (Wennemo 1993; Whitehead 1995). Across jurisdictions, the increased income dispersion associated with labour market polarization appears to suppress the total health status of populations in which incomes are more dispersed relative to those with better income equity, even when the median income of the population is the same.[3]

The rise in non-standard, contingent work and outsourcing are areas of concern for workers' compensation. Perhaps most broadly, the growth in employment insecurity has been associated with reported health problems (Arnetz et al. 1991; Heaney et al. 1994; Ferrie et al. 1995). The growth of outsourcing and non-standard work presents special challenges for health and safety efforts associated with workers' compensation (Quinlan 1997). Recent Australian research indicates that occupational health and safety outcomes may be poorer for self-employed workers (Mayhew et al. 1997). Quinlan suggests this is being driven by three factors: economic and reward factors, disorganization, and increased likelihood of regulatory failure. Reward pressures drive self-employed workers to work excessive hours and cut corners in relation to safety. Contractors unfamiliar with safety procedures may precipitate disorganizing consequences from their actions on other workers at a particular work site. Regulations and compliance programs often fail to address subcontracting and small owner-operator firms.

The casualization of employment is an important part of rising labour force participation for women and may pose a special mental health burden for them (Chung et al., this volume; Santana et al. 1997). Casual workers are more likely to be younger and less risk averse than older, experienced workers; they are less likely to receive health and safety training, and to have specific job knowledge and hazards information in workplaces where they are temporarily assigned – often with some alienation related to being assigned to the least favourable jobs. Recent work from Minnesota in the US suggests that being a contingent worker is associated with longer non-work spells and greater claim submission incentives (Park et al. 1998). On the other hand, contingent workers are often not fully covered by workers' compensation benefits, and they account for a small portion of all claims. The argument is made that contingent workers are more likely to claim since they face higher risk environments, and have higher incentives to file claims because of poorer benefits (including little if any health insurance in the US), poorer monitoring of claims, and poorer employment security. Nonetheless, other evidence (Tarasuk and Eakin 1994; Hogg-Johnson and Cole 1998) clearly suggests that workers who feel their employment tenure is threatened by filing claims experience longer disability durations; contingent workers could be expected to more frequently have this perception.

Other work by Silverstein et al. (1998) in Washington State suggests that the relative rate of musculoskeletal injuries for temporary workers is much higher in a range of industries. Compared to the overall sector, temporary service workers in assembly work have a relative injury rate range between 4.1 and 8.0. For machine operators the range is 4.8 to 7.4. Temporary service health care workers are at 4.7 times the risk for sciatica, and temporary warehousing workers are at 3 times the risk for gradual onset hand-wrist disorders. We need further empirical study to segregate the effects of the relative youth of temporary workers from the effects of safety training and additional job hazards of temporary work. But it is clear that temporary and contingent work present special prevention and liability challenges that warrant a new approach, or possibly some kind of tiered approach to safety and compensation.

Concurrent with labour market shifts in the distribution of income and kind and amount of employment, the kind of injury, disability, and disease faced by workers has changed quite significantly over the last fifty years. Although catastrophic acute injuries, fatalities, and classical occupational disease remain the priority for workers' compensation prevention initiatives, the new world of work is one in which work-related musculoskeletal strains, sprains, and pains constitute most injuries and the majority of costs in North America. Some of the rise in strains and sprains has been associated with the growth of lean production methods in manufacturing and service jobs, but the growth in scale and prevalence of these conditions cannot be fully explained by the pace of production alone. Pace of production and cycle time pressure are important especially in manufacturing, assembly line work, and in work involving urgent deadlines (Wokutch 1992; Lewchuck and Robertson 1996; Brooker et al. 1997; Polanyi et al. 1997). Work-related musculoskeletal disorders (WMSDs) often have a poorly defined physiological pathogenesis and appear sensitive to both biomechanical and psychosocial risk and remedial factors, as described in the chapters by Norman and Wells, Kerr, Hogg-Johnson et al., and Tunks, Crook, and Crook in this volume. They are genuine mind-body problems that appear very sensitive to poor psychosocial work conditions (Toomingas et al. 1997; Kerr et al. 1998). In contrast to acute injuries with obvious discrete tissue damage, WMSDs are often insidious in their onset and require different methods of risk assessment and different approaches to prevention and treatment, matters to which we will shortly turn. In addition, the decline of standard employment arrangements suggests that we need a new and different approach to prevention, adjudication, regulation, and rate-setting for non-standard work, with the corollary new approach to the prevention of injury and disease among contingent workers.

Prevention of Injury and Disease
What makes a difference in preventing injury and occupational disease? The three broad traditional strategies for prevention have included regulatory and enforcement process, incentive mechanisms, and the internal responsibility system. As O'Grady notes in his chapter in this volume, it is less important to consider which one "works best" than it is to strike the right balance between the three approaches. Indeed, there may be a case for rebalancing in favour of firm-level internal responsibility systems and intervention.

As we have pointed out elsewhere, the major challenge of prevention in modern workplaces is no longer simply the exercise of informed individual choice in safety behaviour or health behaviour (Polanyi et al., forthcoming). While there has been progress on the reduction of injury at work over the last few decades, fatalities and disease remain as major challenges. New epidemiological and biomechanical studies, respectively reviewed by Kerr and by Norman and Wells in this volume, highlight areas of promise and challenge in applying what we know about causation to prevention at the firm level. It is one thing to understand the role of biomechanical exposure in injury. It is quite another to intervene in the work process in small or large companies to alter such exposures. It is yet another to introduce threshold limit values to regulate work environments for such exposures.

The bold step recently taken in British Columbia to introduce an ergonomics regulation will be watched closely all over North America for its impact on job design and injury reporting. Even with such a progressive step, one should not be surprised if future declines in injury rates are not dramatic, Lanoie's (1992) study of the short-term effects of health and safety regulation on injury showed little overall effect on injury rates. This weak role for regulation as an effective prevention mechanism was recently underscored in a review by Kralj (forthcoming), who emphasized the role of the internal responsibilities, and firm process alongside system and experience rating in reducing injury rates. There can be little argument that experience rating programs have reduced reported injury rates, but as Thomason points out in this volume, this decline comes with some perverse incentive effects on workers and employers. Moreover, the market model of workers receiving higher wages for higher hazard jobs is one that can be argued to be wrong in some fatality cases (Leigh 1989).

To understand that job structure, decision latitude, psychological demand, effort-reward imbalance, and the social relationships at work all influence the genesis of soft tissue injury is one thing, but as managers at General Motors put it to the researchers following a three-year study there: can you engineer psychosocial factors into the production of cars? Perhaps the first step on the road to altering psychosocial exposure at work is to understand that several psychosocial effects arise from the interaction of job structure and worker perception, as Kerr notes in his chapter. The job structure provides us with one possible modifiable point of prevention, possibly through the internal responsibility system.

Perhaps the biggest challenge in serious prevention research work is to take account of the "long wave" labour force composition changes noted by Gunderson and Hyatt, and Ostry, in this volume. It may be a hollow victory to declare success in the field of prevention when injury rates are already falling owing to a changing sectoral composition in the labour market.

The points of intervention for some of this new prevention work may come from Shannon's review of firm-level factors in this volume. The organizational and management practices of the modern workplace, and the age and experience of its workforce, are powerful predictors of injury rates at the "meso level" of the company or the workplace. The importance of building management commitment to prevention has long been understood in companies like Dupont as Shannon notes. The key role for an empowered health and safety committee is perhaps not surprising. It may be here, once again, that the enlightened activism of joint health and safety committees holds some promise for improving the psychosocial aspects of job structure. By contrast, the prevention of particular diseases and fatalities is an area where education regulation and enforcement will continue to be important.

Taken together, the chapters on prevention in this volume suggest an agenda for a new round of management-level psychosocial and biomechanical intervention in the workplace, alongside rigorous documentation of what works and what doesn't to reduce injury, illness, and disability. Stronger multivariate methods and careful firm-level analysis are sorely required if researchers are to play a helpful role here. Getting the commitment of business, labour, and the insurance industry to engage in partnered research and the application of new research evidence is a formidable challenge that may require additional incentives to proceed on any kind of large scale.

In the minds of some leaders in the field, the most promising pathway to prevention in the workplace may be through the subsequent interventions triggered by injury, and the promise of secondary intervention focused on work-station improvement and disability management (Frank et al. 1996b; Battié 1992; Loisel et al. 1994). It is to these matters we now turn.

Timely, Effective Treatment and Safe Return to Work

The slow rise of soft tissue injury, and particularly low back pain, as the main cause of disability in North American workplaces has only recently been met with a range of high-quality studies on what makes a difference and what doesn't in treating these injuries and promoting rapid recovery. It used to be thought that early aggressive intervention was always the preferred mode, but as Hogg-Johnson et al. and Brooker et al. point out in this volume, careful phasing in of medical rehabilitation is required to promote return to function and return to work. In particular, there are few conventional medical interventions in the early acute stage of low back and other soft tissue injury (the first three to four weeks) that appear to make a difference. Indeed, aggressive medical intervention in the acute stages of uncomplicated soft tissue injury may actually have iatrogenic side effects – slower recovery and delayed return to work (Frank et al. 1998). On the other hand, well-designed, staged interventions involving successive job-linked rehabilitation interventions and offers of job modification in the sub-acute period (six to twelve weeks) for those still off work with low back pain may be quite effective in promoting recovery and return to work (Frank et al. 1996a, 1996b, 1998). Studies by Yassi et al. (1995) and Loisel et al. (1994, 1997) also highlight the importance of individualized and firm-level ergonomic interventions, at the work station and workplace respectively, as being critical to reducing lost time and promoting recovery. Likewise, a people-oriented culture at the workplace, early non-coercive contact with the workplace after injury, the availability of modified work, and unionization are all factors that appear to facilitate early return to work without adverse health effects on the injured worker (Sinclair et al. 1998).

Frank et al. (1998) recently reviewed the key studies for low back pain in the last few years and argue compellingly that much can be done to bring down the burden of this, the largest injury category. Engagement of the major stakeholder audiences – the workplace parties, the health care providers and patients, and the insurers – is crucial to successful secondary prevention. It is these stakeholders who must act in concert to coordinate well-considered medical-, workplace-, insurer-based interventions necessary to promote recovery and return to work.

Primary and secondary preventive interventions for disability from soft tissue injury, and especially mechanical low back pain, now have some base of evidence on which to proceed. And as Hogg-Johnson et al. note, we are beginning to have a clearer picture of the potpourri of medical interventions that are effective for upper-extremity injuries. But what of the treatment effectiveness for chronic pain? There is reason to be cautious about initial return to work as the only indicator of success, since repeated lost time events and the subsequent development of chronic pain create the biggest areas of cost and the most intractable cases. Chronic pain from WMSD has attracted much attention recently. The mixed range of treatment remedies available is carefully reviewed in the chapter by Tunks, Crook, and Crook in this volume. The biggest question regarding chronic pain facing workers' compensation boards in Canada is whether such pain arising from WMSD, in the absence of obvious pathophysiology, should be de-insured by workers' compensation following so-called normal recovery times. Indeed, at the time of writing this issue is topical in Ontario, Alberta, and Nova Scotia. This issue of chronic pain is but one of the challenging issues of entitlement that constitute the final challenge for workers' compensation.

Entitlement, Fairness, and Sustainability in Workers' Compensation
Workers' compensation systems have shared the essential requirement that the injury suffered by the employee must be work-related if the worker is to be compensated. In order for an injury or disease to be compensable under a system of workers' compensation, it must have arisen "out of and in the course of employment." This coverage formula imports legal notions of factual causation into workers' compensation regimes, analogous to the investigation of causation carried out in common-law personal injury actions (Joseph 1983).

With acute physical injury at the workplace, the causal connection between work and harm is readily apparent. Where a hand has been mangled by machinery, a worker has fallen from a scaffold or been burned by a welder, or a foreign object has entered an eye or killed a worker, the causal connection is quite clear. Such cases usually involve readily demonstrable physical trauma or acute pathophysiology, occurring at a specific place and at a definite moment in time, with unequivocal onset and an immediate effect on the worker. There is little room for debate as to causation. These events establish the prima facie case that the injury arose "out of employment" – i.e., that the nature or character of the employment was the origin or cause of the injury. Even the contentious field of entitlement determination for fatal work-related death benefits, as Terry Thomason illustrates in his review in this volume, does not suffer the indeterminacy of most modern injury categories. The determination of death benefits is driven less often toward whether the accident was work-related. Rather, it is more often a struggle over how we should properly pay out the benefit.[4]

Given the rapid process of industrialization under way at the time when most workers' compensation legislation was passed, as well as the kind of work then carried out in the factories, mills, and mines of the day, policy makers were rightly preoccupied with the prevalent hazards of the day. The drafters of early legislation probably had in mind extending coverage to bona fide victims of the new technology of the machine age, and to the particular risks of each occupation (Vinson 1996). Workers' compensation systems were initially conceived primarily in terms of compensating workers for acute injuries sustained in the workplace, and so the requirement of a causal link between the work and the injury did not pose much of a problem.

Similarly, with respect to the coverage of industrial disease, it was originally contemplated that workers' compensation should not turn into a general sick-pay scheme and that coverage should be restricted to physician-diagnosed diseases specific to industry diseases that do not normally result from other causes.

The historical concept of causation that underlies workers' compensation legislation originated in a world where workers performed heavy labour in hazardous conditions and tended to suffer from "hard" or acute injuries such as lacerations, broken bones, severed limbs, or specific intoxications by chemical hazards. While such injuries and diseases have by no means disappeared, the workplace and the nature of work itself have undergone transformations and such injuries no longer constitute the majority of claims and cost. In 1994, 190,557 claims for sprains and strains were accepted by workers' compensation boards and commissions across Canada. In the same year, only 23,457 fracture claims were accepted (Statistics Canada 1995).[5]

Technology has largely (but not completely) replaced hard labour; service industries now employ more people than do the manufacturing or resource sectors; new methods of management, organization, and production have altered workers' traditional roles; and the last fifty years have seen a transition from premature death arising largely from infectious disease to a longer life, but one filled with more chronic disabling conditions. Firm management and workers feel the pressures from their competition and the media to scrutinize non-competitive regulatory practices. The prominent and most reported workplace health problems in contemporary North America are those of soft tissue and repetitive motion injuries, conditions of imprecise etiology, sometimes long latency periods, and often insidious onset, as well as mental health and stress conditions. Similarly, a number (but not all) of the industrial diseases of today are workplace exaggerations of the "natural" diseases of ageing. The consequential challenge to entitlement is skilfully presented in the chapters by Frank and Maetzel, and Gnam, in this volume.

Yet, despite the transition from the unequivocal health conditions of the old world of work to the slow-onset, less specific conditions associated with the new competitive order for which workers tend to be compensated today, and despite our growing understanding of the pervasive role played by occupation and socio-economic status in the causation of disease generally, workers' compensation systems continue to view causation principally in the traditional linear sense of "one cause, one condition."

The relationship between occupational exposures and health conditions may now be grossly characterized as follows (see Table 1.1). Many original industrial accidents had fairly unequivocal occupational causation, so entitlement was not an issue under the original Meredith scheme. With the slow-onset, insidious conditions characteristic of most soft tissue injury, occupational causation, although widely acknowledged, is contentious. More contentious still is evidence that conditions at work may accelerate some major diseases of ageing, creating a significant challenge to the original scheme, which was based on harms arising from occupational causes.

Frank and Maetzel make the case that the work-attributable risk associated with back pain (the single largest claim category for workers' compensation in North America) is comparable, on current epidemiological evidence, to that associated with heart disease and occupationally linked osteoarthritis of the knee and hip. The difference is that these latter two conditions, which are quite prevalent in the working population, are often not recognized in workers' compensation regimes. Were they to be more frequently recognized, the consequence would be a spectacular rise in compensation costs associated with the recognition of these relationships. Modern workers' compensation schemes have to trade off fairness (why are WMSDs compensated when osteoarthritis of the knee and hip and heart disease have comparable work-related risks?) with sustainability. Concerns for sustainability suggest that entitling these latter conditions would generate a dramatic rise in benefits and premium rates (Shainblum et al., forthcoming).

As Gnam argues in his chapter in this volume, the same general argument is made for mental stress claims, especially so-called mental-mental claims. Similarly, the growth of costs is the main motive for restricting coverage for chronic pain arising from WMSD, a move which Tunks et al. (this volume) point out is contentious and difficult to justify, given our knowledge of pain. "Mental-mental" claims are those where the exposures are

Table 1.1

Linking occupational exposure and disease

Nature of occupational causation	Example conditions	Causation	Entitlement status
Unequivocal occupational causation of occupational condition	• Lead poisoning • Asbestosis • Crush, cut, fracture at work	• Clear causation and toxicity specific to occupational exposure • Lung changes leading to respiratory distress • Biomechanical insult	Frequently scheduled as occupational disease and injuries – claims almost always accepted
Occupational-social environments increase risk of occupational/ non-occupational conditions	• "Occupational low back pain" and carpal tunnel syndrome from biomechanical/ psychological loads at work	• Multifactorial causation • Interacting worker-/work-related risk factors exceeding exposure threshold for condition	Contentious scheduling, with frequent individual adjudication — highly variable across jurisdictions and cases
Work environment exposure accelerating chronic diseases of later life	• Heart disease • Osteoarthritis	• Multifactorial causation • Job strain (psychosocial factors) accelerating cardiovascular changes • Job biomechanical exposures accelerating arthritic process	Rarely recognized despite good recent science suggesting occupational causation is important

said to be mental stressors and the health problem caused is some state of general mental stress or strain. As Gnam points out, such claims generated a dramatic rise in claims and cost in the litigious environment of California prior to 1990, fuelling a perception that mental stress claims would easily expand out of control. The absence of an objective physical measurement of impaired body function (e.g., in low back pain) is usually presumably seen as a powerful argument to disallow claims in order to avoid rewarding "fraudulent claims." This mechanistic bias appears notwithstanding the fact that the odds of such injury associated with biomechanical exposure are equivalent to cardiovascular disease associations with robust psychosocial variables such as job strain or effort-reward imbalance (as reviewed by Kerr, and Frank and Maetzel, in this volume).

With most jurisdictions trying to bring down the payroll burden to make local markets attractive to foreign investors and reduce costs, the enlargement of entitlement seems a tough sell. On the other hand, some restriction of entitlement, as was done in the case of stress for the State of California, may allow for the broadening of entitlement when a high threshold of causation evidence is required. Whether or not the epidemiology – not to mention the clinical judgment – is up to such precise hair-splitting, remains a major impediment to the careful and fair restriction of entitlement, as pointed out by Frank and Maetzel, and Gnam, in their essays in this volume.

While WMSDs are fairly well established in case law in most of North America, some investigators are making arguments that the entitlement playing field should be made fair not by levelling up, but by levelling down. Using Ontario data, Johnson et al. (1998) argue that the only way to get something close to an unbiased estimate of occupational back pain (as opposed to an injury rate inflated by perverse incentives) is to discount the benefit level by something in the order of 25 percent for back injuries and possibly other soft tissue injuries as well. Incentive effects are indeed demonstrable in a range of studies of workers' compensation systems (Hirsch 1997), although as Thomason points out in his review in this volume, disentangling perverse incentive effects on workers' claim behaviour and perverse incentive effects on firms' injury reporting appears a formidable challenge. At one extreme end of the continuum, Shorter (1997) has contentiously argued that many modern health complaints including occupational complaints of chronic pain, repetitive strain injuries, and WMSD are shaped and constructed by a culture that did not exist historically, but are analogous to Victorian "hysteria" or "neurasthenia."

Whether entitlement should be levelled up or down is the single most contentious issue in workers' compensation systems and reflects the larger debate surrounding trade liberalization and its effects on harmonization of labour policies and social benefits (Gunderson 1998). This entitlement question is even more vexatious in jurisdictions where unfunded liabilities exist and have driven recent reforms (Bogyo 1995). However, the economists would point out that there is an "efficient" level of wage replacement discernible by economic modelling.

What is rarely noted in the benefit debate is that the cost of any increased benefit is likely to be shifted back to workers. Dungan (forthcoming) recently modelled the macroeconomic effects of a number of workers' compensation benefit level adjustments on the Ontario and Canadian economies. He did show some modest predictable transitional adjustments in jobs and GDP associated with benefit level changes. However, benefit increases create job losses in the short term until these are shifted back to labour as lower wages. In short, he challenges the view of increased payroll costs as "durable" job killers. Something in the order of 80 percent of increased payroll costs come directly out of a worker's wage packet, not the employer's profit (Dahlby 1993). Alternatively, some of the costs of such increases might be passed on through exchange rate mechanisms that ultimately affect the standard of living. Freeman (1994: 105) has argued: "If Canadians want to spend more on occupational health and safety than Americans, and if the cost of such is not shifted back to Canadian workers, Canadian firms will be at a competitive disadvantage at a particular exchange rate. But then the Canadian dollar will depreciate versus the US dollar and all Canadians will bear the cost of the higher health and safety standards through the higher cost of imported goods from the United States." In the new competitive order, higher benefits will be paid for one way or the other. In the tug of war over the level of benefits, the "historic compromise" is now operating in a different industrial power structure than when it originated.

When workers' compensation began, the state (driven by the intercession of the courts and state-sponsored enquiries) mediated bilateral conflict between labour and capital. In a global economy of footloose capital, the moorings of the nation-state have been slipped in favour of a complex range of regional and multilateral trade agreements that bind nation-states. Jurisdictional competition for investment and jobs may well drive investment on some aggregate basis toward the jurisdictions with the least amount of labour regulation. In a liberalized trade environment capital can be footloose, but labour cannot. Skilful multinationals can play off workers and states one against the other to win concessions on wages and benefits. In such circumstances, the regulatory retreat by governments becomes akin to wage concession (Gunderson 1998). In such concessions, it is workers who stand to lose. One difficult role for governments in this new competitive order will be to broker some balance in a workers' compensation world where capital has far greater influence in the political process than it had during William Meredith's time. The modern challenge is to ensure that governments are not disabled in their workers' compensation efforts by the foreign direct investment imperatives of trade liberalization. Rather, the challenge is to bring the best available science to bear to modernize workers' compensation schemes based on an understanding of new forms of work-related disablement, some of which are preventable processes rather than discrete events.

In one of the first case studies of upward regulatory harmonization, Walters (1997) reviewed the implementation of the European Union directive on preventive health and safety services. He concluded that there was some limited legislative and operational impact in Northern Europe, with large gaps still present between Northern and Southern Europe.

In the modernization of workers' compensation there is cause for some optimism. Somehow, despite different political traditions and histories, every province in Canada has provincial monopoly of workers' public compensation regimes with quite similar administrative features built largely from the original principles of Meredith (Bogyo 1995).[6] This soft harmonization of Canadian approaches is driven by historical tradition and political imperative in the absence of any obvious federal or national standard for workers' compensation. All provinces are also now working actively to eliminate or prevent unfunded liabilities.

Recent work on the costs of workers' compensation in Canada and the United States by Terry Thomason and John Burton (forthcoming) suggests that Canadian workers' compensation systems are very competitive with their American counterparts. They conclude that British Columbia, and to a lesser extent Ontario, enjoy a relative cost advantage when compared to the United States after controlling for a number of differential factors including benefit levels, compensation coverage injury rates, the proportion of permanent partial disability claims, and union density. As is the case with health insurance, some forms of public or publicly regulated disability insurance may outperform private and fully competitive insurance markets because of the unique problems of market failure in the health and disability insurance markets (Drache and Sullivan 1999). The challenge is to allow for some competitive pressure in workers' compensation systems to make public agencies more efficient, without foregoing the scale benefits of public monopoly collection and administration.

If one believes Thomason and Burton, the marginally higher benefits afforded by public monopolies in Canada may be preserved if we can meet the challenge of keeping the systems efficient, competitive, and well managed. Our experiments with WCB governance in Canada have perhaps armed us with better models for managing this complex policy area (Thomason et al. 1995). Many problems in the US workers' compensation systems can be traced to the massive shifting of costs for health care, because workers' compensation allows higher benefits and pays more for health care and legal services than most private health insurance, in the largely private US health insurance marketplace. It may indeed be the rela-. tively lower cost of health care in Canada that keeps workers' compensation competitive with US comparators.

In revisiting workers' compensation, it is important to recall its historic purposes: to prevent workers and their families from becoming destitute as a result of injury or disease, and to ensure employers were not bankrupted by the obligation to pay directly for work injury or disease. These twin social objectives would appear to remain important aspects of any future model of workers' compensation. Achieving these objectives must be separated from the means of achieving them. The introduction of competitive processes, new incentive methods, and so on must not be confused with the social objectives of workers' compensation. Like medicare, workers' compensation was developed precisely because of the failure of private insurance markets to adequately protect injured workers. Market mechanisms may represent potential ways of delivering more efficiently on the original social objectives. However, when the means and the ends are conflated we begin to believe it is justified to arbitrarily de-insure or shift the risk for particular disease or injury conditions where good evidence exists of work-relatedness, because private insurance markets work with a range of exclusions and adverse selection processes. It should be possible in the new competitive order to ensure that the original social policy objectives of workers' compensation are served, using a variety of different models of public/private arrangements within this country and elsewhere.

Workers' compensation is an important area of historic compromise largely neglected in social policy studies in Canada. After nearly ninety years of history, it remains an interesting test case of the robustness of the instruments of the modern welfare state. It is perhaps not surprising then that this interesting institutional innovation should constitute a unique window on the cautious process of state sector reform in an era of liberalized trade. Although the long arm of competitive investment and cost reduction is strong in influencing state choices, workers' compensation has continued to mediate the economy of need and the economy of work when they conflict in the lives of injured workers. In our view, the continued vitality of workers' compensation schemes in Canada will turn on their capacity to innovate and meet the four challenges sketched out through the various chapters in this volume.

Notes

1   As a knowledge worker, I (T. Sullivan) am simultaneously working with a stand-alone computer, extracting material from the Internet and library online, corresponding with my office and international colleagues via e-mail, revising legal documents that are arriving on my fax machine, and talking on conference calls. Not atypical in the modern world, my work station and work look a lot different from that of the average worker at the time of Meredith.

2 We owe much to our colleagues at the Institute for Work and Health for shaping our thinking on these matters and their respective formulations of the effects of work environments on health and the effects of labour market experiences on health. An earlier version of the research map is described in *The First Five Years: A Review of the Institute for Work and Health Research Program* (Toronto: Institute for Work and Health, 1996).

3 The longer term solution to this paradox of modernity, as Keating and Hertzman (1999) describe it, is to promote the developmental health of our population (and future workforce) – a challenge for this period of major social and economic transition we are in.

4 In assessing approaches to fatality benefits, Thomason points out that the key issue in setting entitlement is which principles will be used to determine benefit levels. A needs-based system based on number of dependants or a technical determination of life-time disability benefits yield entirely different approaches and different sums of money for death benefits.

5 Not all jurisdictions allow workers compensation for soft tissue injuries with the same conviction as North American jurisdictions (see Yates and Burton 1998). Sweden now discounts back injury after a period and other jurisdictions have minimal exposure threshold requirements.

6 It is worth noting that only six US jurisdictions have such monopoly models.

References

Arnetz, B.B., S.O. Brenner, L. Levi, R. Hjelm, I.L. Petterson, J. Wasserman, B. Petrini, P. Eneroth, A. Kallner, R. Kvetnansky, and M. Vigas. 1991. "Neuroendocrine and Immunologic Effects of Unemployment and Job Insecurity." *Psychotherapy and Psychosomatics* 55 (2-4): 76-80.

Barth, P. 1998. "An International View of Workers' Compensation for Occupational Disease." In *International Examinations of Medical-Legal Aspects of Work Injuries,* ed. E.H. Yates and J.F. Burton, 182-203. London: Scarecrow Press.

Battié, M.C. 1992. "Minimizing the Impact of Back Pain: Workplace Strategies." *Seminars in Spine Surgery* 4 (1): 20-8.

Betcherman, G., and G. Lowe. 1997. *The Future of Work in Canada.* Ottawa: Canadian Policy Research Networks; Renouf.

Blane, D., E. Bruner, and R. Wilkinson. 1996. *Social Organization and Health.* London: Routledge.

Bogyo, T.J. 1995. "Workers' Compensation: Updating the Historic Compromise." In *Chronic Stress: Workers' Compensation in the 1990s,* ed. T. Thomason, G. Vaillancourt, T. Bogyo, and P. Stritch.Toronto: C.D. Howe Institute.

Brooker, A.-S., J. Frank, and V. Tarasuk. 1997. "Back Pain Claim Rates and the Business Cycle, in Contrast to Acute Injuries and Upper Limb Soft Tissue Injuries." *Social Science and Medicine* 45 (3): 429-39.

Chadlader, A. 1992. *The Impact of Royal Commissions on Public Policy: Workers' Compensation in British Columbia 1941-1968.* Vancouver: UBC Press.

Dahlby, B. 1993. "Payroll Taxes." In *Business Taxation in Ontario,* ed. A.M. Maslove. Toronto: University of Toronto Press.

Drache, D., and T. Sullivan, eds. 1999. *Health Reform: Public Success, Private Failure.* London: Routledge.

Dungan, P. Forthcoming. "The Effects of Workers' Compensation and Other Payroll Taxes on the Macro Economies of Canada and Ontario." In *Issues in Workers' Compensation: Foundations for Reform,* ed. M. Gunderson and D. Hyatt. Toronto: University of Toronto Press.

Evans, R.G., M.L. Barrer, and T.R. Marmor, eds. 1994. *Why Are Some People Healthy and Others Not? The Determinants of Health of Populations.* New York: De Gruyter.

Ferrie, J.E., M.J. Shipley, M.G. Marmot, S. Stansfeld, and G.D. Smith. 1995. "Health Effects of Anticipation of Job Change and Non-Employment: Longitudinal Data from the Whitehall II Study." *British Medical Journal* 311: 1264-9.

Fogel, R.W. 1993. "New Sources and New Techniques for the Study of Secular Trends in Nutritional Status, Health, Mortality, and the Process of Aging." *Historical Methods* 26 (1): 5-43.

Frank, J., M.S. Kerr, A.-S. Brooker, S.E. DeMaio, A. Maetzel, H.S. Shannon, T.J. Sullivan, R.W. Norman, and R.P. Wells. 1996a. "Disability Resulting from Occupational Low Back Pain, Part I: What Do We Know about Primary Prevention? A Review of the Scientific Evidence on Prevention before Disability Begins." *Spine* 21 (24): 2908-17.

–. 1996b. "Disability Resulting from Occupational Low Back Pain, Part II: What Do We Know about Secondary Prevention? A Review of the Scientific Evidence on Prevention before Disability Begins." *Spine* 21 (24): 2918-29.

Frank, J., and F. Mustard. 1994. "The Rise in Health of Populations and Historical Change in Population Health." *Daedalus* 123 (4): 1-21.

Frank, J., S. Sinclair, S. Hogg-Johnson, H. Shannon, C. Bombardier, D. Beaton, and D. Cole. 1998. "Preventing Disability from Work-Related Low-Back Pain: New Evidence Gives New Hope – If We Can Just Get All the Players Onside." *Canadian Medical Association Journal* 158 (12): 1625-31.

Freeman, R. 1994. Comment in R. Ehrenberg, *Labor Markets and Integrating National Economies,* 31. Washington, DC: Brookings Institution.

Gunderson, M. 1998. "Harmonization of Labour Policies under Trade Liberalization." *Industrial Relations* 53 (1): 24-54.

Gunderson, M., and C. Riddell. 1996. *The Changing Nature of Work: Implications for Public Policy.* Ottawa: Institute for Research on Public Policy.

Hallqvist, J., F. Diderichsen, T. Theorell, C. Reuterwall, and A. Ahlbom. 1998. "Is the Effect of Job Strain on Myocardial Infarction Risk Due to Interaction between High Psychological Demands and Low Decision Latitude? Results from the Stockholm Heart Epidemiology Program (SHEEP)." *Social Science and Medicine* 46 (11): 1405-15.

Heaney, C., B. Israel, and J. House. 1994. "Chronic Job Insecurity among Automobile Workers: Effects on Job Satisfaction and Health." *Social Science and Medicine* 38 (10): 1431-7.

Hirsch, B. 1997. "Incentive Effects of Workers' Compensation." *Clinical Orthopaedics and Related Research* 336: 33-41.

Hogg-Johnson, S., and D. Cole. 1998. "Early Prognostic Factors for Duration on Benefits among Workers with Compensated Occupational Soft Tissue Injuries." Working Paper 64. Institute for Work and Health, Toronto.

Johnson, J., and E. Hall. 1995. "Class, Work, and Health." In *Society and Health,* ed. B. Amick, S. Levine, A. Tarlov, and D. Chapman Walsh, 247-71. New York: Oxford University Press.

Johnson, W., M. Baldwin, and R. Butler. 1998. "Back Pain and Work Disability: The Need for a New Paradigm." *Industrial Relations* 37 (1): 9-34.

Joseph, L. 1983. "The Causation Issue in Workers' Compensation Mental Disability Cases: An Analysis, Solutions, and a Perspective." *Vanderbilt Law Review* 36 (264): 263-321.

Kaplan, G.A., E. Pamuk, J.W. Lynch, R.D. Cohen, and J.L. Balfour. 1996. "Inequality in Income and Mortality in the United States: Analysis of Mortality and Potential Pathways." *British Medical Journal* 312: 999-1003.

Karasek, R., and T. Theorell. 1990. *Healthy Work.* New York: Basic Books.

Keating, D., and C. Hertzman. 1999. *Developmental Health: The Wealth of Nations in an Information Age.* New York: Guilford Books.

Kennedy, B.P., I. Kawachi, and D. Prothrow-Stith. 1996. "Income Distribution and Mortality: Cross-Sectional Ecological Study of the Robin Hood Index in the United States." *British Medical Journal* 312: 1004-7.

Kerr, M.S, J.W. Frank, H.S Shannon, R.W.K. Norman, R.P. Wells, W.P. Neumann, C. Bombardier, and the Ontario Universities Back Pain Study (OUBPS) Group. 1998. "A Case-Control Study of Biomechanical and Psychosocial Risk Factors for Low-Back Pain Reported at Work." Working Paper 61. Institute for Work and Health, Toronto.

Kralj, B. Forthcoming. "Occupational Health and Safety: Effectiveness of Economic and Regulatory Mechanisms." In *Issues in Workers' Compensation: Foundations for Reform,* ed. M. Gunderson and D. Hyatt. Toronto: University of Toronto Press.

Lanoie, P. 1992. "The Impact of Occupational Safety and Health Regulation on the Risk of Workplace Accidents (Quebec 1983-87)." *Journal of Human Resources* 27 (4): 643-60.

Lavis, J. 1997. "An Enquiry into the Links between Labour Market Experiences and Health." PhD diss., Harvard University.

Leigh, J. 1989. "Compensating Wages for Job-Related Death: The Opposing Arguments." *Journal of Economic Issues* 23 (3): 823-42.

Leigh, J., and T. Miller. 1997. "Ranking Occupations Based upon the Costs of Job-Related Injuries and Diseases." *Journal of Occupational and Environmental Medicine* 39 (12): 1170-82.

Lewchuck, W., and D. Robertson. 1996. "Working Conditions under Lean Production: A Worker Based Benchmarking Study." *Asia-Pacific Business Review* 2 (4): 60-81.

Loisel, P., L. Abenhaim, P. Durand, J.M. Esdaile, S. Suissa, L. Gosselin, R. Simard, J. Turcotte, and J. Lemaire. 1997. "A Population Based Randomized Clinical Trial on Back Pain Management." *Spine* 22 (24): 2911-8.

Loisel, P., P. Durand, L. Abenhaim, R. Simard, J. Turcotte, and J. Esdaile. 1994. "Management of Occupational Back Pain: The Sherbrooke Model." *Occupational and Environmental Medicine* 51: 597-602.

Matthews, S., C. Hertzman, A. Ostry, and C. Power. 1998. "Gender, Work Roles, and Psychosocial Work Characteristics as Determinants of Health." *Social Science and Medicine* 46 (11): 1417-24.

Mayhew, C., M. Quinlan, and R. Ferris. 1997. "The Effects of Subcontracting/Outsourcing on Occupational Health and Safety: Survey Evidence from Four Australian Industries." *Safety Science* 25 (1-3): 163-78.

Meredith, W. 1913. *The Workmen's Compensation Act with Reports on Laws Relating to the Liability of Employers.* Toronto: King's Printer.

Messing, K. 1998. *One-Eyed Science: Occupational Health and Women Workers.* Philadelphia: Temple University Press.

Mustard, F. 1999. "Health, Health Care, and Social Cohesion." In *Health Reform: Public Success, Private Failure,* ed. D. Drache and T. Sullivan, 329-50. London: Routledge.

Park, Y.-S., R. Butler, and B. Zaidman. 1998. "Impact of Contingent Employees on Workers' Compensation Insurance System." Paper presented at Worker Compensation Research Group, East Lansing, MI.

Plumb, J.M., and J. Cowell. 1998. "An Overview of Workers' Compensation." In *Workers' Compensation,* ed. T. Guidotti and J. Cowell. Special issue of *Occupational Medicine* 13 (?): 241-72.

Polanyi, M., D. Cole, B. Beaton, J. Chung, R. Wells, M. Abdolell, L. Beech-Hawley, S. Ferrier, M. Mondloch, S. Shields, J. Smith, and H. Shannon. 1997. "Upper Limb Work-Related Musculoskeletal Disorders among Newspaper Employees: Cross-Sectional Survey Results." *American Journal of Industrial Medicine* 32: 620-8.

Polanyi, M., J. Frank, H. Shannon, T. Sullivan, and J. Lavis. Forthcoming. "Promoting the Determinants of Good Health in the Workplace." In *Settings in Health Promotion: Linking Theory and Practice,* ed. B. Poland, I. Rootman, and L. Green. Newbury, CA: Sage.

Quinlan, M. 1997. "The Implications of Labour Market Restructuring in Industrialised Societies for Occupational Health and Safety." Paper presented at the National Institute for Working Life, Stockholm, 5 September.

Ramazzini, B. 1964. *The Diseases of Workers.* Translated from the 1713 Latin text, *De Mortifice Artificum,* by Wilber Cave Wright. New York: Hafner Publishing.

Rifkin, J. 1995. *The End of Work: The Decline of the Global Labor Force and the Dawn of the Post-Market Era.* New York: Putnam.

Santana, V.S., D. Loomis, B. Newman, and S.D. Harlow. 1997. "Informal Jobs: Another Occupational Hazard for Women's Mental Health." *International Journal of Epidemiology* 26 (6): 1236-42.

Shainblum, E., T. Sullivan, and J. Frank. Forthcoming. "Multicausality, Non-Traditional Injury, and the Future of Workers' Compensation." In *Issues in Workers' Compensation: Foundations for Reform,* ed. M. Gunderson and D. Hyatt. Toronto: University of Toronto Press.

Shorter, E. 1997. "Somatization and Chronic Pain in Historic Perspective." *Clinical Orthopaedics and Related Research* 336: 52-60.

Silverstein, B., M. Foley, and S. Sama. 1998. "Protecting Contingent Workers from Work Related Injury." Paper presented at PREMUS Workshop on Contingent Work, Helsinki, September.

Sinclair, S., T. Sullivan, J. Clarke, and J. Frank. 1998. "A Framework for Examining Return to Work in Workers' Compensation." In *International Examinations of Medical-Legal Aspects of Work Injuries*, ed. E. Yates and J. Burton, 263-300. London: Scarecrow Press.

Statistics Canada, Labour Division. 1995. *Work Injuries 1992-1994*. Ottawa: Statistics Canada.

Stone, D. 1984. *The Disabled State*. Philadelphia: Temple University Press.

Sullivan, T. 1998. "Commentary on Health Care Expenditures, Social Spending, and Health Status." In *Striking a Balance: Health Care Systems in Canada and Elsewhere*, 346-55. Vol. 4 of *Canada Health Action: Building on the Legacy*. St. Foy, QC: Éditions Multimondes.

Sullivan, T., O. Uneke, J. Lavis, D. Hyatt, and J. O'Grady. 1998. "Labour Adjustment Policy and Health: Considerations for a Changing World." In *Determinants of Health – Settings and Issues*, 532-77. Vol. 3 of *Canada Health Action: Building on the Legacy*. St. Foy, QC: Éditions Multimondes.

Tarasuk, V., and J. Eakin. 1994. "Back Problems Are for Life: Perceived Vulnerability and Its Implications for Chronic Disability." *Journal of Occupational Rehabilitation* 4 (1): 55-64.

Thomason, T., and J. Burton. Forthcoming. "The Costs of Workers' Compensation in Ontario and British Columbia." In *Issues in Workers' Compensation: Foundations for Reform*, ed. M. Gunderson and D. Hyatt. Toronto: University of Toronto Press.

Thomason, T., G. Vaillancourt, T. Bogyo, and P. Stritch. 1995. *Chronic Stress: Workers' Compensation in the 1990s: Social Policy Challenge*. Toronto: C.D. Howe Institute.

Toomingas, A., T. Theorell, H. Michelson, and R. Nordemar. 1997. "Association between Self-Rated Psychosocial Work Conditions and Musculoskeletal Symptoms and Signs." *Scandinavian Journal of Work Environment and Health* 23 (12): 130-9.

Vinson, K. 1996. "Disentangling Law and Fact: Echoes of Proximate Cause in the Workers' Compensation Coverage Formula." *Alabama Law Review* 47: 723-73.

Walters, D. 1997. "Preventive Services in Occupational Health and Safety in Europe: Developments and Trends in the 1990s." *International Journal of Health Services* 27 (2): 247-71.

Wennemo, I. 1993. "Infant Mortality, Public Policy, and Inequality: A Comparison of 18 Industrialized Countries 1950-1985." *Sociology of Health and Illness* 15 (4): 429-46.

Whitehead, M. 1995. "Tackling Inequalities: A Review of Policy Initiatives." In *Tackling Inequalities in Health*, ed. M. Benzeval, K. Judge, and M. Whitehead, 22-52. London: King's Fund.

Wilkinson, R. 1996. *Unhealthy Societies: The Afflictions of Inequality*. London: Routledge.

Wokutch, R. 1992. *Worker Protection, Japanese Style: Occupational Safety and Health in the Auto Industry*. Ithaca, NY: ILR Press.

Yassi, A., R. Tate, J. Cooper, C. Snow, S. Vallentyne, and J. Khokhar. 1995. "Early Intervention for Back-Injured Nurses at a Large Canadian Tertiary Care Hospital: An Evaluation of the Effectiveness and Cost Benefits of a Two-Year Pilot Project." *Occupational Medicine* 45 (4): 209-14.

Yates, E., and J. Burton, eds. 1998. *International Examinations of Medical-Legal Aspects of Work Injuries*. London: Scarecrow Press.

Part 2: The Industrial-Epidemiological Shift

The three essays that follow explore the significance of major changes in the sectoral composition of the workforce and their dramatic influences on injury and disabling conditions at work. Aleck Ostry's unique historical and descriptive epidemiology of British Columbia as a case jurisdiction documents the major transition over the last fifty years from chainsaws to keyboards. In the early 1950s, male-dominated resource-sector jobs were characteristic. Today, both genders are overrepresented in service-sector jobs, which constitute the single largest segment of employment. The consequence, as Ostry describes so well, is a dramatic change in the nature and scale of injury and occupational disease in the labour force. This epidemiological transition from acute and unequivocal injuries to slow-onset and sometimes chronic strains and sprains of the muscles, bones, and joints, so-called work-related musculoskeletal disorders, is now the hallmark of most workers' compensation challenges in North America.

Gunderson and Hyatt follow this thread by exploring forward projections on changes in the labour force once again using data from British Columbia to estimate changes in the sectoral composition of employment and the consequences for work injury. They demonstrate in this most compelling analysis that all other things being equal, projected changes in the labour force composition and the growth of service-sector employment, alongside the projected decline of resource-sector jobs will result in significant and important reductions in the costs of work-related injury.

The final essay by Chung et al. explores the important and poorly understood distinctions between men and women in relation to the nature and types of injury, incidence, and duration of disability. Their chapter explores the nature of the employment in which women engage in Canada. It also describes the patterns of work-related injury by employment type and body injury type in Canada. Their chapter offers a number of important reflections on the imperative of serving both genders fairly in a modern labour market in which men and women participate in almost equal proportions.

All in all, using Canadian data, the chapters in Part 2 highlight the profound effects that the nature of work and the sectoral and gender composition of the labour force have on injury and disability patterns.

2
From Chainsaws to Keyboards: Injury and Industrial Disease in British Columbia
Aleck Ostry

In the post-war era, the province of British Columbia, like many Canadian jurisdictions, has moved away from its traditional resource-based economy toward a largely service-based economy. During this time, both the service sector and older resource industries have become highly computerized and mechanized. These industrial and technological shifts have changed the way work is organized and performed in British Columbia and have also been associated with a profound shift in labour demography.

The purpose of this investigation is to describe changes in industrial injury and disease rates from 1950 to 1996 and to link these, where possible, to changes in the infrastructure of the BC economy and labour force. Although epidemiological data are used throughout this report, the method and objectives are largely historical. The intent of this investigation is not to produce epidemiological evidence for association and causation. Rather, it is to develop a broad historical description of changing disease and injury rates mainly using epidemiological data obtained from the Workers' Compensation Board (WCB).

Historical trends in the epidemiology of industrial disease and injury cannot be understood properly unless linked to larger social processes, particularly in the post-war era, which witnessed a reshaping of the provincial economy as it moved away from its traditional resource base toward the service sector. In this investigation, economic and employment data for British Columbia were abstracted from Statistics Canada's historical labour force surveys in order to develop indicators to describe the extent and timing of three major aspects of this transformation: (1) the switch from a resource- to service-based economy, (2) fluctuations in the business cycle, (3) and the entry of women into the labour force.

One of the drawbacks of conducting a study using WCB data is that most of the detailed epidemiological information on injury and disease is based on accepted claims. One cannot obtain underlying rates of industrial disease and injury in the entire working population using data based on accepted injury and disease claims. Although claims acceptance rates are obviously related to underlying disease and injury rates and temporal change in these, the claims acceptance process is an administrative and policy filter that limits the extent to which these data can describe the entire at-risk working population.

In an attempt to more closely examine rates in the population at risk, some emphasis has been placed on describing death and injury report rates, their fluctuation over the study period, and their relationship to the three indicators of labour and economic change. Injury and death report rates are based on the WCB-insured population, which in turn represent much of the working population at risk for industrial disease and injury. A focus on these reporting rates will still lead to under-ascertainment of underlying population rates. The extent of this under-ascertainment will depend on the proportion of the working population that was insured by the WCB at a given time.

Despite the epidemiological limitations regarding claims rates just outlined, these rates are used extensively in this investigation to show changes in the proportions of industrial disease and injury categories over the study period and also to describe changing trends in industrial disease and injury claims experience over the study period.

Methods
Two indicators of the social transformation of the BC labour force and economy were obtained from the *Canadian Labour Force Survey* (Statistics Canada 1953-96). The unadjusted yearly BC unemployment rate was selected as a rough indicator of business cycle activity and the BC female labour force participation rate was used to show the increasing gender shift in the labour force.

Also, using WCB claims data, the number of time loss claims in the forestry and service sectors was abstracted for each year up to 1996 (BCWCB 1950-96). The ratio of the number of forestry-sector time loss claims (class 1) compared to service-sector time loss claims (class 6) was calculated for each year and served as an indicator of the shift away from a resource-based and toward a service-based economy. (Time loss claims are not as accurate an indicator as is the number of workers employed in these two sectors to measure this shift but may be a useful proxy.)

Injury data were obtained from *Annual Reports* for the year 1950 through 1996 (BCWCB 1950-96). Detailed breakdown of industrial disease data was available in the reports from 1959 to the end of 1996 only. Injury and death report rates and accepted injury claim rates were available from 1950 to 1996. The denominator for rates is an estimate of the number of workers insured by the WCB in a given year (BCWCB Statistics Department 1998).

Results

Table 2.1 shows the three major indicators of social transformation in the labour force. British Columbia's unemployment rate in the 1950s and 1960s averaged 6.5 percent, increasing to 8 percent through the 1970s. The recession of the early 1980s pushed this rate over 11 percent for most of the decade. During this forty-three-year span, the BC economy witnessed a secular increase in unemployment of approximately 3.5 percent.

Table 2.1

Three indicators of labour and economic transition in the BC economy, 1953-96

Period	Unemployment rate (%)[a]	Number of service-sector workers per 100 forestry-sector workers[b]	Female labour force participation rate (%)[c]
1953-9	6.1	75	24.6
1960-9	6.9	90	32.9
1970-9	8.0	150	43.9
1980-9	11.3	250	54.6
1990-6	9.4	400	58.9

a   Unadjusted BC unemployment rate.
b   Number of service-sector compared to forestry-sector claims times 100.
c   Number of women in the labour force divided by number of women aged 15-65 in the BC population, times 100.

In the 1950s, for every 100 workers in the forestry sector there were seventy-five service workers. By the 1960s, there was an almost equal number of workers in the forestry and service sectors. In the 1990s, there were 400 service workers for every 100 forestry workers. Used as an indicator, this suggests a rapid and fairly consistent pace in the rate of change from a resource-based to a service economy although the pace appears to have slowed after 1980.

The gender shift in the composition of the BC workforce has been equally dramatic. In 1956, one in four working-age females was in the labour force. By 1979, 50 percent of women of working age were in the labour force; by 1996, the number had grown to approximately 60 percent. The rate of growth of female labour force participation was fastest during the 1960s and 1970s and slowed markedly during the late 1980s and 1990s.

While the economy was undergoing these transformations it was also increasing in size (Table 2.2). The number of workers employed in BC nearly quadrupled between the early 1950s and the late 1990s, as did the number of workers covered by the WCB. And, the number of firms insuring their workers tripled during this period. However, the number of insured workers per firm peaked in the 1960s and 1970s at approximately 13. By the 1980s, this had dropped to 9.1 and by the 1990s, to 6.8, which may indicate that workers of the 1990s are, in general, distributed across more, and smaller firms, with fewer co-workers than they were in the 1960s and 1970s.

Table 2.2

Provincial employment and WCB coverage

Period	Number employed[a]	Number insured[b]	Percent insured[c]	Number of firms[d]
1953-9	490,600	377,718	77.0	30,817
1960-9	664,800	511,900	77.0	66,475
1970-9	1,014,000	801,400	79.0	101,400
1980-9	1,341,200	1,017,600	75.8	93,054
1990-6	1,676,000	1,327,714	79.2	90,673

a   Total number of workers in the BC workforce.
b   Number of workers insured by the WCB. (Estimate obtained from BC WCB Statistics Department.)
c   Percent of workers insured by the WCB.
d   Number of firms covered by the WCB. (Figure obtained from BC WCB *Annual Reports*, 1953-96.)

Insurance coverage at the WCB remained fairly constant between 75 and 80 percent of the workforce with some decrease in coverage during the 1980s. This means that in terms of the epidemiology of injury and industrial disease, the experience of approximately 25 percent of workers in the province will not be captured using WCB statistics.

Deaths Reported to the WCB

Table 2.3 shows that the death report rate to the WCB was 67.3 per one hundred thousand insured workers during the 1950s. This dropped steeply through the 1960s and by the 1970s was less than half that observed in the 1950s. By the 1990s, the death report rate had halved again to 14 per one

Table 2.3

WCB death report rate by decade, 1950-96

Period	Death report rate[a]
1950-9	67.3
1960-9	43.0
1970-9	28.0
1980-9	19.4
1990-6	14.0

a   Reported deaths per year per 100,000 WCB-insured workers.

hundred thousand insured workers. In all, the rate at which deaths were reported to the WCB dropped by 79 percent from the 1950s to the 1990s.

During the post-war era, the BC economy witnessed a major shift from resources to a service economy. The number of time loss claims for the forestry sector compared to the service sector are used, in this investigation, as a crude indicator to illustrate the timing of this shift. Figure 2.1 shows the death report rate in relation to the ratio of the number of forestry- to service-sector claims in BC from 1950 to 1996.

Figure 2.1

Death report rate and ratio of forestry- to service-sector claims by year, 1950-96

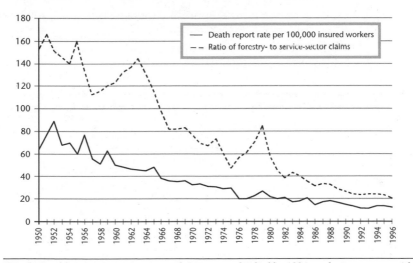

Note: Ratio of forestry- to service-sector claims was multiplied by 100 in order to compare with the death report rate.

This graph indicates that the shift away from the forestry sector toward the service sector roughly parallels the decline in the death report rate. (Although the death report rate declined less quickly than the proportion of forestry- relative to service-sector claims.) The decline appears to be more rapid for both curves from 1950 to the mid-1970s. (The decline is not smooth as there are two time periods, 1957-64 and 1975-79 when the death report rate increases.)

It is possible that the shift toward a service economy could have changed the kinds and intensity of exposures that workers faced. It is likely, for example, that in an economy moving from "chainsaws to keyboards" the proportion of insured workers exposed to extremely dangerous, acute, and potentially deadly hazards has decreased and this trend could, at least partly, explain the drop in the reported death rate. Decreased death report rates might also be attributable to increased safety awareness and prevention. Any determination of this would have to be made after controlling for the large-scale secular changes outlined.

Injuries Reported to the WCB

Table 2.4 shows that the rate at which injuries were reported to the WCB dropped by 29 percent from the 1950s to the 1990s with approximately half the drop occurring during the 1990s. Figure 2.2 shows the injury report rate in relation to the ratio of the number of forestry- to service-sector claims from 1953 to 1996. Over this period, the injury report rate declined, the greatest drop having occurred from the 1950s through the 1960s (unlike the death report rate, there have been no sharp declines in the injury report rate). During the 1970s, the injury report rate increased. In 1980, the rate began to decrease again and by 1992 had reached levels last seen in 1969. Since 1992, the injury report rate has declined slightly.

Figure 2.2

Injury report rate and ratio of forestry- to service-sector claims by year, 1953-96

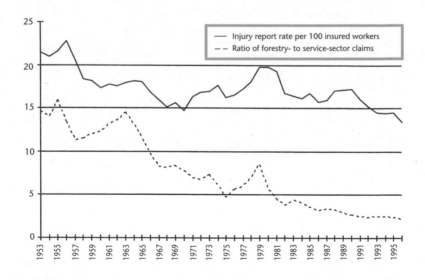

Note: Ratio of forestry- to service-sector claims was multiplied by 10 in order to compare with the injury report rate.

Figure 2.2 indicates that the injury report rate appears not to be linked to the shift towards a service economy. Clearly, a number of factors other than change in the structure of the economy may influence the rate at

Table 2.4

WCB injury report rate by decade, 1950-96

Period	Injury report rate[a]
1950-9	21.3
1960-9	17.1
1970-9	17.0
1980-9	17.1
1990-6	15.1

a Reported injuries per year per 100 WCB-insured workers.

which injuries are reported to the WCB. Injury report rates might also be influenced by WCB, industry, and union education campaigns. They might also be influenced by the changing mix of workers and firms becoming insured by the WCB over time. Also, a number of studies have indicated that claims rates (not injury report rates) may be influenced by the business cycle – the more people who are working, the more claims that are made, and vice versa.

For example, in the United States, several studies have shown that workers' compensation claim rates increase with increased business cycle activity (Kossoris 1943; Robinson 1988; Kossoris 1938; Catalano 1979; Robinson and Shor 1989). In a recent study of back claim rates in Ontario between 1975 and 1993, Brooker used the unemployment rate as a measure of

Figure 2.3

Injury report rate and unemployment rate by year, 1953-96

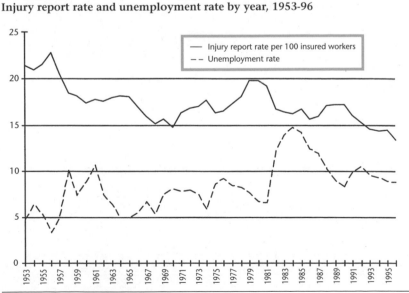

Note: Unemployment rate is the unadjusted BC rate.

business cycle activity. She showed that age- and gender-adjusted back claim rates for the manufacturing, trade, and construction sectors varied inversely with the unemployment rate (Brooker et al. 1997).

Injury report rates may be a more sensitive measure than injury claim rates, because they are less affected by administrative and policy decisions within the WCB. Figure 2.3 compares injury report rates to the unadjusted BC unemployment rate, by year from 1953 through 1996. (It should be noted that unlike the study by Brooker et al. in Ontario, the graph in Figure 2.3 is descriptive as age and gender were not controlled.)

The unemployment and injury report rates appear to vary inversely with each other in a regular pattern year by year over the entire period. This observation deserves further investigation given that other studies have shown a similar pattern with accepted claim rates.

Injury Claims in Relation to the Changing Economy

Injury reports appear to be sensitive to changes in the business cycle (at least as measured by the unemployment rate). Once an injury is reported to the board, the claims process commences. To contextualize the discussion of injury claims in relation to the changing economy, the relationship between injury report rates and time loss claim rates is first illustrated (Figure 2.4).

Both injury report rates and accepted time loss claims rates dropped by

Figure 2.4

Injury report rate and accepted time loss claim rate, 1953-96

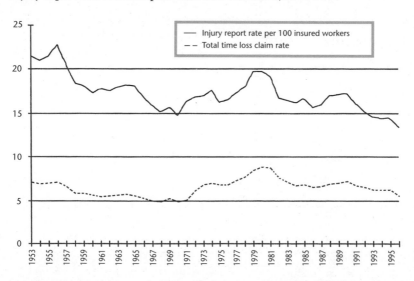

approximately 30 percent between 1953 and 1970. Then, during the 1970s, both rates increased by about 25 percent. Between 1981 and 1996 there was a decrease in both rates except for a small increase in the late 1980s and early 1990s.

Presumably, the relationship between the injury report rate and total claims acceptance rate will be governed by a combination of the seriousness of reported injury and disease and board policy in accepting claims. It would also be interesting to know if the claims rate in British Columbia fluctuates with the business cycle. Figure 2.5 shows the total time loss claim rate and the unemployment rate from 1953 through 1996. (Total time loss claims include short-term and long-term disability claims, industrial disease claims, and fatal claims.)

Figure 2.5

Total time loss claim rates and unemployment rate by year, 1953-96

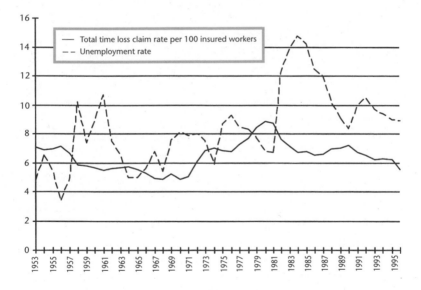

Note: Total time loss claims include short-term and long-term disability claims, industrial disease claims, and fatal claims. Unemployment rate is the unadjusted BC rate.

The inverse relationship between the total time loss claim rate and the unemployment rate is not as visible as in Figure 2.3. The total time loss claim rate appears to decrease during the recessions of 1981-2 and 1990-2, as did the injury report rate. Beyond this observation, more detailed investigation is needed to determine the exact relationship between the business cycle and total time loss claim rates in British Columbia.

The total time loss claim rate will partly reflect board policies toward claimants – changes in such policies may be reflected by change in the proportion of total accepted time loss claims to reported injuries. Figure 2.6 graphs total time loss claims as a percentage of the number of injuries reported by year from 1953 through 1996.

Figure 2.6

Accepted total time loss claims as a percentage of injuries reported by year, 1953-96

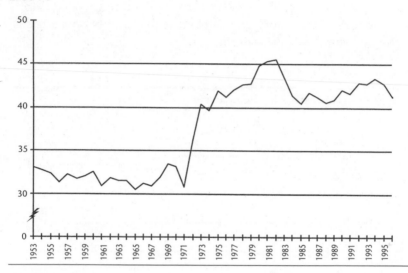

From 1953 until 1971, approximately one-third of injuries reported to the board resulted in an accepted time loss claim. From 1972 until 1975, the percentage of accepted claims increased at a rate of approximately 3 percent per year. The major increase from 1972 to 1973 is most likely due to removal in 1972 of a three-day waiting period for the filing of claims. From 1973 until 1982, the percentage of accepted claims increased at a rate of 0.5 percent per year, peaking at just over 45 in 1982. Over the next three years, to 1985, there was a drop to 40.5 percent. Between 1985 and 1996, the proportion of accepted claims remained in fairly constant fluctuation between 40.5 and 43.7 percent.

The third indicator of social transformation in the labour force, as used in this report, is the changing participation rate of women in the BC economy. Figure 2.7 shows the trend in female participation in the labour force in relation to the shift toward a service economy.

The movement of women into the labour force roughly parallels the move toward a service economy. As women entered the labour force in greater numbers and as the economy shifted away from its traditional

Figure 2.7

**Female participation rate[a] and rate of shift toward a service economy[b]
in British Columbia**

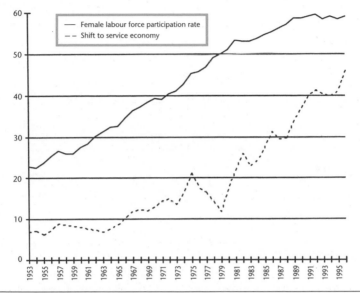

a   Number of employed women divided by total population of women in British Columbia
between ages fifteen and sixty-five, multiplied by 100.
b   Number of service-sector time loss claims divided by number of forestry-sector time loss
claims, multiplied by ten.

resource base what happened to time loss claims for women? Figure 2.8
shows the changing female labour force participation rate in relation to the
proportion of time loss claims awarded to women.

In 1953, approximately 25 percent of women of working age in British
Columbia were in the workforce and women were awarded 7 percent of time
loss claims. Eighteen years later, in 1971, almost 40 percent of women of
working age were in the workforce and female workers were awarded approximately 10 percent of time loss claims, yielding respective rates of increase of
60 and 43 percent from 1953. By 1980, just over 50 percent of working-age
women were in the workforce and women were awarded 15 percent of time
loss claims, representing rates of increase of 25 and 50 percent respectively
since 1971. By 1996, the female labour force participation rate was approximately 60 percent and female workers were awarded 26 percent of time loss
claims, for respective rates of increase of 20 and 73 percent since 1980.

Although the rate of increase in female participation in the labour force
has *decreased* since 1980, the rate of increase in the proportion of time loss
claims awarded to women *increased* during this same period. From these
purely descriptive data it is not clear why with 60 percent of working-age

Figure 2.8

**Female participation rate in the labour force and proportion of
total time loss claims awarded to women by year, 1953-96**

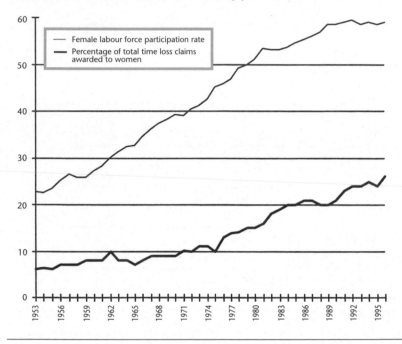

women in the labour force by 1996 that just over 25 percent of claims were
awarded to women (though one ought to keep in mind that the female
labour force participation data are for the whole of the female working
population in British Columbia, while the time loss claim rates are for the
subset of the female working population who are WCB-insured). These
data point to a need to investigate gender issues further, a challenge that is
taken up in some detail in the chapter by Chung et al. in this volume.

Changing Pattern of Injury Claims during the Study Period
Short-term time loss claims represent 94 to 97 percent of total time loss
claims during the study period. Figure 2.9 shows the rates for permanent
disability, fatal claims, and claims for industrial disease. (It should be
remembered when looking at this chart that, although the denominator is
the number of insured workers, its size is different for each category so that
this graph is only useful in showing the relative patterns of fluctuation of
these claim rates over time.)

The pattern of accepted fatal claims over time is similar to that observed
in Figure 2.1 for reported deaths and is understandable as approximately
80 percent of reported deaths result in an accepted fatal claim at the WCB.

Figure 2.9

Injury time loss claim rates by year, 1956-96

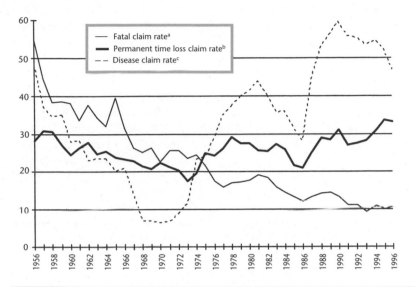

a   Number of permanent time-loss claims accepted per 10,000 insured workers.
b   Number of fatal claims accepted per 100,000 insured workers.
c   Number of accepted industrial disease claims per 10,000 insured workers.

The pattern of accepted permanent time loss claims remains (comparatively) flat over the study period. The pattern of accepted industrial disease claims appears similar to that demonstrated for total time loss claims and injury report rates (see Figure 2.4).

Most injury claims at the WCB are for short-term time loss. Such injuries have been classified into fifteen basic categories over the study period (Appendix A, Table A1). For purposes of this historical analysis, it was felt important to separate strain-based injuries from injuries resulting from impact (such as falls, struck by, stepping on, etc.). Also, the experience of WCBs in most jurisdictions indicates that, as a general category, injuries arising from strain have become increasingly important in the service economy, hence Table A1 shows the reduction, for the purposes of this analysis, of the fifteen basic injury categories into three categories: strain, impact, and miscellaneous.

Some of the fifteen basic categories were added late in the study period. For example, "back strain" appears in the reports separately from "strains and sprains" in 1979 but not earlier. Other categories have changed names and definition. For example, "overexertion" existed as a separate category to 1971 but in 1972 was absorbed into "strains and sprains."

Figure 2.10 shows the proportion of strains, impacts, and miscellaneous injury claims to accepted short-term time loss claims per year from 1952 to 1996. The most rapid increase in strain injuries occurred during the 1970s. During this same period, injuries due to impact decreased at an even more rapid rate. In 1970, approximately 80 percent of the injuries were accounted for by impact injuries and 15 percent by strain injuries. A decade later, in 1980, only 45 percent of injuries were due to impact, and strain injuries as a proportion of all injuries had risen to 45 percent. By 1996, 50 percent of accepted short-term time loss claims were due to strain and only 30 percent to impacts. Back strain injuries represent approximately two-thirds of strain injury time loss claims per year from 1979 to 1996. The proportion of back claims to all injury strain claims was very steady during this time.

Figure 2.10

Proportion of strains, impacts, and miscellaneous injuries to accepted short-term time loss claims per year, 1952-96

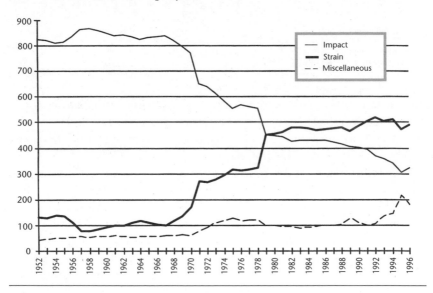

Patterns of Industrial Disease Claims during the Study Period
Figure 2.9 showed the rates of acceptance of industrial disease claims over the study period. The trends for accepted industrial disease claims over time were broadly similar to those for injury report rates and total accepted time loss claims (which are almost completely driven by short-term time loss claims). That is, increases in the 1970s were followed by decreases in

the first half of the 1980s. And, the increases of the last half of the 1980s were followed by declines to 1996.

While this describes trends in rates over time, more detailed information is required to determine whether the kinds of disease compensated have also changed over time. Accordingly, in Table 2.5 we show the average number of accepted industrial disease claims by major category for each decade in the study period. The disease categories were obtained by grouping the WCB industrial disease categories into five large categories: respiratory disease, hearing loss, repetitive stress injury (RSI), dermatitis, and diseases due to radiation exposure, plus an "other" category. The logic for this categorization was to select disease groups that remained fairly significant (mostly above 10 percent of disease claims) throughout the study period. Grouping was also performed on the basis of similarity of exposure and/or outcome.

Table A2 shows these categories in detail and which new industrial diseases were added during this period. Included in the category "other" were

Table 2.5

Average number of industrial disease claims by decade, 1960-96

Period	Respiratory	Hearing loss	RSI	Dermatitis	Radiation	Other	Total
1960-9	93.4	11.9	263.5	373.4	65.3	203.9	1,011.4
1970-9	126.4	192.7	707.8	242.0	279.6	447.0	1,995.5
1980-9	201.0	434.9	2,154.5	266.6	528.0	787.2	4,372.2
1990-6	266.7	722.4	4,252.1	197.7	538.4	1,376.4	7,353.7

allergic reaction, cancer, and stress, for which claims were first awarded in 1992. These form an insignificant portion of the "other" category for these years. These three new categories represent from 3 to 4 percent of total industrial disease claims in the years 1992 through 1996. Of the three new categories, stress claims constitute 90 percent from 1992 through 1996.

Figure 2.11 graphs the proportion of accepted disease claims by major category and decade. The category "other" is not shown but represents approximately 20 percent of industrial disease claims in each decade.

In the 1960s, dermatitis was the largest single category of accepted industrial disease claims, accounting for nearly 40 percent of claims. This was followed by RSI (categorized until 1978 as either bursitis or tenosynovitis), representing 26 percent of claims. The third largest category in the 1960s comprised respiratory disease. By the 1970s, dermatitis had dropped to 10 percent of disease claims and radiation-related disease claims and hearing loss claims had increased to between 10 and 15 percent of disease claims. RSI claims (bursitis and tenosynovitis) represented 35 percent of claims.

Figure 2.11

Proportion of accepted industrial disease claims by category and decade, 1960-96

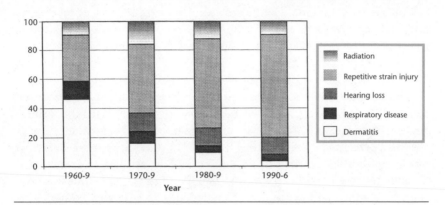

Between 1970 and 1996, claims for bursitis, tenosynovitis, and (after 1979) carpal tunnel syndrome increased from 35 to 55 percent of all industrial disease claims. Because this is the single most important industrial disease category for most of the study period, Figure 2.12 shows the breakdown within this category.

Rates for tenosynovitis double from 0.5 to 1.0 accepted claims per 1,000 insured workers between 1959 and 1979, with all of this increase occurring

Figure 2.12

Accepted repetitive strain disease claim rates per 1,000 insured workers, 1959-96

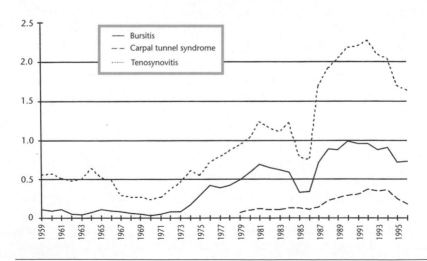

during the 1970s. Between 1979 and 1987, rates declined to 0.75 claims per 1,000 insured workers. After 1987, there was a steep increase, which peaked in 1992 at 2.2 claims per 1,000 insured workers. Since 1992, the rates have declined; by 1996, there were 1.6 claims per 1,000 insured workers. Claims for bursitis and carpal tunnel syndrome appear to follow this same pattern over time.

Conclusion

From the 1950s to the 1990s, the BC economy made a rapid and profound transition from a resource to a largely service economy. During this time, female participation in the labour force more than doubled and unemployment rates underwent a secular increase with a particularly severe increase during the first half of the 1980s. Major changes have also occurred during this time in the number and kinds of injury and industrial disease seen at the WCB. Using broad socio-economic indicators, there appears to be some relationship between major transformations in the economy and changing rates and kinds of injury and disease. For example, there has been a dramatic, 79 percent decline in the rate of reported deaths, which may be associated with the shift away from the resource sector where exposure hazards are more acute relative to the service sector.

As women moved into the labour force at an increasing rate, British Columbia shifted toward a service economy. By 1996, there were more women than ever before in the labour force, most of them working in service-sector jobs. In fact, 60 percent of women of working age were in the labour force by 1996. However, their share of total time loss claims was only 26 percent. Why? It may be that men are exposed to more dangerous working conditions than women. It might be useful to investigate this further by studying the pattern of claims acceptance rates for men and women working in the same occupations where they are more likely to be exposed to similar hazards. More tightly focused empirical studies with an emphasis on gender (and controlling for age and occupation) are needed.

A number of studies have linked claims rates with fluctuations in the business cycle. In this investigation, injury report rates show an inverse relationship with the unemployment rate over the entire study period. This result appears (at least visually) weaker for claims rates and perhaps only for the last half of the study period. These results should be explored further with properly controlled (for age and gender) empirical studies in order to determine the veracity of this apparent association. If claims rates are in fact associated with the business cycle, then this connection has important implications for WCB prevention policy.

Another clear pattern that emerges from this investigation is the dominance by the 1990s of "strain"-related injury and disease claims. After 1980, approximately 50 percent of short-term time loss claims for injury and industrial disease were "strain" related. For the injury claims, after 1980, approximately two-thirds were "back strain," which was the single largest category of strain injuries. These data point to a profound transition in the epidemiology of injury and industrial disease in the British Columbia as it has moved toward a service economy.

There are a number of limitations with the approach taken in this report. The three indicators of social transformation were not developed empirically. They may not be the "best" indicators of the social transformations they claim to measure. Their choice was governed partly by the availability of statistical data for the entire period and partly on commonly accepted ideas about the most significant changes that have occurred in the labour force over the past four decades.

Also, the data have been used in this investigation in an entirely descriptive fashion. As outlined in the introduction, the focus has been historical more than epidemiological. Any associations shown in this investigation are descriptive and must be interpreted as such. Finally, definitions of disease and injury categories have shifted over time. Still, in analysis involving long time periods, use of categories that do not remain exactly the same over time may be useful to show broad temporal patterns. Again these must be interpreted with caution.

In spite of these caveats this investigation does demonstrate two fundamental points. First, this historical approach provides a long time frame over which rates of industrial injury and disease can be traced in order to identify secular trends. This helps to better "locate" the current situation in time. Second, by contextualizing changing patterns of injury and disease within major social transformations in the labour force a first step has been made to further elucidate these patterns. By tracking injury and death report rates versus claims acceptance rates, the impact of social transformations in the labour force becomes more visible. The rate of injury report to the WCB will be less influenced by internal administrative and policy factors than the accepted claims rates so the impact of social change can be more easily isolated.

This investigation shows descriptively that these social transformations taken together with complex administrative and policy changes at the WCB may have an impact on disease and injury trends. That these are intertwined in complex ways is shown in Figure 2.6 where when the three-day waiting period for short-term time loss claims was eliminated, the proportion of accepted claims increased dramatically. This occurred at the time of most rapid labour force transformation with respect to both the move toward a service economy and the pace of increasing female participation in the workforce.

In this investigation, attention has been paid mainly to the impact of social transformation of the labour force on injury and disease. More research needs to be done to better elucidate the impacts of these social processes together with administrative and policy shifts at the WCB. If these factors, and their interactions, are better understood then evaluation and design of appropriate prevention programs can be placed on a firmer theoretical and empirical basis.

Finally, the clear and overwhelming trend toward "strain-related" injuries and disease creates new challenges for adjudication and prevention. The often subjective nature of strain injury and the relationship between psychosocial factors (stress) and back strain and other strain injuries complicates identification and adjudication of these injuries. Identification of "strain-producing" work situations should be a priority. The elucidation of the relationship between "physical" strain injuries and psychosocial work conditions is also very important as increasingly stress has been linked with both attitudinal and physiological outcomes (Fox et al. 1993; Karasek 1989; Sharit and Salvendy 1982).

References

BCWCB. See Workers' Compensation Board of British Columbia.

Brooker A., J. Frank, and V. Tarasuk. 1997. "Back Pain Claim Rates and the Business Cycle." *Social Science and Medicine* 45 (3): 429-39.

Catalano, R. 1979. "Health Costs of Economic Expansion: The Case of Manufacturing Accident Injuries." *American Journal of Public Health* 69 (8): 189-94.

Fox, M.L., D.J. Dwyer, and D.C. Ganster. 1993. "Effects of Stressful Job Demands and Control on Physiological and Attitudinal Outcomes in a Hospital Setting." *Academy of Management Journal* 36 (2): 289-318.

Karasek, R. 1989. "Control in the Workplace and Its Health-Related Aspects." In *Job Control and Worker Health,* ed. S. Sauter, J. Hurell, and C. Copper, 129-59. Chichester, UK: Wiley.

Kossoris, M.D. 1938. "Industrial Injuries and the Business Cycle." *Monthly Labor Review* 46 (3): 579-94.

–. 1943. "Changes in Injury Frequency Rates and Employment in Manufacturing 1936-41." *Monthly Labor Review* 56 (5): 949-54.

Robinson, J.C. 1988. "The Rising Long-Term Trend in Occupational Injury Rates." *American Journal of Public Health* 78 (3): 276-81.

Robinson, J.C., and G.M. Shor. 1989. "Business-Cycle Influences on Work-Related Disability in Construction and Manufacturing." *Millbank Quarterly* 67, supplement 2 (part 1): 92-111.

Sharit, J., and G. Salvendy. 1982. "Occupational Stress: Review and Reappraisal." *Human Factors* 24: 129-62.

Statistics Canada. 1953-96. *Canadian Labour Force Survey.* Ottawa: Statistics Canada.

Workers' Compensation Board of British Columbia (BCWCB). 1950-96. *Annual Reports.* Richmond, BC: Workers' Compensation Board.

3
Workforce and Workplace Change: Implications for Injuries and Compensation
Morley Gunderson and Douglas Hyatt

Labour markets and workplaces are undergoing fundamental transformations as the previous chapter by Ostry outlined. As we shall illustrate, the underlying pressures for these transformations are emanating from the changing nature of work and of the workforce and workplace, as well as the associated labour market institutions that govern the workplace.

These changes are having profound implications in the labour market and the workplace. Policy attention has focused especially on: wage polarization, industrial restructuring toward a service- and knowledge-based economy, increased non-standard and contingent employment, reductions in strike activity, job losses and job displacement, earlier retirement, and youth employment issues.

The purpose of this chapter is to focus on the implications of workplace and workforce changes for workplace injuries and workers' compensation. The various dimensions of occupational health and safety and workers' compensation are considered, including prevention, rehabilitation, return to work, and compensation itself. Particular attention is paid to the implications of expected changes in the industrial composition of the workforce of British Columbia to the year 2005.

In contrast to Ostry's historical and epidemiological analysis of the workforce, this chapter, using British Columbia as the case study, begins with a portrayal of the forecasted changes in the major labour market indicators with particular emphasis on the industrial composition of the workforce. It then outlines other expected workforce changes attributable to factors such as the gender and age composition of the workforce, as well as labour force participation and unemployment, and discusses the implications of these changes for injuries and compensation. The essay then analyzes the changes in the nature of work and the workplace, and their implications for injuries and workers' compensation. It concludes with a summary, which includes a discussion of the key policy implications.

Labour Market Trends

Major Economic and Labour Market Indicators

Table 3.1 provides forecasts of major economic and labour market indicators for British Columbia and compares them with the totals for all of Canada. As the final group of columns ("British Columbia minus all Canada") indicates, British Columbia's performance over the medium term is generally projected to lag behind that of Canada as a whole. Specifically, GDP growth is 0.5 percent lower in British Columbia in 1997, with growth projected to remain slower than the Canadian average (by 0.3 percent) from 1998 through 2002 and again from 2003 through 2005. The low inflation rate (as measured by the consumer price index) of 2 percent or less is projected to continue in both British Columbia and all of Canada for the duration of the study period. Unit labour costs, which are 0.6 percent higher in British Columbia than the all-Canada total in 1997, are forecasted to remain higher in the province, but only by a small margin. Labour force participation rates are projected to remain fairly steady in British Columbia and all of Canada, albeit slightly lower in British Columbia. Employment growth is expected to remain similar in British Columbia and all of Canada. British Columbia's unemployment rate, which has generally been lower than the all-Canada average (0.4 percent lower in 1997), is expected to converge upward toward the rate for all of Canada, remaining in the neighbourhood of 8 percent.

In general, the BC economy, which has gone from significantly better to somewhat poorer performance than all of Canada in recent years, is expected to converge more toward the performance of all of Canada, albeit with slightly slower growth. A conservative projection is that the BC economy is not likely to re-experience its earlier boom relative to Canada as a whole, nor is its recent negative performance likely to continue, though slightly below-average performance in employment growth may be expected.

Industrial Restructuring

Table 3.2 gives the recent and expected employment growth by industry over three seven-year periods, again with comparisons to all of Canada. Overall, the rapid employment growth that British Columbia experienced from 1985 through 1991 has dwindled in recent years (1992 to 1998) and is expected to drop continuously in the near future (1999 to 2005). In essence, British Columbia's employment growth will converge more toward the relatively constant growth that is occurring in all of Canada (as shown in the "All Canada" column) so that the difference between British Columbia and all of Canada will dissipate in the near future (as shown in the "British Columbia minus all Canada" columns).

This declining employment growth in British Columbia is being accompanied by considerable variation in employment growth across the different

Table 3.1

Major economic and labour market indicators, British Columbia and Canada, various years, 1997-2005 (average annual rates of growth)

Industry indicator	British Columbia			All Canada			British Columbia minus all Canada		
	1997	1998-2002	2003-5	1997	1998-2002	2003-5	1997	1998-2002	2003-5
Gross domestic product	3.2	2.5	1.9	3.7	2.8	2.2	-0.5	-0.3	-0.3
Consumer price index	1.8	1.8	2.0	1.6	1.8	2.0	0.2	0.0	0.0
Unit labour cost	1.6	1.7	1.8	1.0	1.6	1.7	0.6	0.1	0.1
GDP/employed worker	1.2	0.6	0.7	1.4	0.9	0.9	-0.2	-0.3	-0.2
Labour force participation rate[a]	65.0	65.5	65.7	64.9	65.6	65.9	0.1	-0.1	-0.2
Employment growth	2.0	1.8	1.2	2.0	1.8	1.2	0.0	0.1	0.0
Unemployment rate[a]	8.8	8.2	8.1	9.2	8.2	8.0	-0.4	0.0	0.1

a   The table entries are rate levels, not growth rates.
Source: Extracted from Canadian Occupational Projection System (1998).

Table 3.2

Actual and projected employment by industry, aggregate industries, British Columbia and Canada, 1985-2005[a]

	British Columbia			All Canada			British Columbia minus all Canada		
	1985-91	1992-8	1999-2005	1985-91	1992-8	1999-2005	1985-91	1992-8	1999-2005
Agriculture	-8.3	2.8	5.2	-5.0	-4.8	4.0	-3.3	7.6	1.2
Construction	51.2	11.9	3.8	20.3	12.0	12.0	30.9	-0.0	-8.1
Finance	13.6	-0.8	4.4	20.2	1.3	3.1	-6.7	-2.1	1.3
Fishing and trapping	18.2	-18.9	15.4	41.5	-13.3	1.2	-23.3	-5.6	14.2
Logging and forestry	-7.8	17.9	2.4	-2.3	18.6	0.8	-5.5	-0.7	1.6
Manufacturing	13.7	15.4	8.1	-5.2	18.4	9.4	18.9	-3.0	-1.3
Mining	-13.3	31.2	3.3	-7.3	17.1	9.4	-6.0	14.1	-6.2
Public administration	6.1	-2.0	6.2	5.2	-10.2	4.6	0.9	8.1	1.6
Services	33.0	30.6	11.6	20.5	17.5	11.7	12.6	13.1	-0.1
Trade	20.7	8.5	6.4	9.0	7.8	6.4	11.7	0.7	-0.0
Utilities	-11.1	1.3	4.0	12.1	-11.2	7.4	-23.2	12.4	-3.4
All industries	22.2	16.6	8.5	10.0	11.1	8.9	12.2	5.4	-0.4

a Percentage change in employment over three seven-year periods: 1985-91, 1992-8, and 1999-2005.
Source: Calculated from data provided in Canadian Occupational Projection System (1998).

industries, reflecting the marked industrial restructuring of the economy. The restructuring is expected to be different in British Columbia compared to Canada as a whole, as indicated by the difference in the "British Columbia minus all Canada" columns.

Specifically, employment growth in agriculture is expected to continue to be below the all-industry average over the study period in both British Columbia and all of Canada, although the differences (both relative to the all-industry average and the BC versus all-Canada difference) are expected not to be as great. For example, while total employment across all industries grew on average by 22 percent in British Columbia between 1985 and 1991, it declined by 8 percent in agriculture over that period. A similar but less severe difference prevailed in all of Canada. However, from 1999 through 2005, employment in agriculture in all of Canada is expected to grow by almost half the all-industry average, and in British Columbia this growth is expected to be slightly more than half the all-industry average.

More marked vicissitudes are expected in fishing and trapping. In British Columbia, employment growth in fishing and trapping was only slightly below the average industrial growth from 1985 through 1991 (although for all of Canada it was four times the average growth, reflecting the expansion of the Atlantic fisheries). From 1992 through 1998, employment in fishing and trapping declined by a dramatic 19 percent in British Columbia compared to an all-industry growth of 17 percent (with a similar pattern for all Canada). A rebound to just over 15 percent is projected in British Columbia for 1999 through 2005 – a rebound that is twice the projected all-industry growth of 8.5 percent for that period.

Logging and forestry are also undergoing dramatic changes. The recent employment expansion between 1992 and 1998 in British Columbia (slightly above the all-industry growth) is projected to fall off dramatically (to one-quarter of a much lower all-industry growth) between 1998 and 2005. This parallels a similar pattern for all of Canada, although logging and forestry are proportionately more important in British Columbia than elsewhere in Canada.

Similarly, the growth spurt of employment in mining from 1992 through 1998 (twice the all-industry employment growth rate) is expected to drop off dramatically between 1999 and 2005.

Manufacturing employment growth in British Columbia appears to be following a steady slower growth than that for Canada as a whole. After the construction boom in British Columbia in the late 1980s, employment growth in that sector fell dramatically. Service-sector employment growth in British Columbia has been substantially higher than the all-industry employment growth in all three periods, albeit the differences have grown smaller over time, as has the difference between British Columbia and all of

Canada. Employment growth in public administration in British Columbia has been slower than the all-industry employment growth in all periods, especially from 1992 through 1998 (although it did not fall in British Columbia as much as in all of Canada over that period).

Overall, a rather complicated picture of employment growth emerges in British Columbia, both across different sectors and with respect to Canada as a whole. At the risk of oversimplification, the main trends appear to be: (1) a slowdown in overall employment growth in British Columbia, both absolutely over time, and relative to all of Canada; (2) substantial fluctuations in the primary, resource-based sectors and construction, with below-average employment growth in those sectors projected for the near future; (3) above-average employment growth in services, with that tendency being even stronger in British Columbia than in all of Canada.

Implications for Injuries and Workers' Compensation
These changes in the economy and the labour market are likely to have important implications for workplace injuries and workers' compensation. Injuries may increase as workers change jobs, moving from the declining sectors to the expanding sectors where they are less familiar with the hazards. Or, during recessions, employers may use their remaining employees more intensively through the increased use of overtime, thereby increasing the exposure of remaining workers to risk of injury or disease (Cole et al. 1998). As well, the slowdown in the BC economy and the greater socioeconomic polarization may give rise to health problems. The growing evidence of the negative effects on health from declining income, higher unemployment, lower occupational and social status, and greater socioeconomic polarization is discussed in Sullivan et al. (1998). Conversely, the slowdown of the BC economy may mean fewer injuries as the pace of work and the "speed-up" are lessened.

The slowdown of the economy will also probably give rise to more pressure to contain costs, including regulatory costs associated with occupational health and safety and workers' compensation, insofar as these costs inhibit the competitiveness of BC firms relative to similar firms in other jurisdictions, and thereby inhibit employment growth.

Most important, employment growth is generally projected to be slower in sectors with high injury rates and workers' compensation costs (primary and resource-based industries and construction) and highest in the service sector, which tends to have low injury rates and workers' compensation costs. This suggests the potential for a reduction in per-capita injury rates and workers' compensation costs over the near future. The possible magnitude of that change and the factors that contribute to it are illustrated in the next section.

Simulations of the Impact of Industrial Restructuring

To highlight the expected impact of changes in the industrial composition of the workforce, we simulated the expected changes in workers' compensation costs that would occur from the forecasted employment growth including the industrial restructuring, and from the industrial restructuring only, assuming no change in overall employment. This required a matching of employment numbers from the Canadian Occupational Projection System (COPS) (1998) with workers' compensation assessment rates and with payroll estimates (AWCBC 1997), all from different data sources. (Details of the matching as well as the methodology used for this exercise can be found in an appendix to our original report to the Royal Commission on Workers' Compensation in British Columbia and is available from the authors on request.)

Because this matching was complicated and involved judgment calls about appropriate aggregations, the calculations here should be regarded as illustrative of the broad trends rather than as precise actuarial-type calculations of expected cost changes. Before the actual estimates are presented, a simplified example is provided to illustrate the methodology.

Hypothetical, Simplified Illustration of Methodology

Table 3.3 illustrates the methodology used, based on a stylized example with three industries: logging and forestry, manufacturing, and services. Logging and forestry have low employment, high wages, and high injury rates and hence high assessment rates. Manufacturing has medium employment, wages, and assessment rates. Services have high employment, low wages, and low assessment rates. Although the example is simplified to illustrate and set the stage for the more complex calculations that follow, its results are designed to mirror the general conclusions that emerge in the subsequent more complete analysis.

The top panel of Table 3.3 illustrates the calculation of total workers' compensation costs for 1995. The employment numbers (column 1) are multiplied by the average annual earnings (column 3) to yield the payroll costs for each industry (column 4). These are then multiplied by the assessment rates for each industry (column 5) to yield the total assessable workers' compensation costs for each industry (column 6). These in turn are summed to yield the total workers' compensation costs across all industries. Dividing this total (in column 6) by the payroll cost total of column 4 yields an implied assessment rate for all industries in the province. In effect, this is the average assessment rate, weighted by the industry payroll costs. It is a measure of the system cost per dollar of payroll. An alternative measure of system cost is indicated by the cost per employee (column 6 divided by column 1) as given in the last row.

The second panel illustrates the same calculation based on forecasted

Table 3.3

Hypothetical changes in workers' compensation costs

Industry	Employment (number of persons) (1)	Distribution of employment (%) (2)	Average annual earnings ($) (3)	Total annual payroll ($) (4) = (1) × (3)	Assessment rates per $1 of payroll (%) (5)	Total workers' compensation costs ($) (6) = (4) × (5)
Current year 1995						
Logging and forestry	2	0.20	40,000	80,000	0.04	3,200
Manufacturing	3	0.30	30,000	90,000	0.03	2,700
Services	5	0.50	20,000	100,000	0.02	2,000
All industries	10	1.00	27,000[a]	270,000	0.029[b]	7,900
Cost per employee	n/a	n/a	n/a	n/a	n/a	790[c]
Forecast to year 2005, employment growth and industrial restructuring						
Logging and forestry	1	0.08	40,000	40,000	0.04	1,600
Manufacturing	4	0.33	30,000	120,000	0.03	3,600
Services	7	0.59	20,000	140,000	0.02	2,800
All industries	12	1.00	25,000[a]	300,000	0.027[b]	8,000
Cost per employee	n/a	n/a	n/a	n/a	n/a	667[c]

▶ *Table 3.3*

Hypothetical changes in workers' compensation costs

Industry	Employment (number of persons)	Distribution of employment (%)	Average annual earnings ($)	Total annual payroll ($)	Assessment rates per $1 of payroll (%)	Total workers' compensation costs ($)
	(1)	(2)	(3)	(4) = (1) × (3)	(5)	(6) = (4) × (5)
Forecast to year 2005, industrial restructuring only, no total employment change						
Logging and forestry	**0.8**	**0.08**	40,000	32,000	0.04	1,280
Manufacturing	**3.3**	**0.33**	30,000	99,000	0.03	2,970
Services	**5.9**	**0.59**	20,000	118,000	0.02	2,360
All industries	10	1.00	24,900[a]	249,000	0.026[b]	6,610
Cost per employee	n/a	n/a	n/a	n/a	n/a	661[c]

Notes: Bold denotes forecast changes in employment and its distribution.
a Calculated as the employment weighted average, that is, the total payroll for all industries from column 4 divided by total employment for all industries from column 1.
b Calculated as total workers' compensation costs for all industries from column 6 divided by total payroll for all industries from column 4.
c Calculated as total workers' compensation costs for all industries from column 6 divided by total employment for all industries from column 1.

employment change to 2005. The total labour force grows by 20 percent, from ten persons to twelve. As well, the distribution of the workforce changes, with a decline in logging and forestry (from two persons to one), a slight increase in manufacturing (from three to four persons), and a large increase in services (from five to seven persons). These changes lead to a decline in the percentage of the workforce in logging and forestry from 0.20 to 0.08, a slight increase in manufacturing from 0.30 to 0.33, and a large increase in services from 0.50 to 0.59. These changes in employment and the distribution of that employment are highlighted in bold in columns 1 and 2 respectively.

The changes in both employment growth and in industrial restructuring result in an increase in total workers' compensation costs from $7,900 in 1995 to $8,000 by 2005. The cost increase occurs solely because of changes in employment and its industrial distribution, since average earnings and assessment rates are held constant. This overall system cost increase occurs because, as documented subsequently, the cost increase from the employment growth outweighs the cost reduction from the restructuring from high-wage, high-assessment rate industries like logging and forestry, to lower-wage, low-assessment rate industries in the service sector. Although the overall system cost has increased, most of this simply reflects the employment growth that has occurred from ten to twelve workers. The average cost per worker falls considerably from $790 in 1995 (i.e., $7,900/10) to $667 per worker in 2005 (i.e., $8,000/12). The fall in the average cost per worker occurs because the employment growth disproportionately occurs in industries of both lower injury and hence assessment rates, as well as in lower-wage industries (where a given assessment rate implies a lower total cost). The fact that the total implied assessment rate (column 5) falls only marginally, from 0.029 in 1995 to 0.027 in 2005, highlights that most of the substantial drop in the cost per worker is accompanied by a corresponding drop in the earnings per worker, so that cost per dollar of payroll does not fall by much.

This does not mean that the reduction in assessment costs (and presumably injuries) is artificial or an artefact of the data. It would reflect a disproportionate employment growth in industries with lower assessment rates (and presumably injuries associated with those lower rates). Hence, the overall average cost per worker falls. But since these growth industries also tend to be lower wage industries, the cost per dollar of payroll does not fall by as much.

The calculations in the bottom panel of Table 3.3 isolate those cost changes resulting from changes in industrial distribution from those resulting from employment growth. This is accomplished by assuming that there is no employment growth, but that the 1995 employment of ten persons is distributed according to the industrial distribution of the workforce for 2005. In essence, the only change is the industrial distribution of the workforce as illustrated in bold in column 1 of the bottom panel.

This yields a total system cost of $6,610 by 2005. This is 16 percent less than the system cost of $7,900 in 1995 (which, as it turns out, corresponds closely to the 20 percent reduction we find in our subsequent detailed calculations based on the "real" employment numbers and forecasts). The cost reduction occurs solely because of the restructuring from high-wage, high-assessment rate industries like logging and forestry, to lower-wage, low-assessment rate industries in the service sector. Since the employment level is assumed to be the same, the average cost per worker drops considerably, from $790 (i.e., $7,900/10) in 1995 to $661 (i.e., $6,610/10) in 2005. Again, since the growth industries also tend to be lower-wage industries, the drop in cost per dollar of payroll is smaller, going from 0.029 percent in 1995 to 0.026 percent by 2005.

The cost calculations of Table 3.3 are hypothetical, simplified, and designed to illustrate the more detailed methodological approach that we use in the following analysis. Nevertheless, they are representative of what occurs in this more complicated set of real calculations as set out in the next section.

Projected Cost Calculations by Aggregate Industry Groups

The cost calculations are summarized in Table 3.4. The cost changes that are expected to occur as a result of changes in both employment growth and the distribution of employment (as previously illustrated in the middle panel of Table 3.3) are given in column 2 for the year 2000 and column 3 for the year 2005. The cost changes that are expected to occur solely as a result of changes in the distribution of employment (as previously illustrated in the bottom panel of Table 3.3) are given in column 4 for the year 2000 and column 5 for the year 2005.

As the all-industries figures of the third-last row of Table 3.4 illustrate, total workers' compensation costs are projected to increase by 10.6 percent to the year 2000 and 16 percent to the year 2005, as a result of both employment growth and changes in the industrial distribution of the workforce. On a per worker basis, the system costs are projected to decrease, however, as indicated in the second-last row of Table 3.4, where cost per worker falls from $700 in 1995 to $694 by 2000, and to $686 by 2005. The drop in the cost per worker reflects the disproportionate employment growth that will occur in sectors with lower workers' compensation costs (and presumably injury rates). As indicated in the last row in Table 3.4, the cost per $100 of payroll is also expected to drop slightly, from 2.26 percent in 1995 to 2.24 percent by 2000, and to 2.22 percent by 2005. Because employment growth is also expected to be disproportionate in lower-wage industries, the apparent cost reduction is negligible when expressed as a percent of payroll.

Table 3.4

Projected workers' compensation costs, British Columbia, 2000 and 2005

	1995 assessment rates (%)	Cost change based on forecasted employment growth and changing distribution of employment (%)		Cost change based on constant 1995 employment and changing distribution of employment (%)	
		2000	2005	2000	2005
	(1)	(2)	(3)	(4)	(5)
Agriculture	3.68	18.93	6.57	23.96	-4.51
Construction	5.84	10.56	11.78	-0.93	-5.76
Finance	0.25	0.86	4.09	-9.62	-12.24
Fishing and trapping	3.22	-7.35	-16.97	6.42	-10.28
Logging and forestry	6.44	-17.53	-26.10	-17.14	-30.14
Manufacturing	3.02	11.54	17.61	-0.05	-0.84
Mining	4.28	34.93	37.84	20.91	16.21
Public administration, municipal	0.88	-0.45	7.49	-10.80	-9.37
Services	1.27	18.55	29.14	6.23	8.88
Trade	1.51	8.13	13.07	-3.10	-4.67
Transportation, storage, and communication	2.93	12.28	19.73	0.61	-0.94
Utilities	2.47	-3.59	-0.34	-13.61	-15.98
All industries	2.26	10.56	16.17	-0.93	-19.81
Cost per worker	$700	$694	$686	$694	$561
Cost per $100 payroll (%)	2.26	2.24	2.22	2.24	1.82

There is considerable variation in those cost projections across industries, reflecting the variation in forecasted employment growth across the different industries. Employment and hence costs, for example, are forecasted to fall in fishing and trapping, and especially in logging and forestry. In contrast, costs are expected to rise disproportionately in mining and services, reflecting the expected growth of employment in those sectors.

Although not shown in the table, our analysis was also performed at more disaggregated industry levels. While the industry aggregates provide a useful summary picture, they mask considerable variation within each industry. For example, although workers' compensation costs are expected to increase by 11 percent overall in manufacturing by 2000, within manufacturing, costs are expected to increase by 114 percent in petroleum and coal products, and to decrease by 11 percent in clothing manufacturing, reflecting the differential forecasts of employment growth in those sectors.

The last two columns of Table 3.4 are the most informative since they indicate the changes in workers' compensation costs that are expected to occur purely because of industrial restructuring, after controlling for the effect of overall employment growth (i.e., total employment is held constant at the 1995 level, with the 2000 and 2005 forecasted industrial distributions of the workforce applied to that employment level in columns 4 and 5, respectively).

The all-industries total in column 4 indicates that, as a result of industrial restructuring, workers' compensation costs are expected to fall by 1 percent between 1995 and 2000, and by a substantial 20 percent between 1995 and 2005 (column 5). This reflects the forecasted restructuring from industries with high assessment rates (and presumably high injury rates) to ones with low assessment and injury rates.

As the separate industry breakdowns indicate, costs are expected to fall by 30 percent in the logging and forestry industry, reflecting the industrial restructuring from that industry associated with its forecasted 2005 distribution of the workforce. Costs are expected to stay about the same in manufacturing, since there is not much restructuring out of that industry, and they are expected to increase by 9 percent in services, reflecting the restructuring to that sector.

As noted earlier, the forecasted cost changes across the different aggregate industry designations can mask the considerable variation that exists within each of these broad industry groups. For example, although the aggregate cost reduction is forecasted to be 1 percent in manufacturing, within that broad aggregate, costs are expected to increase by 82 percent in petroleum and coal products, and to decrease by 30 percent in clothing manufacturing, reflecting the industrial restructuring across those subsectors within manufacturing.

As the second-last row in Table 3.4 indicates, these changes should lead to a reduction in the average workers' compensation cost per worker from $700 in 1995 to $561 by the year 2005. As well, they would lead to a reduction in the cost per $100 of payroll (the implied assessment rate) from 2.26 percent in 1995 to 1.82 percent by 2005. The fact that there is a substantial reduction in cost per $100 of payroll highlights that the industrial restructuring to industries of low assessment and injury rates is not always to low-wage industries. If it were, then the savings in cost per worker would not be reflected in cost per $100 of payroll.

Summary of Impact of Industrial Restructuring
Overall, the industrial restructuring that is forecasted to occur in British Columbia is expected to lead to substantial savings in workers' compensation costs, since the restructuring is generally from industries with high assessment rates to industries with low assessment rates. To the extent that the industry assessment rates reflect the incidence and severity of injuries in each sector, this should also mean a drop in the incidence and severity of injuries in the province.

The cost saving (and injury reduction) will be minor until the year 2000, being in the neighbourhood of 1 percent. However, between 2000 and 2005, a cost saving of 20 percent is projected due to the industrial restructuring. Of course, greater uncertainty prevails about the cost saving further into the future, reflecting the greater uncertainty about the forecasts of the restructuring of employment by industry.

As an alternative way of portraying the expected cost saving, workers' compensation costs per worker are expected to fall from $700 in 1995 to $694 by 2000 and to $561 by 2005. Alternatively, the cost per $100 of payroll (the implied assessment rate for the system as a whole) is forecasted to fall from 2.26 percent in 1995 to 2.24 percent by 2000 and to 1.82 percent by 2005, due purely to the forecasted industrial restructuring of employment. In other words, if the employment numbers stayed fixed at 1995 levels, and the changes were confined solely to industrial restructuring, the overall assessment rate necessary to finance the system would fall from 2.26 percent of payroll in 1995 to 2.24 percent by 2000, and to 1.82 by 2005. The substantial change between 2000 and 2005 highlights the expectation that most of the industrial restructuring will occur over that five-year period. The cost saving is expected to occur because the restructuring will result in proportionately less employment in high assessment rate (and presumably high injury rate) industries to lower assessment rate industries.

The system cost saving due to industrial restructuring, of course, assumes that the assessment rates will remain the same in each of the industries. The growth industries with the low assessment rates (e.g., public administration, services) tend to be ones with non-traditional injuries and diseases such as stress, mental illness, repetitive strain and other disorders, and cardiovascular and musculoskeletal injuries and diseases. To the extent that these injuries become more prominent and compensable, then the assessment rates may well rise in those sectors, thereby offsetting some of the cost saving from industrial restructuring.

An alternative perspective is that the cost saving is largely illusory, and reflects mainly the industrial restructuring from industries where injuries were compensable because of the "hard" nature of the injuries, to industries where they are not as compensable because they reflect "soft" injuries and diseases that are more difficult to measure and assess. The restructuring is not to a safer workforce, but rather to a workforce that is less compensated for its new injuries and diseases. This may well lead to lower assessment costs to employers, but that does not necessarily imply a safer workforce or a lower "true cost" of injuries. It may well reflect a less compensated workforce.

The reasonableness of this interpretation is difficult to assess. The overall generalization that emerges is that the industrial restructuring is expected to lead to substantial cost saving in the system if assessment rates by industry remain unchanged. Whether this implies a safer workforce or one that is simply less compensated for the newer injuries and diseases of the growth industries is beyond the scope of this analysis.

The system cost saving, however, is likely to lead to different pressures. There will be pressure to have the cost savings filter down to a lower overall average assessment rate (i.e., not change the rates by industry) given the pressure to constrain payroll taxes. That emphasis, in turn, emanates from the perception that payroll taxes are "killers of jobs" and that they hinder competitiveness. If payroll taxes are perceived to be shifted back onto workers (DiMatteo and Shannon 1995) in the form of lower compensating wages in return for the benefit of the workers' compensation, then restraining assessment rates would be alleviating wage stagnation.

Pressure will also probably exist to use the system cost savings to increase compensation for emerging diseases and conditions that are associated with the growth industries. If these diseases and conditions are more liberally compensated, then the resulting higher assessment rates in those industries will offset the cost savings that otherwise would have accrued from the restructuring from industries of high to low assessment rates.

Clearly, the industrial restructuring will lead to the potential for cost saving in the system. The ultimate use of that cost saving will depend upon other pressures that will effectively vie for the funds.

Other Changes and Implications for Injuries and Compensation

In earlier papers (Gunderson, forthcoming; Gunderson and Hyatt, forthcoming) we identified a wide range of changes that were occurring in the nature of the workforce, the workplace, workplace practices, and workplace institutions and we illustrated their implications for workers' compensation. They are expanded upon here, with particular attention paid to various functions of occupational health and safety and workers' compensation, including prevention, rehabilitation, return to work, and compensation.

Other Workforce Changes

The ageing workforce (Grover 1998) means that the composition of claims will shift toward older workers. Older workers are more prone to injuries that are age-related, and occupational diseases with long latency periods may become more manifest. This may increase claims costs, and longer life expectancy may increase the duration of claims.

On the other hand, older workers tend to have fewer accidents because of their experience and they may have a greater tendency to take precautions against risks. Their shorter remaining life expectancy may reduce the expected duration of long-term claims.

Return-to-work adjustments are likely to be more difficult for older workers, in terms of both learning new skills and finding alternative employment. Retirement may be a more viable option. Issues of integration with disability benefits for the Canada Pension Plan and other age-related programs will obviously become more important. Vocational rehabilitation will have to be geared to any special needs of older workers.

The ageing workforce also has implications for any unfunded liabilities that may be transferred from older workers to younger workers in pay-as-you-go systems like workers' compensation, which are not mandated to be actuarially fully funded (Gunderson and Hyatt 1998). In such systems, the incumbent workers pay for the benefits of the recipients who are receiving workers' compensation, with the implicit understanding that, if they are injured, they will be covered by new generations of workers and firms who will be paying into the system. Such "pay-as-you-go" (or partial pay-as-you-go) systems are sustainable when population and real wage growth is stable; however, with an ageing workforce and stagnant real wages, the ability of younger generations of workers (and firms) to continue the implicit obligation may be in jeopardy. In such circumstances, contribution rates have to be raised to cover the future expected liabilities, or benefits will have to be reduced. The benefit reductions would not be likely to take overt forms, since that would appear to violate the implicit social contract that is involved. Rather, they may take more subtle forms such as more stringent requirements for employers to accommodate the return to work of injured workers, shifting claimants to other income support systems, tightening eligibility and return-to-work requirements, and pressure for privatization to save on administrative costs and perhaps to require full funding.

In addition to being older on average, the workforce of the future will continue to reflect the increased labour force participation of women and the dominance of the two-earner family, though these trends are levelling off (Grover 1998). They do imply, however, the continuation of the stress issues associated with balancing work and family. To the extent that these contribute to compensable stress-related injuries, diseases, and other conditions in the workplace, then such stress-related problems will continue to loom large in the area of occupational health and safety and compensation.

The workforce of the future will also continue to be characterized by increased ethnic diversity. The main issue here is likely to emanate from information problems associated with language and cultural barriers, especially with respect to information on workplace hazards and workers' rights.

Workplace Changes

Dramatic changes are also occurring in the workplace – that is, within the internal labour market of firms.

Technological change, especially that associated with computer technology and the information economy, continues largely unabated. This should lead to a reduction of conventional, "hard" physical injuries associated with blue-collar, physical labour (along the lines of the industrial restructuring discussed previously). However, technological change will also bring with it a host of heretofore non-traditional diseases and ailments associated with repetitive strain (such as carpal tunnel syndrome) and perhaps stress-related diseases associated with the use of new work technologies.

Technological change can also bring with it new requirements for our approaches to prevention, as noted in the chapters by Kerr, Norman and Wells, Shannon, and O'Grady in this volume. It may also bring about advances in medical diagnostics and treatments, and facilitate reasonable accommodation and return to work when injuries and illnesses do occur.

The growth of small firms will probably continue. While they can be an important source of job creation, they can create particular challenges for occupational health and safety and workers' compensation. Such firms may find it difficult to adopt health and safety programs and to be informed about workplace hazards. They may find it more difficult to hold open jobs for injured workers and to accommodate these workers' return to work. Small firms may be more difficult to monitor for infractions, and they may even be exempt from certain regulations such as those requiring a joint health and safety committee, and workers' compensation experience rating.

The growth of small firms, coming at the same time as increased mergers and acquisitions, means that the workplace may be increasingly characterized by polarization, with large, multinational conglomerates serviced by small subcontractors. This suggests the potential need for a dual strategy especially with respect to enforcement. Fostering the internal responsibility system may be effective for the large firms, given their internal organizational structure and their sensitivity to their public image. Disseminating information and informing workers of their rights and responsibilities, assisting in reasonable accommodation, and facilitating the return to work of injured workers may be more important in the smaller firms.

The restructuring that has been occurring and that will probably continue into the future implies that a substantial number of new firms have been created while others have gone out of business. If there are unfunded liabilities in pay-as-you-go systems like workers' compensation, this means that the firms that go out of business will not have to pay for their workers' compensation liabilities. Moreover, the new firms will be taking on those liabilities. This could discourage the growth of new firms, especially small firms that may find it difficult to take on higher payroll taxes that would be associated with their paying down the liabilities of the previous generation of firms. Of course, this also means that the decline of older firms may slow down, at least to the extent that they are spared the cost of the higher payroll taxes they would be paying for their unfunded liabilities. To the extent that we want firms to pay for the full social costs of their activities, however, we would not want to sustain them in business simply because they do not have to pay for the full costs of their injuries.

The substantial downsizing that is occurring and may well continue also has implications for health and safety and workers' compensation. The threat of potential job loss, and the reality of job loss should it occur, can give rise to stress-related problems. Such problems can also exist for the remaining workforce who do not lose their jobs but often have an increased workload if they are assigned the work of those who have lost their jobs.

Changes in Workplace Practices
Dramatic changes are also occurring in the workplace practices of firms, with important implications for health and safety and workers' compensation.

Job classifications are becoming broader and workers are often expected to do a wide range of tasks as the number of job classifications gets reduced. This could lead to an increase in injuries, as workers may be less familiar with the hazards associated with the different aspects of the job. Broader job classifications may also make vocational rehabilitation more difficult, at least to the extent that multi-skilling is required for the multi-tasking. On the other hand, it may facilitate the return to work of injured workers since a wider range of tasks are available, and it may be easier to reassign the existing workforce to make room for a returning injured worker.

Organizational structures are becoming flatter with vertical hierarchies and supervision being reduced. This could lead to reduced supervision on health and safety issues, enhancing the importance of self-monitoring and responsibility in the area.

The increased emphasis on pay for performance could lead to enhanced stress as the pace of work increases. It may also lead to cutting corners and reduced attention to health and safety, although health and safety issues could be incorporated into the performance requirements. Just-in-time delivery can have similar effects.

The increased emphasis on employee involvement and participation in workplace decision making can provide a potentially important forum for integrating health and safety issues into workplace actions. Employees can be an invaluable source of information and suggestions on workplace issues, including health and safety. Employee involvement is often invoked as a mechanism for self-monitoring and quality control. Quality control could involve not only the quality of the product, but also the quality of the health and safety conditions under which it is produced.

Workplace teams also have the potential to be a focus for health and safety issues and for information dissemination. They could facilitate the return to work of injured workers to the extent that tasks can be reallocated within the team. This could lead to additional pressure on the work team, however, as well as pressure not to report injuries if they would reflect badly on the team, reduce or eliminate any reward associated with maintaining a record of low levels of injury reporting, or provide an additional burden on the team.

There has been increased use of non-standard employment in various forms including part-time work, fixed-term contracts, temporary-help agencies, subcontracting, self-employment, home-based work, and telecommuting. The very intent of this work is flexibility, but as noted by Sullivan and Frank in this volume, that flexibility can enhance problems of coverage, information dissemination, and attribution of the source of injury and especially of it being work-related. Return-to-work and reasonable accommodation requirements can become more difficult in non-fixed work sites, though the enhanced flexibility could also accommodate transitions in the return to work.

Changing Institutions

Substantial changes are also occurring in the labour market institutions that are important in regulating workplace arrangements.

Unions are often on the defensive, having declined in many countries including the United States where the unionization rate at about 16 percent of the workforce is less than half of the rate in Canada. Even if unions have not declined in Canada, they are under pressure given the increased competition that exists with the United States under free trade.

A possible decline in the influence of unions could jeopardize the important role they play, especially with respect to the three Rs: the right to know or be informed about workplace risks; the right to refuse unsafe work; and the right to representation in joint health and safety committees. Unions can also play an important role in the return-to-work decision, although their emphasis on seniority can also make it more difficult to re-assign injured workers.

Restrictions are increasingly being placed on other policy initiatives, in part in response to the pressures on governments to retrench in their expenditures and to minimize costly regulations. Such restrictions in turn can lead to substitutions across programs as recipients find their access and payments reduced in some. Restrictions on unemployment insurance, for example, can induce reallocation to workers' compensation (Fortin and Lanoie 1992). Reallocations can also occur among disability-related programs such as Canada/Quebec Pension Plan disability, private long-term disability, and workers' compensation.

Governments are under increased pressure to cut government spending and taxes. Resistance to payroll taxes like those used to finance workers' compensation is particularly strong in part because of the perception that they are "killers of jobs." If the incidence of such taxes is ultimately shifted back onto workers in the form of lower wages (a strong possibility given that labour is relatively immobile and cannot escape the tax), then the concern is that this will foster continued stagnation in real wage growth.

Pressures on governments to reduce program expenditures will translate into pressure to prevent accidents and to utilize vocational rehabilitation if it is cost effective in facilitating return to work. It will also lead to restraints on benefits, with respect to both restricting the injuries and diseases that will be covered, and the generosity of benefits once they occur. Governments will also be under increased pressure to shift some of the costs onto the private sector by instituting stronger requirements in the area of return to work and the duty to accommodate. They will also be more watchful for efficiencies in the delivery of their services, and perhaps consider alternative forms of service delivery, including privatization.

Much of the increased pressure on governments is occurring because of inter-jurisdictional competition for investment and the jobs associated with that investment (Gunderson 1998). The increased competition among different governments (both across countries and within countries) in turn results from globalization, trade liberalization, and capital mobility. With trade liberalization, companies are more able to move to low-cost countries, or lower-cost jurisdictions within countries, and export around the world given the reduction in tariffs and non-tariff barriers to trade. The investment and plant location decisions of such companies may well be influenced by regulatory costs including those associated with occupational health and safety and workers' compensation. In such circumstances, governments may compete with other governments by reducing the costs of doing business in their jurisdiction.

The concern is that this inter-jurisdictional competition for investment and jobs will lead to a "race to the bottom" or policy "harmonization to the lowest common denominator." Increased attention will be paid to what is happening in other jurisdictions, especially major trading partners. This indeed will occur. However, labour regulations need not always add to the cost of doing business. Health and safety regulations can reduce costly workplace accidents. Workers' compensation is a quid pro quo for giving up the right to sue an employer, thereby saving employers the cost of expensive litigation.

In such circumstances, the pressure will be in the direction of ensuring the cost-effectiveness of regulations, not necessarily on eliminating regulation per se. Pressure may also exist for inter-jurisdictional cooperation in the policy arena so as not to compete on the basis of reducing socially important regulations.

Conclusion

Clearly, dramatic changes are occurring in almost all dimensions of work: the workforce, the workplace, workplace practices, and labour market institutions. These in turn are having important implications for almost all functions associated with occupational health and safety and workers' compensation: prevention, rehabilitation, return to work, and compensation.

Increased attention will be placed on prevention, both as a cost-saving measure and as part of the emphasis on health and well-being. This will be embraced by the ageing population and by the growing knowledge-based workforce with its increased awareness of health and well-being. Prevention measures will require modification from the conventional "hard-hat and guard-rail" emphasis associated with physical injuries in blue-collar work to issues such as ergonomics, stress management, and musculoskeletal injuries associated with the changing nature of work.

Vocational and medical rehabilitation needs will also change, especially because of the ageing workforce. Early retirement may be a viable alternative, just as it is with the non-injured workforce. Vocational rehabilitation will have to place an emphasis on more general training, with an emphasis on multi-skilling and team-based activity, in step with the general training needs in the non-injured workforce.

Return-to-work and accommodation requirements increasingly will be emphasized by governments as a way of enhancing self-sufficiency and reducing their compensation costs by shifting obligations to the private sector. However, the return-to-work and accommodation requirements will be made more difficult because of the ageing workforce, high unemployment, slower growth, rapid technological change, multi-tasking, and the increasing number of small firms. Tensions will continue in this area, though they may be reduced somewhat by other changes such as the flexibility gained by broader-based job classifications and technological change that can facilitate some of the accommodations.

The compensation aspect of workers' compensation is the area that will be most affected by the changes that are occurring. The industrial restructuring that is forecasted to occur in British Columbia is expected to lead to savings in workers' compensation system costs in the order of 20 percent between the year 2000 and 2005. This reflects restructuring that is generally from industries with high assessment rates (e.g., agriculture, fishing, logging and forestry, construction) to industries of low assessment rates, notably services. To the extent that the industry assessment rates reflect the incidence and severity of injuries in each sector, this should also mean a drop in the incidence and severity of injuries in the province.

Of course, there will be various competing pressures for the savings from industrial restructuring. If the historical trends in Ostry's chapter in this volume are any indication, then we might expect a continued rise in soft tissue injury rates. Pressure will exist to use the savings to compensate and deal with the musculoskeletal injuries and stress-related disorders that are more common in the growing service sector. To the extent that these injuries become more prominent and compensable, then the assessment rates may rise in those sectors, thereby offsetting some of the cost saving from industrial restructuring.

Pressure will exist to have the cost saving filter down to a lower overall average assessment rate given the pressure for payroll tax reductions, since they are often perceived as "killers of jobs" and hindrances to competitiveness, especially for the growing small business sector. If unfunded liabilities exist that will be passed to an already over-burdened younger generation of workers, there may be pressure to use the cost saving to reduce any unfunded liability. Demands on the system may also increase in the future to the extent that the greater numbers of older persons are associated with higher system costs.

Competing pressure for any cost saving is likely to be made more complicated because the industrial restructuring is giving rise to new diseases and conditions that are more difficult to diagnose (Frank, forthcoming), diseases and conditions that often have long latency periods, complex interactions, and multiple causes that make it difficult to attribute the cause to work or to a specific employer (Shainblum et al., forthcoming). As well, the dramatic restructuring in labour markets that is occurring is giving rise to a wide range of adjustment consequences – unemployment, job loss, job insecurity, uncertainty, socio-economic polarization – all of which can have negative effects on health (Sullivan et al. 1998). In such circumstances, fundamental rethinking may be necessary with respect to how best to redesign the system to maintain its essential insurance features while at the same time maintaining its financial integrity and encouraging the return to work of injured workers.

The urgency of the matter is heightened as governments and policy makers are also under increased pressures from various sources including taxpayer resistance, fiscal restraint, and inter-jurisdictional competition for investment and the jobs associated with that investment. Those forces will put pressure on governments to ensure that regulations like those pertaining to occupational health and safety and workers' compensation serve their fundamental purposes in a cost-effective fashion.

The changing nature of the workforce and the workplace are giving rise to both new challenges and new opportunities. This is true not only for employers and employees, but also for governments and policy makers. Nowhere are these challenges more prominent than in the areas of occupational health and safety and workers' compensation.

References

Association of Workers' Compensation Boards of Canada (AWCBC). 1997. *Workers' Compensation Industry Classification, Assessment Rates, and Experience Rating Programs in Canada*. Toronto: Association of Workers' Compensation Boards of Canada.

Canadian Occupational Projection System (COPS). 1998. *Macroeconomic Reference Scenario*. Ottawa: Human Resources Development Canada.

Cole, D., D. Hyatt, and S. Sinclair. 1998. "Economics and RSI/WMSD: Coming to Grips with Economic Causes, Costs, and Efficiency." Working Paper, Institute for Work and Health, Toronto.

DiMatteo, L., and M. Shannon. 1995. "Payroll Taxation in Canada: An Overview." *Canadian Business Economics* 3 (4): 5-22.

Fortin, B., and P. Lanoie. 1992. "Substitution between Unemployment Insurance and Compensation." *Journal of Public Economics* 49: 287-312.

Frank, J. Forthcoming. "Paradoxical Aspects of Low Back Pain in Workers' Compensation Systems." In *Issues in Workers' Compensation: Foundations for Reform*, ed. M. Gunderson and D. Hyatt. Toronto: University of Toronto Press.

Grover, G. 1998. "British Columbia Labour Force and Employment Dynamics: A Historical Review." Report prepared for the Royal Commission on Workers' Compensation in British Columbia.

Gunderson, M. 1998. "Harmonization of Labour Policies under Trade Liberalization." *Industrial Relations* 53 (1): 11-41.

–. Forthcoming. "Workers' Compensation in the New World of Work." In *Issues in Workers' Compensation: Foundations for Reform*, ed. M. Gunderson and D. Hyatt. Toronto: University of Toronto Press.

Gunderson, M., and D. Hyatt. 1998. "Intergenerational Considerations of Workers' Compensation Unfunded Liabilities." In *Government Finances and Generational Equity*, ed. Miles Corak, 317-30. Ottawa: Statistics Canada and Human Resources Development Canada.

–. Forthcoming. "Workers' Compensation Unfunded Liabilities." In *Issues in Workers' Compensation: Foundations for Reform*, ed. M. Gunderson and D. Hyatt. Toronto: University of Toronto Press.

Shainblum, E., T. Sullivan, and J. Frank. Forthcoming "Multicausality, Non-Traditional Injury, and the Future of Workers' Compensation." In *Issues in Workers' Compensation: Foundations for Reform*, ed. M. Gunderson and D. Hyatt. Toronto: University of Toronto Press.

Sullivan, T., O. Uneke, J. Lavis, D. Hyatt, and J. O'Grady. 1998. "Labour Adjustment Policies and Health: Considerations for a Changing World." In *Determinants of Health: Settings and Issues*, ed. National Forum on Health, 531-61. St.-Foy, QC: Éditions MultiMondes, for the National Forum on Health.

4
Women, Work, and Injury
Jinjoo Chung, Donald Cole, and Judy Clarke

Women form a growing part of the Canadian labour force and the injuries they experience constitute an increasing proportion of workers' compensation board (WCB) claims. This chapter documents these trends and addresses associated issues. This approach is in keeping with the growing recognition of the importance of gender-based analyses for public policy (Morris 1997). Although many of the data necessary for a full gender-based analysis remain uncollected or unanalyzed, we can nonetheless describe situations in which women have different experiences of work-related injury or illness than men do. In this chapter, we refer to "gender" rather than "sex," recognizing the importance of social conditions and social behaviour (rather than only biological factors) in explaining the different experiences of women and men (Doyal 1995; Messing et al. 1991, 1998). We focus more on analysis of women's situation in the context of comparative analysis. This leads us to challenge the "gender-neutral policy" approach, which assumes that policies, programs, and legislation affect everyone in the same way regardless of gender (Status of Women Canada 1996) and which has historically been the norm in the field of workers' compensation. We argue that the development of policies, programs, and data collection/management strategies that are sensitive to gender issues would be an important step toward more equitable treatment of women by workers' compensation systems.

Gender Differences in the Labour Market
The different roles women and men have played in the workforce are fundamental to understanding gender differences in work and health relationships. Women's participation in the Canadian labour force increased dramatically between 1975 and 1997, from 44.4 percent to 57.4 percent, while men's participation declined, from 78.4 percent to 72.5 percent. Women now make up just less than half of total employment.

Age was associated with gender differences in labour force participation rates. In 1997, 72 percent of women and 79 percent of men aged twenty to twenty-four were in the labour force, whereas the rates were 78 percent and 91 percent respectively for those aged twenty-five to thirty-four, and 79 percent and 93 percent in the thirty-five- to forty-four-year age group.[1] The large gender differences in labour force participation after age twenty-five are probably associated with pregnancy and women's family responsibilities, particularly in the most intensive years of child bearing and child rearing (women made up almost 99 percent of recipients of maternity and parental benefits in 1993) (Statistics Canada 1994). Further, women were more likely to work part-time, with about 29 percent of women so employed in 1997, compared to only 10.5 percent of men.[2]

Significant changes have occurred in the pattern of employment of Canadian workers by industrial sector. The proportion of workers employed in the service (as opposed to goods-producing) sector increased from 64 percent to 72 percent between 1975 and 1998.[3] In 1995, 86 percent of employed women and 63 percent of employed men were in the service sector.[4] The three industrial sectors in which most women worked were services (51 percent of employed women), trade (17 percent), and manufacturing (10 percent), whereas for men the distribution was somewhat different: services (26 percent of employed men), trade (17 percent), and manufacturing (20 percent). The only two places where numbers of women exceeded those of men were in the service sector and the finance, insurance, and real estate sector.

Women and men tend to cluster in certain occupations, respectively. In 1996, women constituted 79 percent of people in health occupations, 72 percent in business, finance, and administrative occupations, and 40 percent in occupations designated as social science, education, government

Table 4.1

Women's top ten occupations in 1961 and 1996

	1961	1996
1	Stenographers, typists, and clerk-typists	Retail sales clerks
2	Clerical occupations not elsewhere classified	Office secretaries
3	Sales clerks	Cashiers
4	Maids and related service workers not elsewhere classified	Registered nurses
5	Schoolteachers	Accounting clerks
6	Bookkeepers and cashiers	Elementary/ kindergarten teachers
7	Nurses, graduate and in-training	Waitresses
8	Farm labourers	Office clerks
9	Waitresses	Babysitters
10	Sewers and sewing machine operators	Receptionists

Source: 1961 data: Wilson (1991). 1996 data: 1996 census analysis by Statistics Canada (cited in "He's a trucker, she types – 1990s just like the 50s," *Globe and Mail*, 18 March 1998, p. A1).

service, and religion.[5] Men made up the major part of the workforce in trades, transport and equipment operators, and related occupations (94 percent), in primary industry (79 percent), and in processing, manufacturing, and utilities (71 percent). More specific occupational categories (Table 4.1) suggest that women's occupations have changed very little over the past three decades in Canada (Fox 1987), although the gap between women's and men's earning capacity narrowed between 1967 and 1994.[6] Thus gender segregation in the labour force implies that the range of overall occupational exposures at work will be different for women and men.

Gender Differences in Compensable Occupational Injuries and Illnesses

We now turn to gender differences in the experience of time loss injuries (and to a lesser extent illnesses). Women accounted for 26.2 percent of time loss injuries in 1996 (Appendix B, Figure B1) with British Columbia (26.1 percent) close to the Canadian average (AWCBC 1999). Consistent with changes in the gender composition of the labour force, the trend from 1982 (the earliest year national data were aggregated) to 1996 is for the women's proportion to increase (from 17.1 percent to 26.2 percent) and for the men's to decline (from 82.9 percent to 73.8 percent[7]). However, women still account for disproportionately few time loss injuries.

Breakdown of the data by industrial sector (Figure B2) allows us to explore this trend. In 1996, the manufacturing sector had most injuries (29.0 percent of all accepted time loss claims in Canada), followed by services (24.5 percent) and trade (17.1 percent). Men's greater labour force participation in manufacturing, transportation, and construction, which together accounted for 46.3 percent of time loss claims (but only 28 percent of those employed) may be part of the reason. In contrast, those sectors in which women's participation was highest, finance and services, together accounted for only 25 percent of time loss claims. In spite of these obvious sectoral differences, we note that across all industrial sectors, men accounted for greater proportions of time loss claims than their labour force participation alone might warrant.

It may appear that these differences are associated with the different occupations held by women and men in the various industrial sectors. Proportions of time loss claims broken down according to occupational groups provide further information. In the four occupational groups accounting for most time loss claims in 1996 (trades and skilled transport and equipment operators; intermediate occupations in transport, equipment operators; labourers in processing, manufacturing machine operators; and processing and manufacturing machine operators), men predominate. In contrast, only three occupational groups in the top ten had higher proportions of women (assisting occupations in support of health services; intermediate sales and service occupations; and elemental sales and service occupations).

Turning to the nature of injuries sustained (Table 4.2), we again note a difference in patterns for men and women, and changes over recent years (Figure 4.1). In 1996, sprains and strains (the most common injury type) constituted 29.6 percent of all time loss claims for men and 12.4 percent, for women. In this injury category, men dropped from 80.5 percent to 70.6 percent of injured workers between 1982 and 1996, with women's proportion increasing correspondingly (19.5 percent to 29.4 percent) (as illustrated in Figure B1). Men tended to have more claims for cuts, lacerations, punctures, fractures, scratches, and abrasions while women were more likely to have inflammation, irritation, non-specified, and other occupational injuries. The latter is consistent with more work-related disorders of the neck and upper limb, known as repetitive strain injuries (RSI) or cumulative trauma disorders, among women. An analysis of Ontario WCB data (Ashbury 1995) found that over the six-year period from 1986 through 1991, RSI rates and claim frequency rates were higher for women than men in each of the job categories with the highest risk for this type of injury. Further, women's rates were increasing.

Figure 4.1

Accepted time loss claims for sprains and strains by gender in Canada, 1982-96

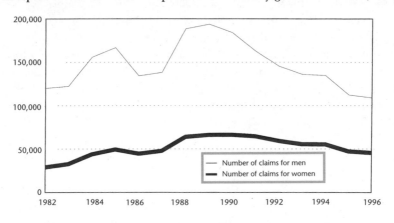

Note: The figures exclude "unknown" and "not coded" claims.
Source: Association of Workers' Compensation Boards of Canada, www.AWCBC.on.ca.

Analysis by part of body affected is consistent with this inference (Table 4.3). Although back injuries were the most common for both genders, proportionately more of women's injuries affected the shoulder(s), arm(s), wrist(s), or multiple body areas than for men. Except when special analyses

Table 4.2

Percentage of accepted time loss injuries by nature of injury and gender in Canada, 1996

Nature of injury	Within genders		Across genders		
	Women	Men	Women	Men	Total
Contusion, crushing, bruises	13.5	15.1	3.5	11.0	14.5
Cut, laceration, puncture	6.4	10.2	1.7	7.5	9.2
Fracture	4.1	6.4	1.1	4.7	5.8
Inflammation or irritation	7.8	4.9	2.1	3.6	5.7
Occupational injury not elsewhere classified	5.5	4.5	1.5	3.3	4.8
Other occupational injury or illness	3.8	2.6	1	1.9	2.9
Scratches, abrasions (superficial wounds)	1.1	3.5	0.3	2.6	2.9
Sprains, strains	46.8	40.2	12.4	29.6	42.0
Others	11.0	12.6	2.9	9.3	12.2
Total	100	100	26.5	73.5	100

Note: These percentage exclude "unknown" and "not-coded" claims.
Source: Association of Workers' Compensation Boards of Canada, www.AWCBC.on.ca

Table 4.3

Percentage of accepted time loss injuries by part of body and gender, 1996

Part of body	Within genders		Across genders		
	Women	Men	Women	Men	Total
Ankle(s)	4.6	5.0	1.2	3.7	4.9
Arm(s)	5.7	4.8	1.5	3.6	5.1
Back	29.7	26.6	7.8	19.6	27.4
Finger(s)	9.3	12.5	2.5	9.2	11.7
Foot (feet)	2.8	3.8	0.7	2.7	3.4
Hand(s)	4.1	4.7	1.1	3.5	4.6
Leg(s)	6.2	8.5	1.6	6.3	7.9
Multiple parts	8.0	4.9	2.1	3.6	5.7
Shoulder(s)	7.9	5.6	2.1	4.1	6.2
Wrist(s)	5.6	3.4	1.5	2.5	4.0
Others	16.1	20.2	4.3	14.8	19.1
Total	100	100	26.4	73.6	100

Note: These percentages exclude "unknown" and "not coded" claims.
Source: Association of Workers' Compensation Boards of Canada, www.AWCBC.on.ca

are done (such as Ashbury 1995), we are unable to provide true gender-based injury rates (numbers of those with time loss injuries divided by numbers of those at risk of injury), since the requisite data have not been reported.

Analysis of labour force and time loss claims data shows that women account for proportionately fewer claims compared to their labour force participation in every industrial sector and that women report injuries consistent with their occupational exposures (Figure B3).

Women and Compensable Injuries
This section explores two potential reasons for women's relatively low claim rates: exclusion of some women under workers' compensation acts and barriers women face when reporting injuries. It then goes on to explore duration of time loss associated with compensable injuries for women.

Women and Exclusions under Workers' Compensation Acts
As with other insurance systems, workers' compensation covers only "eligible" employees. Definitions of eligibility differ across Canada. For example, in Ontario, bank employees, independent operators, self-employed individuals – those who do not employ full- or part-time workers and who operate under a contract for service – are not automatically covered under the act, although employers may voluntarily apply for personal coverage for the costs of compensating their injured workers (Ontario WSIB 1997). On the other hand, in British Columbia, coverage includes bank employees and has fewer restrictions on sectors and types of workers (WCBBC 1997).

Such differences are reflected in the proportion of time loss claims that are awarded in a particular sector. For example, the finance and insurance industry sector (in which women predominate) accounted for only 0.086 percent of time loss claims in Ontario in 1996, compared to 0.49 percent in British Columbia and 0.32 percent in all of Canada.[8] Coverage differs across provinces. Nevertheless, these proportions are considerably lower in both provinces than the estimated proportion of employment in this sector. Thus women in this sector probably have low levels of coverage, yet a careful examination of coverage is required to make such a conclusion.

Low workers' compensation coverage rates in small and non-standardized workplaces can also have significant implications for women, who tend to be overrepresented in such workplaces. Smaller, non-standard workplaces are generally riskier than larger, more formal organizations (Eakin and Weir 1995) and have historically received less attention in safety education and health promotion programs (Eakin 1992). Recent economic restructuring, intense global competition, and rapid technological change have been associated with increased numbers of small businesses in Canada, including large numbers headed by women.[9] In addition, informal workers – those who work without a formal contract, job security, or benefits packages – tend to face greater health risks in labour-intensive jobs but are often excluded from legal protections and workers' compensation (Santana et al. 1997). Women doing domestic service[10] (particularly minority women) and volunteer work (where women are clearly the majority) would be among such informal workers.

Women's greater employment in part-time jobs may also influence their reporting of injuries. Although many women choose to work part-time due to domestic responsibilities or other reasons (Statistics Canada 1994), others may have fewer working hours than they would like, and relatively low wages. For example, in areas such as sales and service occupations, employers tend to hire staff to work for less than 30 hours a week, partly because that is all the time that is needed to meet the employer's needs, and partly because the employer is not required to pay benefits to those who work less than 30 hours a week. In contrast, men doing part-time work tend to have high-power jobs and to choose their own hours of work.[11] Such implied vulnerability on the part of women leads us into a discussion of non-legal barriers to reporting of compensation claims.

Women and Barriers to Claim Reporting and Acceptance

Women may face barriers in reporting and acceptance of claims because of a variety of biases and pressures among workers' compensation board personnel, workplace parties, and health professionals. Ideas about women's occupational injuries and illnesses, particularly those that are not associated with a single event[12] (which account for the majority of women's claims) may influence both the reporting and adjudication process for women's claims. Ideas about "the reality" of women's occupational health problems are shaped by current understandings. Yassi (1981) notes that the creation of evidence may be shaped by the interests of those with the power to fund research and make decisions regarding the circulation and utilization of research results, and in the same vein, Messing (1998: 42) argues that women's health issues have largely been excluded from occupational health research, because "occupational health scientists have been trained and molded by scientific institutions whose evolution has not equipped them to meet the need of women workers." If this is the case in the research community, perhaps it is not surprising that women's occupational health concerns have been inadequately or unfairly dealt with by those with the power to make a difference at a practical level.

When workers' compensation claims are filed, women's claims may meet more challenges and face more suspicion by workers' compensation staff. Carpal tunnel syndrome is a disorder seen more frequently in women than in men (Kelsey 1982). A study of 135 carpal tunnel claims filed in the United States from 1991 to 1995 found that only 19 percent were accepted without a problem (EWWC 1997). The other 81 percent of claims were either

Table 4.4

Percentage of claims accepted, rejected, and pending by gender in Ontario, 1991-6

Year	Men				Women			
	A	P	R	Z	A	P	R	Z
1991	86.68	0.02	11.56	1.73	86.11	0.01	12.02	1.86
1992	85.76	0.02	12.64	1.58	85.16	0.01	13	1.83
1993	84.71	0.02	13.96	1.31	83.56	0.02	14.92	1.5
1994	82.91	0.03	15.91	1.15	79.98	0.02	18.47	1.52
1995	82.84	0.04	15.89	1.23	79.58	0.05	18.84	1.53
1996	82.35	0.11	16.51	1.03	79.23	0.14	19.29	1.34

Note: A = accepted, P = pending, R = rejected, Z = amalgamated.
Source: WSIB (1997).

challenged or ignored by insurers, with some of the cases taking over 1,000 days to resolve. Among women who filed claims for carpal tunnel syndrome, 40 to 42 percent felt that their claims were not dealt with in a fair and satisfactory way. Data from the Ontario WSIB provide detailed information on accepted, rejected, or pending cases by gender, plus amalgamated cases – new claims ruled to be a recurrence – from 1991 to 1996 (Table 4.4). Rates of rejection for women rose from 12 percent in 1991 to 19 percent (almost one in five claims) in 1996. In every year, women's claims had higher rates of rejection than men's, with gender differences since 1994 being consistently greater than in the earlier period.

One Canadian study (Lippel 1995) was able to investigate other reasons for gender differences, based on a review of accepted and refused workers' compensation claims for psychological stress in Quebec. Though stress is different in nature from most injuries, the handling of these claims provides a glimpse of how an important work and health concern for women was dealt with by workers' compensation authorities in one jurisdiction. Among ninety-seven published and unpublished decisions on workers' compensation claims for psychological stress, 51 percent (twenty-five cases out of forty-nine) of women's claims were accepted compared to 66 percent (thirty-six cases out of fifty-five) of men's. Various explanations for women's lower rate of accepted cases were advanced. Women constituted a minority of members on both the Review Board Panel (22 percent) and the Appeal Panels (20 percent). Content analysis of legal documents showed that when women occupied roles stereotypically associated with stress, their cases were often refused on the basis that stress was "normal" to that occupation or workplace. In the process of adjudication, both men and women were asked about their personal lives as part of the test of the work-relatedness of stress experienced. Yet the interpretation of similar personal stressors was different for each gender. A man breaking up with a girlfriend during the period of work stress still received compensation, whereas any statements mentioning difficulties at home (mostly marital difficulties), became barriers to women receiving compensation. In the same vein, a personal trait such as perfectionism was thought to be a mark of good character for men, while the same trait prevented women from receiving compensation. The study concluded that often women's claims were refused because of male domination of decision-making roles and gender-biased perceptions about work and personal traits.

In the workplace, managers may not understand the nature of women's work and work-related illness or injury. In one US study, occupational physicians saw patients at the request of their employer. They found that out of 1,609 individuals with occupational health conditions affecting their wrist, hand, shoulder, or back, only 25 percent filed any claims and that 23 percent of individuals who had lost seven consecutive days from work did not file a claim (EWWC 1997). The Institute for Work and Health (1998) has conducted a study of employees, about half of whom were women, at a large, metropolitan newspaper. They found that about 60 percent of employees surveyed reported having some neck and upper limb pain, with women complaining of more intense and frequent pain than men. Only 29 percent of employees had sought health care for their complaints, and only 22 percent had reported their conditions to the workplace, including some with moderate or worse pain impairing their ability to perform their job duties. A variety of work factors influenced reporting (e.g., repetitive jobs, keyboard layout, deadlines), but women were still more likely to report their pain to the workplace. When asked whether fear of lay-off, unemployment, or harassment stopped them from reporting their problem to management, 6 percent of symptomatic employees answered "yes" (there were no gender differences in response to this question). When asked for other reasons for not reporting, 17 percent of those with moderate or worse symptoms reported that the problem was not severe enough, and 7 percent attributed symptoms to non-work factors. In this same group, women were more likely than men to express uncertainty as to whether the problem was RSI or whether it would be taken seriously by the employer (seven women versus one man); men were more likely to simply answer "no" to the question about other reasons (thirty-seven men versus nineteen women). Such findings indicate that multiple barriers will have to be dealt with in the workplace for adequate reporting to occur and thus to permit early job modification, or to provide support to those with RSI.

For the newly emerging disorders such as RSI, which are more common in women, a lack of research evidence may prevent practitioners from accurately assessing the work-relatedness of the disorder (Yassi 1981). Half of a group of UK doctors who were asked by the courts to report on individual cases believed that RSI was not a genuine disease entity (Diwaker and Stothard 1995). A study in the United States (Niemeyer 1991) showed that historically when women attempted to explain their RSI pains to health professionals, doctors tended to see their pains as "the outcome of thwarted urges or neglected duties of the peculiarly female kind." Such biases have a long history in physicians' characterization of occupational injuries and diseases among women (Bammer and Matin 1994; Hopkins 1990). Women are often perceived as psychologically or physiologically more "frail." For example, primary care physicians and hospital interns incorrectly classified a higher proportion of non-disturbed women as "disturbed" than was the case for a similar group of men (Redman et al. 1991). Women's reports of their injuries have been more likely to be regarded as "complaining," "malingering," or women-specific health behaviours than as preventable work-related conditions (Dembe 1996).

Gender biases in the workplace among health professionals and workers' compensation staff may result in less frequent or later reporting and fewer accepted claims. Such biases may cause the compensation process to be more prolonged, slow the course of recovery for women, and delay or deflect preventive measures.

Women and Recovery from Occupational Injuries
We have previously noted that women file relatively few workers' compensation claims. However, most workers' compensation studies indicate that once a claim is filed, women tend to remain off work for longer than do men (Bigos et al. 1986; Johnson et al. 1990). Reasons for this may lie in gender-differentiated aspects of medical care, household situation, or occupational role.

In previous health care studies not related to work issues (e.g., Cleeland et al. 1994; Bernard et al. 1993), systematic gender differences have been demonstrated, with poorer pain management, longer hospital stays, and less technologically intensive care for women. Recent studies of rehabilitation programs for injured workers have suggested different response patterns for women. Results from an Ontario study indicate that women with claims for soft tissue injuries were equally likely to attend a WCB-designed physiotherapy program (Sinclair et al. 1997). However, upon completion of the program, they were more likely to be judged as needing continuing physical work restrictions or further assessment than were men (Hogg-Johnson et al. 1998).

The association of marital status with duration on compensation benefits differs by gender. Married women are on benefits for longer than other women, unlike married men, whose absences are shorter than those of other men (Johnson et al. 1995). The greater responsibility for domestic work assumed by married women (Statistics Canada 1994) may be a contributing factor, as may the lesser earning potential of women, which we have previously described. In general, workers in lower income groups where women predominate are slower to return to work than those with higher income.

Women's Broader Health and Work Experience
Women's concerns about the effect of work on their health are broader than would be expected if one considered only compensation statistics, as the hazards they describe are not always recognized or accepted under the current system. We review some of these here, as well as the potential implications for workers' compensation systems.

Working Women and their Primary Health Concerns
When asked about significant work-related health concerns (Walters 1992), Canadian women cited stress, depression, and anxiety. In focus groups, working women cited stress as the most important health issue, followed

by RSIs, harassment, and violence, and the double workday (Feldberg et al. 1996). Most of the focus group participants were in female-dominated occupations such as nursing, teaching, and child care. When asked to identify "the most important health problems, both physical and mental, for women who work in a job like yours," 49 percent indicated stress.

Data from the General Social Survey (Statistics Canada 1994), involving a structured questionnaire and more traditional health and safety hazards, suggest that women and men perceived different risks differently (Figure B4). For women, the most frequent responses were working in proximity to a computer screen or terminal, and excessive worry or stress due to job demands (36 percent and 25 percent of employed women respectively). For men dust/fibres in air and loud noises (more "traditional" workplace hazards common in men's occupations) were most important (41 percent and 36 percent of employed men respectively). Differential exposure as the consequence of occupational segregation by gender certainly contributes to explaining for work and health concerns.

To support this argument, the health effects of adverse working conditions showed almost no gender differences in a study of women and men in similar jobs with comparable working conditions (Loscocco and Spitze 1990). A total of 2,260 non-supervisory employees were recruited from twenty-seven different plants in seven manufacturing industries in the state of Indiana. Four aspects of work were documented: job demands, job deprivations and rewards, physical environment, and work-related social support. All of these factors affected the well-being of men and women, with almost no gender differences.

Women's special concerns about RSI and stress are supported by other evidence on prevalence. Several studies have documented higher prevalence rates of RSI and more severe symptoms in women (Polanyi et al. 1997; Tanaka et al. 1988). In the analysis of RSI among newspaper employees (Institute for Work and Health 1998) gender differences in demographic, physical, and psychosocial factors partially accounted for women's tendency to have more severe symptoms. Women tended to have less formal post-secondary education, and more of them were touch typists, spent more time on the phone, and believed that a poorly designed work station could cause RSI. In an earlier study, Shadbolt (1988) reported that women who suffered from RSI had higher levels of psychological strain and psychosocial stress. Women's jobs both at work and at home contribute to their RSI (Meekosha and Jakubowicz 1986). Nevertheless, doctors, family members, co-workers, and managers may be slow to recognize the work-relatedness of their symptoms (Reid et al. 1991).

National Population and Health Survey data showed that Canadian females in all age groups over twelve in the general population had a higher prevalence of depression in 1995.[13] Three large cross-sectional population surveys of employed people conducted in Canada and Sweden also found gender differences in mental health. These studies have used the concepts of psychological work demands, job control, and other psychosocial job characteristics (Karasek and Theorell 1990, 1996) to partially explain such gender differences in mental health. In Sweden, Hall (1989) documented the highest levels of job control among white-collar men in male-dominated jobs, while the lowest were found among blue-collar women in male-dominated jobs. Men in jobs traditionally regarded as "women's work" had a higher level of job control than women in the same jobs. Women working in the lowest stratum of jobs and with a majority of men were likely to have the greatest work stress. In a Canadian study using survey methods (Roxburgh 1996), women were exposed to lower substantive complexity and job control, although the lower job control did not directly lead to women's distress. Women were more vulnerable to the negative effects of job routinization, one dimension of psychological demands in Karasek's model. In an analysis of Canadian data from the 1994-5 National Population and Health Survey (NPHS) (Scott et al. 1998), women workers reported significantly less decision latitude and more psychological demands than men. Furthermore, women with higher job strain (high demands and low control), greater job insecurity, and higher chronic stress were significantly more likely to have poorer general health. Women who reported their main activity as working for pay or profit *and* caring for family reported more job strain, while job insecurity was more important for those working for pay and profit only. These findings indicate the complex interplay between work and home stressors in predicting the nature and impact of women's stress (Lowe 1989).

Hidden Work-Related Health Risks for Women

Uncovering health risks involved in women's work is an ongoing challenge where the tradition has been to focus on men's occupational health concerns in jobs typically held by men. Historically, women's role in reproduction and its relation to work has been an important focus. The US National Institute of Occupational Safety and Health estimated the number of workers exposed each year to nine known or suspected reproductive hazards (mostly to women) and on this basis argued that adverse reproductive outcomes should be included in the top ten occupational diseases (CDC [NIOSH] 1985). Consultants to the Canadian Royal Commission on New Reproductive Technologies (1993) extrapolated these figures to an estimated 1.5 million Canadian workers similarly exposed to a range of biological, chemical, and physical hazards each year. Since 1981, Quebec's health and safety law has contained a provision for physician-authorized protective reassignment of pregnant or breast-feeding women to work that would not pose a risk to the woman or her baby. If no such work is available, compensated time off can be authorized by the Work Health and Safety Commission (Commission de Santé et Securité au Travail, CSST). Over 80 percent of women compensated have been in their second or third trimester, and ergonomic hazards have been the main reason (62 percent of cases) (Groupe de travail "Pour une maternité sans danger" 1993). Biomechanical exposures or stressors acting on women during pregnancy have been associated with reduced gestational age and birth weight, while work scheduling (e.g., issues such as shift work) has been associated with pregnancy loss (Infante-Rivard 1993).

Some work-related risks are also associated with musculoskeletal strains, but the nature of this association has been perceived differently for women and men. Daycare workers lifting children, waitresses carrying heavy trays, or check-out cashiers repetitively lifting items such as bottles of milk and juice were perceived as not handling manual material in the same sense as truckers loading boxes were.[14] This is in spite of the fact that the total weight handled each day in each job may be very similar and may cause musculoskeletal strains in each case. Even the same occupation may pose different health risks for each gender. Among employees working in poultry factories, bakeries (Dumais et al. 1993), and the cleaning industry (Messing et al. 1993), women and men have been found to occupy different roles and do different tasks, with women tending to do more repetitive work. Relying solely on a job title as a proxy for exposure in the judgment of work-relatedness of women's health conditions may thus introduce inaccuracy and bias (Messing et al. 1994). Lack of consideration of the different health risks associated with different tasks, may lead to the conservative notion of women as the "weaker sex" rather than identifying aggravating work factors (Mergler et al. 1987).

Many women in Walters's (1992) study, considered stress to be "part of life" rather than the result of particular workplace hazards. The conceptual shift in definition of the source of women's health problems, from general life conditions or their particular physiology (particularly reproductive) to hazardous working conditions, has required gender sensitivity. For example, researchers have documented that irregular menstrual periods can be associated with work stress or working in cold areas (Mergler and Vézina 1985). Review of job descriptions, as part of pay equity work, raised the issues of RSI and stress for women workers at an Ontario newspaper (TARP 1994). The 1993 Statistics Canada Violence Against Women Survey (cited in Feldberg 1996) found that in the twelve months prior to the survey, 6 percent of employed women experienced sexual harassment, while over their entire work life 23 percent of women reporting injuries had experienced workplace harassment at some point.

"Caring" or "emotional" work (Hochschild 1983) is being recognized by some (e.g., Messing 1998) as a potential health risk. Emotional work is defined as "the labour involved in dealing with other people's feelings, a core component of which is the regulation of emotions" (James 1989: 15, cited in Yyelland 1994). Since service workers primarily deal not with things but clients, "the facilitation and regulation of the expression of emotion in the public domain appear to be the core nature of work" (Stelling 1994). Women's frequent employment as teachers, nurses, waitresses, or public servants highlights this component of their jobs. For example, a good bedside manner is required in nurses. Nonetheless, nurses are often caught between structural constraints (such as downsizing and changing administrative practices) and patients' and their families' demands to provide a better quality of care (Yyelland 1994). Because emotional work is often perceived as consistent with the feminine character and work that women do at home, it may not be regarded as a legitimate occupational health risk.

Thus, an increasingly broad range of health conditions are being linked by researchers to work, with recognition of the multiple causes that may give rise to each condition. These are "work-related diseases" according to definitions developed by the World Health Organization since they are "aggravated (aggravation of pre-existing conditions), accelerated, or exacerbated by workplace exposures" (WHO 1985, cited in Jeyaratnam 1992: 5-6). Reluctance on the part of policy makers to recognize the broader scope of work-related health impacts among women may result in the growth of future "epidemics" of claims that could have been foreseen.

Key Issues and Potential Avenues
Currently, information by gender is limited to numbers of claims in particular categories, that is, numerator information. To compare rates of injury or disease by gender, one needs better denominator information. At the most superficial level, this would include gender-specific information on employment within each sector and occupation. At present, such information comes from sources that may not truly represent the workforce covered by workers' compensation and must be integrated with claims information to provide rates of injury for men and women in the various categories (Hébert 1993). Availability of such analyses is limited, rather than being part of the ongoing data available for monitoring equity in the workers' compensation system.

However, the use of sector or occupation as a proxy for exposure to hazards may be inappropriate, because men and women often do different work within the same occupational group. One way of obtaining gender-specific information on hazards is by doing periodic hazard surveys. This information could also, however, be extracted from systematically organized and recorded inspection and enforcement data (including gender), collected by workers' compensation boards or ministries of labour. More detailed information on jobs and exposures, if collected in a routine manner in the future (as per Rest and Ashford 1992) would permit more realistic comparison of exposures for women and men.

The links between work and health now extend beyond the former notions of injury (e.g., mine fatalities) in occupations that have traditionally been dominated by men. The recognition of a wider range of work-related health hazards may be due to changes in technology (e.g., increased computerization), availability of research evidence (e.g., the link between psychosocial factors such as job demand and control and health), and composition of the workforce (e.g., the larger service sector). In sectors and jobs where women predominate, slower onset, partially disabling conditions arising out of the nature of employment (e.g., work-related musculoskeletal disorders of the neck and upper limb or RSI) are increasingly being seen. Work-related health problems among women tend to be caused not only by the physical characteristics of jobs but also by the psychosocial dimensions of women's work. Women's jobs in the service sector involve much "emotional work," a major source of stress. Yet at present, stress-related disorders are seen as problematic areas of compensation, and as better dealt with via health promotion rather prevention programs.

Workplace programs that support early reporting and intervention for work-related musculoskeletal disorders are an option that may prove beneficial in shortening the course of these slow-onset conditions. Movement toward an ergonomic standard that includes the organization of work as well as biomechanical demands and anthropometric standards is an important step in dealing with this wider range of hazards. Some jurisdictions (e.g., Denmark) have developed inspection protocols for psychosocial hazards, similar to ones for physical or chemical hazards. The considerable experience with compensation of stress-related disorders in other jurisdictions (see chapter by Gnam in this volume) may prove useful in the refinement of guidelines for Canadian workers' compensation systems.

In contrast to acute injuries, the most prevalent health problems related to women's work have multiple potential causes, that is, they are non-specific. Assessment of their work-relatedness requires knowledge of relevant work factors and documentation of an occupational history, with inquiry into specific work-related hazards. Few health care providers have the appropriate training to make this connection and gather the relevant information, nor have the incentives to do so been provided them. Hence, conditions such as carpal tunnel syndrome (which are more common among older women for a variety of reasons), may not be linked to workplace exposures, but mistakenly attributed to biological (e.g., hormonal) factors.

The provision of additional training on the wider range of hazards as evidenced in the current literature linking work and health is a potential solution. In addition to health professionals, claims adjudicators and consultants drawn in to judge work-relatedness would benefit from such training. Other means of encouraging the documentation of hazardous working conditions of women include: providing specific billing incentives for documentation of these factors (Yassi 1981), increasing the numbers of publicly funded clinical occupational health personnel knowledgeable in such matters, and promoting recruitment and advancement of women in occupational health and safety agencies and workers' compensation boards (Rest and Ashford 1992).

In the number of follow-up studies of compensable soft tissue injuries, women took longer to return to work than men. Potential explanations include: a greater degree of disability among women because of barriers to reporting, greater home demands that interfere with the recovery process, or less willingness on the part of employers to provide substantially modified work for women. We have suggested some ways that reporting barriers could be dealt with. Dealing with women's disproportionate role as family caregivers and home workers is a more daunting task. Some workplaces, recognizing that workers whose domestic responsibilities are respected are more productive and absent less often, have initiated family-friendly policies such as flexible working hours and part-time arrangements. Perhaps greater flexibility in return-to-work arrangements for women is required, in order to promote recovery equity.

Conclusion

The increasing role of women in the labour force and expanding knowledge about the different mix of workplace hazards, compensated conditions, work/family roles, and patterns of recovery that women experience suggest that adjustments in current work, safety, and compensation practices are required if health inequities experienced by women in the workforce are to be reduced. The adaptation of information systems to allow for gender-based analyses will greatly improve our capacity to track gender-related hazards and factors influencing recovery. Greater emphasis on research in the health, safety, and compensation field that includes gender analyses would then be facilitated. The hiring of more women in the workplace inspection and prevention area, and training of health and safety personnel, health care providers, and agency staff on gender issues would enhance both understanding and practice. We expect that, ultimately, these activities should support policy shifts in the recognition of the work-relatedness of conditions, their compensability, and the supports for recovery that reflect women's different experiences of health and work.

Notes
1   Statistics Canada 1997. *Labour Force Characteristics by Age and Sex.* CANSIM, Matrix 3472, http://www.StatCan.CA/english/Pgdb/People/Labour/labor20a.htm. [18 February 1998].
2   Statistics Canada 1997. *Full-Time and Part-Time Employment.* CANSIM, Matrix 3472,

http://www.StatCan.CA/english/Pgdb/People/Labour/labor12.htm. [18 February 1998].
3 Statistics Canada 1999. CANSIM, Matrix 3472 Labour Force Annual Averages, Canada, Service Sector D984662, Labour Force Goods-Producing Sector D984656. http://www.Stat Can.CA/english [19 March 1999].
4 Statistics Canada 1995. *Employment, by Detailed Industry and Sex 1995.* Catalogue no. 71F0004XCB. http://www.StatCan.CA/english/Pgdb/People/Labour/labor10a.htm. [18 February 1998].
5 Statistics Canada 1996. *Labour Force 15 Years and Over by Occupation 1996 Census,* http://www.StatCan.CA/english/Pgdb/People/Labour/labor45a.htm.1996 Census Nation tables [27 March 1997].
6 Statistics Canada 1994. *Average Earnings by Sex.* Catalogue no. 13-217-XPB. http://www.Stat Can.CA/english/Pgdb/People/Labour/labor01a.htm. [18 February 1998].
7 Statistics Canada 1996. *Distribution of Employed People by Industry.* CANSIM, Matrices 3472-3482, http://www.StatCan.CA/english/Pgdb/People/Labour/labor21a.htm. [25 March 1998].
8 Statistics Canada 1996. *Employment in the Finance and Other Service Industries.* CANSIM, Matrices 4285, 4299, 4313, 4327, 4341, 4355, 4369, 4383, 4397, 4411, 4425, 4439, and 4453. http://www.StatCan.CA/english/Pgdb/Economy/Finance/fin14a.htm. [1998].
9 Statistics Canada 1996. *Labour Force 15 Years and Over by Class of Worker 1996 Census,* http://www.StatCan.CA/english/Pgdb/People/Labour/labor43a.htm. [27 March 1997].
10 Also unpaid family workers (those who worked without pay in a family farm, business, or professional practice owned or operated by a related household member) should be included here. Men and women accounted for 0.3 and 0.8 percent, respectively, of this category. Statistics Canada 1996. *Labour Force 15 Years and Over by Class of Worker 1996 Census.* http://www.StatCan.CA/english/Pgdb/People/Labour/labor43a.htm. [27 March 1997].
11 *Globe and Mail.* "Part-Time Work Stats Questioned." 18 March 1998. p. A6.
12 Due to a lack of studies that deal with gender differences, we include studies on occupational diseases experienced mainly by women, and a few studies in which gender differences are shown.
13 Statistics Canada 1995. *Prevalence of Depression, by Age and Sex 1995.* http://www.Stat Can.CA/english/Pgdb/People/Health/health35.htm. [2 February 1998].
14 See articles in Messing et al. (1995).

References
Association of Workers' Compensation Boards of Canada (AWCBC). Various years. www.AWCBC.on.ca.
Ashbury, Fredrick D. 1995. "Occupational Repetitive Strain Injuries and Gender in Ontario 1986 to 1990." *Journal of Occupational and Environmental Medicine* 37 (4): 479-85.
Bammer, G., and B. Martin. 1994. "Repetition Strain Injury in Australia: Medical Knowledge, Social Movement, and De Facto Partisanship." *Social Problems* 39 (3): 219-37.
Beaton, D.E. 1995. "Examining the Clinical Course of Work-Related Musculoskeletal Disorders of the Upper Extremity Using the Ontario Workers' Compensation Board Administrative Database." MSc thesis, University of Toronto.
Bernard, Annette M., Rodney A. Hayward, Judith S. Rosevear, and Laurence F. McMahon, Jr. 1993. "Gender and Hospital Resource Use: Unexpected Differences." *Evaluation and the Health Professions* 16 (2): 177-89.
Bigos, S.J., D.M. Spengler, N.A. Martin, J. Zeh, L. Fisher, and A. Nachemson. 1986. "Back Injuries in Industry, a Retrospective Study, III: Employee Related Factors." *Spine* 11 (3): 252-6.
Bolaria, B. Singh, and Rosemary Bolaria. 1994. *Women, Medicine, and Health.* Halifax: Fernwood Publishing.
Centres for Disease Control (CDC), National Institute for Occupational Health and Safety (NIOSH). 1985. "Leading Work-Related Diseases and Injuries – United States. Disorders of Reproduction." *MMWR* 34 (35): 537-40.
Choi, Bernard, Marianne Levitsky, Roxanne D. Lloyd, and Ilene M. Stones. 1996. "Patterns and Risk Factors for Sprains and Strains in Ontario, Canada, 1990: An Analysis of the

Workplace Health and Safety Database." *Journal of Occupational and Environmental Medicine* 38 (4): 379-89.

Clarke, Judy, Jinjoo Chung, and Donald Cole. 1999. "Gender and Return to Work from Lost Time Work-Related Soft Tissue Disorders: Relationships with Health Factors." Unpublished paper, Institute for Work and Health, Toronto.

Cleeland, Charles S., René Gonin, Alan K. Hatfield, John H. Edmonson, Ronald H. Blum, James A. Stewart, and Kishan J. Pandya. 1994. "Pain and Its Treatment in Outpatients with Metastatic Cancer." *New England Journal of Medicine* 330 (9): 592-6.

Dembe, A.E. 1996. *Occupation and Disease: How Social Factors Affect the Conception of Work-Related Disorders*. New Haven: Yale University Press.

Diwaker, H.N., and J. Stohard. 1995. "What Do Doctors Mean by Tenosynovitis and Repetitive Strain Injury?" *Occupational Medicine* [Oxford] 45 (2): 97-104.

Doyal, Lesley. 1995. *What Makes Women Sick? Gender and the Political Economy of Health*. New Brunswick, NJ: Rutgers University Press.

Dumais, L., K. Messing, A.M. Seifer, J. Courville, and N. Vézina. 1993. "Forces for and against Change in the Sexual Division of Labour at an Industrial Bakery." *Work, Employment, and Society* 7 (3): 363-82.

Eakin, J. 1992. "Leaving It up to the Workers: Sociological Perspective on the Management of Health and Safety in Small Workplaces." *International Journal of Health Services* 22: 689-704.

Eakin, J., and N. Weir. 1995. "Canadian Approaches to the Promotion of Health in Small Workplaces." *Canadian Journal of Public Health* March-April: 109-13.

Ewan, C., E. Lowy, and J. Reid. 1991. "'Falling out of Culture': The Effects of Repetitive Strain Injury on Sufferers, Roles, and Identity." *Sociology of Health and Illness* 13 (2): 168-92.

Ed Welch on Workers Compensation (EWWC). 1997. "'Some Workers Don't File': A Significant Number of People May Be Passing Up Their Right to Comp." *Ed Welch on Workers Compensation* 7 (10): 1-3.

Feldberg, Georgina, David Northrup, Mike Scott, and Tracey Shannon. 1996. *Ontario Women's Work-Related Health Survey Descriptive Summary*. Toronto: Centre for Health Studies and Institute for Social Research, York University.

Fox, Bonnie. 1987. "Occupational Gender Segregation of the Canadian Labour Force 1931-1981." *Canadian Review of Sociology and Anthropology* 24: 374-97.

Groupe de travail "pour une maternité sans danger." 1993. *Pour une maternité sans danger: Assez de recherche. Rapport soumis au directeur général de l'IRRST*. Montréal: IRRST.

Hall, E.M. 1989. "Gender, Work Control, and Stress: A Theoretical Discussion and an Empirical Test." *International Journal of Health Services* 19: 725-45.

Hébert, François. 1993. Denominators Workshop: The Construction of Appropriate Rates of Injury, Claims, and Disability Materials. Sponsored by the Workers' Compensation Institute, 28 April, Queen's University, Kingston, ON.

Hochschild, A.R. 1983. *The Managed Heart*. Berkeley: University of California Press.

Hogg-Johnson, S., D. Cole, and Early Claimant Cohort Design Group and Prognostic Modeling Workgroup. 1998. "Early Prognostic for Duration of Benefits among Workers with Compensated Occupational Soft Tissue Injuries." Institute for Work and Health (IWH), Toronto.

Hopkins, A. 1990. "The Social Recognition of RSI: An Australian and American Comparison." *Social Science and Medicine* 30 (3): 365-72.

Infante-Rivard, C. 1993. "Pregnancy Loss and Work Schedule during Pregnancy." *Epidemiology* 4 (1): 73-5.

Institute for Work and Health (IWH). 1998. "A Final Report Prepared by RSI Watch Committee." Toronto: Institute for Work and Health.

Jeyaratnam, J. 1992. *Occupational Health in Developing Countries*. Oxford: Oxford University Press.

Johnson, W.G., R.J. Butler, and M.L. Baldwin. 1995. "First Spells of Work Absences among Ontario Workers." In *Research in Canadian Workers' Compensation*, ed. Terry Thomason and R.P. Chaykowski, 73-84. Kingston, ON: IRC Press.

Johnson, W.G., and Ondrich, J. 1990. "The Duration of Post-Injury Absences from Work." *Review of Economics and Statistics* 72: 578-86.

Karasek, R.A., and T. Theorell. 1990. *Healthy Work: Stress, Productivity, and the Reconstruction of Working Life*. New York: Basic Books.

Kelsey, J.L. 1982. *Epidemiology of Musculoskeletal Disorders*. New York: Oxford University Press.

Lippel, Katherine. 1995. "Watching the Watchers: How Expert Witnesses and Decision-Makers Perceive Men's and Women's Workplace Stressors." In *Invisible: Issues in Women's Occupational Health*, ed. Karen Messing, Barbara Neis, and Lucie Dumais, 265-91. Charlottetown: Gynergy Books.

Loscocco, Kayrn N., and Glenna Sptze. 1990. "Working Conditions, Social Support, and the Well-Being of Female and Male Factory Workers." *Journal of Health and Social Behavior* 31: 313-27.

Lowe, Graham S. 1989. "Women, Paid/Unpaid Work, and Stress: New Directions for Research." Paper prepared for the Canadian Advisory Council on the Status of Women.

Meekosha, H., and A. Jakubowicz. 1986. "Women Suffering RSI: The Hidden Relations of Gender, the Labour Process, and Medicine." *Journal of Occupational Health and Safety* [Australia, New Zealand] 2: 390-401.

Mergler, D., C. Brabant, N. Vézina, and K. Messing. 1987. "The Weaker Sex? Men in Women's Working Conditions Report Similar Health Symptoms?" *Journal of Occupational Medicine* 29: 417-21.

Mergler, D., and N. Vézina. 1985. "Dysmenorrhea and Cold Exposure." *Journal of Reproductive Medicine* 30: 106-11.

Messing, Karen. 1991. "Occupational Safety and Health Concerns of Canadian Women: A Background Paper." Prepared for the Women's Bureau, Labour Canada.

–. 1998. *One-Eyed Science: Occupational Health and Women Workers*. Philadelphia: Temple University Press.

Messing K., G. Doniol-Shaw, and C. Haentjents. 1993. "Sugar and Spice and Everything Nice: Health Effects of the Sexual Division of Labour among Train Cleaners." *International Journal of Health Services* 23 (1): 133-46.

Messing, Karen, Julie Courville, Micheline Boucher, Lucie Dumais, and Ana-Maria Seifert. 1994. "Can Safety Risks of Blue Collar Jobs Be Compared by Gender?" *Safety Science* 18 (2): 95-112.

Messing, Karen, Barbara Neis, and Lucie Dumais, eds. 1995. *Invisible: Issues in Women's Occupational Health*. Charlottetown: Gynergy Books.

Messing, K., F. Tissot, M. Saurel-Cubizolles, M. Kaminski, and M. Bourgine. 1998. "Sex as a Variable Can Be a Surrogate for Some Working Conditions." *Journal of Occupational and Environmental Medicine* 40 (3): 250-60.

Morris, Marika. 1997. *Gender-Based Analysis Backgrounder*. SP-100-01-97-E. Ottawa: Human Resources Development Canada.

Niemeyer, Linda Ogden. 1991. "Social Labeling, Stereotyping, and Observer Bias in Workers' Compensation: The Impact of Provider-Patient Interaction on Outcome." *Journal of Occupational Rehabilitation* 1 (4): 251-69.

Polanyi, M., D.C. Cole, D.E. Beaton, J. Chung, et al. 1997. "Upper Limb Work-Related Musculoskeletal Disorders among Newspaper Employees: Cross-Sectional Survey Results." *American Journal of Industrial Medicine* 32: 620-8.

Redman, S., G.R. Webb, D.J. Hennrikus, J.J. Gordon, and R.W. Sanson-Fisher. 1991. "The Effects of Gender on Diagnosis of Psychological Disturbance." *Journal of Behavioral Medicine* 14 (5): 527-40.

Reid, J., C. Ewan, and E. Lowy. 1991. "Pilgrimage of Pain: The Illness Experiences of Women with Repetition Strain Injury and the Search for Credibility." *Social Science and Medicine* 32 (5): 601-12.

Rest, Kathleen M., and Nicholas A. Ashford. 1992. *Occupational Safety and Health in British Columbia: An Administrative Inventory*. Richmond, BC: Workers' Compensation Board of British Columbia (5M 12/92).

Roxburgh, Susan. 1996. "Gender Differences in Work and Well-Being: Effects of Exposure and Vulnerability." *Journal of Health and Social Behaviour* 37 (3): 265-77.

Royal Commission on New Reproductive Technologies. 1993. *Proceed with Care: Final Report of the Royal Commission on New Reproductive Technologies.* 2 vols. Catalogue Z1-1989-3E. Ottawa: Minister of Government Services Canada.

Santana, Vilma S., Dana Loomis, Beth Newman, and Siobán D. Harlow. 1997. "Informal Jobs: Another Occupational Hazard for Women's Mental Health?" *International Journal of Epidemiology* 26 (6): 1236-42.

Scott, F., S.A. Ibrahim, H.S. Shannon, D.C. Cole, J. Eyles, and V. Goel. 1998. "Canadian Working Women: Job Stress and Self-Reported Health: An Analysis of the 1994-5 National Population Survey." Working Paper, Institute for Work and Health.

Shadbolt, B. 1988. "The Severity of Life Strains and Stresses Reported by Female RSI Sufferers." *Journal of Occupational Health and Safety* [Australia, New Zealand] 4 (3): 239-49.

Sinclair, S.J., S. Hogg-Johnson, M.V. Mondloch, and S.A. Shields. 1997. "The Effectiveness of an Early Active Intervention Program for Workers with Soft-Tissue Injuries: The Early Claimant Cohort Study." *Spine* 22 (24): 2919-31.

Statistics Canada. 1994. *Women in the Labour Force.* Occasional. Catalogue no. 75-507E. Ottawa: Statistics Canada.

–. 1995. *Employment, by Detailed Industry and Sex.* Catalogue no. 71F0004XCB. Ottawa: Statistics Canada.

Status of Women Canada. 1996. *Gender-Based Analysis: A Guide for Policy-Making.* Ottawa: Status of Women Canada.

Stelling, Joan. 1994. "Nursing Metaphors: Reflections on the Meaning of Time." In *Women, Medicine, and Health,* ed. B. Singh Bolaria and Rosemary Bolaria, 205-17. Halifax: Fernwood Publishing.

Tanaka, Shiro, Paul Seligman, William Halperin, et al. 1988. "Use of Workers' Compensation Claims Data for Surveillance of Cumulative Trauma Disorders." *Journal of Occupational Medicine* 30 (6): 488-92.

Technological Adjustment Research Program (TARP) Newspaper Project, prepared by Elisa Pane. 1994. *Machine Bites Dog: A Study of Technology and Work in Ontario's Newspaper Industry.* Toronto: Southern Ontario Newspaper Guild.

Theorell, T., and R.A. Karasek. 1996. "Current Issues Relating to Psychosocial Job Strain and Cardiovascular Disease Research." *Journal of Occupational Health Psychology* 1 (1): 9-26.

Thurston, Wilfreda E., Cathie M. Scott, and Barbara A. Crow. 1996. "Social Change, Policy Development, and the Influence on Women's Health." Paper presented at the Fifth National Health Promotion Research Conference, Halifax, June 1997.

Walters, Vivienne. 1992. "Women's Views of Their Main Health Problems." *Canadian Journal of Public Health* 83 (5): 371-4.

Walters, Vivienne, Rhonda Lenton, and Marie Mckeary. 1995. "Women's Health in the Context of Women's Lives: A Report Submitted to the Health Promotion Directorate, Health Canada."

World Health Organization (WHO). 1985. *Identification and Control of Work-Related Diseases.* WHO Technical Report Series 714. Geneva: WHO.

Wilson, S.J. 1991. *Women, Families, and Work.* Toronto: McGraw-Hill Ryerson.

Workers' Compensation Board of British Columbia (WCBBC). 1997. http://www.wcb.bc. ca/resmat/websites.htm [10 February 1998].

Workplace Safety and Insurance Board of Ontario (WSIB). 1997. http://www.wcb.on.ca/ wcb/wcb.nsf/public/AbouttheWCB [10 February 1998].

Yassi, Annalee. 1981. "Occupational Disease and Workers' Compensation in Ontario." Report prepared for Professor Paul C. Weiler, study of workers' compensation in Ontario.

Yyelland, Byrad. 1994. "Structural Constraints, Emotional Labour, and Nursing Work." In *Women, Medicine, and Health,* ed. B. Singh Bolaria and Rosemary Bolaria, 231-40. Halifax: Fernwood Publishing.

Part 3: Prevention

In this section, the significant challenge of preventing work-related injury and disability is explored. The opening chapter by Kerr highlights the significant base of evidence that now identifies measurable psychosocial risks as factors for a range of work-related health problems including cardiovascular disease and work-related musculoskeletal problems. Although challenging, the issues of job design, decision latitude, control, and effort-reward imbalance in the workplace are now recognized as being associated with a range of variation in work-related health problems. The major challenge is to translate this knowledge into workable prevention and intervention strategies in a world in which job design and organization are rarely seen as being the direct task of prevention.

Robert Norman and Richard Wells take up the prevention challenge with an equally compelling portrait of the importance of ergonomic interventions for the reduction of musculoskeletal disorders. Acknowledging the balanced contribution of psychosocial and biomechanical factors, Norman and Wells review the spectrum of promising new biomechanical studies highlighting the importance of "participatory" and macro-ergonomics in finding solutions to the problem of work injury in modern work environments.

Harry Shannon reviews the short list of important high-quality quantitative studies that, using a number of screening criteria, have highlighted management and organizational characteristics associated with high and low levels of work injury. He emphasizes the importance of management commitment, delegation of health and safety activities, and the structure of the labour force as key elements associated with reduced injury rates.

Picking up from Shannon's chapter, John O'Grady reviews the legislative and policy regime for occupational health and safety committees in

Canada. O'Grady argues strenuously that the separation of industrial relations conflict and health and safety committee activities is an artificial distinction. He carefully reviews the limited range of Canadian studies documenting the relationships between health and safety activities and a reduction of injury and disability. O'Grady concludes with a call for a rededicated focus on occupational disease entities, and a need to adjust the internal responsibility system to the structural changes in the labour market, in particular the challenges associated with the growth of non-standard employment and the decline of unionization in Canada.

5

The Importance of Psychosocial Risk Factors in Injury

Michael Kerr

In many compensation jurisdictions, reported injury rates have been decreasing over the last few years (AWCBC 1997). Embedded within these substantial reductions in overall claims has been a similar, and perhaps even slightly stronger overall downward trend for sprain and strain injuries, the most common type of work-related musculoskeletal disorder (WMSD). What is driving these downward trends? A number of speculative arguments can be put forward to explain the apparent declines: they might simply be misleading statistical artefacts, since lower *numbers* of claims do not necessarily mean lower injury *rates;* they could be the result of a business cycle effect, where lower claims rates are observed during times of higher unemployment (a similar reduction in claims occurred between 1982 and 1984); they may be the consequence of changes in compensation policy that could, for example, either discourage potential claimants through lower benefit levels, or encourage the availability of modified work, which, in turn, could result in fewer time loss claims. They might represent genuine reductions in injury rates, which are perhaps indicative of either the changing nature of work, as discussed by Ostry, and Gunderson and Hyatt, in this volume, or they may also represent the dividends that have begun to accrue from investments in workplace prevention programs, such as those with a focus on ergonomic improvements.

Throughout this recent period of reductions in overall claims, musculoskeletal injuries have steadfastly maintained their rank as the most common occupational injury, consistently representing about half of all claims filed, even after accounting for the recent drop in the number of claims (AWCBC 1997). WMSDs are also believed to account for well over half of all the direct compensation costs paid out (Frank et al. 1996). Clearly, there is a case to be made for singling out these injuries for special attention. The substantial burden of illness attributable to WMSDs, including the immense financial, personal, and societal costs associated with them, has provided the rationale for extensive research into the underlying causes of these disorders and the disability that often accompanies them (Frank et al. 1996).

This chapter summarizes the current state of research into the non-biomechanical workplace "causes" of these WMSD conditions (etiologic research). While not negating the role of the physical demands of work (see Norman and Wells, this volume), this review is intended to highlight a need for the recognition of the additional contribution that other workplace factors can have. In particular, this chapter reviews the factors contributing to the onset of the most common musculoskeletal conditions encountered in the workplace, with a special focus presented on recent developments involving research on the psychosocial work environment. This chapter is deliberately structured to convey some sense of the relative importance of the different types of risk factors found to be associated with WMSDs, as determined by the weight of the current scientific evidence available on the topic. The review also highlights the potential for reducing injury rates (i.e., primary prevention) through intervention programs that attempt to change the workplace psychosocial environment. Finally, in addition to encouraging a broader understanding of the underlying causes of the disorders and the possibilities for their prevention, this review highlights the need for more workplace-based research, including in particular, the development of new, practical tools that can better measure the most important aspects of the work environment thought to be associated with the onset of WMSDs.

The most frequently occurring musculoskeletal disorders, which consist primarily of sprain and strain problems of the back, neck, shoulder, and arm (including the wrist), are often caused or aggravated by workplace factors, hence the commonly used acronym WMSD for work-related musculoskeletal disorders (Hagberg et al. 1995). While all of these conditions are also known to have non-work causes, such as sports and motor vehicle injuries, pregnancy, and certain congenital conditions such as scoliosis, this review will focus primarily on an examination of their work-relatedness, since this is of particular relevance to workers' compensation. In addition to these work-related factors, note that a number of individual characteristics (e.g., height, weight, age, etc.) have also been examined in relation to WMSDs. These will be discussed briefly in the section on risk factors. Finally, it is recognized that organizational or firm-level practices, such as the presence of a joint health and safety committee, or management commitment to safety, can also have an impact on employee health, including the rate of time loss injuries such as WMSDs (Robson et al. 1998). These organizational factors will not be covered in this chapter but are well covered in the chapters by Shannon and O'Grady in this volume.

This chapter will not discuss the factors that contribute to disability or chronicity once the condition occurs (prognostic research). A distinction needs to be drawn between etiologic and prognostic research since there can easily be confusion between what causes (or contributes to) these conditions, and what is more likely a consequence (or sequelae) of them. Consider, for example, the study of a psychological variable such as depression as a risk factor for back pain. In many, if not most studies examining the causes of WMSDs, the exposures (possible risk factors, like depression) and the outcomes (possible injuries, like back pain) are measured at the same point in time. This can possibly obscure cause-and-effect relationships by making it difficult to determine whether the depression precipitated the back pain (i.e., possibly a risk factor) or whether it was a consequence of the pain (and thus possibly a prognostic factor).

This overlap between the factors related to the etiology and prognosis of musculoskeletal conditions is illustrated in Figure 5.1. Since one of the aims of this overview is to highlight the potential for intervention programs aimed at modifying true risk factors (to prevent the occurrence of WMSDs), recognizing a distinction between risk and prognostic factors is essential. It would not, for example, be very helpful or cost effective for a workplace to focus prevention efforts on trying to change something that ultimately turns out to be a consequence of injury, rather than an underlying cause for it. Treatment programs or disability management that necessarily focus on these consequences as part of secondary prevention efforts are properly aimed at improving return-to-work and functional abilities markers. For the purpose of this chapter, however, Figure 5.1 is presented to indicate an exclusive focus on factors related to preventing WMSDs in the first place, rather than a discussion about the disability they can produce. (See Bombardier et al. 1994 for a more complete discussion.)

Figure 5.1

Etiologic versus prognostic factors in injury

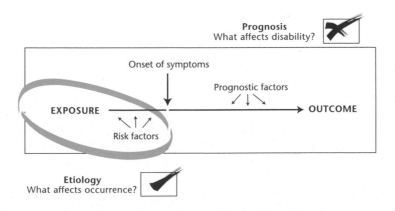

Risk Factors for Musculoskeletal Disorders

The etiologic research on WMSDs has usually taken one of two general approaches: biomechanical or psychosocial (Frank et al. 1996). In biomechanical studies, the underlying conceptual model implies that WMSDs are the result of tissue damage or pain produced when a worker is exposed to physically demanding work. Problems can be the result of either high peak loads that can affect tissues directly, or repeated physical loading at lower levels that ultimately leads to a lowered pain tolerance in the exposed tissue (i.e., a threshold shift). The recent emphasis on psychosocial research, the second general approach to WMSD studies, may have been instigated by a recognition that claims rates for WMSDs have increased or remained persistently high in the face of widespread changes in workplaces that, over time, are believed to have eliminated most "heavy" work. This seeming contradiction has been interpreted, understandably, as a clear demonstration of the importance of factors beyond the physical demands of work in determining the onset of these disorders (Hadler 1997). Only recently have studies begun to consistently adopt a more comprehensive approach to the issue by combining the key aspects from both the biomechanical and psychosocial perspectives.

Note that because of the confusion that can result when the term *psychosocial research* is inconsistently applied, the "catch-all" definition described above – that is, all things not overtly related to the physical demands of work – has not been particularly helpful in furthering our understanding of the issue. In the eyes of some, misuse of this term can lead to a notion that the emphasis is being shifted away from an objective analysis of the work being done toward a more subjective focus on who is doing the work. In this chapter, the term *psychosocial* is used in reference to a wide range of work environment factors that are believed to be associated with the onset of WMSDs, such as job control, job satisfaction, or the balance between the efforts and rewards associated with work. A distinction needs to be made between these more work-related psychosocial variables and psychological states, such as anxiety or depression, which are related more to the individual worker than they are to the work environment. As stated earlier, while factors such as anxiety or depression are probably very important in determining recovery from the disorder once it has occurred, it can be argued that they are more likely a consequence of WMSDs, rather than a cause of the original problem (Bombardier et al. 1994). Similarly, psychological "traits," sometimes associated with particular health problems, are often overstated as causes and almost certainly less amenable to constructive intervention than work environment factors.

While the psychosocial and biomechanical rubrics may adequately describe the approaches to etiologic research, the risk factors for WMSDs themselves are perhaps better described within four main categories (see

Table 5.1): (1) individual factors, such as a person's height and weight, and smoking habits and personality traits; (2) physical (or biomechanical) factors, such as vibration, heavy lifting, and awkward postures; (3) psychophysical factors, which refer to an individual's perceptions about the physical demands of work, over and above what may have been measured in (2); and (4) psychosocial factors, which describe elements of the work environment and the work-worker interface, such as job control and job satisfaction. In order to better represent the relative impact of the various risk factors on the overall incidence of WMSDs, and thereby provide some context for the influence that psychosocial factors may be exerting, each of these four categories are reviewed below.

Table 5.1

Categories of risk factors and examples from low back pain research

Category	Example for low back pain
1 Individual characteristics and personality traits (e.g., height, weight, smoking habits)	Previous back pain is a strong predictor of who will develop it in the future
2 Physical (biomechanical) factors (e.g., vibration, heavy lifting ,and awkward postures)	Workers who report back pain found to have higher measured levels of lumbar spine forces (e.g., peak shear)
3 Psychophysical factors (i.e., an individual's perceptions about the physical demands of work, over and above what may have been measured in category 2)	Workers who self-rate physical demands of work to be excessive are more likely to report back pain
4 Psychosocial factors (e.g., elements of the work environment and the work-worker interface, such as job control and job satisfaction)	Workers who report back pain also more likely to report negative workplace social environment (e.g., more conflicts, less pleasant atmosphere, etc.)

Source: Kerr et al. (1998).

In addition to the four broad groups of factors in Table 5.1, which are typically measured at the individual level, there are firm- or organizational-level factors, such as the presence of a joint health and safety committee and the adoption of a "safety culture" that can affect the occurrence of injury. However, few if any studies have examined these factors in relation to WMSDs specifically.

This brief review of risk factors summarizes the results of recent epidemiological studies rather than case reports, laboratory studies, or expert opinion.
While the evidence from these other sources should not be ignored, as it can
contribute significantly to the hierarchy of evidence required to establish
causation systematically, the ultimate test for the hypotheses these efforts
develop is to try to link them to real workplace injury and exposure data.
Hence the reliance on epidemiological studies (Egilman et al. 1996; Bombardier et al. 1994). This review is also limited mainly to an examination of the
exposures thought to be most relevant to occupational settings, particularly
those with the potential for change through workplace interventions.
Several general and more in-depth reviews of specific WMSD epidemiology
are also available (Burdorf and Sorock 1997; National Institute for Occupational Safety and Health 1997; Hales and Bernard 1996; Hagberg et al. 1995;
Armstrong et al. 1993; Frank et al. 1996). The purpose here is to supplement
these reviews with a focus on recent developments in the field of psychosocial risk factor research. Because physical and psychosocial factors tend to be
poorly defined and measured in most published WMSD studies, we note
some recent articles that thoroughly review the methods and issues of concern for assessing risk factors in the workplace (Veazie et al. 1994; Burdorf et
al. 1997; Winkel and Mathiassen 1994; Bongers et al. 1993; Burdorf 1992).

Finally, this chapter presents a general set of risk factors that are applicable
to the majority of musculoskeletal disorders encountered in the workplace,
most of which could be categorized as soft tissue sprains and strains. In other
words, rather than singling out specific conditions and then detailing the
list of possible risk factors associated with each one, the risk factors presented are assumed to be applicable across the full group of disorders combined into the common and burdensome WMSD category. This is not to
suggest that unique pairings of specific risk factors and musculoskeletal disorder do not exist – they undoubtedly do, as with the association between
compression of the intervertebral discs and the onset of low back pain
(Norman et al. 1998). However, the extent of the overlap between the risk
factors identified in the published literature for the various WMSD sub-con-
ditions, whether physical or psychosocial, was deemed sufficient enough to
justify the unified approach taken here. A further advantage to this
approach, apart from the obvious parsimony it affords, is the recognition of
common threads between some of the underlying causes of these conditions, which could allow for the development of more broadly based intervention programs targeted at WMSDs in general, rather than the splintering
of programs along specific sub-condition lines.[1]

Individual Factors

A number of individual risk factors (i.e., personal characteristics) have been
studied, though very few have been clearly established as risk factors for

WMSDs. The strongest and most consistent association has been reported for prior occurrence of a WMSD, with somewhat less well established associations for age, obesity, smoking, and gender (Garg and Moore 1992; Kelsey and Golden 1988; Riihimäki 1991; Hildebrandt 1987). The lack of a clear association with age is perhaps surprising, but may be the result of experience or seniority issues in the workplace confounding the relationship. That is, older workers often do not have the same job demands as younger workers and are typically more risk averse and cautious (Hales and Bernard 1996). Females have been shown to have higher rates of most WMSDs, but there is also evidence to suggest that this may be more of a reporting phenomenon, since the level of unreported symptoms is often higher among men (Polanyi et al. 1997; National Institute for Occupational Safety and Health 1997). Although previous reporting of WMSD, especially for low back pain, is probably the most established of the individual factors examined, this association has sometimes been interpreted as representing an underlying personality trait, such as "compensation neuroses" or "hysteria" (Bigos et al. 1992; Frank et al. 1995; Ford 1997). However, it could also be indicative of a reduced threshold for injury or pain in tissues that have been repeatedly injured over time. Additionally, there is very little evidence supporting an association between the occurrence of WMSD and general fitness or muscular strength levels, the presence of pre-morbid X-ray abnormalities, or the presence of psychological disorders such as depression and anxiety (Gibson 1988; Battié et al. 1989a, 1989b; Bigos et al. 1991). While some of the factors from this category are known to affect recovery time once someone has a WMSD, their role in the onset of these conditions remains to be established. As noted, few if any of these individual factors are readily modifiable, especially in the workplace, thus they may be of little use in prevention strategies specific to WMSD (Frank et al. 1996).

Physical Factors
The evidence linking the physical demands of work with WMSD comes mostly from cross-sectional studies, such as surveys[2] (Bombardier et al. 1994). There are a number of concerns with the quality of such studies, over and above the difficulty of establishing a cause-and-effect pathway using such data (Leamon 1994; Frank et al. 1995). Taken individually, most of the published studies on WMSD provide only modest evidence of causation. However, the evidence from any one study is only part of the overall picture of what is known to contribute to the disorders (Egilman et al. 1996). Two observations support the conclusion that there is a causal relationship between musculoskeletal problems and workplace physical exposures: (1) the consistency of the published evidence, whereby certain variables (such as heavy lifting and whole body vibration) have been reported over many different types of studies and study settings as being

linked to WMSD; and (2) the strength of the associations observed for more generalizable characteristics of the physical demands of work that are objectively measurable, such as repetitive use and awkward postures (Hales and Bernard 1996). In a number of studies, the risk of developing a WMSD has been reported to be several times higher for workers exposed to physically demanding work compared to those who have not been exposed to such work (NIOSH 1997).

Some of the best evidence substantiating the link between workplace biomechanical exposures and WMSDs comes from recent studies that have used detailed, direct measurements of the physical demands of work on each individual in the study, rather than using self-reported data or the assignment of exposure status from group measures or crude categories such as job title (Norman et al. 1998; Polanyi et al. 1997; Kerr 1997; Punnett et al. 1991; Marras et al. 1995). Based on these newer studies, and the existing body of evidence from older studies, the best established risk factors for WMSDs are reported to be: posture, including awkward and prolonged postures, as well as bending, twisting, and overhead work; vibration of the whole body and the hand/arm region; and lifting, including high forces (i.e., "heavy" lifts) as well as cumulative or repetitive forces. As has been suggested recently, some variables in this list may in fact be surrogate measures of more direct biomechanical forces (Wells et al. 1997). For example, while heavy lifting has been identified in many studies as a risk factor, it may in fact be just a risk marker for the high levels of disc compression in the low back that result from the lifting process (Kerr 1997). While certain conditions, such as hand/arm vibration syndrome may have very specific risk factors, elsewhere there is considerable overlap in the physical demands of work that have been reported as risk factors for the major WMSDs. As previously mentioned, such risk factor congruence could have practical implications for the scope of interventions aimed at preventing WMSDs in the workplace, whereby an overall strategic approach to WMSD prevention programs might be used to complement injury-specific ones.

Most of the evidence for the physical demands of work has been provided by studies that did not control for the workplace psychosocial environment, thus the relative contribution of these respective factors is still unclear. However, the overall quality of recent studies and the strengths of the associations observed for physical demands factors appear to indicate that physical risks are contributing substantially to the occurrence of WMSD. It is also possible that in certain work environments, particularly those where exposure to heavy physical demands is common, these factors would in fact be the primary risk factors of concern, since the effects of psychosocial factors might be overshadowed in such conditions (Theorell 1995). To better present the relative effects of the factors from these two major categories, the few studies that have attempted to simultaneously measure biomechanical and psychosocial risk factors are discussed later under the psychosocial rubric. Note, however, that these studies have generally found that the physical demands factors produced substantial increases in risk that were significantly, and more consistently associated with WMSD than psychosocial factors, again underscoring the link between WMSDs and the physical demands of work.

Psychophysical Factors
The evidence in support of the relationship between WMSDs and workers' perceptions of the physical demands of the job comes mostly from laboratory studies of material handling, which have often not linked these perceptions to risk of injury (Snook 1988). Despite this qualification, psychophysical data form the cornerstone of existing lifting guidelines (Borg 1982; Waters et al. 1993; Snook 1978). Recent evidence that has demonstrated the importance of workers' perceptions of the physical demands of work comes from a Canadian study of risk factors for low back pain among autoworkers, which found an independent contribution for the perceptions of job loading even when direct ("objective") measurements of job demands were taken into account (Kerr 1997). The findings of this study support a considerable body of earlier work reporting a link between the self-reported assessment of work load and WMSD (NIOSH 1997). It is a unique finding however, in that the strength of the reported association, combined with the study's statistically controlling for direct measures of at least some of the physical demands of work, imply that such information could have an important role to play in workplace interventions. These results also suggest that psychophysical assessment of work load is a more complex construct than simply a self-assessed rating of job-related physical demands. It is almost certainly affected by a number of other dimensions, possibly including but not restricted to such elements as pain and endurance thresholds, and the extent of the available support network, among other things.

Psychosocial Factors
The complex relationship that appears to exist between work-related psychosocial factors, such as the amount of job control available to workers, and the physical demands of work they experience, such as spinal loading, make it difficult to reach definitive conclusions about the relative importance of work-related psychosocial factors to the risk of developing WMSDs. Bongers et al., in a thorough review of the literature on this topic, concluded that the "studies do not present conclusive evidence due to high correlations between psychosocial factors and physical load and [because of the] difficulties in measuring dependent and independent variables" (Bongers et al. 1993). A similar finding was reported more recently

by the US National Institute of Occupational Safety and Health (NIOSH 1997). Despite these qualifications, there appears to be growing research evidence pointing toward a link between certain psychosocial factors and WMSDs, such as monotonous work, a poor workplace social environment, low job control, high perceived workload, and time pressure.

This conclusion has been reached based on the findings of a number of recent studies specifically designed to examine the role psychosocial factors might have in the onset of WMSDs. For example, an analysis of routinely collected survey data in the Netherlands reported a significant association between psychosocial stressors (high work pace and lack of intellectual discretion) and musculoskeletal complaints after taking self-reported physical work stressors and worker characteristics into account (Houtman et al. 1994). Similar results were obtained in the recent case-control study of back pain among autoworkers in Canada, where substantial effects were observed for negative perceptions of the work environment, low job control, and a perceived mismatch between one's education and the job held, even after controlling for the directly measured physical demands of work, which were themselves strongly, and independently associated with back pain (Kerr 1997). In this study, the relative contribution of psychosocial and physical load factors to the risk of reporting back pain was reported to be roughly equivalent.

Further support for a link between psychosocial factors and soft tissue musculoskeletal problems at work comes from two recent studies at major newspapers in the US and Canada involving non-production workers (i.e., office workers often required to do extensive computer work on the job). Both of these studies reported independent associations between the presence of musculoskeletal symptoms and the physical and psychosocial aspects of work, most notably keyboard height and posture, and high psychological workload and low job control (Polanyi et al. 1997; Faucett and Rempel 1994). The US study also examined the issue of possible interactions between physical and psychosocial risk factors, reporting that the effect of combined exposures was greater than might be expected based on the strengths of the independent associations for the separate factors.

Job dissatisfaction has also been examined as a psychosocial risk factor for WMSD. However, the published evidence in support of this association is weak and contradictory (Kerr 1997; NIOSH 1997; Bigos et al. 1991; Krause et al. 1997). The Boeing Study of predictors for back injuries in airplane assembly workers is often cited to support the association between job-related psychosocial factors and WMSDs (Bigos et al. 1991). The main finding of this prospective three-year follow-up study was that, apart from a prior history of back pain reports, worker dissatisfaction with job tasks was the only work-related risk factor associated with subsequent reporting of back pain. None of the variables assessing the physical demands of work significantly predicted who reported back pain. However, it is possible that the ability of this study to identify biomechanical risk factors was limited by a misclassification error resulting from a reliance upon group-level biomechanical assessments to the study subjects, which were performed once only, at baseline, often well before the worker developed back pain.[3] It should also be noted that this study could predict only a small proportion of the observed cases even when all measured risk factors were combined (Bigos et al. 1992). Given these caveats, dissatisfaction with work, at least as measured in the Bigos et al. study, does not appear to be a very strong risk factor for WMSDs.

Finally, a number of new studies of risk factors for WMSDs have been launched in Europe recently, that, like the Canadian study of low back pain in autoworkers, were specifically designed to address the relative contribution of biomechanical and psychosocial factors. The results of these studies have not yet been published, as most have not yet been completed. However, based on preliminary results presented at international conferences, these studies once again seem to be demonstrating that both the psychosocial and the physical demands of work are important risk factors for WMSDs (Theorell 1996; Bongers and Houtman 1996). In particular, the variables assessing job control, psychological job demands, and social support appear to have the strongest relationship with the onset of WMSDs. However, based on the currently available evidence, including a recent comprehensive and systematic review by the National Institute for Occupational Safety and Health, it should be reiterated that the link between the physical demands of work and the onset of WMSDs appears to be better established than it does for workplace psychosocial factors (NIOSH 1997).

Based on the available literature, then, the best-established risk factors for WMSDs would be: a prior WMSD history; self-rated perceptions of heavy physical demands of work; jobs requiring heavy lifting or physically demanding or repetitive work; awkward postures; and vibration. While the evidence is less compelling for the psychosocial factors, there is nevertheless increasing evidence that these factors have an independent contribution to the onset of WMSDs. The most notable factors include limited job control, monotonous work, psychologically demanding work, and low workplace social support. There is also emerging evidence to suggest that an imbalance in the efforts and rewards associated with work may also be affecting the incidence of WMSDs (Siegrist 1996).

While knowledge of risk factors for WMSD can be an important first step in the development of preventive and therapeutic interventions, note that detailed knowledge of causal mechanisms has not always been a prerequisite for action in terms of developing and implementing strategies for prevention. For example, while the exact mechanism for the relationship between smoking and lung cancer may not be entirely understood, smoking cessation campaigns have still been launched, and they have often had significant success in reducing smoking-related illness, including cancer and heart disease (Blair 1995). The same potential for change could be argued as the rationale for interventions aimed at preventing musculoskeletal disorders in the workplace. While the exact mechanism linking injury with the demands of work is still not known, the extent of the WMSD burden combined with the strength of the evidence that is available linking WMSDs to the workplace should provide sufficient rationale for the development and implementation of primary prevention efforts.

Causal Mechanisms for Psychosocial Risk Factors

It is relatively easy, because of everyday life experience with aches, pains, and physical activity, to imagine how physically demanding work could possibly result in a WMSD. It is not quite as intuitive perhaps to comprehend how the psychosocial work environment could also be triggering these events. As might be expected, based on the body of evidence described above, the theoretical and conceptual underpinnings are not nearly as well developed for the psychosocial model of WMSD etiology as they are for the biomechanical model (Bongers et al. 1993). One of the best known psychosocial risk factor models, and one that receives extensive research attention, was first proposed by Karasek, with later modifications in conjunction with Johnson and Theorell (Karasek and Theorell 1990). Their demand-control-support model of work-related psychosocial stress, shown in Figure 5.2, has been widely studied, particularly for cardiovascular disease (CVD) (Reed et al. 1989; Karasek et al. 1988; Alfredsson et al. 1983). It has only recently been extended to other health outcomes, most notably WMSD research (Theorell et al. 1991; Houtman et al. 1994). This model predicts that jobs with low demand, high control, and high support are relatively protective of health, whereas jobs with high demands, low control, and low social support raise the risk of a range of poor health outcomes.

In the Karasek model, the job-control construct combines elements of skill discretion, such as creativity, with elements of decision latitude, such as the freedom to make decisions about how work is done. The psychological job-demands scale is constructed to address the concepts of work pace and cognitive demands, although recent evidence indicates that the scale may in fact be overlapping with self-ratings of the physical demands of work (Kerr 1997). The social-support scale combines elements of the active encouragement and assistance of co-workers and supervisors as well as the provision of a social environment conducive to work. In the Karasek model, the people at highest risk are those who have the most job strain (i.e., low job control together with the high psychological demands), and the least amount of workplace support. For a more thorough discussion of this model, see Karasek and Theorell 1990.

Figure 5.2

The Karasek-Theorell demand-control-support model

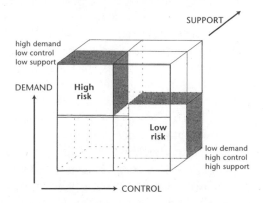

Research studies in several different occupational settings have established a clear but modest association between CVD and the job-strain model, especially for the degree of job control available to the worker (presumably to modify work demands). Similar findings have been reported for workers with a poor workplace social support network (good support is believed to help mediate job strain) (Theorell and Karasek 1996). These reported associations between CVD and elements of the job-strain model have been shown to persist even after study results have been adjusted for all the established CVD risk factors, such as smoking, cholesterol, and age (Johnson et al. 1996). This independent relationship between CVD and work has been very elegantly demonstrated recently in a large cohort study of CVD among British civil servants (Marmot et al. 1997). The study, based at Whitehall, first showed the existence of a strong gradient for CVD incidence according to civil service rank. The authors then reported that the proportion of the observed gradient that could be accounted for by traditional risk factors for CVD in a multivariate statistical model including smoking, age, obesity, physical inactivity, and high cholesterol was no greater than that which could be attributed to differences in job control between the occupational grades. In other words, the effect attributed to the psychosocial work environment, in the form of job control, persisted even after taking the individual risk factor differences into account. While the Whitehall study has found a similar effect in a study looking at job rank and low back pain, the relationship is not yet as clearly established for musculoskeletal conditions, possibly because fewer studies have examined it, and possibly because WMSDs are not as easily defined (or diagnosed) as CVD (Bongers et al. 1993).

One of the most recent developments in the field of workplace stress research, shown in Figure 5.3, is a conceptual model by Siegrist that examines the perceived imbalance between the efforts and rewards associated with work (Siegrist 1996).[4] In this model, Siegrist argues that the greatest risk to health occurs where people experience a mismatch between high costs spent and low gains received in occupational life. While this model has shown some promise in identifying work-related causes of stress, as with the demand-control model, it has also not been extensively used in studies of musculoskeletal injuries. However, it is noteworthy that some physiological responses of stress, including changes in blood levels of neuroendocrine "messengers" such as cortisol and adrenaline/noradrenaline, have systemic effects on several other body organs, including the muscles (e.g., the effects observed with the "fight-or-flight" response). This supports the notion that there may be overlap between the causal mechanisms for WMSDs and CVD, and thus indicates there may be a general effect (e.g., non-specific "stress") produced by a negative psychosocial work environment (Peter and Siegrist 1997; Theorell 1995).

Figure 5.3

The effort-reward imbalance model

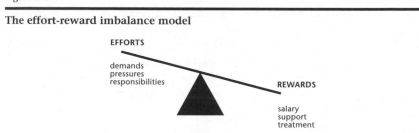

Source: Siegrist (1996).

As discussed above, some of the controversy surrounding the acceptance of psychosocial variables as risk factors for WMSDs may result from difficulty in conceptualizing them as a part of a direct causal mechanism. Recently, however, studies have begun to explore the biological pathways (pathomechanisms) that may explain the proposed association between WMSDs and psychosocial stressors. Although the evidence is still very limited, there is some new research, particularly from electromyography (EMG) studies, indicating that direct biological effects of "stress" are possible on the musculoskeletal system (Theorell 1995; Lundberg et al. 1989). Some of these effects are similar to those seen from biomechanical stressors (Lundberg et al. 1994) such as increased muscle tension, while others may be responses specific to psychological stressors such as increased blood levels of cortisol or changes to the pain receptors (Theorell et al. 1991). It is also likely that some factors labelled as psychosocial variables, such as job control, could influence WMSD risk indirectly by modifying exposure to biomechanical risk factors (either attenuating or amplifying these risk factors), which then directly affects WMSD onset.

As shown in Figure 5.4, the possible injury mechanisms underlying the two main risk factor models for WMSDs may be the result of direct or indirect effects from exposure to either type of risk factor, psychosocial or biomechanical. The uncertainty surrounding these mechanisms, and the restrictions imposed by the rather narrow risk factor focus of much of the prior WMSD etiologic research, led to the broad-based approach to assessing workplace exposures that has been adopted by the more recent WMSD studies. It is hoped that the results of these new studies will help clarify the relative importance of biomechanical and psychosocial workplace factors in the genesis of WMSDs.

Figure 5.4

The interaction of physical and psychosocial factors in the occurrence of WMSDs

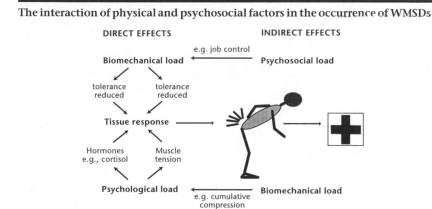

Potential for Interventions

While some intervention work has been done in trying to reduce or eliminate risk factors for WMSDs, it has almost exclusively been directed toward either changing the workers themselves, often through behavioural or education programs, or changing the physical demands of work, such as with the introduction of lift-assists. However, as outlined in the companion piece by Norman and Wells (this volume), very few interventions have been properly evaluated in order to determine their effectiveness, particularly in relation to their costs and benefits, an important prerequisite for the broader uptake of any prevention program. Even rarer still are interventions that have been specifically focused on changing the psychosocial work environment (Hurrell and Murphy 1996).

Having stated these caveats on the quality and amount of the published research, however, it is necessary to comment on the difficulty of demonstrating the scientific effectiveness of workplace interventions. Did a "package" achieve its desired effect or effects (Silverstein 1992)? Intervention effectiveness depends on a number of factors, and few if any of these can be carefully controlled by researchers in the workplace. In addition to internal concerns about efficacy, coverage, compliance, and ascertainment within the intervention, researchers must also contend with many extraneous factors that might influence effectiveness, such as economic disruptions in the workplace (e.g., lay-offs), industrial engineering factors (product or processing changes), and labour-management problems (e.g., strikes). Given the litany of potential pitfalls, it is not surprising that there are so few well-evaluated interventions claiming to be able to effectively reduce the rates of WMSDs. It has been argued that such research might be better focused on taking advantage of natural experiments rather than attempting the direct workplace modifications typically required by rigorous experimental guidelines (Silverstein 1992).

In spite of the difficulties that can arise, some work on psychosocial interventions has been done in the area of work stress and cardiovascular disease, as well as general health promotion programs. However, most of these efforts have been directed toward helping workers to cope with work stress, rather than being aimed at changing the work process or the work environment. While these types of interventions have shown some beneficial effects, especially in high-risk populations (e.g., stress reduction for people exhibiting "type A" behaviour), they may focus too narrowly on the individuals and thereby possibly ignore the contribution of the work environment. Fortunately, a few workplace studies have examined the direct biomedical effects of changes in occupational factors believed to be associated with stress. For example, Orth-Gomer et al. (1994) showed significant serum-lipid-lowering effects (reductions in mean triglycerides and apolipoproteins B/AI ratios) indicative of lowered CVD risk by randomly assigning 129 Swedish health care service workers either to a control group (35 subjects) or an intervention group (94 subjects). In this study, the intervention was designed to recognize and change work-related risk factors specifically associated with the demand-control model. Groups of workers set up action plans consisting of a list of problems to improve, together with the actions to be taken and the people responsible for initiating and evaluating the intervention. The main objective of the program was to decrease job strain (without decreasing productivity), mainly by increasing job control and social support in the workplace. In addition to the serum lipid effects reported above, some improvement was also seen in the levels of psychosocial risk factors. While the program was clearly focused on CVD risk, such interventions could also have beneficial effects on WMSD rates given the potential systemic effects for the observed physiological responses.

Another example of the potential for interventions with a psychosocial focus is a recent German study of stress management in bus drivers (who are also known to be at high risk of WMSDs). This pilot study, which included an intensive therapy intervention as well as recommendations for workplace change, concluded that an intervention program based on recognizing the risks in the workplace psychosocial environment can indeed show beneficial health effects, perhaps through combined changes to individual and structural measures that improve coping and thereby lessen the need for control (Aust et al. 1997). It is hoped that in the future, such interventions will include components in their design that can directly assess the impact on WMSDs as well.

While some of the more recent studies have demonstrated potential beneficial effects from modifying work-related psychosocial factors, it seems unlikely that programs aimed at modifying the psychosocial work environment only will be successful. The same would be true for programs focused exclusively on the physical demands of work. A more comprehensive approach is required that integrates modifications to the physical as well as the psychosocial work environments, since risk factors have now been identified from both domains (Baker et al. 1996). Although this may sound like an unrealistic challenge – to change the overall work environment to satisfy concerns about risk factors for WMSDs – some programs have been launched elsewhere that have attempted to do just this.

In the Danish PRIM study (Project on Research and Intervention in Monotonous work), researchers are trying to examine the health effects of monotonous repetitive work as well as strategies to reduce exposures to this type of work. While some preliminary results have indicated that WMSD symptoms are reversible and may be influenced by job reallocation to less monotonous and repetitive work, the results of the main intervention study have not yet been produced (Schibye et al. 1995). The authors of this work have adopted a pragmatic approach to determining program effectiveness, whereby they tend not to combine an etiologic component with the intervention (i.e., one that seeks to establish causation), which simplifies the prevention effort to one that can focus on exposure as the only outcome measure (Skov and Kristensen 1996). The PRIM study is one of the only prevention efforts with a particular focus on psychosocial factors and WMSDs, although even here the overlap with biomechanical factors is extensive. A similar interrelationship exists in the studies discussed in the companion paper on ergonomics interventions by Norman and Wells (this volume), where it is proposed that improvements in psychosocial factors could accrue largely as a consequence of ergonomic-based interventions.

Conclusion

The evidence summarized in this chapter suggests that psychosocial risk factors are important in the etiology of work-related musculoskeletal disorders. There is growing evidence of a link between workplace psychosocial factors and cardiovascular disease, and this type of research is now being extended into other health-related outcomes, including general work absenteeism, as with the Whitehall study of British civil servants. Recent examinations of the links between WMSDs and psychosocial factors are beginning to indicate that there is indeed evidence for a causal relationship, although more research needs to be done to better clarify both the extent of this relationship and the biological pathways (or pathomechanisms) that may be behind it. While it is recognized that there are limitations to the quality of the evidence on psychosocial risk factors, there is good reason to believe that interventions that include components addressing psychosocial risk factors could help reduce the incidence of WMSDs.

Despite the growing indications that psychosocial factors may directly influence the onset of WMSDs, the overall weight of the evidence from published research on risk factors for WMSDs clearly indicates that the physical demands of work cannot be ignored in the search for successful prevention programs. In summarizing the full weight of the available literature on the topic, its is apparent that the association between workplace physical demands and musculoskeletal disorders is a more strongly established link than the one between the psychosocial work environment and musculoskeletal disorders. Better understanding the nature of the interrelationships between the two work-related risk factor models will require more workplace research that gives equal emphasis to measurements of both types of factors. It will also require more basic research into the effective measurement of these factors and the possible biological pathways (or pathomechanisms) leading toward the onset of WMSDs. Because of the purported link to the workplace environment, much of this work will need to be performed in workplaces themselves, which have traditionally been a difficult place for researchers to gain access. A discussion of the ways and means to improve this access, such as compensation premium incentives or rebates for companies permitting researchers access to their workplaces, could greatly facilitate the kind of research needed to help resolve the remaining controversies regarding causation and prevention of WMSDs.

Notes

1   The argument in favour of combining the major conditions together in the discussion of risk factors in this chapter may seem somewhat simplistic. It is not meant to imply that a narrow range of exposures causes all cases of a wide range of conditions. Rather, it is meant to convey the idea that common themes are present in many of the risk factors and that exploring these themes in more detail could have potential benefits. Certain musculoskeletal disorders, especially the less common conditions, but also including some of those that are relatively common, like carpal tunnel syndrome or epicondylitis, may benefit from very specific prevention programs aimed a narrow range of factors, such as specific hand tool redesign. The argument presented here is that a broad-ranging program that recognizes the extensive overlap in the etiology of WMSDs is most likely to effect the greatest change. For a more thorough discussion of the issues of the nature and burden of WMSDs,

including topics of staging and phasing of the major WMSDs as well as factors of relevance to recovery from them, see the companion chapter in this volume by Hogg-Johnson et al.

2 Cross-sectional studies select subjects at a single point in time. Therefore, a mixture of people with chronic and acute WMSDs are usually enrolled. This can make the results difficult to interpret since distinguishing between factors that cause a problem and factors that are a consequence of it is problematic. Prospective cohort studies, which follow a large number of healthy people (the cohort), can usually avoid this difficulty. However, their high cost, driven by their larger sample sizes, limits their use. They may also suffer from a problem of intervening changes between the time of measuring exposure and measuring outcome. These changes can severely cloud a relationship when current and past exposures differ strongly. Because of their lower cost and greater flexibility, cross-sectional studies, including case-control studies that compare a predetermined number of cases and comparison subjects, are the most common form of WMSD study, with the latter providing the more robust design for investigating causality. See Bombardier et al. 1994 for a more thorough discussion of etiologic study design options.

3 Biomechanical data were collected for the Boeing Study only for "job types" employing twenty or more workers. The remaining subjects were assigned the exposure values based on this site-specific job classification scheme. (See Bigos et al. 1992 for more information.)

4 The model also addresses several other key points including "intrinsic" efforts (e.g., competitiveness, irritability) as well as status control (e.g., security, prospects).

References

Alfredsson, K., R. Karasek, and T. Theorell. 1983. "Myocardial Infarction and Psycho-Social Work Environment: An Analysis of the Male Swedish Working Force." *Social Science and Medicine* 16: 463-7.

Armstrong, T.J., P. Buckle, L.J. Fine, M. Hagberg, B. Jonsson, A. Kilbom, I. Kuorinka, B.A. Silverstein, G. Sjogaard, and E. Viikari-Juntura. 1993. "A Conceptual Model for Work-Related Neck and Upper-Limb Musculoskeletal Disorders." *Scandinavian Journal of Work, Environment, and Health* 19 (2): 73-84.

Association of Workers' Compensation Boards of Canada (AWCBC). 1997. *Work Injuries and Diseases Canada 1994-1996.* Mississauga: AWCBC.

Aust, B., R. Peter, and J. Siegrist. 1997. "Stress Management in Bus Drivers: A Pilot Study on the Model of Effort-Reward Imbalance." *International Journal of Stress Management* 4: 297-305.

Baker, E., B.A. Israel, and S. Schurman. 1996. "The Integrated Model: Implications for Worksite Health Promotion and Occupational Health and Safety Practice." *Health Education Quarterly* 23 (2): 175-90.

Battié, M.C., S.J. Bigos, L.D. Fisher, T.H. Hansson, M.E. Jones, and M.D. Wortley. 1989. "Isometric Lifting Strength as a Predictor of Industrial Back Pain Reports." *Spine* 14 (8): 851-6.

Battié, M.C., S.J. Bigos, L.D. Fisher, T.H. Hansson, A.L. Nachemson, D.M. Spengler, M.D. Wortley, and J. Zeh. 1989. "A Prospective Study of the Role of Cardiovascular Risk Factors and Fitness in Industrial Back Pain Complaints." *Spine* 14 (2): 141-7.

Bigos, S.J., M.C. Battié, D.M. Spengler, L.D. Fisher, W.E. Fordyce, T.H. Hansson, A.L. Nachemson, and M.D. Wortley. 1991. "A Prospective Study of Work Perceptions and Psychosocial Factors Affecting the Report of Back Injury." *Spine* 16 (1): 1-6.

Bigos, S.J., M.C. Battié, D.M. Spengler, L.D. Fisher, W.E. Fordyce, T.H. Hansson, A.L. Nachemson, and J. Zeh. 1992. "A Longitudinal, Prospective Study of Industrial Back Injury Reporting." *Clinical Orthopaedics and Related Research* 279: 21-34.

Blair, S.N. 1995. "Noneconomic Benefits of Health Promotion." In *Worksite Health Promotion Economics: Consensus and Analysis,* ed. R.L. Kaman, 33-54. Champaign, IL: Association for Worksite Health Promotion, Human Kinetics.

Bombardier, C., M.S. Kerr, H.S. Shannon, and J.W. Frank. 1994. "A Guide to Interpreting Epidemiologic Studies on the Etiology of Back Pain." *Spine* 19 (18, supplement): 2047S-56S.

Bongers, P.M., C.R. De Winter, M.A.J. Kompier, and V.H. Hildebrandt. 1993. "Psychosocial Factors at Work and Musculoskeletal Disease." *Scandinavian Journal of Work, Environment, and Health* 19 (5): 297-312.

Bongers, P.M., and I.L.D. Houtman. 1996. "Psychosocial Factors and Musculoskeletal Symptoms: First Results of the Dutch Longitudinal Study." 25th International Congress on Occupational Health, 16-20 September, Stockholm. Book of abstracts 2: 79.

Borg, G.A.V. 1982. "Psychophysical Bases of Perceived Exertion." *Medicine and Science in Sports and Exercise* 14 (5): 377-81.

Burdorf, A. 1992. "Exposure Assessment of Risk Factors for Disorders of the Back in Occupational Epidemiology." *Scandinavian Journal of Work, Environment, and Health* 18 (1): 1-9.

Burdorf, A., M. Rossignol, F.A. Fathallah, S.H. Snook, and R.F. Herrick. 1997. "Challenges in Assessing Risk Factors in Epidemiologic Studies on Back Disorders." *American Journal of Industrial Medicine* 32: 142-52.

Burdorf, A., and G. Sorock. 1997. "Positive and Negative Evidence on Risk Factors for Back Disorders." *Scandinavian Journal of Work, Environment, and Health* 23 (4): 243-56.

Egilman, D., L. Punnett, E.W. Hjelm, and L. Welch. 1996. "Evidence for Work-Related Musculoskeletal Disorders." *Journal of Occupational and Environmental Medicine* 38: 1079-80.

Faucett, J., and D. Rempel. 1994. "VDT-Related Musculoskeletal Symptoms: Interactions between Work Posture and Psychosocial Work Factors." *American Journal of Industrial Medicine* 26: 597-612.

Ford, C.V. 1997. "Somatization and Fashionable Diagnoses: Illness as a Way of Life." *Scandinavian Journal of Work, Environment, and Health* 23 (supplement 3): 7-16.

Frank, J.W., M.S. Kerr, A.S. Brooker, S.E. Demaio, A. Maetzel, H.S. Shannon, T. Sullivan, R.W. Norman, and R.P. Wells. 1996. "Disability Resulting from Occupational Low Back Pain, Part I: What Do We Know about Primary Prevention? A Review of the Scientific Evidence on Prevention before Disability Begins." *Spine* 21 (24): 2908-17.

Frank, J.W., I.R. Pulcins, M.S. Kerr, H.S. Shannon, and S. Stansfeld. 1995. "Occupational Back Pain: An Unhelpful Polemic." *Scandinavian Journal of Work, Environment, and Health* 21 (1): 3-14.

Garg, A., and J.S. Moore. 1992. "Prevention Strategies and the Low Back in Industry." *Occupational Medicine* 7: 629-40.

Gibson, E.S. 1988. "The Value of Preplacement Screening Radiography of the Low Back." *Occupational Medicine* 3 (1): 91-108.

Hadler, N.M. 1997. "Workers with Disabling Back Pain." *New England Journal of Medicine* 337: 341-43.

Hagberg, M., B. Silverstein, R. Wells, M.J. Smith, H.W. Hendrick, P. Carayon, and M. Perusse. 1995. *Work Related Musculoskeletal Disorders (WMSDs): A Reference Book for Prevention*. London: Taylor and Francis.

Hales, T.R., and B.P. Bernard. 1996. "Epidemiology of Work-Related Musculoskeletal Disorders." *Orthopedic Clinics of North America* 27: 679-709.

Hildebrandt, V.H. 1987. "A Review of Epidemiological Research on Risk Factors of Low Back Pain." In *Musculoskeletal Disorders at Work*, ed. P.W. Buckle, 9-16. London: Taylor and Francis.

Houtman, I.L.D., P.M. Bongers, P. Smulders, and M.A.J. Kompier. 1994. "Psychosocial Stressors at Work and Musculoskeletal Problems." *Scandinavian Journal of Work, Environment, and Health* 20 (2): 139-45.

Hurrell, Jr., J.J., and L.R. Murphy. 1996. "Occupational Stress Intervention." *American Journal of Industrial Medicine* 29 (4): 338-41.

Johnson, J.V., W. Stewart, E.M. Hall, P. Fredlund, and T. Theorell. 1996. "Long-Term Psychosocial Work Environment and Cardiovascular Mortality among Swedish Men." *American Journal of Public Health* 86: 324-31.

Karasek, R., and T. Theorell. 1990. *Healthy Work: Stress, Productivity, and the Reconstruction of Working Life*. New York: Basic Books.

Karasek, R.A., T. Theorell, J. Schwartz, P.L. Schnall, C.F. Pieper, and J. Michela. 1988. "Job Characteristics in Relation to the Prevalence of Myocardial Infarction in the US, HES, and HANES." *American Journal of Public Health* 78: 910-8.

Kelsey, J.L., and A.L. Golden. 1988. "Occupational and Workplace Factors Associated with Low Back Pain." *Occupational Medicine: State of the Art Reviews* 3 (10): 7-16.

Kerr, M.S. 1998. "A Case-Control Study of Biomechanical and Psychosocial Risk Factors for Low-Back Pain Reported in an Occupational Setting." PhD diss., University of Toronto.

Kerr, M.S, J.W. Frank, H.S Shannon, R.W.K. Norman, R.P. Wells, W.P. Neumann, C.

Bombardier, and the Ontario Universities Back Pain Study (OUBPS) Group. 1998. "A Case-Control Study of Biomechanical and Psychosocial Risk Factors for Low-Back Pain Reported at Work." Working Paper 61. Institute for Work and Health (IWH), Toronto.

Krause, N., D.R. Ragland, B.A. Greiner, S.L. Syme, and J.M. Fisher. 1997. "Psychosocial Job Factors Associated with Back and Neck Pain in Public Transit Operators." *Scandinavian Journal of Work, Environment, and Health* 23 (3): 179-86.

Leamon, T.B. 1994. "Research to Reality: A Critical Review of the Validity of Various Criteria for the Prevention of Occupationally Induced Low Back Pain Disability." *Ergonomics* 37: 1959-74.

Lundberg, U., M. Granqvist, T. Hansson, M. Magnusson, and L. Wallin. 1989. "Psychological and Physiological Stress Responses during Repetitive Work at an Assembly Line." *Work and Stress* 3 (2): 143-53.

Lundberg, U., R. Kadefors, B. Melin, G. Palmerud, P. Hassmen, M. Engstrom, and I.E. Dohns. 1994. "Psychophysiological Stress and EMG Activity of the Trapezius Muscle." *International Journal of Behavioral Medicine* 1: 354-70.

Marmot, M.G., H. Bosma, J. Hemingway, E. Brunner, and S. Stansfeld. 1997. "Contribution of Job Control and Other Risk Factors to Social Variations in Coronary Heart Disease Incidence." *Lancet* 350: 235-9.

Marras, W.S., S.A. Lavender, S.E. Leurgans, F.A. Fathallah, S.A. Ferguson, W.G. Allread, and S.L. Rajulu. 1995. "Biomechanical Risk Factors for Occupationally Related Low Back Disorders." *Ergonomics* 38 (2). 377-410.

National Institute for Occupational Safety and Health (NIOSH). 1997. *Musculoskeletal Disorders and Workplace Factors: A Critical Review of Epidemiologic Evidence for Work-Related Musculoskeletal Disorders of the Neck, Upper Extremity, and Low Back.* Baltimore: US Department of Health and Human Services.

Norman, R., R. Wells, P. Neumann, J. Frank, H. Shannon, M. Kerr, and the Ontario Universities Back Pain Study (OUBPS) Group. 1998. "A Comparison of Peak vs Cumulative Physical Work Exposure Risk Factors for the Reporting of Low Back Pain in the Automotive Industry." *Clinical Biomechanics* 13 (8): 561-73.

Orth-Gomer, K., I. Eriksson, V. Moser, T. Theorell, and P. Fredlund. 1994. "Lipid Lowering through Work Stress Reduction." *International Journal of Behavioral Medicine* 1 (3): 204-14.

Peter, R., and J. Siegrist. 1997. "Chronic Work Stress, Sickness Absence, and Hypertension in Middle Managers: General or Specific Sociological Explanations?" *Social Science and Medicine* 45: 1111-20.

Polanyi, M., D.C. Cole, D.E. Beaton, J. Chung, R. Wells, M. Abdolell, L. Beech-Hawley, S.E. Ferrier, M.V. Mondloch, S.A. Shields, J.M. Smith, and H.S. Shannon. 1997. "Upper Limb Work-Related Musculoskeletal Disorders among Newspaper Employees: Cross-Sectional Survey Results." *American Journal of Industrial Medicine* 32: 620-8.

Punnett, L., L.J. Fine, W.M. Keyserling, G.D. Herrin, and D.B. Chaffin. 1991. "Back Disorders and Nonneutral Trunk Postures of Automobile Assembly Workers." *Scandinavian Journal of Work, Environment, and Health* 17: 337-46.

Reed, D.M., A.Z. Lacroix, R.A. Karasek, D. Miller, and C.A. Maclean. 1989. "Occupational Strain and the Incidence of Coronary Heart Disease." *American Journal of Epidemiology* 129: 495-502.

Riihimäki, H. 1991. "Low-Back Pain, Its Origin, and Risk Indicators." *Scandinavian Journal of Work, Environment, and Health* 17 (1): 81-90.

Robson, L.S., M.F. Polanyi, M.S. Kerr, and H.S. Shannon. 1998. "How the Workplace Can Influence Employee Illness and Injury." Working Paper 8. Institute for Work and Health (IWH), Toronto.

Schibye, B., T. Skov, D. Ekner, J.U. Christiansen, and G. Sjogaard. 1995. Musculoskeletal Symptoms among Sewing Machine Operators." *Scandinavian Journal of Work, Environment, and Health* 21 (6): 427-34.

Siegrist, J. 1996. "Adverse Health Effects of High-Effort/Low-Reward Conditions." *Journal of Occupational Health Psychology* 1: 27-41.

Silverstein, B. 1992. "Design and Evaluation of Interventions to Reduce Work-Related Musculoskeletal Disorders." Paper presented at the International Scientific Conference on Prevention of Work-Related Musculoskeletal Disorders PREMUS, Stockholm, 12 May.

Skov, T., and T.S. Kristensen. 1996. "Etiologic and Prevention Effectiveness Intervention Studies in Occupational Health." *American Journal of Industrial Medicine* 29 (4): 378-81.

Snook, S.H. 1978. "The Design of Manual Handling Tasks." *Ergonomics* 21 (12): 963-85.

–. 1988. "Approaches to the Control of Back Pain in Industry: Job Design, Job Placement, and Education/Training." *Occupational Medicine: State of the Art Reviews* 3 (1): 45-59.

Theorell, T. 1995. "Possible Mechanisms beyond the Relationship between the Demand-Control-Support Model and Disorders of the Locomotor System." In *Beyond Biomechanics: Psychosocial Aspects of Musculoskeletal Disorders in Office Work*, ed. S.D. Moon and S.L. Sauter, 65-74. Bristol: Taylor and Francis.

–. 1996. "Association between Psychosocial Factors and Work-Related Musculoskeletal Disorders: MUSIC Stockholm." 25th International Congress on Occupational Health, Stockholm, 16-20 September. Book of abstracts 2: 79.

Theorell, T., K. Harms-Ringdahl, G. Ahlberg-Hulten, and B. Westin. 1991. "Psychosocial Job Factors and Symptoms from the Locomotor System: A Multicausal Analysis." *Scandinavian Journal of Rehabilitation Medicine* 23: 165-73.

Theorell, T., and R.A. Karasek. 1996. "Current Issues Relating to Psychosocial Job Strain and Cardiovascular Disease Research." *Journal of Occupational Health Psychology* 1: 9-26.

Veazie, M.A., D.D. Landen, T.R. Bender, and H.E. Amandus. 1994. "Epidemiologic Research on the Etiology of Injuries at Work." *Annual Review of Public Health* 15: 203-21.

Waters, T.R., V. Putz-Anderson, A. Garg, and L.J. Fine. 1993. "Revised NIOSH Equation for the Design and Evaluation of Manual Lifting Tasks." *Ergonomics* 36 (7): 749-76.

Wells, R., R. Norman, P. Neumann, D. Andrews, J.W. Frank, H.S. Shannon, and M. Kerr. 1997. "Assessment of Physical Work Load in Epidemiologic Studies: Common Measurement Metrics for Exposure Assessment." *Ergonomics* 40: 51-61.

Winkel, J., and S.E. Mathiassen. 1994. "Assessment of Physical Work Load in Epidemiologic Studies: Concepts, Issues, and Operational Considerations." *Ergonomics* 37: 979-88.

6
Ergonomic Interventions for Reducing Musculoskeletal Disorders
Robert Norman and Richard Wells

The social and monetary costs of occupationally related injury and illness must be reduced. The question is, can production or service processes and practices, tools, equipment, materials, work space layout, task, job, and work organization be designed to minimize ill health outcomes and, at the same time, maximize productivity, quality, and profit? As noted in the introductory chapter by Sullivan and Frank, musculoskeletal disorders account for more than one-half of all workers' compensation costs.

Recent reviews have reaffirmed a strong work-related component for many upper limb and low back pain cases (Hagberg et al. 1995; NIOSH 1997). The work-related portion of the injuries and resulting disability is potentially preventable. It is important to identify interventions that are effective in reducing both the incidence of initial work-related musculoskeletal disorders (WMSDs) and the resulting disability, as well as the personal and monetary costs associated with them (Frank et al. 1996). This chapter will focus on evidence for the utility of "ergonomic interventions" in the reduction of WMSDs or disability arising from them and suggest some future directions for how such interventions might be applied.

Ergonomics is the process of designing, modifying, or organizing tools, materials, equipment, work spaces, tasks, jobs, products, systems, and environments to match peoples' psychological, social, anatomical, biomechanical, and physiological abilities, needs, and limitations. Thus, the scope of ergonomics or human factors (we will use the terms synonymously), includes physical, biophysical, cognitive, social, and organizational aspects of work. Moreover, ergonomics includes interventions aimed at improving work at both the level of individuals (microergonomics) and at the level of work organization (macroergonomics as discussed by Kerr and Shannon in this volume). Clearly, these levels interact with each other. The objectives of ergonomics are to design work to improve productivity and the quality of the product or service provided without compromising employee health, safety, or the quality of working life. Ergonomics is about human-centred design of work: it focuses on people in the process of the production, maintenance, and use of goods or services.

Interventions that change physical, cognitive, social, and organizational factors are of potential use in the reduction of musculoskeletal disorders. Factors from all four areas that affect work and the workforce have been shown to be related to the development of musculoskeletal disorders. Interventions are normally aimed at reducing or eliminating risk factors for injury.

Risk Factors for WMSDs

On the basis of a number of recent critical reviews of the literature (Burdorf 1992; Winkel and Mathiassen 1994; Hagberg et al. 1995; NIOSH 1997; Punnett and Bergqvist 1997), many types of musculoskeleletal disorders have been shown to have substantial work-related components. This is especially true where exposure levels are high and conditions adverse, for example, high frequency of lifting loads with the arms outstretched.

There is strong evidence that low back disorders are associated with lifting, high exertion, and awkward back postures (e.g., Punnett et al. 1991; Marras et al. 1993). Whole-body vibration has also been found to be strongly related to low back pain. Studies that used direct measures to quantify work exposures, worker by worker, generally showed stronger relationships than studies that used less precise methods such as job titles applied to many workers in a group. For example, a recent study using an extensive battery of both psychosocial and biomechanical exposure measures found that both types of variables were important, independent contributors to the reporting of low back pain in the automobile assembly industry. Specifically, higher peak and cumulative forces on the spine, higher forces on the hands, bent trunk postures, and perceptions of a poor work social environment, low decision latitude, good co-worker support, high job satisfaction, and high physical demands were all important, independent risk factors for reporting low back pain (Kerr 1998; Norman et al. 1998). This study provided consistent evidence of an association between workplace biomechanical factors and low back pain (LBP) and independent, if less consistent contributions for psychosocial factors. These observations were different from those reported by Bigos et al. (1991), who found that only job dissatisfaction was significant. However, their estimates of physical demands were done only at a group level or by job title.

There is strong evidence that non-neutral posture, especially overhead work, as well as high forces and high frequency movements are associated with development of neck and shoulder disorders. For the arm, combinations of forceful actions, awkward postures, and high frequency movements are associated with the development of carpal tunnel syndrome and tendinitis.

These findings typically come from industrial work activities. There is also a growing recognition that office tasks, especially those associated with visual display terminals (VDTs) can lead to musculoskeletal disorders. Disorders of the hand and wrist appear to be related to long-term use of the keyboard; the mechanism appears to be repetitive finger motion and sustained muscle activity in the forearm. For many body areas there is good to strong evidence that work exposures are associated with the development of injury and that the relative risk of certain work exposures is high; this is true for shoulder and hand/wrist tendinitis, low back pain, carpal tunnel syndrome, hypothenar hammer syndrome, tension neck syndrome, as well as localized but non-diagnosed pain in general. Plausible biological mechanisms for why these risk factors result in musculoskeletal disorders have been proposed. Our best evidence points to a complex interaction of physical, psychosocial, and individual factors in the production of musculoskeletal disorders at work.

Note that while the literature is clear on the main risk factors for injury, details of mechanisms of injury and injury threshold values are often unclear. For example, recent epidemiological studies have indicated that as the time spent using a visual display terminal increases, the risk of developing musculoskeletal disorders of the shoulders and arm also increases (Punnett and Bergqvist 1997). Cumulative compressive force on the spine is an independent risk factor for LBP (Kerr 1998; Norman et al. 1998). However, it is not possible to reduce the time using a VDT to zero; data must still be entered. Nor is it possible to reduce cumulative compression on the spine to zero. The spine is in some level of compression while just sitting or standing. Until there is a better understanding of tolerable durations or rates of working with VDTs or loading the low back and, in general, how time-related factors such as work rates or work durations cause tissue damage, it is difficult to understand exactly how long-term VDT use elevates injury risk, and it is difficult to produce effective mice, keyboards, work schedules, or job designs.

Types of Ergonomic Interventions

WMSDs have multiple risk factors spanning the individual, interpersonal, and physical environment, and the organization of work. Investigators from different disciplinary backgrounds, each with their own taxonomy, have approached interventions in a variety of ways. In this essay, we shall use the terms *engineering, administrative,* and *behavioural interventions.* Table 6.1 illustrates some ways in which interventions have been categorized.

Of course in any situation, multiple interventions may be made simultaneously or sequentially. Recent reviews by Goldenhar and Schulte (1994), Grant et al. (1995), Zwerling et al. (1997), and Westgaard and Winkel (1997), include many examples of interventions.

Table 6.1

Taxonomy of interventions to reduce WMSD

Level of analysis	Organizational design and management taxonomy	Ergonomic taxonomy	Industrial psychology taxonomy
Organizational structure and environment at firm or unit level	Macroergonomics	Administrative controls	Organizational structure
Job/task factors	Microergonomics	Engineering controls	Job design
Individual factors	Personal protective equipment and training	Personal protective equipment and behaviour	Interpersonal relations

Engineering interventions are physical manipulations of hazards or routes of exposure to physical hazards. Typical examples may be the provision of lift tables to prevent lifting from ground level, or adjustable office equipment. Administrative interventions concentrate on changing the duties or the design of the job such as the introduction of job rotation or job enlargement, use of work cells, changes in production line speed, or changes in policies – for example, requiring at least two persons to lift patients in a hospital. Behavioural interventions focus on the individual worker's behaviours or capacity. For example, a behavioural (or personal) intervention may focus on increasing fitness or strength, on stress-reduction workshops, or on educational courses to improve work methods or safety awareness. Requiring the use of personal protective equipment is a combination of all three types of intervention and is commonly used in safety and industrial hygiene.

The main difficulty with effecting administrative and behavioural changes and use of personal protective equipment is compliance. A rush job will probably mean that the worker cannot wait for a co-worker's assistance, does not tighten or wear the back belt, or cannot use the educational information on proper manual handling in the workplace. Engineering changes, on the other hand, tend to be more permanent, affect all workers on that job, and are unlikely to be bypassed under time pressure. For these reasons, engineering changes are usually recommended as a first approach and administrative controls are recommended only if job-design changes cannot be instituted or further risk reduction is required. The last resort should be behavioural and personal protective equipment changes.

There are many possible outcomes by which ergonomic interventions may be evaluated. Classically, these range from efficacy determined under ideal conditions on selected groups in a laboratory or field setting, through effectiveness measured under field conditions on larger groups, to cost-effectiveness or cost-benefit studies. Intermediate outcomes such as the intensity of the intervention (e.g., how many hours of training) or the compliance of people with the interventions (process measures) are important in understanding how the intervention affects the outcome of interest. An example may serve to illustrate these issues.

Within one year, a small company had two low back injury cases in a department with heavy lifting. Powered lifting assists were introduced as an engineering intervention. One year later, no reductions in the costs associated with back claims were found. The intervention was assessed as a failure. A review of the specifications of the lift assists showed that in efficacy tests in the laboratory the hoists reduced low back loads for the weights of interest. Feedback from supervisors and workers, however, determined that many people in the department were not familiar with the use of the lift assists and, as a result, the compliance with using them was low. In addition, breakdowns meant that they were not available much of the time. These process measures indicated that both the intensity of the intervention and compliance were low. This may have led to poor effectiveness of the intervention on the plant floor. A measure of the number of back strains from WCB claims and the first aid logs would have been useful in determining effectiveness. On review of the cost data, it was determined that most of the costs were due to an injury that had occurred in the previous year. Cost data were also deemed to be unstable due to the small size of the company and the limited follow-up time. The original conclusion, "no effect," was not warranted. This example and the other examples found in Table 6.2 illustrate the challenges facing both the introduction of interventions for reduction of WMSDs and their evaluation.

Several experimental designs can be implemented to study the effectiveness of ergonomic interventions, some statistically better than others, and some more practical than others in the workplace. These include pre/post designs, pre/post designs with control groups, and randomized controlled trials (RCTs). As we progress down this list, the designs allow a more unbiased assessment of the intervention's effectiveness. Unfortunately, randomized control trials, although regarded as the "gold standard" in many fields, are expensive and difficult to conduct in field settings. Sound experimental designs are characterized by randomization of assignment of people or other units of analysis to control and treatment groups. Studies reported on the evaluation of interventions in the workplace are rarely able to comply with randomization criteria of good research and often use a measurement on the same group before intervention as a control, if there is any control group at all. The problem with this so-called historical control group is that changing conditions unrelated to the intervention, but that affect the outcome, can occur during the course of the intervention (e.g., change in the economy). A before/after experiment cannot account for the effects of these changing conditions and the intervention may be credited with a change that it did not cause.

A sampling of recent reviews of interventions for reducing WMSDs, safety, and mental health outcomes reveals two main threads. First, the reviews catalogue studies that have attempted to change employee relations, task requirements, and organizational structures and that also have had an evaluation process (Kilbom 1988; Goldenhar and Schulte 1994; Grant and Habes 1995; Zwerling et al. 1997). Second, the reviews have noted that there has been a lack of rigorous experimental design and evaluation methodology used in the intervention literature.

As a result, some of the reviewers have set out criteria for appropriate evaluation (Goldenhar and Schulte 1994, 1996; Malmivaara 1997; Westgaard and Winkel 1997). Those who have had experience in attempting to conduct ergonomics research in workplaces, we among them, have come to

Table 6.2

Assessing intervention effects aimed at reducing WMSD: Necessary conditions for success of intervention and evaluation of interventions

	Some necessary conditions for success of intervention and evaluation of interventions	*Example 1* Engineering: introduction of lift assists to reduce patient lifting in health care	*Example 2* Administrative: introduction of job rotation in an assembly line operation to reduce working with arms outstretched	*Example 3* Training: "anatomy and proper lifting technique" for manual material handlers
Action/indicator/ outcome				
Efficacy	Intervention reduced exposure to hazards, or increased the person's capacity to tolerate them. Short-term laboratory or classroom changes in response, e.g., strength, EMG, discomfort, knowledge or performance.	Peak loads on the spine reduced when using mock-up with healthy volunteer "patients."	Reduced time spent with the arms extended in front of the body when rotating between selected tasks.	Increase in knowledge or skill occurred.
Effectiveness	Intervention was transferred to the field. Very short term (~1 day) field changes in response, e.g., strength, EMG, discomfort, emotional strain or performance.	Loads when handling patients under normal operating conditions were reduced as demonstrated by, e.g., EMG or biomechanical model.	A rotation scheme was implemented that allowed rotation between tasks with different demands as measured, e.g. with EMG or posture recording.	Knowledge increase resulted in behaviour changes which reduced exposure. This may have required engineering or administrative changes to the workplace.

▶ *Table 6.2*

Assessing intervention effects aimed at reducing WMSD: Necessary conditions for success of intervention and evaluation of interventions

Action/indicator/ outcome	Some necessary conditions for success of intervention and evaluation of interventions	Example 1 Engineering: introduction of lift assists to reduce patient lifting in health care	Example 2 Administrative: introduction of job rotation in an assembly line operation to reduce working with arms outstretched	Example 3 Training: "anatomy and proper lifting technique" for manual material handlers
Short term (~4 weeks) field response, e.g., strength, EMG, discomfort, emotional strain or performance.	Intervention was of sufficient intensity to produce an effect.	Use of the lifting assist continued in order to reduce exposure.	Rotation was maintained, with rotation among tasks with different demands.	Newcomers were trained to maintain intensity of intervention.
Long-term (+1 year) changes in reported MSD, pain, performance, emotional strain, quality, scrap, etc.	Intervention was sustained with high intensity and compliance. Outcomes were measured in treatment group and preferably a comparison group.			
Cost-benefit Long-term (+1 year) changes in cost of MSD, performance, quality, scrap, etc., and costs associated with intervention.	Costs assigned to all musculoskeletal health and absence outcomes (compensation and sickness absence costs).			
	If the treatment group is small or many have disorders at the start of the study, effects may take a number of years to become detectable even if the intervention is effective.			

believe that randomized control trial rigour, however desirable statistically, is usually impractical. The recommendation is a tiered approach whereby interventions would first be studied by simpler, cheaper, and faster, but less statistically sound research approaches. Only those interventions that looked most promising would be tested with the most rigorous and expensive experimental design approaches. These recommended strategies for performing workplace ergonomic intervention studies, while not as methodologically sound as RCTs, would inform best practice (Kilbom 1988; Silverstein 1987; Polanyi et al. 1996; Zwerling et al. 1997). Notwithstanding the experimental design limitations described above, the literature on ergonomics interventions is informative.

The mid-1990s have seen an increasing interest in documenting the effectiveness of interventions to prevent musculoskeletal disorders at the primary and secondary level. This is driven by the high costs of these disorders and the growing interest in regulatory approaches, for example, British Columbia (BCWCB 1998) and Occupational Health and Safety Administration in the United States.

The National Safety Council (1982) lists a wide range of engineering interventions, contributed by various companies, to solve occupational health and safety problems. Unfortunately, most of the interventions lack formal evaluation. Grant and Habes (1995) summarized twenty-four engineering interventions to reduce ergonomic risk factors for the low back and upper limbs. For example, Gallimore and Brown (1993) intervened to reduce visual fatigue and body discomfort in VDT users. Analysis indicated that awkward static work postures were contributing factors. VDT screens were fitted with a screen that moved the image further from the eye. This led to reduced glare, and improved neck posture for bifocal wearers.

The majority of the evaluations were short-term efficacy-type studies. The reduction in exposure to risk factors (efficacy) was assessed by many means including postural improvement (most evaluations), reduced muscle activity, reduced tissue loads, and reduced vibration. In a few studies, performance, such as productivity and errors, was assessed. In almost all examples, the intervention reduced exposure to risk factors.

Only a few engineering intervention studies have followed workers over longer time frames with end points such as musculoskeletal sick-leave. Aarås and Westgaard (1987) followed the workforce of a telephone manufacturing facility over eight years. The introduction of adjustable work surfaces, arm rests, and other engineering changes to reduce postural load during assembly of wiring panels reduced both muscular demand on the shoulder region, as measured by electromyography, and musculoskeletal sick-leave. There was no comparison group to help control for other long-term changes that occurred over the eight-year project. A study in a health care facility, although aimed at secondary prevention to prevent time loss resulting from low back pain, reported substantial reductions in the incidence of time loss claims, possibly resulting from spillover from the ward where the interventions were made (Yassi et al. 1995).

Administrative interventions often change the duties of workers by job assignment changes or rotation, or they change break schedules. The concept of microbreaks, or frequent (every ten minutes) short (thirty-second) breaks has been advocated for workers in both industrial and office environments. These breaks may be either passive (sit or stand quietly) or active (combine the break with stretching or simple exercises). Studies in the field and laboratory indicate that the approach has merit in reducing discomfort. Genaidy et al. (1995) reported that four weeks of active microbreaks led to a statistically significant reduction in perceived discomfort among twenty-eight workers at a meat packing plant. Henning et al. (1997) studied two sites where microbreaks were introduced for a four- to six-week period for workers who used computers. The introduction of microbreaks alone did not lead to any improvement in productivity or well-being, but Henning et al. reported that productivity and eye and leg comfort improved when the short breaks included stretching. These short-term studies by Genaidy et al. and Henning et al. suggest that active microbreaks may be required to realize the benefits of any changes to breaks; however, longer-term studies are not currently available.

Behavioural/personal interventions have been the most studied. This may be because interventions such as education or personal protective equipment allow for large-scale and even randomized trials more easily than workplace equipment changes. A small body of evaluation focuses on work methods training using peer group feedback, video, or electromyographic feedback. For example, Parenmark (1988) used electromyographic feedback to train work methods with low shoulder demand in newly hired and experienced assemblers. A control group was used in each case. A follow-up after one year showed that the new employees trained by feedback had less musculoskeletal sick-leave in the shoulder region but that the experienced workers had no statistically significant decrease. Smith and co-workers used a peer training process in the meat packing industry to improve work methods (Smith 1994). In the following year, a reduction in reported injuries was observed. However, a pre/post design without a comparison group was used.

Most of the behaviour/personal ergonomic intervention research is focused on back pain. The literature identifies three major types of interventions: education or "back schools," exercise, and mechanical supports (wrist splints or "back belts"). One of the better studies on back pain and exercise (Gundewall et al. 1993) compared twenty-eight hospital workers who performed back-specific exercises with a control group of thirty-two similar workers. The two groups were followed up for thirteen months. The exercise group had fewer back pain complaints (53.9 versus 94.3) and fewer mean days lost from work (1.0 versus 4.84). The consensus of recent critical reviews is that exercise has some effect in the prevention of low back pain (Lahad et al. 1994; van Poppel et al. 1997).

Education for prevention of musculoskeletal disorders may be a short didactic presentation or a more comprehensive program. Content is typically organized around anatomy, risk factors, and work technique or "proper" body mechanics. Many of the interventions that utilized education also included another component. For example, in the study of Walsh and Schwartz (1990), which evaluated back supports, one group also received a one-hour educational program stressing lifting technique. A test showed that those who took the educational program scored higher on low back pain knowledge. This indicated that the educational program was effective in increasing knowledge. On six-month follow-up, however, there was no difference in absenteeism noted between the group who received the educational program and the control group. Similar results were found in the study of Daltroy et al. (1993) except that they also noted that despite the increased knowledge about low back pain, two and a half years later they did not detect changes in the work behaviours targeted by the program, such as postures of the arm and back. In this case, the increased knowledge did not translate into changed behaviour with reduced physical exposures, perhaps for the reasons described before, that is, time pressures, poor workplace layout, etc.

Overall, the reviews of Lahad et al. 1994 and van Poppel et al. 1997 found that there was not good evidence that education was effective in the prevention of low back pain. On the other hand, Engels et al. (1998) recently reported that twelve nurses who had participated in an ergonomics education program showed significant reductions in the number and percentage of harmful postures and errors while performing standardized nursing tasks compared with a control group of twelve who had not had the training. Whether this improved technique was transferred to actual nursing tasks on a ward, given typical pressures to work fast, was not known.

One can hypothesize many reasons for equivocal results on the effectiveness of ergonomic education programs. These hypotheses could include poor content or poor pedagogy in the course, jobs whose inherent design does not allow safe work regardless of the knowledge of the worker about injury risk, previously injured workers whose tissues have low resistance to re-injury regardless of job or work-station design or utilization of good technique, and a host of other possibilities. Few would argue that improved education about injury risk, mechanisms, and avoidance strategies is a bad thing. However, reasons for success or failure of educational interventions in reducing risk and cost of injury in the workplace remain to be understood.

Frequently, multiple-focus interventions are made simultaneously. For example, Grant and Habes (1995) and Zwerling et al. (1997) described over thirty published studies where the effectiveness of a variety of control strategies in reducing musculoskeletal disorders and discomfort was evaluated. The studies were of widely different methodological quality and the results ranged from being ineffective, to being unable to evaluate the intervention, to being effective. In almost all cases the interventions combined engineering, administrative, and behavioural/personal approaches. This makes identification of critical aspects of the intervention difficult. Kilbom (1988) suggests that job redesign (engineering change) is best, but suggests that as physical environment improves, work organizational and psychological factors become more important. Research would be helpful on the effects of deliberate attempts to take advantage of the interactions among engineering, administrative, and behavioural interventions, rather than attempting to study the effects of each in isolation. For example, engineering improvements in job design may result in improvements in the perceptions of workers about their workplace social environment and permit utilization of safer work practices that the workers have learned about in educational programs.

Combinations of biomechanical, psychological, and physiological factors operating at the level of the individual employee are clearly influenced by company organization, policies, production schedules, financial viability, and a host of other factors that mould a work social climate or culture. Worker attitudes, behaviours, abilities, and limitations undoubtedly feed back on, and modify the culture. Some of these interacting factors can be visualized in Figure 6.1. Here, personal characteristics of workers, their perceptions about their work, and ergonomic aspects of the design of work are all superimposed on a background of workplace organizational factors. All four categories of factors interact to affect productivity, the quality of goods and services, risk of injury, and decisions by a worker to report pain, go off work, and whether or when to return to work.

Hendrick (1991) and others advocate a systems approach to harmonizing the technical and personnel subsystems in an organization, an approach referred to as macroergonomics. For example, Smith and Carayon (1996) propose a plausible, but not entirely new, systems model in which they, by admission, speculate that both psychological and physical stress perceived by video display terminal users can result in WMSD because of imbalances among elements in the work system. Their five elements include: technology, job/task design, work (social) environment, organization of work, and the individual (at the centre). Imbalances among these elements, they suggest, result in adverse physical and psychological reactions that are expressed, for example, as direct injury to tissue, elevated muscular tension resulting in chronic fatigue or hormonal sensitization to pain because of psychological stress, inappropriate work methods as a result of low morale

Figure 6.1

Organizational factors in work injury

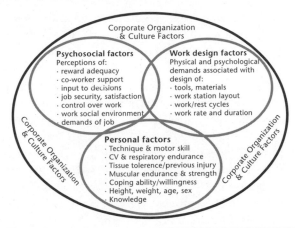

and indifference, etc. The imbalances are caused by deficiencies in one or a combination of the elements of the work system. These authors state (1996: 36): "There currently is no scientific evidence or valid hypothetical biological mechanism that can logically define physical stressors as superordinate to work organization stressors in causing CTDs [cumulative trauma disorders], or inversely, as subordinate to work organization stressors in causing CTDs." Our study on biomechanical and psychosocial risk factors for lower back pain (LBP) supports this position (Kerr 1998; Norman et al. 1998).

Smith (1997) proposes that interventions should start with organizational support, arguing that this increases motivation and feelings of security in the workforce, reduces stress, and reduces resistance to change. Furthermore, he suggests that "employee participation" is an essential aspect of technology implementation. Indeed, there is an increasing advocacy of "participatory ergonomics" by ergonomists, a psychosocial intervention process.

Wilson (1995: 1071) explains that participation within an ergonomics management program at work can be taken to be "the involvement of people in planning and controlling a significant amount of their own work activities, with sufficient knowledge and power to influence both processes and outcomes in order to achieve desirable goals." Kourinka (1997) defines participatory ergonomics as practical ergonomics with participation of the necessary actors in problem solving. The participation is not limited to worker participation but rather, includes all levels of the hierarchy with first-hand experience about the problem at hand. It may be formal or informal participation. Thus, it is a means of using an organization's experience to devise the best interventions, be they administrative, behavioural, or engineering. Participatory interventions are also reported to result in improved communication among stakeholders that has positive results substantially beyond the issues at hand (Saari 1992). Thus, participatory ergonomics is a psychosocial intervention in itself.

Vink et al. (1992) commented that although many people had experience with participatory ergonomics at that time, the underlying theories and methods were not well developed. More recently, Kourinka (1997) has noted that the methodology in participatory ergonomics is not a solid body of knowledge based on a theoretical construct. It is merely a collection of structures and approaches that have shown their usefulness in the hands of a competent ergonomics practitioner. There are several models of participation. One is that workers participate fully in all aspects of the process of improving the working environment, from problem identification to data gathering, analysis of information, solution invention or selection, implementation, and evaluation. Advantages are stated to be that workers know their work best and worker-generated solutions will facilitate acceptance. Disadvantages are that management is neither convinced nor committed to the process or the outcomes. An alternative model is that workers formulate solutions and management makes the final selection. This is reported to help solve both the problem of the threatened authority of management and the risk to labour members on the participating team of implementation of unpopular or faulty solutions.

Several, mainly qualitative studies on participatory ergonomics have appeared in the scientific literature. Kourinka et al. (1994) used a participatory process for the redesign of the front seat of police cars to determine if such a process would influence perceptions and create more realistic attitudes toward LBP. The outcome was enthusiastic and committed participation by members of all groups but no affect on attitudes toward low back pain although the authors stated that they "could not reject the hypothesis" of changed attitudes toward LBP.

Moore and Garg (1996, 1997a, 1997b) reported that a participatory ergonomics program in the red meat packing industry, an industry with high incidence and severity of WMSD, resulted in high ratings of satisfaction with the process by the ergonomics team members in all aspects except "solution implementation." The authors themselves point out that the study was a demonstration project rather than an experimental project and, as such, the design was a "post-test only with non-equivalent groups," a quasi-experimental design. This is one of the more extensive descriptions of a quasi-experimental approach to addressing the effectiveness of participatory ergonomics and the study is weak from an experimental design perspective.

A more quantitative study on a participatory ergonomic process of improving office work was reported by Vink and Kompier (1997). The work stations of people who entered salary data at high speeds in a large government office were studied before and after the introduction of adjustable chairs, tables, and other "ergonomic" equipment. Five months later, deviation from the "ideal" work-station layout was measured. There were significant improvements in comfort for back and neck complaints with the new work stations for almost all employees. The authors commented on the difficulty of conducting and controlling conditions of the experiment in the workplace because of continual interruptions to the participants, sickness absence on evaluation days, and other practical problems usually not encountered in the laboratory.

One of the more extensively reported participatory interventions is not in ergonomics but in the area of occupational safety. It is a combined participatory and behaviour modification approach to attempt to reduce workplace accidents by involving workers in the development of a housekeeping checklist, monitoring the number of "opportunities for improvement" frequently, and posting the results of each audit for all in the workplace to see (Saari and Nasanen 1989; Saari 1992). The scoring is simply the number of "yes" (tidy) ticks on the checklist as a percent of the total possible "yes" responses. Baselines are typically about 60 percent and rise over a period of six to eight weeks to 90 percent. These authors have shown the effect to persist for up to three years following withdrawal of the graphical feedback. The interesting finding, according to the authors, is that although one might expect a reduction in accidents of about 25 percent from improved housekeeping, the number of accidents often reduces by 70 to 90 percent. The reasons for this dramatic improvement are speculative, but plausible explanations are that people generalize the learned (safety) behaviour to other hazards and either remove those risks or are more careful in risky environments.

Engaging all stakeholders in taking charge of their own workplace health and safety in a participatory process is intuitively appealing. However, once again, the evidence base is thin and probably not convincing for sceptical employers. None of these studies has employed true experimental designs. Some are qualitative; most are before/after quasi-experimental designs with no true control group; none is randomized; usually groups are targeted for intervention because they have high injury rates, absenteeism, or some other feature that needs improvement. There are two good participatory ergonomics studies that will be discussed later (Narayan and Rudolph 1993; Lanoie and Tavenas 1996), both with positive outcomes. Continued research on the effectiveness of participatory ergonomic interventions is certainly needed.

In spite of continual calls for cost-benefit or cost-effectiveness analyses of ergonomic interventions for the purposes of "making the business case," relatively few studies of economic analyses of ergonomic interventions can be found in the scientific literature; there are many case study reports in professional periodicals. Cost-benefit analyses typically weigh the economic costs against the economic benefits of an intervention. Cost-effectiveness analyses weigh the costs against a non-monetary benefit such as a reduction in the number of adverse movements of the upper limbs or torso, reductions in absenteeism, or labour turnover rates attributable to an intervention.

Andersson (1992a, 1992b) points out that economic evaluations of ergonomic solutions can be effectively used in the formal accept/reject decision of a particular solution or in choosing among several, in ranking several project proposals, or in controlling the costs of implemented interventions against budget. Several economic indicators can be calculated depending on the type of input data available. They include the calculation of net present value (the present value equivalent of all cash inflows less all cash outlays associated with a project); the internal rate of return (the rate of interest that would equate the discounted present value of expected future receipts to the present value of the cash outlays for the intervention with an expectation that the interest rate would exceed some minimum expected for return on investment, e.g., 20 percent); and the payback period (the time usually expressed in years to regain the cost of the intervention). Each of these economic ratios has its strengths and weakness and requires different assumptions and input data. There are excellent descriptions of these methods and discussions of their strengths and weakness in several articles aimed at non-economists (e.g., Oxenburgh 1991; Andersson 1992a, 1992b; Riel and Imbeau 1996, 1997).

The paper by Riel and Imbeau (1997) is important for the thorough description of processes, methods, and an example of their economic analysis applied to ergonomic decision making. The example was in a helicopter manufacturing plant and required the manual handling of heavy dies. There were many overexertion and bodily reaction types of injuries. One of the important aspects of this study was Riel and Imbeau's demonstration that their economic analysis could be applied to a single work station for the purpose of deciding whether to implement an intervention of a particular type or not. The intervention was the purchase of a hydraulic table and set of rollers to reduce the manual handling. A number of points of interest were developed in the paper. They include the notion that economic analyses make the implicit assumption that economic aspects of potential accidents are linked to a particular work station; that uncertainty as to type of accident that may ensue affects the cost projections (some injuries are more costly than others) and that uncertainty considerations are often missing from economic analyses; and that when considering insurance costs, costs in the first year of a study are reflections of several previous years, not just the current year and that benefits of reduced insurance costs will persist several years beyond the investment at year one. Therefore, the horizon ought to span a time period that corresponds to the entire life of the intervention (equipment in this case) within reason. Their analysis showed that if only medium-term effects were considered, the investment in the hydraulic table and rollers ($10,000) was not attractive but if a longer-term horizon was considered, with all of its assumptions, the project desirability is likely to increase.

There are many health and safety magazine and conference proceeding descriptions of case studies on versions of economic analyses of ergonomic interventions. For example, Darcangelo (1989) reported that Northern Telecom in Calgary saved $95,000 in less than two years as a result of reductions in repetitive strain injuries on one production line for a cost of intervention of $23,000. The intervention included an employee awareness program, injury treatment protocols, a workplace assessment, and recommendations for change. Time loss accidents dropped from twenty to four. The savings were reported to result from a $29,600 increase in productivity and reductions of $54,600, $6,900, and $4,700 in the costs of injuries, fatigue, and material handling, respectively. There was no explanation of how costs attributable to "fatigue" or the other factors were calculated or a description of what changes in the workplace actually occurred.

Most case studies, if not all, suffer from lack of appropriate control groups and sketchy descriptions of exactly what the intervention was. Also, the case study literature probably has reporting bias of successful interventions, a problem also with the scientific literature. Even in the presence of these problems, there are enough success stories on which to base testable hypotheses about the potential utility of ergonomic interventions of various types.

There are some interesting examples of economic analyses in the scientific literature. Aarås and Westgaard (1987), alluded to earlier, showed that work-station redesign in a telephone exchange and cable assembly operation in Norway resulted in a reduction in the number of musculoskeletal sick-leaves on one of the jobs from 25 percent of the female workers employed from zero to two years on that job, to zero percent for this group working on a new ergonomically designed work station. For those who had been working for more than five years, the reduction was from 60 percent to 30 percent of the workers, possibly an effect of a group with WMSD that could now not be eliminated regardless of the quality of design of the new system. The mean duration of sick-leave dropped from seventy-two to forty-seven days on the redesigned work station, which Aarås and Westgaard showed, via electromyography, required lower muscular demand than the old system. Spilling, Eitrheim, and Aarås (1986) used these data and showed a cost savings against cost of intervention of about $60,000 per year (1986 Canadian dollars) for twelve years. The major saving was a dramatic reduction in the employee turnover rate that appreciably reduced recruiting and retraining costs. Over the prolonged duration of this study, a number of economic changes occurred in the country and in the plant, the major problem with a before/after study design. However, interviews with workers indicated that they thought that perhaps 50 percent of the reduction in costs and improvements in retention of the workforce could be attributed to the ergonomic intervention.

Narayan and Rudolph (1993) reported that ergonomic improvements in a medical device assembly plant that had high upper limb and some low back WMSDs resulted in a dramatic reduction in incidence and especially in the severity of injury on the jobs that had been redesigned. The jobs required very fine finger manipulation of materials and tools in prolonged awkward, static postures of the torso and wrists. Seating, lighting, and work-space layout were generally poor. The company used a participatory approach to the analysis of design problems and work-station redesign, including mock-ups of prototype work stations, following a one-day ergonomics awareness program for plant staff. Plant-wide reduction in time loss from 155 to sixty-eight days per 200,000 worker-hours over a one-year period occurred although as the company started implementing design changes the reporting of injury increased. This resulted in lower than hoped for statistics on incidence but the duration of time loss days decreased. The participatory process was successful in leaving the plant with the capability of assessing its operations on an ongoing basis. The economic analysis was simple and relatively informal. As an example, costs for one job (twenty workers) included the research on the work stations, some redesign charges, and the cost of new equipment such as chairs and footrests ($23,600). Benefits included compensation and time loss cost savings ($127,300). The payback period was 2.3 months.

Lanoie and Tavenas (1996) also implemented a participatory ergonomics program to attempt to reduce back-related disorders among warehouse packers who handled boxes full of liquor. A formal analysis of the costs and benefits of the intervention was described. A joint group of management and labour received five days of ergonomics training and subsequently met once a week to discuss safety problems and their solutions. Solutions included changes such as the purchase of a new "truck" seat, pallet movers, and a mechanized plastic wrapper. In the end, the program did not have a significant impact on the total number of accidents but it did reduce back-related injuries. In fact, the focus was on this type of injury but there was no spillover effect of the participatory approach reported by Saari (1992). A strike interrupted the project and may have destroyed the improved communication between management and labour that participatory approaches have been reported to facilitate. The economic analysis showed that the net present value was slightly negative (-$8,000) but became strongly positive ($188,000) if costs and benefits were projected over a five-year amortization period of the capital outlay. Although this study identified benefits of a participatory ergonomic intervention, its main value is the thorough description of the economic analysis that was done with considerable effort to include as many costs as possible and to discuss possible non-tangible bene-fits in addition to those that could be measured.

Perhaps the most ambitious of the economic analyses of ergonomic interventions is that reported by Oxenburgh and Guldberg (1993). They attempted to estimate the costs and financial benefits to industry in an entire country, Australia, to comply with a "safe manual handling code of practice" prior to the introduction of legislation. The draft code contained many features intended to reduce the incidence, severity, and costs of occupational injury. One of the proposed requirements was a load limit of 16 kg. Therefore, the authors attempted to determine the costs to compa-nies of having to comply with a 16 kg load limit and the expected reduc-tions in injuries and their costs if a 16 kg load limit was in place. They selected the sectors that collectively accounted for 80 percent of workplace manual handling injuries. These sectors also accounted for 56 percent of the Australian workforce (manufacturing, construction, wholesale and retail trade, transportation, hospitals/nursing homes). Twelve interviewers conducted interviews with more than 200 managers of randomly sampled companies in these sectors. They sought information about work stations where manual handling occurred, accident statistics, tasks that caused injuries, and managers' estimations of the costs of complying with a 16 kg load limit. These costs might include purchase of hand carts, fork lifts, con-veyers, cranes, etc. Where possible, the interviewers observed and assessed the relevant work stations to make their own judgments.

The authors reported that due to sample size the capital cost estimate was subject to an error of about 20 percent. On the benefit side, the draft code was estimated to reduce the total manual handling injuries by about 27 percent. Monetary benefits from this size of reduction were then esti-mated from known average costs of these injuries but no attempt was made to estimate any changes in productivity that might result from intro-duction of the code. The calculations showed that about 74 percent of the initial capital cost to comply was to reduce lifting in the heavier range of lifts – above 34 kg – with the greater share being borne by small manufac-turing industry. While managers complained about having to comply with lifting limits below 16 kg, few argued that 34 kg was acceptable.

It was estimated that the code would save about A$156 million per year against recurrent annual costs of about A$245 million, for a net cost of about A$89 million. However, only the direct, not the indirect costs of injuries were included in the estimates. Indirect costs of absenteeism have been estimated by numerous authors to vary from about 1.5 to ten times the direct costs. Furthermore, only the weight lifted was taken into account, not the injury problems encountered when light weights are handled in adverse trunk postures or injury-related repetitive handling of lighter loads. The authors argue that since there was resistance in the country to a code based on loads less than 35 kg and since there was no clear evidence for effectiveness of such codes to prevent injury, the strategic thing to do would be to introduce a 35 kg limit initially and gradually move to a code with a lower load limit as acceptance of the original code accumulates. Unfortunately, cost estimates like these are extremely difficult to make and the consequences of gross errors of estimate can be substantial from the point of view of policy development and implementation.

Conclusion

Ergonomic interventions must be targeted to reduce or eliminate known risk factors for work-related injury. Knowledge of low back and upper limb injury mechanisms is improving but there is much more that needs to be learned. There is accumulating, high-quality laboratory and epidemiological evidence about risk factors that shows that a combination of physical demands of tasks and workers' perceptions of their job and the work environment interact to elevate risk of reporting pain of work-related musculoskeletal disorders.

Because musculoskeletal disorders have multiple risk factors, it is highly unlikely that intervening to reduce, or even eliminate, only one of these factors will prevent reporting of WMSDs. This is even more true if the outcome of concern is a reduction in work absence or an improvement in productive and sustained return to work of injured employees. The multi-factor nature of the problem suggests that for effective intervention, the organization has to be considered as a whole, with intervention at several levels simultaneously, before costs will decline. Intervention at only one place in the system will not account for sufficient variance to show a difference in prevention of initial injury, recurrence, or disability, and almost certainly not on the costs of injury-related work absence. For example, intervening by convincing senior management to publicly commit to reducing injury incidence and severity is necessary, but not sufficient, in the absence of introducing risk-reducing job design changes at the level of the individual worker.

Unfortunately, there is very little research on interventions that is sufficiently well designed and implemented to be unequivocal in its conclusions. There are good reasons for this state of affairs. This type of research is very difficult to do for many reasons including: a work environment that changes more rapidly than the time it takes to complete a randomized control trial; the difficulty in finding proper control groups for the duration of a study, as well as the ethics and natural change in the workplace that inhibit maintenance of such groups; the high costs of studying sufficiently large groups to obtain enough data to be confident that lack of observed differences between intervention and control groups are real; inducing companies to get involved in this type of research given inevitable interruptions and the risk of finding results perceived by management or labour to be adverse or costly. However, in a rapidly changing business environment, it is not possible to wait for completion of gold-standard research designs, for example, randomized control trials of evaluations of particular strategies. It has taken about a decade to reach the current (generally negative) evaluation of the effectiveness of "back belts" in preventing low back injury in the workplace. This clearly cannot be taken as a model for evaluation of other specific products. Compromise on the rigour of the research design by both the research teams and users of the information must be made.

There is considerable efficacy research at the level of biomechanical indicators carried out by researchers in laboratories or in workplaces that shows, usually under ideal conditions, reduced physical demands as a result of various interventions such as tool or job redesign. There is some, but much less, effectiveness research carried out under normal working conditions in plants and businesses by workplace personnel; there is a little, but very little, research on the costs and benefits of ergonomic intervention in the workplace. There are many case studies at all of these levels that show benefits of interventions of various types. Where interventions can be more easily applied to large numbers of people, typically training, personal protective equipment, or administrative interventions, more robust evaluation is available. In fact a number of randomized trials are now available. These have permitted better evaluation of these interventions for organizationally important outcomes such as absenteeism, back injury incidence, and back pain (e.g., van Poppel et al. 1997).

Much more needs to be learned about risk factors, in particular, about the interaction of various types of risk factors and much more needs to be learned about the effectiveness of ergonomic interventions in reducing injury and increasing quality and productivity. Determining risk factors for WMSDs has been mainly a researcher-led effort. It is not clear that the next phase of the effort, prevention of work-related musculoskeletal disorders, can continue in the same way because of the intrusion of outsiders intervening in the business of the workplace. Employers and labour have to take the lead, with the assistance of researchers. However, in the experience of the authors, it has been difficult to engage employers in risk-factor research for the reasons noted above. Obtaining commitment and active involvement from both management and labour in more intrusive, ergonomic intervention research may be even more of a challenge. One possible way would be through direct financial incentives of temporary reductions in WCB premiums or penalties.

Additional, but equally important questions that must be answered are what minimal level of research evidence rigour is necessary to convince various parties in a position to reduce the social and monetary costs of work-related injury (e.g., management, labour, compensation boards, legislators) to change current practices? How much money can a company expect to save through intervention and what is the evidence? It is recognized that intermediate outcome measures in all studies are essential but it is unrealistic to avoid dealing with monetary aspects of health and safety. Cost and benefit considerations must be included in as many intervention studies as possible. This issue also points to the need for management, business, and economic expertise on most intervention research teams and the need for management cooperation in revealing financial information and assisting in selecting relevant outcome indicators of costs, profits, productivity and quality, and interpretation of data.

Despite a sophisticated international research expertise in the measurement of injury risk of jobs, companies do not yet have tools of established reliability and usefulness available to them for addressing risk factors for musculoskeletal disorders such as are found in occupational hygiene. Development and application of a range of methods, from checklist to instrumented measures is needed to help organizations identify hazards, implement controls, and manage their own workplaces.

The majority of efforts over the last two decades have been devoted to determining the work-relatedness of musculoskeletal disorders. In our opinions, the conclusion to be drawn is that there is moderate to strong evidence that many musculoskeletal disorders have a substantial work-related component. This is not to imply that injury mechanisms, exposure thresholds, and dose-response relationships of risk factors are clear. They need continued research. However, future directions must include good studies on the development, implementation, and evaluation of the effectiveness of various approaches to interventions to reduce risk of injury, and to reduce social and monetary costs. There is some research evidence and many case studies that suggest that ergonomic interventions, indeed, reduce risk and cost of occupational injury but the study designs have generally been weak. Furthermore, we suggest that the specific research question(s), the experimental design, the plan for data acquisition, interpretation, and dissemination must be planned with the potential user groups if utilization of results, even at a local level, is to be realized.

Recent reviews of priorities in occupational health research in the United Kingdom (Harrington and Calvert 1996), in the Netherlands (van der Beek et al. 1997), and in the United States (Rosenstock 1996) all concluded that musculoskeletal disorders were major problems in these advanced economies. The Netherlands and the United States have targeted the design, implementation, and evaluation of interventions in work-related musculoskeletal disorders as being of great importance, particularly their cost-benefit analysis. We concur.

References

Aarås, A., and R.H. Westgaard. 1987. "Further Studies of Postural Load and Musculo-Skeletal Injuries of Workers at an Electro-Mechanical Assembly Plant." *Applied Ergonomics* 18 (3): 211-9.

Andersson, E.R. 1992. "Economic Evaluation of Ergonomic Solutions: Part I: Guidelines for the Practitioner." *International Journal of Industrial Ergonomics* 10: 161-71.

–. 1992. "Economic Evaluation of Ergonomic Solutions: Part II: The Scientific Basis." *International Journal of Industrial Ergonomics* 10: 173-8.

Bigos, S.J., M.C. Battié, D.M. Spengler, L.D. Fisher, W.E. Fordyce, T.H. Hansson, A.L. Nachemson, and M.D. Wortley. 1991. "A Prospective Study of Work Perceptions and Psychosocial Factors Affecting the Report of Back Injury." *Spine* 16 (1): 1-6.

Burdorf, A. 1992. "Exposure Assessment of Risk Factors for Disorders of the Back in Occupational Epidemiology." *Scandinavian Journal of Work, Environment, and Health* 18 (1): 1-9.

British Columbia Workers' Compensation Board (BCWCB). 1998. Occupational Health and Safety Regulation 296/97.

Daltroy, L., M. Iversen, M. Larson, J. Ryan, C. Zwerling, A. Fossel, and M. Liang. 1993. "Teaching and Social Support: Effects on Knowledge, Attitudes, and Behaviours to Prevent Low Back Injuries in Industry." *Health Education Quarterly* 20: 43-62.

Darcangelo, J. 1989. "Repetitive Strain Injuries: A Strategy that Works." *Occupational Health and Safety Canada* 5: 3.

Engels, J., J. van der Gulden, T. Senden, J. Kolk, and R. Binkhorst. 1998. "The Effects of an Ergonomic Educational Course, Postural Load, Perceived Physical Exertion, and Biomechanical Errors in Nursing." *International Archives of Occupational and Environmental Health* 71: 336-42.

Frank, J., A.-S. Brooker, S. Demaio, M. Kerr, A. Maetzel, H. Shannon, T. Sullivan, R. Norman, and R. Wells. 1996. "Disability Due to Occupational Low Back Pain: What Do We Know about Primary Prevention?" *Spine* 21 (24): 2908-17.

Gallimore, J., and M. Brown. 1993. "Effectiveness of the C-Sharp: Reducing Ergonomic Problems at VDTs." *Applied Ergonomics* 24 (5): 327-36.

Genaidy, A., E. Delgado, and T. Bustos. 1995. "Active Microbreak Effects on Musculoskeletal Comfort Ratings in Meat Packing Plants." *Ergonomics* 38 (2): 326-36.

Goldenhar, M., and P. Schulte. 1994. "Intervention Research in Occupational Health and Safety." *Journal of Occupational Medicine* 36 (7): 763-75.

–. 1996. "Methodological Issues for Intervention Research in Occupational Health and Safety." *American Journal of Industrial Medicine* 29: 289-94.

Grant, K., D. Habes, and S. Schneider. 1995. "Summary of Studies on the Effectiveness of Ergonomic Interventions." *Applied Occupational and Environmental Hygiene* 10 (6): 523-30.

Gundewall, B., M. Liljeqvist, and T. Hansson. 1993. "Primary Prevention of Back Symptoms and Absence from Work: A Prospective Randomized Study among Hospital Employees." *Spine* 18 (5): 587-94.

Hagberg, M., B. Silverstein, R. Wells, R. Smith, P. Carayon, H. Hendrick, M. Perusse, I. Kuorinka, and L. Forcier, eds. 1995. *Work-Related Musculoskeletal Disorders (WMSD): A Handbook for Prevention.* London: Taylor and Francis.

Harrington, J.M., and I.A. Calvert. 1996. "Research Priorities in Occupational Medicine: A Survey of United Kingdom Personnel Managers." *Occupational and Environmental Medicine* 53: 642-4.

Hendrick, H. 1991. "Ergonomics in Organizational Design and Management." *Ergonomics* 34 (6): 743-56.

Henning, R., P. Jaques, G. Kissel, A. Sullivan, and S. Alteras-Webb. 1997. "Frequent Short Rest Breaks from Computer Work: Effects on Productivity and Well-Being at Two Sites." *Ergonomics* 40 (1): 78-91.

Kerr, M.S. 1998. "A Case-Control Study of Biomechanical and Psychosocial Risk Factors for Low-Back Pain Reported in an Occupational Setting." PhD diss., University of Toronto.

Kilbom, A. 1988. "Intervention Programs for Work-Related Neck and Upper Limb Disorders: Strategies and Evaluation." *Ergonomics* 31 (5): 735-47.

Kuorinka, I. 1997. "Tools and Means of Implementing Participatory Ergonomics." *International Journal of Industrial Ergonomics* 19: 267-70.

Kuorinka, I., M.-M. Côté, R. Baril, R. Geoffrion, D. Giguere, M.-A. Dalzell, and C. Larue. 1994. "Participation in Workplace Design with Reference to Low Back Pain: A Case for the Improvement of the Police Patrol Car." *Ergonomics* 37 (7): 1331-6.

Lahad, A., A. Malter, A. Berg, and R. Deyo. 1994. "The Effectiveness of Four Interventions for the Prevention of Low Back Pain." *Journal of the American Medical Association* 272 (16): 1286-91.

Lanoie, P., and S. Tavenas. 1996. "Costs and Benefits of Preventing Workplace Accidents: The Case of Participatory Ergonomics." *Safety Science* 24 (3): 181-96.

Malmivaara, A. 1997. "Evidence-Based Intervention for Musculoskeletal Disorders." *Scandinavian Journal of Work, Environment, and Health* 32: 161-3.

Marras, W.S., S.A. Lavender, S.E. Leurgans, S.L. Rajulu, W.G. Allread, F.A. Fathallah, and S.A. Ferguson. 1993. "The Role of Dynamic Three-Dimensional Trunk Motion in Occupational-Related Low Back Disorders: The Effects of Workplace Factors, Trunk Position, and Trunk Motion Characteristics on Risk of Injury." *Spine* 18 (5): 617-28.

Moore, J.S., and A. Garg. 1996. "Use of Participatory Ergonomics Teams to Address Musculoskeletal Hazards in the Red Meat Packing Industry." *American Journal of Industrial Medicine* 29: 402-8.

–. 1997a. "Participatory Ergonomics in a Red Meat Packing Plant, Part I: Evidence of Long-Term Effectiveness." *American Industrial Hygiene Association Journal* 58: 127-31.

–. 1997b. "Participatory Ergonomics in a Red Meat Packing Plant, Part II: Case Studies." *American Industrial Hygiene Association Journal* 58: 498-505.

Narayan, M., and L. Rudolph. 1993. "Ergonomic Improvements in a Medical Device Assembly Plant: A Field Study." Proceedings of the Human Factors and Ergonomics Society, 812-6. Santa Monica, CA: Human Factors Society.

National Institute for Occupational Health and Safety (NIOSH). 1997. *Musculoskeletal Disorders (MSDs) and Workplace Factors: A Critical Review of Epidemiologic Evidence for Work-Related Musculoskeletal Disorders of the Neck, Upper Extremity, and Low Back.* Cincinnati: US Department of Health and Human Services.

National Safety Council. 1982. *Making the Job Easier: An Ergonomics Idea Book.* Chicago: National Safety Council; Stockholm: Swedish Work Environment Fund.

Norman, R., R. Wells, P. Neumann, J. Frank, H. Shannon, and M. Kerr. 1998. "A Comparison of Peak vs Cumulative Physical Work Exposure Risk Factors for the Reporting of Low Back Pain in the Automotive Industry." *Clinical Biomechanics* 13: 561-73.

Oxenburgh, M.S. 1991. *Increasing Productivity and Profit through Health and Safety.* Sydney: CCH International.

Oxenburgh, M.S., and H.H. Guldberg. 1993. "The Economic and Health Effects on Introducing a Safe Manual Handling Code of Practice." *International Journal of Industrial Ergonomics* 12: 241-53.

Parenmark, G., B. Engval, and A.-K. Malmqvist. 1988. "Ergonomic On the Job Training of Assembly Workers: Arm-Neck-Shoulder Complaints Drastically Reduced among Beginners." *Applied Ergonomics* 19 (2): 143-6.

Polanyi, M., J. Eakin, J. Frank, H. Shannon, and T. Sullivan. 1996. "Creating Healthier Work Environments: A Critical Review of Health Impacts of Workplace Organizational Change Interventions." Working Paper 39. Institute for Work and Health (IWH), Toronto.

Punnett, L., and U. Bergqvist. 1997. "Visual Display Work and Upper Extremity Musculoskeletal Disorders: A Review of Epidemiological Findings." National Institute for Working Life – Ergonomic Expert Committee Document 1.

Punnett, L., L.D. Fine, W.M. Keyserling, G.D. Herrin, and D.B. Chaffin. 1991. "Back Disorders and Nonneutral Trunk Postures of Automobile Assembly Workers." *Scandinavian Journal of Work, Environment, and Health* 17: 337-46.

Riel, P.F., and D. Imbeau. 1996. "Justifying Investments in Industrial Ergonomics." *International Journal of Industrial Ergonomics* 18: 349-61.

–. 1997. "The Economic Evaluation of an Ergonomic Investment for Preventive Purposes: A Case Study." *Journal of Safety Research* 28 (3): 159-76.

Rosenstock, L. 1996. "The Future of Intervention Research at NIOSH." *American Journal of Industrial Medicine* 29: 295-7.

Saari, J. 1992. "Successful Implementation of Occupational Health and Safety Programs in Manufacturing for the 1990s." *International Journal of Human Factors in Manufacturing* 2 (1): 55-66.

Saari, J., and M. Nasanen. 1989. "The Effect of Positive Feedback on Industrial Housekeeping and Accidents: A Long-Term Study at a Shipyard." *International Journal of Industrial Ergonomics* 4: 201-11.

Silverstein, B. 1987. "Evaluation of Interventions for Control of Cumulative Trauma Disorders." In *Ergonomic Interventions to Prevent Musculoskeletal Injuries in Industry,* ed. D.B. Chaffin, 87-99. Chelsea, MI: Lewis Publishers.

Smith, M. 1994. "A Case Study of a Participatory Ergonomics and Safety Program in a Meat Processing Plant." Proceedings of the International Ergonomics Association Congress, 6. Santa Monica, CA: Human Factors Society.

–. 1997. "Psychosocial Aspects of Working with Video Display Terminals (VDTs) and Employee Physical and Mental Health." *Ergonomics* 40 (10): 1002-15.

Smith, M., and Carayon, P. 1996. "Work Organization, Stress, and Cumulative Trauma Disorders." In *Beyond Biomechanics: Psychosocial Aspects of Cumulative Trauma Disorders,* ed. S. Moon and S. Sauter, 23-42. London: Taylor and Francis.

Spilling, S., J. Eitrheim, and A. Aarås. 1986. "Cost-Benefit Analysis of Work Environment Investment at STK's Telephone Plant at Kongsvinger." In *The Ergonomics of Working Postures,* ed. N. Corlett, J. Wilson, I. Manenica, 380-97. Philadelphia: Taylor and Francis.

van der Beek, A., M. Frings-Dresen, F. van Dijk, and I. Houtman. 1997. "Priorities in Occupational Health Research: A Delphi Study in the Netherlands." *Occupational and Environmental Medicine* 54: 504-10.

van Poppel, M., B. Koes, T. Smid, and L. Bouter. 1997. "A Systematic Review of Controlled Clinical Trials on the Prevention of Back Pain in Industry." *Occupational and Environmental Medicine* 54: 841-7.

Vink, P., and M. Kompier. 1997. "Improving Office Work: A Participatory Ergonomic Experiment in a Naturalistic Setting." *Ergonomics* 40 (4): 435-49.

Vink, P., E. Lourijsen, E. Wortel, and J. Dul. 1992. "Experiences in Participatory Ergonomics: Results of a Roundtable Session during the 11th IEA Congress, Paris." *Ergonomics* 35 (2): 123-7.

Walsh, N., and R. Schwartz. 1990. "The Influence of Prophylactic Prostheses on Abdominal Strength and Low Back Injury in the Workplace." *American Journal of Physical Medicine and Rehabilitation* 69: 245-50.

Westgaard, R.H., and J. Winkel. 1997. "Ergonomic Intervention Research for Improved Musculoskeletal Health: A Critical Review." *International Journal of Industrial Ergonomics* 20: 463-500.

Wilson, John R., and E. Nigel Corlett. 1995. *Evaluation of Human Work.* 2nd ed. London: Taylor and Francis.

Winkel, J., and S.E. Mathiassen. 1994. "Assessment of Physical Work Load in Epidemiologic Studies: Concepts, Issues, and Operational Considerations." *Ergonomics* 37: 979-88.

Yassi, A., R. Tate, J.E. Cooper, C. Snow, J. Vallentyne, and J.B. Khokhar. 1995. "Early Intervention for Back-Injured Nurses at a Large Canadian Tertiary Care Hospital: An Evaluation of the Effectiveness and Cost Benefits of a Two-Year Pilot Project." *Occupational Medicine* 45: 209-14.

Zwerling, C., L. Daltroy, L. Fine, J. Johnson, J. Melius, and B. Silverstein. 1997. "Design and Conduct of Injury Intervention Studies: A Review of Evaluation Strategies." *American Journal of Industrial Medicine* 32: 164-79.

7

Firm-Level Organizational Practices and Work Injury

Harry Shannon

Traditionally, occupational health and safety (OHS) has been concerned with chemical, physical, and biological hazards in the workplace. Thus, for example, physical hazards can include lighting and temperature; chemical hazards include airborne contaminants such as lead or vinyl chloride; and biological hazards in certain work groups include infection passed onto a worker through contact with others, through needle stick injuries or other routes. Physical hazards that may result in accidental injuries have also been a major concern for OHS practitioners. In most industrialized countries, these concerns have diminished over the years, and increasing attention has been paid to "psychological" or "psychosocial" issues as reviewed by Kerr in this volume. Attention has been paid to the "stress" of the workplace,[1] and in some instances attempts have been made to redesign the nature of the work being done by each worker.

This chapter, though, will look at a different type of evidence. It will examine factors at the level of the workplace, rather than the level of the individual. I will begin by describing the meaning of "firm-level organizational practices," and go on to review various types of evidence that link such factors to workplace safety. This will be followed by a discussion of the policy implications, especially on how to secure management commitment to safety in the workplace.

Work Organization and Workplace Organization

Many workplaces have become concerned with stress. To deal with stress, employers have commonly used stress-management programs, which attempt to show workers how they can deal with what are often seen as almost inevitable stressors in work, as well as daily life. These approaches have been criticized because they do nothing to relieve the workplace stressors that create the stress. A sceptical view is that these programs "teach people how to feel good about feeling bad." As well, there is even a report that suggests that stress-management programs can be harmful where the individual has no control over his or her stressful situation (Dolan 1994).

This has led people to consider the relevance of factors at the workplace level. How much do organizational practices, and in particular safety culture, influence the number and types of accidents and injuries that occur? There is perhaps a fairly fine line between work-level and firm-level factors. In particular, the way in which the workplace as a whole is organized is critical in determining the organization of work at an individual level. An obvious example of this is the difference between assembly-line automobile manufacture versus the policy adopted by Volvo of having small groups of workers take responsibility for assembling a car from start to finish.

What can we identify as relevant in examining this issue? We can specify several components that make up what we call workplace or firm-level organization. These include organizational structure and philosophy; organizational philosophy on OHS; labour markets and unions; internal responsibility systems (the philosophy underlying much OHS legislation in Canada and elsewhere, which relies on labour and management working together "internally" to solve OHS problems); organizational demography; risk and physical conditions; and financial performance and profitability.

Broad Evidence Linking Organizational Factors and Safety

An obvious question is why we might believe that these factors could make a difference in safety performance. For now I will look at some data that suggest at a broad level that workplace factors may be important. Later I will examine evidence on which particular factors may make a difference.

The first set of data concerns five automobile assembly plants in Ontario. Essentially, these do the same type of work, putting together cars, vans, and trucks. Yet there the similarities end. Data from these plants for three successive years show a consistent pattern across the companies: Despite the similar nature of the work there is about a fivefold difference between the best and the worst companies in their workers' compensation time loss claim rates. Interestingly, this does not occur just for back pain or upper extremity problems for which some discretion in reporting might be considered as an explanation, but the same pattern occurs also for acute injuries, which are much less likely to be susceptible to such reporting bias.

The next piece of evidence concerns the apparently limited effectiveness of health and safety approaches adopted during the 1980s in Canada. Most jurisdictions in Canada adopted new health and safety legislation in the late 1970s or early 1980s. Public attention focused on these issues and political pressure on governments to act ensued. Thus, more intensive attention was paid to OHS. However, when the time loss claim rates for Canada generally and Ontario in particular are examined for the period between the late 1970s and 1990, little evidence of a decline is seen. This, in fairness, is not true for fatal accidents or all accidents (including non-time-loss), both of which did decline significantly. If the traditional approaches to OHS had been effective, we would expect to have seen a drop in time loss claim rates. That this did not occur raises questions about our current approaches to OHS.

The drop since 1990 was probably associated with the recession in the early part of the decade. This is supported by the work of Brooker et al. (1997), which showed in time series analyses an inverse relationship between the employment rates in different sectors and the workers' compensation claim rates.

At an even broader level, there are differences across different jurisdictions. Fatal accident rates per 100,000 employee-years are lower in Scandinavian countries than in North America, where rates are in turn lower than those in developing countries. While differences may be due to a number of factors, including cultural attitudes, types of industry, legislation, etc., the figures do show that improvements are indeed possible. However, this "big picture" view is somewhat beyond the scope of this chapter, which concentrates on the intermediate level (the workplace), which falls between the macro-level (state, province, country) and the micro-level (the individual).

It is not just in the auto industry that major differences between organizations exist. Some companies in almost all types of business have consistently better safety performance than others. Accident rates can vary by ten- or even a hundredfold within "rate groups" (groups of companies in the same type of business). There are a number of possible explanations for such differences, among them reporting; workforce characteristics; chance findings; or real differences. I will examine arguments and evidence in favour of and against each of these possible explanations. And, in particular, if the conclusion is that real differences exist, then the obvious question is why? What is being done differently by the good companies? As I have already noted, this type of question differs from that posed by more traditional scrutiny and research on accidents and injuries, which tends to focus on the individual worker.

The Increasing Attention to Organizational Factors
This newer approach of looking at company-level variables has become fairly common, albeit only recently. As Feyer and Williamson (1998) point out: "the search for the major causes ... of occupational accidents has really moved now to concentrate on the systemic and organizational aspects of work rather than on the immediate circumstances and behaviours that lead up to each individual accident."

Hale and Hovden (1998) consider attention to the management systems and culture to constitute the "third age of safety." The "first age of more scientific study of safety concerned itself with the technical measures" to prevent injuries. Research focusing attention on the individual worker started the second age. The rise of ergonomics and concern with probabilistic risk analysis in the 1960s and 1970s produced a linking of these two approaches.

Hale and Hovden note the increased dissatisfaction in the 1980s with the notion that health and safety could be captured simply by matching the individual to technology. They identified several reasons for the increased interest in organizational factors and management systems in the late 1980s. These reasons included major disasters (including Bhopal, Seveso, the crash of the Challenger Space Shuttle, etc.), several of which occurred in settings with apparently well-developed safety systems but which also showed clearly the role of organizational factors. Another reason was the shrinking role of government because of budget cutbacks, leading to less detailed regulation and less inspection of OHS in the workplace itself. Regulatory authorities wanted to find indicators of appropriate self-regulation by companies and they looked for these in the scope and functioning of the management systems.

Interestingly, those who study organizations have long realized the difficulty of changing the organization by changing individuals. Over thirty years ago, Katz and Kahn wrote: "Attempts to change organizations by changing individuals have a long history of theoretical and practical failure ... Its essential weakness can be labelled the *psychological fallacy*, the concentration on individuals without regard to the situational factors that shape their behaviours ... it is a great over-simplification" (Katz and Kahn 1966). The "situational factors" are, of course, what I have been labelling firm-level organizational practices.

Types of Evidence Available

I now move on to discuss evidence on which features (factors) of the organization and approaches to OHS are related to better safety performance. Before doing so, I first note that a number of attempts, often based on little or no scientific evidence, have been made to list organizational factors related to safety. This is not to say that experienced safety professionals are not correct in their judgments of what works and what does not work in safety. But as the Advisory Committee on the Safety of Nuclear Installations (ACSNI) Human Factors Study Group wrote: "Before committing an organization to widespread change, however, it would be wise to consider evidence more objective than mere opinion. The first part of the report has described the history of safety management as perceived by employers, managers, and regulators. A striking feature of this history has been the small amount of research evidence that has been quoted to support the beliefs that have evolved" (ACSNI 1993).

Case Studies

There are a number of companies known to have outstanding performance in health and safety. In some, injuries (or at least serious injuries) appear to have been virtually eliminated. One example of the literature scrutinizing such companies is the work by Stewart (1996, 1994, 1993a, 1993b), which has set out to identify characteristics of these outstanding companies. Stewart drew particularly on the experience of DuPont, the chemical manufacturer. In Canada, DuPont's injury frequency in the mid-1980s was 0.08 per 200,000 exposure-hours, compared with the industry average of 0.40, and a rate in Ontario manufacturing of 7.0. Certainly, the nature of work in the chemical industry is different from that in other manufacturing (e.g., automobile manufacturing, where assembly-line work entails repetitive work in awkward postures with the consequent risk of back pain or upper extremity disorders). However, the chemical industry is well aware of the potential for disastrous accidents and has paid considerable attention to OHS. Its safety record, and DuPont's in particular, is notable compared with other industries.

Stewart's experience at DuPont led him to list several "keys to managing for superior safety." The first was that excellence in safety and in business performance can coexist. As well, top management must be committed to safety and to the view that all injuries can be prevented. The "message" to all levels of the organization must be clear and aimed to engage the workforce. Safety must be accepted as a line responsibility with strong leadership from the CEO down. Safety systems, structures, and processes should be in place, with well-trained resource people. Safety standards and rules should be understood by all and developed by those who will live with them, and discipline should reinforce the rules. Finally, all employees should be involved in safety activities.

Comparative Case Studies

One limitation of case studies is that they include no comparison. Thus, while the characteristics of outstanding companies are identified, there is no guarantee that those characteristics are any different from those of companies with mediocre or poor safety records. This is not to say that the findings of these reports are to be dismissed, but they should be interpreted with caution. From a research methodology point of view, the ideal is to have in-depth studies of a large number of companies with both good and bad safety performance. In practice, though, a balance must be struck between the sample size (i.e., the number of companies studied) and the amount (or the depth) of information obtained on each company.

Verma et al. (1994) investigated several plants in the auto industry to understand differences in organizational practices in those plants with better and those with worse safety records. They studied four companies, collecting data via site visits using direct observation, interviews with key informants representing several levels of the organizational hierarchy, and the retrieval of organizational documents. Verma et al. summarized their conclusions about what contributed to the success of the OHS programs under six key points.

First, where there had been improvements, there was some motivation to make changes. Indeed, they believed that these motivators were important in explaining the differences between organizations (i.e., why some workplaces do not use available knowledge to improve health and safety). In the plants studied, motivation came from poor safety performance history, or sometimes poor safety audits, or both. In one case, the possibility of plant closure led management and union to collaborate on a wider range of measures for improvement.

Second, Verma et al. noted that one factor that contributed to better safety performance was "local autonomy" in the workplace. This allowed those directly affected to take action as and when needed. In this respect, they noted that perceptions of safety differed depending on proximity to situation. Thus, a plant manager could have difficulty identifying appropriate changes throughout the plant. This meant it was important for workers to be able to use formal and informal channels to promote safety.

Third, another factor contributing to the success of OHS programs "was the joint [i.e., from both labour and management] nature of response to safety and health issues." (It should be noted that all plants in the Verma et al. survey were unionized. The authors were unable to conduct similar explorations in non-unionized plants.) The authors listed a number of ways in which labour and management collaborated. They noted that the mechanism by which joint action works was not identified – it was not a focus of the study – but indirect information led them to suggest that "the message of safety is conveyed more effectively to workers when it comes jointly from both the union and the management."

Fourth was an appropriate mix of formal procedures as well as flexible practices within those structures. Thus, certain activities such as formal audits were considered important and dealt with conscientiously; and when action was needed more rapidly, the parties involved were able to use more informal mechanisms to ensure that what was needed got done.

Fifth was accountability. Where performance was better, all parties – managers, union leaders, and workers – were involved in creating a safe environment. One plant manager in particular took leadership in developing a safety culture and made others in the plant accountable for implementing recommendations from safety audits.

Sixth was the use of incentives to improve safety standards. In the authors' sample, none of the plants offered rewards, but rather recognized high safety performers. An unusual "incentive" given to one plant by the company's head office was a financial "cushion" to allow for changes in the assembly line. This allowed a slowdown of the line during the changeover from one model to another, a period which the literature suggests is associated with a higher number of accidents.

In their overall conclusions, Verma et al. pointed out that a "joint governance system ... provides a foundation for effective health and safety performance." They argued that new models of workplace governance might be needed, and suggested the need for future research to focus on this. In particular, they considered the view that health and safety issues are ones on which both labour and management can easily agree to be "simplistic." This they felt meant new governance processes were needed even more strongly.

Quantitative Studies

As noted above, an alternative to studying a small number of companies in depth is to examine a large number of companies, but with comparatively less information on each. My colleagues and I at McMaster University conducted one such study (Shannon et al. 1996, 1992), which was sponsored by the Industrial Accident Prevention Association (IAPA) in Ontario, and covered manufacturing and retail sectors.

We began with the list of factors comprising firm-level organizational practices noted above. Our primary approach was via a survey of companies. The questionnaire was designed to refer to practices at the workplace level. We asked questions based on our theoretical understanding of the topic as well as the aims of the study, and we copied or adapted questions from other surveys. We developed separate questionnaires, one to send to workers and the other to management. The management questionnaire was long even after substantial editing, so we divided it into three sections. This was to allow its completion by different people, depending on their position, expertise, and knowledge. The targeted respondents were the senior manager, the human resources manager, and the management co-chair of the joint health and safety committee (JHSC). The questionnaire for workers was directed to the worker co-chair of the JHSC. Some questions were identical in both the worker and management questionnaires. The questionnaire was pilot tested and appropriate revisions made. Since we wanted to make comparisons between workplaces with different levels of safety performance, we used workers' compensation time loss frequency rates to identify companies with "low," "medium," and "high" rates. We defined "low" as a rate less than or equal to 50 percent of the average injury rate of the rate group (a group of comparable businesses). Similarly, we called "high" a rate more than 50 percent above the rate group average. We identified six rate groups in manufacturing, and two in retail. We considered only companies with more than fifty employees (in retail, more than twenty), and divided organizations into those with fewer than 100 and 100 or more employees.

Overall, we chose roughly 1,000 workplaces. We received completed questionnaires from 54 percent of the retail organizations, with a higher response (58 percent) from the manufacturing companies. Our phone call reminders to workplaces had suggested that the questionnaire length was a barrier to its completion in non-respondents. Therefore, from the original survey we took a short list of questions that could be answered in a five- to ten-minute interview. We telephoned non-respondents to ask them to complete this shorter questionnaire, and roughly 75 percent of 200 companies randomly sampled from non-respondents did so. Their answers to these questions were very similar to those obtained from the mail survey. As well, the response rate was very similar in companies with low, medium, and high frequency rates. We therefore concluded that comparisons we made between these three groups were valid.

Our main analysis compared each variable across the three groups. We looked for overall differences, as well as a possible "trend" across the three groups. We also conducted multiple regression using the time loss frequency rate as a percentage of the rate group average as our outcome.

Among the variables related to lower claim rates (at least in manufacturing, where the sample size was much larger) were: delegation of authority; a high degree of worker autonomy and participation; and encouragement of career commitment. On the approach to OHS in particular, factors related to lower claim rates included: health and safety being defined in each manager's job description; health and safety constituting an important component of managers' annual appraisals; participation of the workforce in health and safety decisions; and provision of group (but not individual) safety incentives. In contrast, factors related to higher rates included high employee turnover and number of grievances per 100 union members. Regarding the internal responsibility system, several variables were related to higher claim rates: little training for labour JHSC members; labour threats to take issues outside the JHSC; management threats of sanctions; and work refusals in the previous three years. As well, the state of worker-management relations was important, with more cooperative workplaces having lower rates, based on responses from management representatives. (A similar trend was seen with the responses of the worker representative, although it was not statistically significant.)

While this study was being conducted, a number of similar projects were also in progress. In a second report (Shannon et al. 1997), these and other reports are synthesized and variables consistently (from study to study) related to lower claim rates are identified. I now describe briefly each of these studies and their findings, concentrating on factors reported in more than one of the studies.

The earliest study we identified was one conducted in Michigan (Simonds and Shafai-Sahrai 1977; Shafai-Sahrai 1973). In a monograph adapted from his doctoral dissertation, Shafai-Sahrai and his supervisor identified eleven matched pairs of companies in the state. Each member of the pair was in the same industry and of roughly the same size, but had quite different accident rates. The ratios of accident rates of the two paired companies ranged from 1.3 to 4.5, with an average of roughly 3.0. All companies were visited and workplaces observed. Various executives were interviewed and relevant records were examined. The factors studied could be classified into four groups: involvement of management, various promotional efforts, characteristics of the workforce, and physical conditions. Of twenty-six companies contacted, twenty-two agreed to take part in the study, an excellent response rate. The companies ranged in size from eighty to 650 employees. As well as the interviews, the researchers used a rating form for the observed physical plant conditions. A number of factors were related to lower injury frequency rates: involvement of top management in safety, better recording systems for injuries, use of accident cost analyses, fewer workers under the aegis of each supervisor, existence of recreational programs for employees, higher average age of employees, higher percentage of workers who were married, longer mean duration of employment with the company, better machinery safety protection, and roomy and clean shop environment. Factors not related to injury frequency included efforts to promote safety through the families of workers and the quality and quantity of safety rules.

In the mid-1970s, a number of studies were conducted by the National Institute for Occupational Safety and Health in the United States (Cohen et al. 1975; Cohen 1977). One of these (Cohen et al. 1975) met the eligibility criteria for inclusion in our overview. Using Wisconsin firms from six different industries, ninety-six matched pairs of companies were identified. Fifty-two percent responded, with no difference in response proportions between high and low injury rate companies. As well, accident rates were similar in respondents and non-respondents. Data were used from forty-two pairs. The primary data available came from self-administered questionnaires completed by safety personnel. The study defined within-pair high rate firms as those with at least double the accident rate of low rate firms. (Rates were of accidental injury requiring more than first aid treatment.) While many of the results were not statistically significant, the authors described a number of factors and their relationship to accident rates as "suggestive." Factors related to lower accident rates included: active role of top management, conduct of safety audits, safety incentives, safety training on a regular basis, use by company of community and family to promote health and safety, and use of personal protective equipment. Use of discipline was, if anything, related to higher accident rates. Factors unrelated to claim rates included number of workers per supervisor, completeness of accident investigations, presence of safety rules, and monitoring of unsafe behaviours of workers.

As noted above, the NIOSH group conducted other studies. These included a review (Cohen 1977) of relevant research including, of course, their own. Cohen concluded that strong management commitment to safety and frequent close contact between workers, supervisors, and management on safety matters were "the two most influential and dominant factors."

In 1988, Chew reported a study from Thailand, India, and Singapore (Chew 1988). Firms of moderate size (fifty to 200 workers) from six different industries were identified, and eighteen matched pairs were "selected" (the number eligible was not reported). Structured, unblinded interviews of the chief executive and safety personnel of the company were conducted. Further information was obtained by observation in a "walk through" of the plant. Using the combined fatality and time loss injury rate, a high rate firm was one whose rate was two- to fourfold higher than that of the low rate firm in the pair – where pairs were matched by nation, industry, and number of workers. Factors related to lower claim rates included: active role of top management, safety audits, and amount of safety training. Also important were good housekeeping and safety controls on machinery. Safety incentives and numbers of workers per supervisor were not related to accident rates, while presence of safety rules and use of personal protective equipment were each significant in one of the three countries.

Simard and colleagues (Simard and Marchand 1994; Simard et al. 1988) identified Quebec industrial firms with more than seventy employees. They selected from a random sample until 100 firms were willing to take part in the study. (To reach this number, they approached 258 firms, so their response rate was 39 percent.) Self-administered questionnaires were given to a variety of individuals in the company: managers, personnel directors, supervisors, safety personnel, management and union JHSC co-chairs, worker safety representatives, and the union president. The researchers identified firms with a below average time loss accident rate in each of two years (1986 and 1987). These companies were labelled as "more effective"; all other companies were considered "less effective." The analysis was quite theoretical, but in terms of factors considered by other studies Simard et al.'s data showed that lower accident rates were related to safety audits, correction of hazards, completeness of accident investigations, and younger age. (This was the only study that suggested younger people had lower accident rates. In general, studies show a reduced accident rate in older workers; see, e.g., Laflamme and Menckel 1995.) Use of personal protective equipment, low turnover, and level of perceived risks by management were not significantly related to accident rate.

A second study of Quebec workers by Tuohy and Simard (1993) was carried out in Quebec workplaces with more than twenty employees in nine industrial sectors. Of the 921 companies approached, 352 (38 percent) responded, and 117 had usable data (13 percent). Injury rates for three years were used to define a company's status relative to its class (of companies in the same type of business). Self-administered questionnaires were completed by management joint health and safety committee representatives. Companies whose workers had more seniority and were older tended to have lower accident rates. However, a number of factors were not significantly related to injury rates. These included: the representation of senior management on the JHSC, the presence of a safety director, worker and manager as co-chairs of the JHSC, and the use of threats to take matters outside the JHSC by members of the committee. Interestingly, some factors were both positively and negatively related to accident rates, depending on the subgroup of companies studied. Such factors included: institutionalized procedures for operation of the JHSC, a broad scope of activity for the committee, collective strategies to problem solving on the JHSC, and the profitability of the organization.

The authors explained the different results for smaller and larger companies by considering the timing of the formation of the JHSC. Larger companies, they argued, had had JHSCs in place for some time, sufficiently long for their effect to be noticeable. However, for smaller companies, the committees were more recent, and companies with poor safety records were using them to help solve their safety problems. The committees in such companies thus had much to do, so they had a broad range of activities.

For our overview, we identified a study conducted in US coal mines employing at least 150 underground miners (Mines Safety and Health Administration 1983). Forty companies participated, apparently all of those selected. Questionnaires were completed by various employees and management representatives. Injury incidence rates were used to distinguish high and low accident rate companies. Only three of the factors measured overlapped with those in the other studies in our overview. None of these was significantly related to injury rates: equipment well maintained, active role of top management, and the relative importance attached to safety compared with production.

Interestingly, after publishing our overview, I received a letter from Robert Peters who had conducted a similar type of review for the US Bureau of Mines (Peters 1989). He identified a number of unpublished reports, although only the one just described was common to our review and his. All the other comparable studies he referenced were government documents outside the published, peer-reviewed literature and were not found in our bibliographic search. In his summary of findings, Peters noted that ideally studies should use longitudinal designs, control groups, and multivariate analyses. He commented on the difficulty of finding companies willing to take part in research, and he also pointed out that "best practices" at large companies might not be feasible or practical for smaller mines and vice versa. Nevertheless, he identified some variables statistically significantly related to lower accident rates in multiple studies: better labour-management relations, greater employee involvement in decision making, management's ability to communicate to the miner that they truly consider employee health and safety a top priority, and several aspects of first line supervisors' interactions with miners. Peters observed that "most of the variables that appear to be playing a significant role in achieving a good mine safety record are within management's ability to control."

Tuohy and Simard (1993) studied not only Quebec companies, but also firms in Ontario with more than twenty workers. They selected a random sample of "about" 3,000 workplaces, of whom "2,000" responded, and 920 provided usable data (31 percent). Self-administered questionnaires were sent to one worker member and one management member of each JHSC. A company's safety performance was defined by its injury rate relative to its SIC (Standard Industrial Classification) group over a five year period. Seniority and low turnover were significantly related to lower injury rates; so too were number of workers represented on the JHSC, worker and manager as co-chairs on the committee, duration of training of JHSC members, institutionalized procedures for the operation of the JHSC, and a broad scope of activity for the committee. Factors not significantly related to the claim rate included senior management representation on the JHSC, presence of a safety director, executive/decision-making status of the JHSC, advisory/decision-making status of the JHSC. Other variables produced ambivalent results depending on the size of company in the subgroup.

Researchers at the Upjohn Institute have conducted two studies of organizational factors. The first one (Habeck et al. 1991) studied Michigan firms with at least fifty workers (more than 100 in the health services field) who had at least some claims, and came from one of four different industries. Of 284 companies, 124 (44 percent) responded. There were no clear differences in response by number of workers or industry. Respondents, though, did have 20 percent fewer claims than non-respondents. Self-administered questionnaires were sent to each chief executive officer. Compensation claim rates were used to define those with high rates (in the top 15 percent) and those with low rates (bottom 15 percent). A considerable number of variables were significantly related to lower claim rates: direct channels of communication and information, empowerment of the workforce, existence of profit sharing, presence of an employee assistance program, active involvement of top management in safety, monitoring of unsafe worker behaviours, safety training on a regular basis, company committing resources to employee health, employee health screening, use of modified work following injury, low turnover, more seniority, and larger workforce. Presence of a union was related to higher claim rates.

Executive/decision-making status of the JHSC was not significantly related to claim rates; also not related were high grievance rates, supervisor training in interpersonal skills, presence of safety incentives, and several post-injury behaviours.

In a later study from the same team (Hunt et al. 1993), Michigan firms with over 100 workers were identified in seven different industries. This time the random sample was 477, of which 220 (46 percent) responded. Self-administered questionnaires were sent to the chief executive officer or the director of human resources. The study used both claim rates and severity rates (lost work days per 100 workers) as outcomes. Factor analyses of the questions was conducted followed by a regression analysis of the injury rate against the identified factors. Among variables in constructs that were related to lower claim rates were: direct channels of communication and information, empowerment of the workforce, encouragement of a long-term commitment of the workforce, and good relations between management and workers. Specific factors for health and safety approaches that were associated with reduced claim rates included: evaluation of safety hazards, monitoring of unsafe worker behaviours, employee health screening, and provision of modified work. This latter factor was found in both Michigan studies, but in no others. This is because workers' compensation applies in Michigan only after seven days' lost time. Thus, if successful efforts are made to return injured employees to work quickly, a compensation claim will not be made. Hunt and his colleagues also found that good housekeeping and safety controls on machinery were related to lower injury rates. Unlike almost all other studies, an active role in safety of top management was not significantly related to claim rates, nor were safety audits, hazard correction, or safety's being important in performance appraisals.

Another small study, by Lewchuk and his colleagues (Lewchuk et al. 1990), examined the effectiveness of "Workwell," an Ontario program that gives companies a financial incentive to change practices and advises companies on what the new practices should involve. Workwell is linked to experience rating and encourages companies to employ formal health and safety programs. The results of audits help determine if companies will have a surcharge imposed on their Workers' Compensation (now Workplace Safety and Insurance) premium or receive a rebate on the premium. The authors examined four types of companies: (1) those with continuing high costs/claim rates that passed their audit, (2) those with high costs that passed their audit, but that had reduced their accident frequency rate by at least 50 percent in the previous twelve months, (3) those with very low claim costs that passed their audit, and (4) those with very low costs that failed their audit. The first was considered a group not responding to the Workwell program, while the others were considered likely to help understand how companies could reduce their accident rates and associated costs.

For example, group 4 consisted of companies that had avoided reported accidents despite the lack of a formal OHS program (measured by the audit) and this might point to alternative safety approaches.

Although there were only seven companies in each of groups 3 and 4, and no formal statistical tests were conducted, the pattern of results led the authors to several conclusions. They noted that formal OHS programs "were most successful when there was a strong managerial commitment and when employees were allowed to participate in decision making." In contrast, formal programs tended to be unsuccessful when these conditions were not present. Interestingly, the former (successful) situation occurred mainly with a largely male workforce, aged between twenty-five and fifty, and with at least two years' seniority. The unsuccessful programs were typically in companies with "a marginal work force" – young females with short seniority and with limited communication ability in English.

Joint Health and Safety Committees
I have found two studies that considered just one factor: the presence of joint health and safety committees. Boden et al. (1984) found "virtually no effect" in a sample of manufacturing companies in Massachusetts. Interviews in a small sub-sample suggested that successful committees were characterized by commitment of management and labour, rather than by "objective" measures.

Lewchuk et al. (1996) conducted a time series analysis of Ontario manufacturing and retail companies, taking into account when the companies set up their joint health and safety committees. The manufacturing sector was required to have such committees from the early 1980s but retail operations had to do so only from 1990. In contrast to Boden et al., the authors' results suggested that committees were linked to lower claim rates.

A report submitted in late 1997 to the BCWCB (Havlovic and McShane 1997) had as its primary aim to look at characteristics of joint health and safety committees, health and safety training, and management initiatives in forest product mills in British Columbia in relation to injury rates. A secondary purpose was to look at corporate and mill characteristics in relation to safety; such variables were described as covariates in relation to the main questions. In this preliminary report, covariate analyses were not shown.

Data were received from 106 management and fifty-nine employee representatives at 137 mills. The response rate was not stated, although this may be partially due to incorrect information in the records from which the list of BC mills was taken. The authors reported relationships with both minor and serious accidents. Interestingly, some classes of variables were more strongly associated with minor accidents (compared with serious ones), others with serious (rather than minor) accidents.

Overall, approximately 200 correlations were shown for each of minor and serious accidents. The authors concluded that there was "some support for the idea that structured JHSC activities help to reduce accident rates." As well, better relations in various contexts between labour and management were related to some lower injury rates. The authors noted that mills with lower rates of serious accidents generally offered more training to management representatives on the JHSC, but there was no clear pattern for training offered to employee JHSC representatives. Finally, mills that were unionized had lower rates, particularly of serious accidents.

Although the studies described can be considered quantitative, the data they provided did not allow a summary measure to be computed (e.g., via a meta-analysis) of the strength of each factor. Rather, the overview (Shannon et al. 1997) looked for consistency of the factors across the studies. Those consistently related to lower injury rates included: empowerment of the workforce, encouragement of a long-term commitment of the workforce, good relations between management and workers, active role of top management, delegation of safety activities, conduct of safety audits, monitoring of unsafe worker behaviours, safety training – initial and continuing, low turnover and longer seniority, and good housekeeping. Factors not related to lower rates included: representative of senior management on the health and safety committee, written safety rules, and education/literacy of the workforce.

I should note that, even allowing for their design, the studies had certain limitations. For example, response rates were disappointing. Most did not state their power; in the smaller studies it would have been fairly low. Several had not been published in peer-reviewed journals and thus had not been through that "quality filter." As well, the fact that each study considered its own set of variables (factors) with its own questionnaire makes comparison difficult, as does the different analysis conducted by each. Given these issues, it seems remarkable that we found as much consistency as we did. It suggests perhaps that the relationships found are strong ones, and some "real" ones may have been missed.

Workplace Interventions

Studies discussed up to this point show factors related to injury rates. However, correlation does not necessarily imply causation. Thus, modifying these factors is not guaranteed to improve safety. We can, though, draw on data from interventions in the workplace that have been evaluated. Methodologically thorough evaluations, unfortunately, are relatively rare. It is unclear why this is so. It could be that those not reported were unsuccessful, or that companies consider such information to be proprietary and potentially a competitive advantage. In most cases, perhaps, evaluations are simply not done.

Nevertheless, Guastello (1993) has attempted to summarize the literature on what we really know about what works in safety. He identified published papers reporting on the effectiveness of safety interventions. By computing an effect size, he was able to pool data from a variety of published reports. (By effect size he meant the proportional reduction in injury rate, taking into account the equivalent reduction in a comparison group.) He classified the interventions according to ten types. Several he identified could be considered interventions at the workplace level. Three categories that had substantial effect sizes (46 to 49 percent) included management procedures (based on three studies), comprehensive ergonomics (four studies), and a cooperative compliance program (seven studies). The last refers to an approach in California in the construction industry that can perhaps most concisely be described as intermediate between a regulatory approach and internal responsibility.

The International Safety Rating System attempts to look at the policies and procedures in place in a company with regard to safety. Four studies were identified that evaluated the system's effectiveness, which was modest (17 percent). The presence of safety committees was examined in six studies, giving an average effect size of 24 percent. Interestingly, the combined results of thirty studies that examined the effect of personnel selection (attempting to identify "accident-prone" workers and either not hire them or place them in lower risk jobs) showed only a negligible effect (3 percent).

As well, considering health rather than safety, Polanyi and colleagues (Polanyi et al. 1996) reviewed evidence on workplace interventions instigated to improve employee health. Eligible interventions were those aimed at changing the workplace as a whole or the workplace organization, rather than attempting to change the individual (as is the case for smoking cessation or exercise programs, for example). As with safety interventions, the number of studies identified was disappointingly small and of limited quality. Nevertheless, the recommendations at the firm level may have some applicability to safety. The authors argued that organizational changes to improve workers' health should involve unions or employee representatives, management and (if possible) outside researchers; and they should allow sufficient time for discussion of the interventions and their implications. Interventions should start with an assessment of current status and should be broadly based, taking into account a wide variety of factors. Finally, they suggested that large firms could make comparative, best-practice demonstrations in different organizational units of their company. They also pointed to the lack of good evaluations of interventions that had been implemented.

In his review, Guastello (1993) required some aspects of good study design to be fulfilled for a paper to be eligible, but did not report a formal evaluation of each study. Good evaluations of OHS interventions, particularly more complex ones, are sadly lacking. Furthermore, many of those that are reported are of relatively poor quality. An editor of a safety journal told me that he often receives papers that do not follow basic methodological criteria. Yet these criteria are well known and some colleagues and I have written a paper to help readers understand how to identify a good quality study (Shannon et al. 1999).

Alternative Explanations of the Results

Earlier I noted some alternative explanations for the differences in injury claim rates between companies. One was that these might be differences in workforce characteristics. For example, anecdotally it is believed that among automobile plants those with lower rates (may) have younger workforces who are less susceptible to back and other musculoskeletal disorders. Yet, as I noted above, the differences between companies persists for acute traumatic injuries, for which younger workers typically have higher rates. Thus, this seems an implausible explanation. As well, some studies adjusted for workforce characteristics and still found organizational factors related to injury rates.

The play of chance is another possibility. However, the factors identified in the studies were statistically significantly related to injury rates. While such significant relationships could have occurred by chance in perhaps one, maybe two, of the studies, the very purpose of the overview was to look for variables that were consistently related to safety performance in multiple studies, so that chance findings could be ruled out.

The issue of reporting – a third possibility – is of concern. Certainly, it is known that compensable accidents that should legally be reported are not and it is often argued that some compensation claims are made fraudulently. Thus, injury rates can be under- or over-reported. Measuring over-reporting is well-nigh impossible, while one study in Ontario (Research and Evaluation Branch, Ontario WCB, 1992) suggested the under-reporting was relatively minor. If the misreporting as a whole is indeed minor, then it could not have materially affected the McMaster study (for example) in which there was at least a threefold difference in claim rates between the high and low accident rate firms. Further, for misreporting to have biased the results, it would have to have been related to the factors under consideration. This could have been the case for some variables but probably not for others. "Random" misreporting, unrelated to the factors, will have introduced "noise" into the data, probably reducing the number of factors found to be significant but not changing substantially the estimates of correlations, etc.

In short, then, while I do not have the space to do justice to the problem of misreporting, I believe it very unlikely to have seriously affected the results. This applies particularly to variables that were consistently related to injury rates in several studies across time and place. We are thus left with the fourth explanation: a real relationship between firm-level factors and injury rates.

Summary of Data

Several primary factors seem relevant. Perhaps most important among them is top management's commitment to safety. Regardless of the type of study, the finding that such commitment is important is consistently supported by study after study. It can perhaps be seen as the sine qua non for safety, since top management sends signals (of greater or lesser subtlety) on what it considers most important. Supervisors and workers will quickly determine whether the real priority is production. This, of course, leads to the question of how to obtain management commitment, which may be more easily said than done.

Although it is somewhat beyond the scope of this chapter, the literature review shows that management commitment is such an important question that I will address it briefly.

Stewart (1993a) found a strong commitment to safety in companies that had a long history of such commitment or had a particular reason for acting – for example, a fatality or serious accident had occurred or some other significant event had created an appropriate climate. Verma et al. made a similar point in their report. But neither explains how such commitment can be obtained in more ordinary circumstances. The only systematic and detailed attempt to investigate this issue that I am aware of is a book by Hopkins, based on his experience and research in Australia, entitled *Making Safety Work* (Hopkins 1995). He first examines the "safety pays" argument, that it is in the company's economic interest to improve safety. Hopkins points out that this does not always work, and indeed that if it really did, there would be little or no need for regulations since it would be in management's interest to deal well with safety. (Stewart argues that safety may well pay in very poor climates, but beyond a certain point the cost of injuries will not drive safety.) Hopkins describes his qualitative research as showing that experience rating may lead to claims management rather than to safety or disability management. The latter effect, he points out, calls into question the validity of time loss claim rates.

Hopkins states that managers can be motivated by a belief in their obligation to obey the law – a wish to be seen to be doing the proper thing – and real concern for the welfare of (or at least lack of harm to) workers. He believes that government intervention is the best way to focus management attention on safety. From his interviews, he points out that small businesses are typically unaware of experience rating, but they do remember a visit from health and safety inspectors. Indeed, he goes further and states that such visits are the only thing that draws the attention of small employers to health and safety matters.

He discusses the enduring dilemma for government agencies of whether to punish or persuade. The consensus of his contacts was that the best policy uses both punishment and persuasion, depending on local conditions.

He argues strongly that there is a substantial impact of inspections. He further points out that, when they occur, prosecutions are most effective if they get senior managers (or company directors) onto the witness stand in court to explain company policy. He reports that many managers told him that fear of personal liability was by far the most important motivating factor to attend to. In a no doubt deliberately provocative statement, he writes that "a few show trials ... would be extremely salutary." Hopkins supports his argument by noting that when risk management consultants make their pitch for their services to management, they emphasize personal liability ahead of financial benefits of improved safety.

Overall, Hopkins's arguments, being based on direct interviews with many managers, are quite persuasive. They do, though, promote approaches that are currently not fashionable and would probably be resisted strongly. To counter this, it could be argued that companies that obey the law and look after the safety and health of their employees have little to fear from a policy of prosecuting senior company officials.

One important limitation is that the most common types of work-related injuries – back pain and upper extremity disorders – are musculoskeletal. These typically result from chronic exposures and while they can be quite disabling, are not life-threatening in the way that traumatic injuries can be. Further, they may have a non-occupational component to their etiology, so will not seize the attention of managers and others as proposed by Hopkins, who was considering very severe or fatal accidents.

Another approach that has been used to try to change behaviour in other fields is to produce "league tables" of performance. Thus, claim rates could be publicized, a policy that would draw attention to companies with poor records. This, though, might encourage managers to engage in claims management, rather than safety management. Hopkins quotes several examples of attempts to suppress reporting of injuries, rather than to prevent the injuries from occurring. And to the extent that time and resources are limited, attention to claims management will probably detract from the ability to engage in injury prevention. Nevertheless, showing physicians how their adherence to certain guidelines compares with that of their colleagues has proven effective in changing their behaviour. Such an approach might well be useful in safety, provided the information reaches those with the power to take decisions and make changes.

Conclusion

I have attempted to show how workplace organizational factors are related to safety performance. This is now accepted by many researchers and practitioners in the safety field, and represents a shift in focus from the individual worker to the workplace, that is, the context in which the worker operates. It does seem, though, that there are obstacles to applying the evidence toward accident prevention. I have already discussed the issue of obtaining management commitment. Another is that many interventions applied in the workplace are not properly evaluated and reported. Sometimes is seems "obvious" that the intervention should be successful (and in many cases it may well be) or those promoting or implementing it may have a vested interest in its success and be reluctant to put it to the test. For example, a safety professional may have worked hard to persuade management to pay attention to safety and implement a preventive measure at greater or lesser cost. In such cases, there is little incentive to open up the possibility that the measure was not effective. Evans (1985), though, in the road safety field, has collated evidence showing the net effect of interventions can be nil or even that they do more harm than good! This shows that there is indeed an ethical reason to do quality evaluations.

Of course, in many cases the measures may be evaluated, but results of the evaluation are not widely reported. Companies may feel that effective measures give them a competitive advantage, or that there is no benefit to telling the world about measures that did not work as anticipated. Yet this would be useful as it could prevent others from repeating the same mistakes; a careful examination of why the intervention failed could suggest revisions to the content or implementation of the safety measure.

How, then, can the conduct and reporting of evaluations be encouraged? One possibility is that companies that allow researchers to come in to their organizations, do the evaluations, and report them could be charged a reduced workers' compensation premium. As well, publicity could be given to their willingness to contribute to the general good of the workforce.

In short, then, I am encouraging a climate in which safety measures are based on high quality evidence. Only in this way can we truly learn about what does and does not work in occupational safety and distinguish between studies of efforts to reduce claims of injuries from those that truly improve occupational health and safety.

Acknowledgments
I thank my colleagues at McMaster University with whom I conducted two of the studies described in this chapter. My thinking has also been strongly influenced by others at the Institute for Work and Health in Toronto.

Note
1 The term "stress" is ambiguous, since it is used to refer to both the factors in the workplace that create a response and the outcome of (response to) the workplace factors. I use the term "stressors" to refer to the workplace factors.

References

Advisory Committee on the Safety of Nuclear Installations (ACSNI). 1993. *Organising for Safety.* London: HMSO.

Boden, L.I., J.A. Hall, C. Levenstein, and L. Punnett. 1984. "The Impact of Health and Safety Committees." *Journal of Occupational Medicine* 26 (11): 829-34.

Brooker, A., J.W. Frank, and V.S. Tarasuk. 1997. "Back Pain Claim Rates and the Business Cycle." *Social Science and Medicine* 45: 429-39.

Chew, D. 1988. "Effective Occupational Safety Activities: Findings in Three Asian Developing Countries." *International Labour Review* 127: 111-24.

Cohen, A. 1977. "Factors in Successful Occupational Safety Programs." *Journal of Safety Research* 9: 168-78.

Cohen, A., M. Smith, and H.H. Cohen. 1975. *Safety Program Practices in High versus Low Accident Rate Companies.* Cincinnati: National Institute for Occupational Safety and Health.

Dolan, S.L. 1994. "Stress Management Intervention and Assessment: An Overview and an Account of Two Experiences." In *Human Dilemmas in Work Organisations: Strategies for Resolution,* ed. A.K. Korman, 37-57. New York: Guilford Press.

Donchin, M., O. Woolf, L. Kaplan, and Y. Floman. 1990. "Secondary Prevention of Low-Back Pain: A Clinical Trial." *Spine* 15 (12): 1317-20.

Evans, L. 1985. "Human Behavior Feedback and Traffic Safety." *Human Factors* 27: 555-76.

Feyer, A.M., and A. Williamson. 1998. *Occupational Injury: Risk, Prevention, and Intervention. Part Four: Organizations, Management, Culture, and Safety: Introduction.* London: Taylor and Francis.

Guastello, S.J. 1993. "Do We Really Know How Well Our Occupational Accident Prevention Programs Work?" *Safety Science* 16: 445-63.

Habeck, R., M.J. Leahy, H.A. Hunt, F. Chan, and E.M. Welch. 1991. "Employer Factors Related to Workers' Compensation Claims and Disability Management." *Rehabilitation Counselling Bulletin* 34: 210-26.

Hale, A.R., and J. Hovden. 1998. "Management and Culture: The Third Age of Safety. A Review of Approaches to Organizational Aspects of Safety, Health, and Environment." In *Occupational Injury: Risk, Prevention, and Intervention,* ed. A.M. Feyer and A. Williamson. London: Taylor and Francis.

Havlovic, S.J., and S.L. McShane. 1997. *The Effectiveness of Joint Health and Safety Committees (JHSCs) and Safety Training in Reducing Fatalities and Injuries in British Columbia Forest Product Mills.* Burnaby: Workers' Compensation Board of British Columbia.

Hopkins, A. 1995. *Making Safety Work: Getting Management Commitment to Occupational Health and Safety.* St. Leonard's, NSW, Australia: Allen and Unwin.

Hunt, H.A., R.V. Habeck, B. Vantol, and S.M. Scully. 1993. *Disability Prevention among Michigan Employers 1988-1993.* Kalamazoo, MI: W.E. Upjohn Institute for Employment Research.

Katz, D., and R.L. Kahn. 1966. *The Social Psychology of Organizations.* New York: Wiley.

Laflamme, L., and E. Menckel. 1995. "Aging and Occupational Accidents: A Review of the Literature of the Last Three Decades." *Safety Science* 21: 145-61.

Lewchuk, W., D. Brown, M. Groom, and C. Watson. 1990. *Workwell and Formal Health and Safety Programs: Report Prepared for Workers' Compensation Board of Ontario.* Hamilton: Strategic Policy and Analysis Division, Research Evaluation Branch, McMaster University.

Lewchuk, W., A.L. Robb, and V. Walters. 1996. "The Effectiveness of Bill 70 and Joint Health and Safety Committees in Reducing Injuries in the Workplace: The Case of Ontario." *Canadian Public Policy* 22: 2-20.

Mines Safety and Health Administration. 1983. *Factors Associated with Disabling Injuries in Underground Coal Mines.* Washington, DC: US Department of Labor, US Government Printing Office.

Peters, R.H. 1989. *Review of Recent Research on Organizational and Behavioural Factors Associated with Mine Safety.* Washington, DC: US Department of the Interior.

Polanyi, M., J. Eakin, J. Frank, H. Shannon, and T. Sullivan. 1996. *Creating Healthier Work Environments: A Critical Review of the Health Impacts of Workplace Organizational Change Interventions.* Ottawa: National Forum on Health.

Research Policy and Evaluation Branch, Strategic Policy and Analysis Division, Ontario

Workers' Compensation Board (WCB). 1992. "Workplace Accident Reporting Practices Study: Main Report." Workers Compensation Board, Toronto.

Shafai-Sahrai, Y. 1973. *Determinants of Occupational Injury Experience*. East Lansing: Michigan State University.

Shannon, H.S., J. Mayr, and T. Haines. 1997. "Overview of the Relationship between Organizational and Workplace Factors and Injury Rates." *Safety Science* 26: 201-17.

Shannon, H.S., L.S. Robson, and S.J. Guastello. 1999. "Criteria for Evaluating Occupational Safety Intervention Research." *Safety Science* 31: 161-79.

Shannon, H.S., V. Walters, W. Lewchuk, J. Richardson, L.A. Moran, T. Haines, and D. Verma. 1996. "Workplace Organizational Correlates of Lost-Time Accident Rates in Manufacturing." *American Journal of Industrial Medicine* 29: 258-68.

Shannon, H.S., V. Walters, W. Lewchuk, J.L. Richardson, D.K. Verma, T. Haines, and L.A. Moran. 1992. *Health and Safety Approaches in the Workplace: Research Report and Appendices*. Toronto: Industrial Accident Prevention Association (IAPA).

Simard, M., C. Lévesque, and D. Bouteiller. 1988. "Safety Management Effectiveness: Main Results of Research in the Manufacturing Industry." Unpublished essay.

Simard, M., and A. Marchand. 1994. "The Behaviour of First-Line Supervisors in Accident Prevention and Effectiveness in Occupational Safety." *Safety Science* 17 (3): 169-85.

Simonds, R.H., and Y. Shafai-Sahrai. 1977. "Factors Apparently Affecting Injury Frequency in Eleven Matched Pairs of Companies." *Journal of Safety Research* 9: 120-7.

Stewart, J. 1996. "World Class Safety and Outstanding Business Performance: It Is Possible to Have Both." *CIB Perspectives* 4.

Stewart, J.M. 1993a. "The Multi-Ball Juggler." *Business Quarterly* 57 (4): 32-9.

–. 1993b. "Future State Visioning: A Powerful Leadership Process." *Long Range Planning* 26: 89-98.

–. 1994. "The Planning Forum, the International Society for Strategic Management and Planning." *Planning Review* 22 (2): 1-48.

Tuohy, C., and M. Simard. 1993. *The Impact of Joint Health and Safety Committees in Ontario and Quebec. Prepared for the Canadian Association of Administrators of Labour Law*. Toronto: Ontario Ministry of Labour.

Verma, A., and D. Irvine. 1994. "A Qualitative Study Investigating the Firm Characteristics That Are Associated with Variation in Employee Claims Frequency and Duration Rates among Auto Assembly Plants." Unpublished essay.

8
Joint Health and Safety Committees: Finding a Balance
John O'Grady

Joint health and safety committees (JHSCs) are part and parcel of the system of internal responsibility. This system places primary responsibility for preventing workplace accidents and occupational disease on cooperative action by workers' representatives and local managers. For Drache and Glasbeek (1992), the system of joint committees and the philosophy of internal responsibility serve chiefly to dilute management's ultimate responsibility without changing the balance of power in the workplace. Other observers see joint committees as significantly improving conditions in the workplace. The purpose of this chapter is to examine both the potential and the limits of joint committees and, in particular, to consider the external factors that augment or diminish the impact of these committees.

Workplace Injuries and Strategies for Change
Over the fifteen years from 1983 to 1997, accepted time loss injuries per 1,000 workers in Canada fell by approximately one-third, as can be seen in Figure 8.1. However, the experience across provinces differed markedly. In British Columbia, for example, the injury rate declined by only 18 percent, whereas in Ontario and Quebec the rate fell by 37 percent and 35 percent, respectively. The contrast is significant. Public policy in Ontario and Quebec is strongly committed to the philosophy of internal responsibility and to the role of joint health and safety committees. In both provinces, the period from 1983 to 1997 saw a considerable strengthening of legislative and administrative support for joint committees. This begs the question: were joint committees a significant factor in the improved workplace health and safety performance of Ontario and Quebec?

Assessing the role of JHSCs in reducing workplace injuries is a complex task. No jurisdiction in Canada relies wholly on joint committees. Indeed, one of the arguments of this chapter is that the functioning of the internal responsibility system must be considered in the context of the regulatory

Figure 8.1

Accepted time loss injuries per 1,000 workers, Canada, 1983-97

Note: The source for employment data, Statistics Canada's *Survey of Employment Payroll Hours* (SEPH), measures *paid* employment and therefore excludes the self-employed. Note that some workers in federal jurisdiction, such as employees of chartered banks, will be counted in SEPH but are not covered by workers' compensation boards. Conversely, some boards permit self-employed persons to take voluntary coverage.
Sources: Injuries data derived from AWCBC (1997, Table 1); employment data from Statistics Canada (1998).

system and the incentives and cross-subsidies that are embedded in the premium structure of the workers' compensation system.

The internal responsibility system emerged in the unionized mining industry in the 1950s and 1960s and, to a lesser extent, in the manufacturing industry. The system was described in some detail in the 1976 *Report of the Royal Commission on the Health and Safety of Workers in Mines* (the Ham Report) (Ontario 1976). The Ham Report set out four principles. First, the internal responsibility system required joint health and safety committees. Second, the joint committees should have the power to inspect, investigate, and, in some readings of the report, the power to make decisions respecting health and safety. Third, individual workers should have the right to refuse unsafe work. Fourth, workers should have the right to be informed of substances used in the workplace that could be harmful. In one way or another, the Ham Report's internal responsibility principles inform health and safety legislation in all jurisdictions. There are, however, significant differences in how these principles are applied. Legislation differs in the authority conferred on joint committees and on the extent to which committees are

mandatory. In some jurisdictions, committees must be certified and committee members must be trained. The right to refuse is circumscribed in
some provinces. Finally, the role of the health and safety inspectorate differs
across jurisdictions. In some provinces, the inspectorate performs its classical enforcement role. In others, the inspectorate is mandated to carry out a
mediating role and to facilitate the operation of joint committees.

A study done for the Macdonald Royal Commission concluded that "the
adoption of the internal responsibility system ... was one of the key developments in the 1970s" (Digby and Riddell 1985). In Ontario, the *Report
of the Royal Commission on Matters of Health and Safety Arising from the Use of
Asbestos in Ontario,* prepared by the Dupré Commission, described the internal responsibility system as "the cornerstone of the Ontario *Health and
Safety Act*" (Ontario 1984). In Quebec, the Beaudry Report had a comparable
impact and set forth similar principles.

Jurisdictional Comparisons

Prior to the mid-1970s, the preponderant view was that provincial responsibility for labour relations led to inconsistency and a tendency to restrict
changes, so as not to impair a jurisdiction's competitive position. Weiler
challenged this view. He argued that, in the Canadian context, federalism
promoted innovation, not rigidity (Weiler 1980). The evolution of health
and safety policy conforms to Weiler's paradigm.

Table 8.1 compares the adoption of the Ham Report's internal responsibility principles (the "Ham Principles") across the thirteen Canadian jurisdictions, as of 1998.

The general position as of 1998 may be summarized as follows. In all thirteen jurisdictions, the right to know is operative, largely through the adoption of the Workplace Hazardous Materials Information System (WHMIS).
The right to refuse unsafe work applies, at least in some form, to a significant proportion of the workforce, especially in the private sector. Joint
health and safety committees are required by statute for most classes of
workplaces in all but four jurisdictions – Northwest Territories, Alberta,
Prince Edward Island, and Newfoundland – where authority is vested in the
minister of labour to require the establishment of a committee. (In Quebec,
joint committees may be initiated by a union request or by the request of
10 percent of an employer's workforce at a particular establishment.) The
right to participate is tied to the establishment of a joint committee. Only
in Alberta do the rights of committee members not extend to inspection
and evaluation.

Internal Responsibility and Adversarialism

One of the issues that colours the expectations of joint committees and the
evaluation of their impact is the relationship of the internal responsibility

Table 8.1

Adoption of "Ham Principles" of internal responsibility by jurisdiction

	Mandated joint committee[a]	Right to know[b]	Right to participate[c]	Right to refuse unsafe work[d]
Federal	X	X	X	X
Yukon	X	X	X	X
Northwest Territories	See note e	X	See note g	X
British Columbia	X	X	X	X
Alberta	See note e	X	See note g	X
Saskatchewan	X	X	X	X
Manitoba	X	X	X	X
Ontario	X	X	X	X
Quebec	See note f	X	X	X
New Brunswick	X	X	X	X
Nova Scotia	X	X	X	X
Prince Edward Island	See note e	X	See note g	X
Newfoundland	See note e	X	See note g	X

a Joint committees are statutorily required, in at least some classes of workplace.
b Statutory requirement on employer to disclose use of substances or generation of by-products that may be hazardous. Effectively enforced through adoption of Workplace Hazardous Materials Information System (WHMIS).
c Right of members of joint committees (or health and safety representatives) to participate in detection, evaluation, and formulation of strategies to reduce workplace hazards.
d Right of an individual worker to refuse to do work that he or she judges to be unsafe, without risk of discipline, subject to final determination by a government health and safety inspector. The right may be limited with respect to some types of workplaces and some occupations.
e Joint committee is established at ministerial discretion.
f Joint committee is established on union initiative or at request of 10 percent of workers.
g Right to participate is tied to the establishment of a joint committee.
Source: Updated from Bernard (1985).

system to the adversarialism that characterizes employer-employee relations in many workplaces. Proponents of the internal responsibility system frequently see workplace health and safety as non-conflictual, in comparison with the economic issues that are front and centre in collective bargaining. Critics of internal responsibility see joint committees as an attempt to paper over fundamental conflicts of interest. In consequence, critics of the internal responsibility system attach more importance to regulation and enforcement.

The Ham Report explicitly rejected the view that labour and management interests were in conflict in the area of workplace safety. Thus, the commission wrote that "since both parties desire the good of the individual worker, confrontation can and must be set aside with respect both to accidents and to health-impairing environmental exposure" (Ontario 1976: 105). Elsewhere, in the same report, the commission wrote, that "there is emphatically no place for the adversary system of collective bargaining in dealing with matters of health and safety" (Ontario 1976: 157). A similar view was advanced in the *Report of the Joint Federal-Provincial Inquiry Commission into Safety of Mines and Mining Plants in Ontario* (the Burkett Report). This report spoke of the need to develop "the capability to deal with day-to-day health and safety concerns in a co-operative and consultative manner within the context of a free collective bargaining system" (Ontario 1981: vol. 1, 117). The Burkett Report asserted that unions and management should accept that "day-to-day attention to health and safety matters is distinct and apart from the other aspects of the union-management relationship" (Ontario 1981: vol. 1, 87). Indeed, the Burkett Report recommended that worker members of joint committees be constrained from engaging in "partisan union political activity of any kind" (Ontario 1981: vol. 1, 69).

The alternative view – that workplace health and safety is inextricably bound up with conflictual labour-management relations – rests on three pillars: history, the theory of compensating wage differentials, and the practical matter of dealing with the costs.

From the perspective of history, JHSCs did not arise ex nihilo. Prior to the system of internal responsibility, it was a common union strategy to establish such committees through contract negotiations. Contractually founded joint committees were the dominant model in the mining industry, which was the focus of the Ham Report. Viewed against this history, removing these committees from their context of conflictual labour-management relations has little prospect of succeeding.

With regard to compensating wage differentials, a central premise of the economic theory of wages is that, in some degree, risks to health and safety are factored into wage rates (Digby and Riddell 1985: 294). Other factors being held constant, jobs that entail greater risk will command a wage premium. However, as Dickens notes, "every study of differences between union and nonunion compensation for exposure to deadly hazards has found that union members receive much larger [compensating differentials] than nonunion workers" (Dickens 1988: 320). In light of the strong evidence of a wage effect, especially in unionized workplaces, it is difficult to see how health and safety can be removed from conflictual labour-management relations.

On the matter of costs, remedying an occupational health and safety deficiency may be exceedingly high. Reducing noise pollution, dust, or fumes can involve significant capital expenditures. Replacing hazardous substances in a production process may involve a costly re-engineering of production processes. Altering job designs or changing work organization to reduce individual exposure to risk may have significant implications for wages or efficiency. These costs must be borne by someone – if not by consumers in the form of higher prices, then by workers as lower wages or shareholders as lower profits. As Doern notes, "the private firm has a strong built-in bias to err on the side of less costly changes." Doern concludes that "all protestations and assertions to the contrary, occupational and environmental health is a bargainable item" (Doern 1977: 18).

The view that workplace health and safety is a shared interest leads to a preference for a problem-solving modus operandi on joint committees. In contrast, the view that workplace health and safety is shaped by the conflicting interests of labour and management leads to an expectation that joint committees will be an extension of the collective bargaining relationship. Kochan et al. highlighted the difference between a problem-solving orientation and a negotiating style (Kochan et al. 1977: 45ff). The analysis is based on earlier work by Walton and McKersie (1965 and 1993). In the Walton and McKersie analysis, problem solving and bargaining are stages in a relationship, rather than alternative modes of conduct. The relationship proceeds in two phases. The first is characterized by problem solving. In this phase, the parties share information, engage in full and open communication, identify alternative solutions or priorities, and define the joint gains (or losses). The parties seek to maximize the amount of information exchanged and avoid coercive or threatening tactics. The second phase involves the actual bargaining. In this phase, the parties attempt to select one of the alternative solutions or priorities and determine the precise distribution of gains or costs. Behaviour necessarily changes in this phase. The parties limit their communication and rely on principal spokespersons. Either or both parties may engage in bluffing, attempt to establish their firm commitment to a particular position, or use various forms of coercive behaviour, such as warning, promises, and threats. Issues that otherwise stand alone may be linked in an effort to configure a bargain. Kochan et al. found from a survey of fifty-one unionized plants in New York State that "while management apparently adopts either a problem-solving or a negotiating style of behaviour [throughout the interaction], union representatives are more likely to engage in both strategies at the same time or neither strategy at all" (Kochan et al. 1977: 8-9).

The conclusion that problem solving and bargaining are phases in a relationship argues strongly against imputing to health and safety issues the unique property of standing above the conflicting interests of labour and management. If this perspective is accepted, it is unreasonable to expect the internal responsibility system to eliminate sharp disagreements, especially when these are based on different interests and priorities. Conflict is not evidence that the JHSC system is failing. Rather, it is evidence that the parties have moved to the difficult stage of choosing among alternative solutions and dealing with the costs involved.

Table 8.2

Workplaces covered by mandatory joint health and safety committees

	First enactment	Original coverage	Current coverage: mandatory or voluntary[a]	Current coverage: scope[b]
Federal	1978	Designation by minister	Mandatory	Twenty or more employees
Yukon	1973	Mandatory: twenty or more employees	Mandatory	Same as original: twenty or more employees
Northwest Territories	1977	Mandatory: ten or more employees	Subject to direction of chief safety officer	Subject to direction of chief safety officer
British Columbia	1977	Mandatory: • High hazard: twenty or more employees • Low hazard: fifty or more employees	Mandatory	Same as original: • High hazard: twenty or more employees • Low hazard: fifty or more employees
Alberta	1977	Designation by minister	Designation by minister	Designation by minister
Saskatchewan	1972	Mandatory: ten or more employees	Mandatory	Same as original: ten or more employees
Manitoba	1977	Designation by cabinet	Mandatory	Twenty or more employees
Ontario	1976 and 1978	• Designation by minister • Designated substances: twenty or more employees	Mandatory	• Designated substances • Twenty or more employees • Office and retail from 1990
Quebec	1979	• Subject to risk factors • Union may trigger committee	Mandatory in designated sectors	Twenty or more employees in designated sectors

New Brunswick	1977	Mandatory: twenty or more employees	Mandatory	Same as original: twenty or more employees
Nova Scotia	1986	Mandatory: twenty or more employees	Mandatory	Same as original: twenty or more employees
Prince Edward Island	1985	Designation by minister	Designation by minister	Designation by minister
Newfoundland	1978	Designation by minister	Mandatory	Ten or more employees

a Most jurisdictions assign to the minister or a chief inspector the power to require establishment of a joint committee if the provisions of the statute do not otherwise require such a committee.

b Most jurisdictions partially or fully exempt certain types of workplaces or occupations where protection of the public is a factor.

Source: Workplace Health and Safety Agency (1994: 5, Table 1).

Comparisons of Coverage of Joint Heath and Safety Committees

While all jurisdictions provide for joint health and safety committees, there are significant differences in the "trigger conditions" that make it mandatory to establish a committee. Most jurisdictions exempt small workplaces, drawing the cut-off line typically at twenty employees, although Saskatchewan and Newfoundland use a ten-employee threshold. Some jurisdictions distinguish between workplaces using hazardous substances and those that do not. In Quebec, the procedure is to designate sectors rather than specific employers. Currently, nine sectors are designated. In some jurisdictions, where hazardous substances are not used, the employment threshold may be higher. This is the case in British Columbia. Alternatively, the requirement to establish a committee may be subject to ministerial discretion. Alberta and Prince Edward Island stand alone in relying entirely on ministerial discretion. Table 8.2 summarizes requirements for joint committees in each of the thirteen jurisdictions.

Underlying policies on coverage are assumptions of the type of problem to be addressed by joint committees. For example, to require the establishment of JHSCs in workplaces where hazardous substances are used, but to exempt other workplaces, is to implicitly see the primary role of joint committees as auditing exposure to designated substances. Such policies implicitly assume that occupational disease and injury are essentially "blue-collar" problems. The data do not support this view. On a national basis, approximately 47 percent of injuries were accounted for by other than "blue-collar" industries. Policies that view joint committees as relevant chiefly in "blue-collar" industries miss not only more than half of the workforce, but almost half of all workplace injuries.

Comparisons of Functions and Rights of Joint Health and Safety Committees

Generally, all jurisdictions provide for members of JHSCs to have three rights: (1) Members have a right to be present when government inspections are undertaken, (2) members have a right to participate in the investigation of complaints or instances when the right to refuse unsafe work is invoked. And finally, (3) members must have access to necessary information, such as accident reports, investigation reports, and technical data on machinery and equipment, and substances used or produced in the workplace. In Ontario and Quebec, the right to specific types of information is explicit in the statute. In other jurisdictions, the right to information is implicit. Table 8.3 compares the role, powers, and functions of joint committees and joint committee members.

Some jurisdictions require JHSCs to undertake regular inspections of the workplace, independent of government inspections. In Ontario, this must be done monthly. In Alberta, an internal inspection is required coincident

Table 8.3

Comparison of roles, powers, and functions of JHSCs and committee members as set out in legislation

	Role in complaints	JHSC inspections	Government inspections	Maintenance of records	Role in right to refuse cases	Recommendations	Access to information	Development of programs
Federal	•		•	•	•		•	•
Yukon	•	•	•	•			•	•
Northwest Territories					•	•		
British Columbia		•	•	•	•	•	•	
Alberta		•	Limited					
Saskatchewan	•		•	•	•	•	•	•
Manitoba	•		•	•	•	•	•	•
Ontario		•	•	•		•		•
Quebec	•		•	•	•	•	•	
New Brunswick	•	•	•	•	•	•	•	•
Nova Scotia	•		•	•	•	•	•	•
Prince Edward Island	•		•			•	•	•
Newfoundland			•	•	•	•	Limited	•

JHSC = Joint Health and Safety Committee

with every meeting of the committee. British Columbia requires "regular inspections." Swinton, however, notes that some labour representatives complain that employers reduce internal inspections to "walk-arounds" that afford little opportunity for actual inspection (Swinton 1983: 155). All jurisdictions, except Alberta and the Northwest Territories, require records to be kept of meetings, recommendations, and investigations. Some jurisdictions require minutes to be posted. Nine of the thirteen jurisdictions direct committees to undertake safety education and promotion in the workplace; the exceptions are Nova Scotia, Ontario, British Columbia, and the Northwest Territories. Only Ontario requires that two members of the committee – one management and one labour representative – receive approved training. Manitoba, New Brunswick, and Saskatchewan allow committee members to take a leave of absence to obtain training. All jurisdictions, except British Columbia, Alberta, and Prince Edward Island require employers to provide paid time for committee functions. Only four jurisdictions – Newfoundland, Prince Edward Island, Quebec, and Saskatchewan – require meetings to be held during regular working hours. Most jurisdictions stipulate a minimum number of meetings per year, typically three to four. Prince Edward Island, Nova Scotia, and Alberta do not specify a minimum number of meetings.

Quebec is unique in conferring on joint committees the right to choose a physician approved by a designated hospital or community health centre to prepare and monitor a work-site plan and to be in charge of health services in the establishment. The designated physician is a non-voting member of the joint committee. This has led to a relationship with health professionals that is among the most advanced in Canada.

With only one partial exception, the legislation in all thirteen Canadian jurisdictions provides that committees only make recommendations to senior management. Time limits may apply. For example, the 1990 amendments to Ontario's statute require that management respond to recommendations within twenty-one days. Parsons regards the advisory role of joint committees as a dilution of the "direct responsibility" advocated in the Ham Report. (Parsons 1988: 26). Fidler, however, offers a more conservative reading of Ham: "Under Ham's proposed 'internal responsibility system for the performance of work,' management was to define safety standards and supervise their implementation. Worker safety representatives were to 'audit' safety conditions and be front-line advisors to both the inspectorate and company supervisors. The joint labour-management committees were to play a 'consultative and advisory role,' 'communicating management intentions' to the workers and enabling management to 'benefit from the insight of workers'" (Fidler 1985: 337). It is acknowledged by all commentators that the internal responsibility system did not diminish managerial prerogative. Swinton's comments on the Ontario statute apply to other jurisdictions: "The legislation's commitment is to consultation, but no more. There is a strongly held belief that health and safety come within management's prerogative, unless bargained away, and the *Occupational Health and Safety Act* was not meant to shift the balance of power in the workplace to the worker side, either by granting actual decision-making power to joint health and safety committees or by turning government inspectors into interest arbitrators" (Swinton 1983: 153).

The partial exception is Quebec's legislation, which gives joint committees the right to select individual protective devices and equipment "best adapted to the needs of the workers in their establishment." Management is required to assume the cost of these purchases, though it may be presumed that the employer's representatives on the joint committee would not act without sanction from senior management.

Digby and Riddell argue that "if the internal responsibility system is to be highly effective, functional authority should be vested in these committees. They may have only limited efficacy if they are restricted to an advisory role" (Digby and Riddell 1985: 313). Digby and Riddell point out that many workplace hazards are intrinsically linked to the type of machinery installed and the type of equipment used. The design of jobs, especially insofar as they require the repetition of certain motions, is also likely to be a contributor to industrial injury both in the physical strain to which repetitive procedures give rise and their effect on overall attitudes to the work process.

Scandinavian "work environment" legislation affords employee representatives a greater say in the approval of new machinery and equipment, though falls short of conferring a right to veto new machinery or equipment that the employee representatives regard as failing to take adequate account of health and safety needs. Closer to the Canadian legal tradition would be an application of the "duty to bargain in good faith," which is found in labour relations statutes and which applies to formal collective bargaining. As various labour boards have commented, the "duty to bargain" pertains to process, not to outcome. The duty to bargain does not imply an obligation to settle, nor is it a bar against "hard bargaining." The duty to bargain is generally held to require that the parties meet, that they exchange relevant information, and that they make proposals to settle their differences. Labour boards have identified "surface bargaining" as a violation of the requirement to bargain in good faith. "Surface bargaining" is distinguished from "hard bargaining" by a pattern of conduct that may be characterized as perfunctory or evasive. Many collective agreements provide for a duty to consult. Labour boards regard the duty to bargain as a significantly more substantive obligation than an obligation to consult. The view of George Adams, writing as chair of the Ontario Labour Relations Board in *Consolidated Bathurst Packaging Ltd. and International Woodworkers of America* (4 CLRBR NS [1983]), is representative of labour boards in all jurisdictions. Adams characterized this duty to consult as being "many shades lighter in content than the duty to bargain in good faith." The Canada Labour Code, it should be noted, already confers a duty to bargain on the introduction of new technology during the life of a collective agreement. The code requires an employer to bargain to resolution or impasse over the effects of that change. After a limited period of time, this duty to bargain expires and the employer can act unilaterally. There is no right to take industrial action nor any right to arbitrate. However, a failure to bargain in good faith can be the subject of a complaint to the Canada Labour Relations Board.

Consideration should be given to introducing into the internal responsibility system a standard comparable to the "duty to bargain in good faith" found in labour relations statutes. Introducing such a standard would communicate a public policy expectation that the interaction of the parties on JHSCs should be no less focused or substantive than that expected in formal collective bargaining. Applying a standard comparable to the "duty to bargain in good faith" would also provide scope for remedy to managerial (or union) disregard for the internal responsibility system, through reference to the labour board.

Effectiveness of Joint Health and Safety Committees

This section will review the empirical literature on the effectiveness of joint health and safety committees. It was observed earlier that the internal responsibility system is only one of three broad strategies for achieving a reduction in occupational injuries and disease. This context is important to keep in mind. Similar policies respecting internal responsibility can be associated with strikingly different results, if the principles of regulation differ significantly or if there are marked differences in the extent of cross-subsidization in WCB premiums.

In reviewing the literature on the effectiveness of joint committees, we will consider first those studies that were done of Canadian experience and subsequently studies that were done in jurisdictions outside Canada. In general, only studies completed after 1990 are discussed. More recent studies are considered first.

Canadian Studies on Impact of Joint Health and Safety Committees

Lewchuk et al. (1996) identified 637 of the manufacturing and retail workplaces studied in 1991 by Shannon et al. (1992) and surveyed the co-chairs of joint committees at these workplaces for information on when the committee was established. These workplaces were then cross-linked with WCB data on accepted time loss injuries. Survey and WCB data were available for 206 workplaces. These comprised a mix of manufacturing and retail workplaces. The distinction is important because the retail sector was not initially subject to the requirement to establish JHSCs. Lewchuk et al. pose two questions. First, were there differences between the change in injury performance in the manufacturing and retail sectors that became evident with the implementation of the Occupational Health and Safety Act? Second, within the manufacturing sector, were there differences in the change in injury performance arising from whether the joint committee was established prior to or after the statutory requirement? Lewchuk et al. hypothesize that committees that were established prior to the legislative requirement were voluntary and reflected a higher degree of management commitment. Committees established in the period 1978-80 were put in place to comply with the legislated obligation. Those established after 1980 were set up following a period of non-compliance.

Lewchuk et al. find strong support for the proposition that, following enactment of the Occupational Health and Safety Act, injury rates in the manufacturing sector fell more significantly than in the retail sector. Since the requirement to establish JHSCs did not apply to the retail sector, this provides prima facie support for the view that joint committees had an impact on injury performance. The estimating equation used by Lewchuk et al. suggests that "the reduction in lost-time accident frequencies implied by [the adoption of the Occupational Health and Safety Act] is in the order of 18 percent" (Lewchuk et al. 1996: 235).

The analysis of the manufacturing sector data indicates significant results. The data indicate that "where workplaces moved towards the internal responsibility system either before they were mandated or immediately upon the state indicating they were likely to be mandated, joint health and safety committees improved a workplace's health and safety record. However, where workplaces moved toward the internal responsibility system only reluctantly, sometimes after a period when they were in contravention of existing legislation, the formation of a committee had no clear effect" (ibid.: 234). Lewchuk et al. conclude that "the internal responsibility system ... can lead to significantly lower injury and illness rates ... This system of health and safety regulation works and should be encouraged" (ibid.: 235). At the same time, the authors emphasize that "these improvements are neither automatic, nor enjoyed by all workplaces. Simply mandating committees is unlikely to have much effect at workplaces where the internal responsibility system and the co-management of health and safety matters is not embraced by management and/or labour" (ibid.: 235-6).

Lévesque (1995) surveyed seventy-one unionized Quebec manufacturing establishments that had joint health and safety committees. The survey involved direct interviews with labour and management and focused on the tactics they each employ in joint committees and their perception of the tactics used by the other party. Tactics were classified as either "coercive" or "persuasive." Two questions were posed by Lévesque: what is the incidence of coercive versus persuasive tactics, and what are the external correlates of a propensity to use coercive tactics?

Lévesque's data suggest that most members of JHSCs, whether employer or labour representatives, typically use both coercive and persuasive tactics. In only 18 percent of joint committees did both parties confine themselves to persuasive tactics. In an insignificant number of committees, both parties used chiefly coercive tactics. Overall, 64 percent of management respondents and 56 percent of labour respondents relied on a mix of coercive and persuasive tactics (Lévesque 1995: 223-4). These findings lend support to the earlier suggestion that workplace health and safety cannot be divorced from the broader context of conflicting interests and priorities between labour and management. Lévesque also found that the propensity to use coercive tactics correlated to conflict over production goals. Thus, he observes that "the tensions over production objectives overlap with safety" (ibid.: 226). This, too, suggests that Ham and Burkett may have been on the wrong track when they argued that health and safety should be severed from the broader context of employer-employee relations and employer objectives.

The survey for the Workplace Health and Safety Agency (1994) was based on a mailed questionnaire to joint committee co-chairs in 3,000 workplaces. The response rate was 71.7 percent. The purpose of the survey was to assess compliance with the procedural requirements of the (Ontario) Occupational Health and Safety Act, to appraise the functioning of joint committees, and to evaluate the impact of the "core certification training." Under the 1990 amendments to the act, mandatory JHSCs were extended to most workplaces and a certification obligation was established. Among the requirements for certification was the completion of "core certification training" by one management and one labour member of the joint committee. The Workplace Health and Safety Agency was established to develop the core certification training and administer the certification process.

Overall, the survey, highlights of which were prepared by SPR Associates (SPR 1994), found a comparatively high level of compliance. The study concluded that approximately 80 percent of workplaces were in compliance on 80 percent of the requirements. Table 8.4 summarizes the incidence of low levels of compliance. The most noteworthy of these, as discussed immediately following, are highlighted in bold.

The data show a significant compliance problem in small workplaces (i.e., workplaces with fewer than 100 employees) and in the retail, hospitality, and other service industries. The level of non-compliance among non-unionized workplaces reflects workplace size, sectoral factors, and union status. The SPR report also confirmed other findings on the relation between workplace size and injury rates. As Table 8.5 shows, the reported injury rate was approximately 50 percent higher in small workplaces.

The SPR report revealed that in 25.5 percent of workplaces, worker repre-

Table 8.4

Incidence of low levels of compliance with procedural requirements for JHSCs

	Compliance rate (%)
Number of employees	
20-49 employees	**44.4**
50-99 employees	**34.5**
100-499 employees	23.7
500+ employees	10.8
Industrial sector	
Manufacturing	28.4
Mining and resources	20.4
Public sector	22.3
Retail/hospitality/other services	**54.2**
Workplace	
Non-unionized	**44.4**
Unionized	20.9

Note: Bold indicates noteworthy examples.
Source: SPR (1994: 56).

Table 8.5

Injury rates per 100 employees, by workplace size

Number of employees	Injury rate
20-49 employees	2.9
50-99 employees	2.3
100-499 employees	2.3
500+ employees	2.0

Source: SPR (1994: 51).

sentatives to JHSCs were selected by management. Two-thirds of the joint committees were not in compliance with the requirement for monthly inspections of the workplace.

The SPR report revealed a continuing need for training of JHSC members. Thirty-five percent of worker members and 41 percent of management members reported having received no training whatsoever in health and safety matters. Among the issues in which a need for training was cited were stress reduction, reduction of repetitive strain injuries, improvement of air quality, and control of hazardous substances. The report also showed that a lack of training of new employees was commonplace (see Table 8.6).

The SPR report found that joint committee members "generally reported co-operative relationships in their committee work. This was reflected

Table 8.6

No training provided to new employees as reported by management and worker members of JHSCs

	Management members (%)	Worker members (%)
New production employees	48.1	64.3
New office employees	63.0	80.0
New technical/professional employees	62.0	80.5
New sales/service employees	73.5	85.4

Source: SPR (1994: 23).

particularly in the predominance of problem-solving committee actions, as compared to negotiating committee actions" (SPR 1994: 32). Overall, 14.9 percent of management members and 21.3 percent of worker members reported having engaged in one or more "negotiating actions" (SPR 1994: 33). The tenor of joint committees was both affected by the general character of labour relations and also a factor in influencing labour relations. Forty-three percent of management members and 41.5 percent of worker members reported that their work had improved labour-management relations. Fewer than 5 percent of either group reported that joint committee work had worsened labour-management relations. However, 9.6 percent of management members would disband the joint committee if they were not required by legislation to have one in place.

Table 8.7 summarizes the incidence of specific changes that were judged to contribute to a safer work environment. Table 8.7 also separates the incidence of specific changes between committees in which a worker had completed the core certification training versus committees in which this training had not begun. The first tier of the core certification training comprised a forty-hour training program following a prescribed text.

The breadth and sophistication of the reported changes tracked in Table 8.7 is significant. These findings are among the most compelling evidence of the positive impact of joint committees. Table 8.7 also shows a strong correlation between implementing specific changes and completing the core certification training program.

Compared with an earlier survey conducted for the Advisory Council on Occupational Health and Occupational Safety (ACOHOS 1986), the SPR report on the 1994 survey found a perception of significant improvements in committee performance among both management and worker members. Table 8.8 compares results from the two surveys. As can be seen, by all measures, the performance of committees improved between the two surveys.

The Workplace Health and Safety Agency was a bipartite body, established primarily to oversee delivery of health and safety training and to certify joint committees. The agency was established in 1990 by the then Liberal

Table 8.7

Specific changes related to occupational health and safety as reported by worker members of JHSCs

	All committees (%)	Core certification training completed (%)	Core certification training not begun (%)
Improved frequency and/or procedures for inspections	28.3	38.1	27.1
Identified controls for toxic substances	19.3	35.3	26.4
Improved health hazard detection or monitoring	26.3	40.6	28.4
Improved personal protective equipment	36.9	53.0	38.2
Made specific work practices more safe	48.1	64.3	49.4
Improved ergonomic design of work activities	27.7	48.9	31.5
Reduced stress in specific jobs	14.3	25.2	13.4
Improved engineering (ventilation, etc.)	28.6	49.4	31.3
Improved preventive maintenance procedures	30.9	45.7	32.7
Applied health and safety statistics to solve a problem	21.1	42.0	24.7
Began new health and safety training for workers or managers	33.1	45.7	32.8

Source: SPR (1994: 33).

Table 8.8

Perceptions of committee performance as reported by management and worker members of JHSCs

	Worker members		Management members	
	1985-6 (%)	1994 (%)	1985-6 (%)	1994 (%)
Overall record in improving safety	59.4	76.8	56.2	76.3
Overall record in reducing health hazards	58.9	74.1	60.3	77.9
Success in inspections	67.6	85.9	66.5	87.4
Joint committee works well or extremely well	57.3	61.1	61.7	68.5
High rating of workers' knowledge of act	16.6	23.7	18.8	25.9
High rating of workers' contribution to joint committee	42.5	59.1	45.0	64.1
Joint committee viewed as cooperative	71.9	84.1	89.4	91.0
Management selects worker members of joint committee	35.2	25.5	–	–

Sources: 1985-6 data: ACOHOS (1986); 1994 data: SPR (1994: C2, Appendix C).

government and disbanded in 1995 by the newly elected Progressive Conservative government. In a 1994 study, the agency analyzed accident, time loss, and fatality data for the period 1972-89, comparing Ontario's experience to the rest of Canada (WHSA 1994). The agency found that the decline in Ontario exceeded the decline in the rest of Canada. In Ontario, accidents declined at an average annual rate of 0.21 incidents per 100 workers, versus 0.18 in the rest of Canada. There was no statistically significant correlation to unemployment. Fatalities evidenced a greater annual rate of decline in Ontario than in the rest of Canada, averaging 0.50 per 100,000 workers in Ontario versus 0.19 per year outside Ontario. This decline was largely attributable to a reduction in fatal accidents. Deaths arising from occupational disease increased over the period, although this reflected a more liberal recognition of fatality claims by the WCB.

The Workplace Health and Safety Agency's findings are consistent with those of Lewchuk et al. (1996). However, the Lewchuk et al. study carries the analysis further by contrasting the manufacturing and retail sectors and by controlling for the year in which a joint committee was established.

The study by Tuohy and Simard (1993) was in fact two separate studies. The first, by Tuohy, examined the Ontario experience, the second, by Simard, examined the Quebec experience. The studies sought to isolate the impact of joint committees. More specifically, the studies considered whether joint committees have an effect on the injury rate and whether committees reduce the requirement for government enforcement.

The Ontario study relied on a survey, based on pooled data for the period 1980-5, that was conducted for the Advisory Council on Occupational Health and Occupational Safety (ACOHOS 1986). This survey examined the functioning of JHSCs in terms of indicators such as frequency of meetings, record maintenance, number of inspections, depth of management participation, and formulation of recommendations. Tuohy correlated these data with administrative data on accepted injury claims, ministry of labour inspections, and compliance orders. A total of 920 complete observations form the basis for the study.

Tuohy found that by far the most important variable explaining lower relative injury rates was the presence of an experienced, stable workforce. This is an important finding, since many employers are increasing the proportion of part-time, casual, and agency-supplied employees in their total workforce. Tuohy also found that "committee capacity" was another important factor. "Committee capacity" is a composite variable reflecting principally: scope of committee activity, access to information, training, institutionalized procedures, and decision-making role. While injury rates were the most important factor determining the frequency of inspections, Tuohy found that inspectors relied on committees in lieu of inspections, based on the nature of management representation on the committee and the age of the committee. However, this pattern of enforcement by the inspectorate is not well supported by the data. Tuohy comments that "we did not find the age of the committee, or the presence of senior managers on the committee in small and non-union workplaces, to be directly related to lower injury rates, yet these were factors which reduced the likelihood of inspection" (Tuohy and Simard 1993: 10). "Protagonistic relations" between labour and management were associated with a higher compliance order rate but with a lower injury rate. Factors, such as age of the committee and "committee capacity" were strongly associated with an increased propensity by senior management to accept recommendations. No separate appraisal, however, was made of the quality or significance of these recommendations.

The Simard study in Quebec drew on 117 usable survey returns correlated to administrative data. The survey was conducted in 1985-6 and assessed commmittees in terms of certain performance and capacity indicators. Like Tuohy, Simard found "a general tendency for workplace factors to have a greater impact, when compared to committee factors." He points out that this "remind[s] us that occupational health and safety performance results form a complex of factors that lie beyond the usual realm of committees" (ibid.: 22). For workplaces with more than seventy-five employees, the impact of joint committees is positive for all injury performance measures. In smaller workplaces, this pattern does not hold. This is attributed by Simard to differences in the age of committees in large and small workplaces. Joint committees are generally of longer standing in workplaces with seventy-five or more employees. Supporting this interpretation, Simard found that there is a lag in the impact of JHSCs on injury rates. In part this arises from characteristics of the Quebec legislation. In Quebec, committees are established automatically in nine sectors, if requested by a union or 10 percent of employees. Outside of these sectors, committees are established by mutual consent. In this context, newer committees typically arise in response to particular incidents or higher than average injury rates. Thus, in the initial years, the presence of a committee may actually be associated with above average injury rates until the committee's efforts and recommendations have an impact on injury performance. Simard also found that outside of the designated sectors, where committees were established by mutual consent, there was no evidence that the existence of a joint committee had any discernible impact in the absence of a union.

Tuohy and Simard summarize their joint findings: "The most important result of the joint study is the finding that committees with bipartite structures, broad scopes of activities and institutionalized procedures reduce injury rates and improve problem-solving capabilities at the workplace level" (ibid.: 47). Finally, Tuohy and Simard note that "both studies found that adversarial relations between management and labour formed part of a factor which was associated with lower injury rates in unionized workplaces." In Ontario, however, "adversarial and collaborative strategies were linked" (ibid.: 44). This is consistent with Lévesque's findings and lends further weight to the view that occupational health and safety issues cannot be divorced from the broader context of labour relations and the conflicting interests and priorities that characterize those relations.

The Saari et al. (1993) study bears only indirectly on joint committees. The study examined the preferences of companies in the transportation equipment and machinery sector in Quebec with respect to complying with WHMIS training requirements. The study tracked the preferences of ninety-two plants, all of which were members of a bipartite sector association. The study also monitored indicators of commitment to a safety culture, such as the evidence of senior management participation in health and safety matters, the presence of joint committees, and accident prevention activities. The survey was undertaken in 1989-90. The sector association offered companies the option of training employees directly through a four-hour course in WHMIS at only nominal cost for provision of materials or training a company instructor in a two-day course. Companies that chose the latter course would then provide training internally. This was judged by Saari et al. to be the costlier choice for most companies as it required a greater commitment of staff time and financial resources. The general finding was that companies with a stronger safety culture evidenced a marked preference to internalize WHMIS training, while companies with a weaker culture opted for the less costly compliance strategy. The study suggests that sector-based organizations may provide a useful role in providing basic training to companies that do not, for whatever reason, see a value in internalizing the health and safety training function or have the means to do so.

The Shannon et al. (1992) study was undertaken for the (Ontario) Industrial Accident Prevention Association (IAPA) and is reported in Shannon's chapter in this volume. IAPA is an employer association. The study was based on a survey of 1,000 employers in eight sectors, supplemented by interviews. Each survey involved four sub-surveys: worker co-chair of joint committee, management co-chair, senior manager, and human resources director. Forty-four percent of surveyed firms completed all four surveys. Survey respondents were cross-tabulated with their accepted time loss frequency rate, based on WCB data. Firms were categorized as having low, medium, or high time loss frequency rates.

As with Tuohy and Simard, Shannon et al. found that the most important determinants of time loss frequency rates were factors related to the characteristics of the workforce. Workplaces with low time loss frequency rates employed more workers over the age of fifty and fewer workers under the age of twenty-five. They also employed more workers with a least five years' seniority and fewer workers with under two years' seniority. Finally, firms with low time loss frequency rates also had lower rates of labour turnover (Shannon et al. 1992: 107, Table 9.1).

The survey confirmed that joint committees typically engaged in advisory and reactive roles and did not exercise executive authority. However, "workplaces with low lost-time frequency rates were more likely to have joint health and safety committees with executive duties" (ibid.: iii). Union structure was also a factor of some consequence. Each additional steward per 100 members reduced time loss frequency rates by almost 8 percent. This result suggests that unions that push responsibility downward are more likely to have a positive impact through their structure than more centralized unions. The study found that "there was also evidence that committees where labour members received some health and safety training, or where labour members had access to external professional assistance, such as a union financed health and safety specialist, had lower lost-time frequency rates" (ibid.: 108). Finally, the study confirmed the findings of other surveys that there were high levels of cooperation and conflict concurrent in joint committees. Interviews, subsequent to the survey, found that managers acknowledged that "economic constraints can influence what is done in health and safety-trade-offs are commonly made" (ibid.: 174). This is consistent with the view that health and safety issues cannot be divorced from the conflicting interests and priorities of workers and management. Nevertheless, the interviews also found a reiteration of the theme that some JHSC members did not want "problems in the latter [i.e., industrial relations] spilling over and affecting safety" (ibid.: 174).

Havlovic (1991) analyzed fatality data in the BC logging industry from 1940 to 1989. Havlovic noted that British Columbia achieved lower accident and fatality rates in logging and achieved declines in rates sooner than was the case in California, Oregon, or Washington, where the industry faced similar conditions. This superior injury performance was attributable to a mix of safety committees, training programs, enforcement, penalties, and changes in managerial priorities. While acknowledging the contribution of safety committees, Havlovic does not isolate their impact from other factors.

In 1985-6, approximately five years after the requirement to establish joint committees, the ACOHOS survey (ACOHOS 1986) was undertaken by SPR Associates for the (Ontario) Advisory Council on Health and Occupational Safety. The survey was based on questionnaires mailed to 3,000 labour and management members of joint committees and a separate survey of management in 3,800 workplaces. Response rates were 76 percent among joint committee members and 93 percent among managers.

Overall, the ACOHOS survey found a high level of nominal compliance with the procedural requirements. Joint committees had been established in 93 percent of workplaces in which committees were mandatory. Among the procedural requirements in the Occupational Health and Safety Act were regular meetings, posting of minutes, and investigation of accidents and refusals. The survey found that "most firms comply fully with most features of the *Act*, but few are in full compliance" (ACOHOS 1986: 107). However, compliance with specific provisions of the Act was uneven: "Only 22 percent of workplaces with joint health and safety committees appear[ed] to be in full compliance with the *Act*" (ibid.: v).

The ACOHOS survey found that JHSCs were functioning well in 58 percent of workplaces, adequately in 30 percent of workplaces, and poorly in 12 percent. Survey results, however, highlighted the difficulties experienced by joint committee members – principally labour members – in obtaining what they regarded as the necessary information to perform their tasks. Twenty-eight percent of worker members and 9 percent of management members reported not having adequate information. The ACOHOS survey also highlighted the absence of training in health and safety among JHSC members. A striking 19 percent of worker members and 13 percent of management members were not aware of the health and safety implications of designated substances. Overall, the survey found that 19 percent of management members and 39 percent of worker members of joint committees had received no training whatsoever on key issues in occupational health and safety, including hazard recognition, control of designated substances, investigation procedures, requirements under the act, and problem-solving techniques.

The results of the ACOHOS survey were instrumental in shaping subsequent amendments to Ontario's Occupational Health and Safety Act. As discussed above, these amendments addressed the coverage of mandatory committees, their access to information, and the need for committees to be certified.

International Studies on Impact of Joint Health and Safety Committees

Boden et al. (1984) based their study on a sample of seventy-nine Massachusetts manufacturing plants. The number of inspections and the number of "serious" citations by inspectors are used as a proxy for the level of hazard in the workplaces. Boden et al. found no general effect of JHSCs, that is, the presence of a joint committee was not a reliable predictor of whether a plant had a high or low level of hazard. However, the researchers did find that when committees were separated between those perceived as effective by their members and those not so perceived, there was a discernible effect. Effective joint committees functioned as a substitute for Occupational Health and Safety Agency (OSHA) enforcement.

Cooke and Gautschi (1980) surveyed 113 manufacturing plants in Maine to estimate the impact of OSHA inspections and the establishment of joint union-management safety programs at the plant level. The study found that plant-specific programs, jointly administered with unions, reduced lost days. Moreover, "plant-specific efforts have been more effective on average in reducing injuries than have been outside regulatory activities" (Cooke and Gautschi 1980: 256). The impact of plant-specific programs was approximately double that of external regulation.

Kochan et al. (1977) surveyed labour and management co-chairs of JHSCs in fifty-one unionized manufacturing plants in New York State. All of these committees were voluntary. The degree of committee activity was largely determined by the priority assigned to it by the union. Kochan et al. found that the involvement of OSHA inspectors had different effects on union and management members of committees. The study concluded that the involvement of OSHA inspectors moved management from a negotiating style of interaction to a problem-solving style. The opposite, however, was true of the union (ibid.: 50). This finding should not be surprising, since the involvement of an OSHA inspector typically is occasioned by a union request and reflects a decision by the union to use a coercive tactic. While Kochan et al. regarded joint committees as valuable innovations, they concluded that "major safety improvements appear to be less a function of union participation in a safety committee than on the direct pressure of OSHA regulations" (ibid.: 72).

Reilly et al. (1995) relied on 1990 data generated by the third Workplace Industrial Relations Survey (WIRS) in the United Kingdom. WIRS is a systematic review of industrial relations practices. After sample attrition, 432 establishments were included in the analysis. The study found that JHSCs in which employee representatives were chosen by unions had the greatest injury reducing effect compared with both no such committee and committees otherwise configured. Table 8.9 summarizes these results.

Beaumont and Leopold (1982a, 1982b) document the failure of voluntarism to lead to a satisfactory diffusion of JHSCs in the United Kingdom. This failure led to the adoption in 1974 of legislation permitting unions to

Table 8.9

Injuries per 1,000 employees as reported in UK Workplace Industrial Relations Survey (WIRS), 1990

JHSC status	Injury rate per 1,000 employees
No committee	10.9
Joint committee, union appoints all employee representatives	5.3
Joint committee, some employee representatives not appointed by union	7.5
Joint committee, no employee representatives appointed by union	6.1

Source: Reilly et al. (1995: 282, Table 2).

appoint health and safety representatives with inspection powers and requiring employers to establish a joint committee on application by a union (Atherley et al. 1976).

Pragnell (1994) conducted an analysis based on the Australian Workplace Industrial Relations Survey (AWIRS) carried out in 1989-90 in New South Wales. Legislation provides for the establishment of a joint committee if directed by the Work Cover Authority or on application by a recognized trade union. The Australian system is thus intermediate between a voluntarist model and a mandatory model and functions in a manner similar to that in Quebec. In manufacturing, 59 percent of establishments had established joint committees, while in the wholesale and retail sector the proportion was only 36 percent. Eighty-three percent of companies with 200 or more employees had committees compared to 26 percent of companies with twenty to forty-nine employees. The likelihood of a committee being established declined as the proportion of part-time employees increased. Only 9 percent of non-unionized workplaces had committees. Pragnell concludes that "less voluntaristic arrangements, for instance mandatory committees as is the case in Canada, might be considered to overcome the lack of penetration of committees" (Pragnell 1994: 37).

With regard to factors influencing the effectiveness of JHSCs, the Ontario Advisory Council on Occupational Health and Occupational Safety concluded that "unless fully developed through careful legislation and implementation, through training and education, and unless fully integrated with the workplace, the joint health and safety committee leads not to self-regulation, but rather self-deception" (ACOHOS 1986: 169-70). This conclusion is supported by the analytical literature. Lewchuk et al., for example, found that in Ontario there was a marked difference between committees established with management support and those established without such support. Similarly, Boden et al. found no significant effect from the presence of joint committees per se, but noteworthy effects when committee capacity was taken into account.

In the foregoing, a number of factors have been identified as contributing to the effectiveness of joint committees. Two clearly stand out. The first is access to information. The second is training for members of joint committees, and in particular for the co-chairs.

The 1986 ACOHOS survey underscored the difficulties of labour members in obtaining information. Inadequate access to information was cited by 28 percent of worker members. Surprisingly, 9 percent of management members had the same concern. By the time of the 1994 SPR report, this issue largely had been put to rest. It may be inferred, therefore, that the current provisions of the Ontario statute have addressed this problem.[1]

The second critical factor is training committee members. Survey evidence in 1986 showed that one out of five management members and two out of five employee representatives had received no training whatsoever. Equally striking was the finding that 19 percent of worker members and 13 percent of management members were not aware of the health and safety implications of designated substances. The need for committee members to be trained is a theme that runs through the analytical studies. Ontario devised its core certification program to address this deficiency. The 1994 SPR report found a marked contrast between the performance of committees where core certification training had been completed and where it had not yet commenced.

Empirical studies have broadly identified managerial commitment as an important factor in the effectiveness of committees. The difficulty with managerial commitment is that, while it is undeniably important, there are no obvious policy instruments to compel or encourage such commitment. Legislation can specify monthly inspections and regular meetings. Legislation can also set time limits for responding to recommendations. Useful as these provisions may be, they are unlikely to engender commitment where it would otherwise be lacking. It was suggested earlier that occupational health and safety legislation might be strengthened by porting over the "duty to bargain in good faith" that has been a longstanding feature of labour relations statutes. This would provide a partial remedy to what in the labour relations arena would be termed "surface bargaining." Also potentially important is the structure of WCB premiums and related penalties for poor health and safety injury performance.

There may also be scope to occupy an intermediate position between vesting executive responsibility in joint committees and confining committees to a purely advisory role. The Quebec statute, for example, assigns to joint committees decision-making power on personal protective equipment and the selection of an external medical advisor. Safety policy might also be assigned to joint committees, though in the event of an impasse, the legislation would have to determine whether the employer's position or adjudication prevailed. A role could also be defined for joint committees in overseeing occupational health services. There has been some movement in this direction in the European Union (Gevers 1983, 1985). The provisions of the Canada Labour Code respecting mandatory bargaining over the introduction of new technology might be adopted, at least in respect of the occupational health and safety implications of new machinery and equipment. As discussed earlier, the code requires employers to bargain over the *effects* of technological change, but allows the employer to proceed after a period of time if bargaining reaches an impasse. As a restriction on an employer's ability to make decisions, there is little substantive difference between consultation and a duty to bargain along the lines of the Canada Labour Code's treatment of new technology. However, in terms of process, the duty to bargain establishes a higher standard that is consistent with the intent of occupational health and safety legislation.

The availability of impartial expertise may also strengthen a JHSC by enhancing its overall capacity to deal with occupational health and safety issues. The Quebec statute is unique in directing committees to establish a relationship with a qualified medical professional. There has been little systematic exploration of the effect of this provision. Nevertheless, a comparison of injury trends in Quebec and British Columbia suggests that the Quebec model has yielded benefits that must be given weight.

Finally, it is important to the functioning of joint committees that the health and safety inspectorate adopt an appropriate operating philosophy. We turn to this topic separately, in light of its complexity.

The Health and Safety Inspectorate
A contentious policy issue is the relationship between the health and safety inspectorate and the system of internal responsibility. There are three areas of potential conflict that can require the intervention of inspectors. The first, and most obvious, involves an employer that has no commitment to the internal responsibility system. In these circumstances, enforcement through inspectors is essential. Weak enforcement signals other similarly minded employers that non-compliance is the most expedient course. A second area of conflict relates to the cost implications of addressing a particular risk to occupational health or safety. Where addressing the risk of occupational injury or disease involves significant potential costs, there is a strong likelihood of conflict between employee and management members of joint committees. Finally, acceptance that disease pathologies result from the workplace will also be contentious, given the uncertain liabilities that may arise. For all of these reasons, conflict between labour and management members should be expected. Such conflict should be seen not as evidence that the internal responsibility system is failing, but as evidence that the system has approached its limits. Kochan et al., it will be recalled, found that the intervention of inspectors positively altered the approach of management representatives in JHSCs.

What then should be the relationship of health and safety inspectors to the internal responsibility system? The predominant view in government has been that inspectors should only intervene when they are satisfied that a joint committee cannot resolve the matter. This has often led to a perception of weak enforcement. Fidler has described the conflicts that arose in Ontario over the role of the inspectors and their complaints that they were directed to defer to the joint committees, long after it was apparent that problems were not being resolved internally (Fidler 1985). In Ontario, concerns with the health and safety inspectorate led to the appointment of a special review (Ontario 1987).

The difficulty in striking a balance between premature and delayed intervention is compounded by two factors. Many governments have seen the internal responsibility system as a means of reducing public expenditures on compliance. The conclusion drawn by critics of the internal responsibility system, namely, that it substitutes for enforcement and waters down compliance, may be well founded in some jurisdictions. Most governments have also assigned to their inspectorate responsibility for supporting the internal responsibility system by acting as mediators and facilitators to joint committees. In labour relations, it has usually been judged important to maintain a clear-cut distinction between the mediation and facilitation role and the adjudication role. Only in consensual proceedings does one find a mediator-arbitrator. In statutorily founded proceedings, the distinction between mediation and arbitration is invariably maintained. The failure to reflect this separation of roles in occupational health and safety was unsound. Indeed, in principle, there is no reason to believe that a technically qualified inspector will have the skills of a mediator or conversely that a mediator will have the technical understanding required to make enforcement decisions. It would be appropriate, therefore, to divide the mediation roles from the enforcement roles.

Limitations of Joint Health and Safety Committees

The research findings reviewed in this chapter have supported, often with qualifications, the adoption of the internal responsibility system. It is important, however, to recognize the limitations that are inherent in the internal responsibility system. Broadly similar internal responsibility systems will have significantly different effects, if the regulatory regimes differ or if there are perverse incentives in the structure of WCB premiums.

A finding that was reiterated in more than one study was the overriding importance of broad labour market and workforce characteristics as determinants of injury rates. These observations echo the points made by Sullivan and Frank, Ostry, and Gunderson and Hyatt in this volume. Other things being equal, a workforce that is older, full-time, and has a low rate of turnover will have a lower injury rate than a workforce that is younger, has a high proportion of workers who are not full-time or not permanent, and has a high turnover. The term "non-standard" characterizes divergences from the pattern of full-time, permanent employment. Betcherman has documented a secular trend toward an increased reliance on non-standard workers by Canadian employers. Total non-standard employment increased from approximately 23.75 percent in 1975 to 29.25 percent in 1993 (Betcherman 1995). The share of non-standard employment tends to increase during economic downturns and to remain at a higher plateau during the subsequent economic expansion. It is likely that, by now, the share of non-standard employment has crossed the 30 percent threshold. The trend toward a greater share of non-standard employment in total employment will increase the risk of occupational injury.

The research findings examined also found a correlation between union-ization and the effectiveness of the internal responsibility system. JHSCs were more likely to be found in unionized workplaces and are more active in those workplaces. Tucker has estimated that over 90 percent of work refusals occur in unionized workplaces (Tucker 1986). We should not be surprised by that fact. Without the protection of a grievance system, few workers will be inclined to exercise their statutory right to refuse to perform unsafe work. Similarly, only a small minority of non-union members of health and safety committees will summon inspectors to rectify persistent non-compliance with standards. While near universal unionization was not a presumption of the internal responsibility system, widespread unionization – at least in high incidence sectors – was an unstated premise of that system. Indeed, trying to understand the system of internal responsibility and the role of the right to refuse without recognizing the central importance of unions is like trying to put on a production of *Hamlet,* but leaving out the ghost.

Trends in unionization have not been favourable to the internal respon-sibility system. Since 1976, unionization in the resource industries has *declined* by 16.7 percent. In the manufacturing sector, unionization has fallen by 22.9 percent (Galarneau 1996: 46, Table 2). Moreover, those segments of manufacturing that have seen growth in both absolute and relative terms – industries such as plastics or electronics – are almost entirely non-unionized. Not simply in relative terms, but in absolute terms, there are fewer unionized workers in manufacturing and resource industries today than there were in 1976. In 1997, according to the *Canadian Labour Force Survey,* two-thirds of workers in the goods-producing industries were not members of a trade union (Statistics Canada 1997). For an increasing number of workers – increasing both absolutely and relatively – the unstated premise of the inter-nal responsibility system, that is, the presence of a union, no longer holds.

The research findings canvassed in this chapter also showed a lower degree of compliance with statutory obligations in the private service sector. In part, this arises from the conventional wisdom that occupational health and safety is a "blue-collar" problem. Joint committees are less common in the private service sector and their capacity is less developed. At the same time, there is increasing recognition that occupational disease arising from stress and from repetitive strain is not confined to the "blue-collar" industries. The joint committee model historically arose in the resource and manufacturing sector. The transfer of this model to the highly unionized public sector was relatively successful. Porting the joint committee model over to the private service sector will prove far more difficult. There is no tradition in the private service sector of joint committees, nor is there a well-developed health and safety culture. To extend the internal responsibility system to the private service sector will require a commitment to enforcement and training that exceeds what is currently typical in most jurisdictions.

A further distinction that arose in some of the studies reviewed was between occupational safety and occupational disease. Safety issues typically involve such matters as workplace procedures, the use of protective clothing or equipment, and installing safety devices on machinery (e.g, shut-off switches, guards, etc.). The internal responsibility system has undoubtedly made a significant contribution in promoting workplace safety, especially when safety issues can be addressed without a significant capital expenditure. Indeed, safety issues lend themselves to problem-solving and to jointly developed solutions. Arguably, safety issues were predominant in the thinking of those who initially framed the system of internal responsibility. While joint workplace committees have had a positive impact on safety, their efficacy in the prevention of industrial disease is another matter altogether. Yet, it is in the prevention of industrial disease that future gains in workplace health must be made. Indeed, in the service sector, stress-related occupational disease is likely to be more important than work-related injuries as a cause of illness and lost time.

The critical importance of industrial disease, whether it arises from repetitive strain, stress, or from prolonged exposure to contaminants, needs no elucidation. Statistics Canada's *General Social Survey* found that among manufacturing sector workers, 34 percent reported that they were exposed to dangerous chemicals or fumes. Fifty-eight percent said they were exposed to dust or fibres in the air they breathed while at work (Grayson 1994: 42). Perhaps in some situations, the remedy can be identified easily and will entail only a small cost. However, those circumstances are likely to be the exception, not the norm. By far the more common situation is one in which there will be lengthy dispute over the workplace contribution to a pathology and a reluctance on the part of an employer to accept the implied liability. Addressing repetitive strain, as noted by Norman and Wells, and Kerr, in this volume, may require a major redesign of jobs and possibly of machinery. Similarly, the elimination of contaminants can involve significant capital expenditures and the re-engineering of production processes.

Preventing industrial disease will entail greater reliance on standard setting and epidemiological research. With each iteration of standards, there will be a need to provide training to the members of joint committees. It should be recalled that, prior to the introduction of core certification training in Ontario, a disturbingly high proportion of worker members and management members of joint committees were not aware of the health and safety implications of designated substances.

Conclusion

Since the 1970s, the internal responsibility system has been the defining feature of workplace health and safety policy in Canada. In adopting the internal responsibility system, governments typically sought to insulate occupational health and safety from the conflict that characterizes labour relations. This approach is profoundly flawed. History, economic logic, and the need to deal with potentially costly changes in plant and equipment all make it inevitable that the internal responsibility system will be characterized as much by conflict as by problem solving. A policy that views conflict as evidence of failure will only lead to disappointment and frustration. Indeed, the mistaken view that conflict should be avoided diverts attention from the real tasks, which are to manage conflict and balance interests. This is the classical view of the function of an industrial relations system. It has served us well. Workplace health and safety policy would be better served by accepting the realism of the classical view.

The evidence from empirical research is that joint health and safety committees can play an important role in improving workplace health and safety. However, there is also broad agreement that joint committees per se do not lead to improved injury performance. The critical factor is the capacity of these committees. Key determiners of capacity are the right of committee members to information and mandatory training of committee members. Equally important are the regulatory environment and the structuring of economic incentives. Internal responsibility is not a substitute for standard setting, nor for enforcement, though the operation of joint committees may reduce the overall reliance on penalties and enforcement orders. Standard setting and regulatory enforcement are particularly important in workplaces where managerial commitment to improved health and safety is lacking.

The future of the internal responsibility system cannot be separated from structural changes in the labour market. Injury rates are lower among full-time, permanent workers. The trends in the labour market, however, are away from full-time, permanent employment as the norm. Similarly, high rates of unionization were an unstated premise of the system of internal responsibility. In much of the economy, however, that premise is invalid. This may point to the need to adapt the European works council model to the Canadian context.

The system of internal responsibility and the concurrent strengthening of regulatory standards brought about a significant reduction in workplace injury rates. Iterations of this model may lead to further improvement. Structural trends in the labour market, however, are unfavourable. The growth of non-standard employment and the decline of unions, especially in the private sector, will weaken the efficacy of the internal responsibility system. Significant future improvements will require institutional innovation, not simply adjustments in policy.

194 *John O'Grady*

Note

1 The act reads as follows:

Sec. 9(18) Powers of committee – It is the function of a committee and it has power to:
(d) obtain information form the constructor or employer respecting,
  (i) the identification of potential or existing hazards of materials, process or equipment, and
  (ii) health and safety experience and work practices and standards in similar or other industries of which the constructor or employer has knowledge;
(e) obtain information from the constructor or employer concerning the conducting or taking of tests of any equipment, machine, device, article, thing, material or biological, chemical or physical agent in or about a workplace for the purpose of occupational health and safety.

As well, the committee is to be consulted on the preparation of a hazardous materials inventory (Sec. 36[2][b]).

References

Advisory Council on Occupational Health and Occupational Safety (ACOHOS). 1986. *An Evaluation of Joint Health and Safety Committees in Ontario.* Eighth annual report, vol. 2. Prepared by SPR Associates. Toronto: Queen's Printer.

Appleton, William, and Joe Baker. 1984. "The Effect of Unionization on Safety in Bituminous Deep Mines." *Journal of Labour Research* 5 (2): 139-47.

Association of Workers' Compensation Boards of Canada (AWCBC). 1998. "Number of Accepted Time-Loss Injuries by Province, 1982-1997." In *Work Injuries and Diseases,* 1. Mississauga, ON: AWCBC.

Atherley, G.R.C., R.T. Booth, and M.J. Kelly. 1976. "Workers' Involvement in Occupational Health and Safety in Britain." *International Labour Review* 111 (6): 469-82.

Bacow, L.S. 1980. *Bargaining for Job Safety and Health.* Cambridge, MA: MIT Press.

Beaumont, P.B., and J.W. Leopold. 1982a. "A Failure of Voluntarism: The Case of Health and Safety Committees in Britain." *New Zealand Journal of Industrial Relations* 7: 61-75.

–. 1982b. "Joint Health and Safety Committees in the United Kingdom: Participation and Effectiveness – a Conflict?" *Economic and Industrial Democracy* 3: 263-84.

Belous, Richard S. 1989. *The Contingent Economy: The Growth of the Temporary, Part-Time, and Sub-Contracted Workforce.* Washington, DC: National Planning Association.

Bernard, Elaine. 1995. "Canada: Joint Committees on Occupational Health and Safety." In *Work Councils: Consultation, Representation, and Cooperation in Industrial Relations,* ed. Joel Rogers and Wolfgang Streeck, 351-74. Chicago: University of Chicago Press.

Betcherman, Gordon. 1995. "Inside the Black Box: Human Resource Management and the Labor Market." In *Good Jobs, Bad Jobs, No Jobs,* ed. Roy J. Adams et al., 70-102. Toronto: C.D. Howe Institute.

Boden, Leslie, et al. 1984. "The Impact of Health and Safety Committees: A Study Based on Survey Interview and Occupational Safety and Health Administration Data." *Journal of Occupational Medicine* 26 (11): 829-34.

Broyles, Robert, Pran Manga, and Gil Reschenthaler. 1981. *Occupational Health and Safety: Issues and Alternatives.* Ottawa: Economic Council of Canada.

Bryce, George, and Pran Manga. 1985. "The Effectiveness of Health and Safety Committees." *Industrial Relations* 40 (2): 245-57.

Burton, John, and James Chelius. 1997. "Workplace Safety and Health Regulation: Rationale and Results." In *Government Regulation of the Employment Relationship,* ed. Bruce Kaufman, 253-93. Madison, WI: Industrial Relations Research Association.

Butler, Richard, and John Worral. 1983. "Health Conditions and Job Hazards: Union and Nonunion Jobs." *Journal of Labor Research* 4 (4): 339-47.

Chew, David. 1988. "Effective Occupational Safety Activities: Findings in Three Asian Developing Countries." *International Labour Review* 127 (1): 111-24.

Codrington, Caroline, and John Henley. 1981. "The Industrial Relations of Injury and Death: Safety Representatives in the Construction Industry." *British Journal of Industrial Relations* 19: 297-315.

Cooke, William, and Frederick Gautschi. 1980. "OSHA, Plant Safety Programs, and Injury Reduction." *Industrial Relations* 20 (1): 245-57.

Coyle, J.R., and J.W. Leopold. 1981. "Health and Safety Committees: How Effective Are They?" *Occupational Safety and Health* 11 (11): 20-2.

De Matteo, Bob. 1991. "Health and Safety Committees: The Canadian Experience." *New Solutions* 1 (4): 11-15.

Denton, Margaret, and Vivienne Walters. 1980. "Workers' Knowledge of Their Legal Rights and Resistance to Hazardous Work." *Industrial Relations* 45 (3): 531-47.

Dickens, William. 1988. "Differences between Risk Premiums in Union and Nonunion Wages and the Case for Occupational Safety Regulation." *American Economic Review* 74 (2): 320-3.

Digby, Caroline, and Craig Riddell. 1985. "Occupational Health and Safety in Canada." In *Labour-Management Cooperation in Canada,* ed. Craig Riddell, 285-319. Toronto: University of Toronto Press; Royal Commission on the Economic Union and Development Prospects for Canada; Canadian Government Publishing Centre, Supply and Services.

Doern, G. Bruce. 1977. "The Political Economy of Regulating Occupational Health: The Ham and Beaudry Reports." *Canadian Public Administration* 20: 1-35.

Drache, Daniel, and Harry Glasbeek. 1992. *The Changing Workplace: Reshaping Canada's Industrial Relations System.* Toronto: James Lorimer.

Fairris, David. 1992. "Compensating Payments and Hazardous Work in Union and Nonunion Settings." *Journal of Labor Research* 13 (2): 205-21.

–. 1995. "Do Unionized Employers Reappropriate Rent through Worsened Workplace Safety?" *Eastern Economic Journal* 21 (2): 171-85.

–. 1998. "Institutional Change in Shopfloor Governance and the Trajectory of Postwar Injury Rates in US Manufacturing 1946-1970." *Industrial and Labor Relations Review* 51 (2): 187-201.

Fidler, Richard. 1985. "The Occupational Health and Safety Act and the Internal Responsibility System." *Osgoode Hall Law Journal* 24 (2): 314-52.

Frayn, C., and R. Shaughnessy. 1986. "Process and Structure." In *Conflict or Consensus and the Joint Health and Safety Committee: Conference Proceedings,* ed. Industrial Accident Prevention Association and Ontario Federation of Labour. Toronto.

Fuess, S. 1991. "The Impact of Safety and Health Legislation on 'Union Effectiveness.'" *Eastern Economic Journal* 27 (4): 417-23.

Galarneau, Diane. 1996. "Unionized Workers." *Perspectives on Labour and Income* 8 (1): 43-52. Statistics Canada 75-001.

Gersuny, C. 1991. *Work Hazards and Industrial Conflict.* Hanover, NH: University Press of New England.

Gevers, J.K.M. 1983. "Worker Participation in Health and Safety in the EEC: The Role of Representative Institutions." *International Labour Review* 122 (4): 411-28.

–. 1985. "Worker Control over Occupational Health Services: The Development of Legal Rights in the EEC." *International Journal of Health Services* 15 (2): 217-29.

Grayson, J. Paul. 1994. "Perceptions of Workplace Hazards." *Perspectives on Labour and Income* 4 (1): 41-7. Statistics Canada 75-001.

Havlovic, Stephen. 1991. "Safety Committees and Safety Education in Reducing Risk of Death: The Experience of the British Columbia Logging Industry (1940-1989)." In *Proceedings of the 28th Conference of the Canadian Industrial Relations Associations,* ed. D. Carth, 403-7. Kingston, ON: IRC Press.

Hebdon, Robert, and Douglas Hyatt. 1996. "The Impact of Industrial Relations Factors on Health and Safety Conflict under the Internal Responsibility System." Unpublished essay.

Hugentobler, Margrit, Thomas Robins, and Susan Schurman. 1990. "How Unions Can Improve the Outcomes of Joint Health and Safety Training Programs." *Labor Studies Journal* 15 (4): 16-38.

Kaufman, Bruce. 1993. *The Origins and Evolution of the Field of Industrial Relations in the United States.* Ithaca, NY: ILR Press; Cornell University Press.

Kochan, Thomas, Lee Dyer, and David Lipsky. 1977. *The Effectiveness of Union-Management Safety and Health Committees.* Kalamazoo: W.E. Upjohn Institute for Employment Research.

Lévesque, Christian. 1995. "State Intervention in Occupational Health and Safety: Labour-Management Committees Revisited." In *Proceedings of the XXXIst Conference of the Canadian Industrial Relations Association,* ed. A. Giles, A. Smith, and K. Wetzel, 217-31. Toronto: CIRA.

Lewchuk, Wayne, A. Leslie Robb, and Vivienne Walters. 1996. "The Effectiveness of Bill 70 and Joint Health and Safety Committees in Reducing Injuries in the Workplace: The Case of Ontario." *Canadian Public Policy* 23 (3): 225-43.

Lewis, David. 1974. "Worker Participation in Safety: An Industrial Relations Approach." *Industrial Law Journal* 3: 96-104.

Marshall, Ray. 1997. "The Role of Management and Competitive Strategies in Occupational Safety and Health Standards." In *Government Regulation of the Employment Relationship,* ed. Bruce Kaufman, 253-93. Madison, WI: Industrial Relations Research Association.

Moser, Cindy. 1991. "Committees Score High – the Results Are in: Joint Committees Are Playing an Important Role in the Protection of Worker Health and Safety." *OH&S Canada* 7 (4): 62, 315.

Nichols, Theo. 1991. "Labour Intensification, Work Injuries, and the Measurement of Percentage Utilization of Labour (PUL)." *British Journal of Industrial Relations* 29 (4): 569-91.

Ontario. 1976. *Report of the Royal Commission on the Health and Safety of Workers in Mines* [Ham Commission]. Toronto: Queen's Printer.

–. 1981. *Towards Safe Production: Report of the Joint Federal-Provincial Inquiry Commission into Safety of Mines and Mining Plants in Ontario.* K.M. Burkett, chair. 2 vols. Toronto: Queen's Printer.

–. 1984. *Report of the Royal Commission on Matters of Health and Safety Arising from the Use of Asbestos in Ontario* [Dupré Commission]. Toronto: Queen's Printer.

–. 1987. *Report on the Administration of the Occupational Health and Safety Act.* Toronto: Ontario Ministry of Labour.

Ontario Ministry of Labour. 1991. *A Guide to the Occupational Health and Safety Act.* Toronto: Queen's Printer.

Parsons, Michael. 1988. "Worker Participation in Occupational Health and Safety: Lessons from the Canadian Experience." *Labor Studies Journal* 13 (4): 22-32.

Pragnell, Bradley. 1994. *Occupational and Health Committees in NSW: An Analysis for the AWIRS Data.* Sydney: Australian Centre for Industrial Relations Research and Teaching.

Reilly, Barry, Pierella Paci, and Peter Holl. 1995. "Unions, Safety Committees, and Workplace Injuries." *British Journal of Industrial Relations* 33 (2): 275-88.

Reschenthaler, G.B. 1979. *Occupational Health and Safety in Canada: The Economics and Three Case Studies.* Montreal: Institute for Research on Public Policy.

Robinson, James. 1988. "Workplace Hazards and Workers' Desires for Union Representation." *Journal of Labor Research* 9 (3): 237-49.

Rodgers, G., and J. Rodgers, eds. 1989. *Precarious Jobs in Labour Market Regulation: The Growth of Atypical Employment in Western Europe.* Geneva: International Labour Organisation (International Institute for Labour Studies).

Saari, J., S. Bédard, V. Dufort, J. Hryniewcki, and G. Thériault. 1993. "How Companies Respond to New Safety Regulations: A Canadian Investigation." *International Labour Review* 132 (1): 65-75.

Sass, Robert. 1986. "Workplace Health and Safety: Report from Canada." *International Journal of Health Services* 16 (4): 565-82.

Schurman, Susan J., David Weil, Paul Landsbergis, and Barbara Israel. 1998. "The Role of Unions and Collective Bargaining in Preventing Work-Related Disability." In *New Approaches to Disability in the Workplace,* ed. Terry Thomason, John F. Burton, and Douglas E. Hyatt, 121-54. Industrial Relations Research Association Series. Madison, WI: Industrial Relations Research Association.

Shannon, Harry, et al. 1992. *Health and Safety Approaches in the Workplace: A Report Prepared by the Interdisciplinary Health and Safety Research Group of McMaster University in Hamilton, Ontario.* Toronto: Industrial Accident Prevention Association (IAPA).

Simard, Marcel, and Carolyn Tuohy. 1993. *The Impact of Joint Health and Safety Committees in Ontario and Quebec.* Toronto: Canadian Association of Administrators of Labour Law.

Smith, Robert S. 1992. "Have OHSA and Workers' Compensation Made the *Workplace Safer?*" In *Research Frontiers in Industrial Relations and Human Resources,* ed. D. Lewin, O. Mitchell, and P. Sherer, 527-86. Madison, WI: Industrial Relations Research Association.

SPR Associates Incorporated (SPR). 1994. *Highlights of the 1994 Ontario Survey of Occupational Health and Safety and Joint Health and Safety Committees.* Toronto: SPR Associates and Workplace Health and Safety Agency.

SPR Associates Incorporated/National Mail Surveys Incorporated. 1986. "An Evaluation of Joint Health and Safety Committees in Ontario: As Based on Mail Surveys of Worker and Management Members to Joint Health and Safety Committees in Over 3,000 Industrial, Mining, Educational, and Health Workplaces." In *Government of Ontario, Advisory Council on Occupational Health and Occupational Safety, Eighth Annual Report* [1 April 1985-31 March 1986]. Vol. 2. Toronto: Queen's Printer.

Statistics Canada. 1997. *Canadian Labour Survey.* Ottawa: Statistics Canada

Swinton, Katherine. 1983. "Enforcement of Occupational Health and Safety Legislation: The Role of the Internal Responsibility System." In *Studies in Labour Law,* ed. Ken Swan and Katherine Swinton, 145-60. Toronto: Butterworths.

Taylor, D.H., and Waldie, K.G. 1994. *Bipartism: The Case of Health and Safety in Ontario.* Kingston: IRC Press.

Tucker, Eric. 1986. "The Persistence of Market Regulation of Occupational Health and Safety: The Stillbirth of Voluntarism." In *Essays in Labour Law,* ed. G. England, 219-62. Don Mills, ON: CCH Canadian.

–. 1992. "Worker Participation in Health and Safety Regulation: Lessons from Sweden." *Studies in Political Economy* 37: 95-127.

Tuohy, Carolyn. 1984. *Decision Trees and Political Thickets: An Approach to Analysing Regulatory Decision-Making in the Occupational Health Arena.* Toronto: University of Toronto Press.

–. 1990. "Institutions and Interests in the Occupational Health Arena: The Case of Quebec." In *Policy Communities and Public Policy in Canada,* ed. William Coleman and Grace Skogstad, 239-65. Toronto: Copp Clark Pitman.

—. 1995. *Ministerial Review of the Workplace Health and Safety Agency.* Toronto: Ministry of Labour.

Tuohy, Carolyn, and Marcel Simard. 1993. *The Impact of Joint Health and Safety Committees in Ontario and Quebec: A Study Prepared for the Canadian Association of Administrators of Labour Law.* Toronto: Available from the authors.

Walters, Vivienne. 1983. "Occupational Health and Safety Legislation in Ontario: An Analysis of Its Origins and Content." *Canadian Review of Sociology and Anthropology* 20 (4): 413-34.

–. 1985. "The Politics of Occupational Health and Safety: Interviews with Workers' Health and Safety Representatives and Company Doctors." *Canadian Review of Sociology and Anthropology* 22 (1): 57-79.

Walters, Vivienne, and Margaret Denton. 1990. "Workers' Knowledge of Their Legal Rights and Resistance to Hazardous Work." *Industrial Relations* 45 (3): 531-47.

Walton, Richard E., and Robert B. McKersie. 1993. *A Behavioral Theory of Labor Negotiations.* Ithaca, NY: ILR Press. [Originally published in 1965.]

Weil, David. 1992. "Building Safety: The Role of Construction Unions in the Enforcement of OSHA." *Journal of Labour Research* 13 (1): 121-32.

Weiler, Paul. 1977. "The Virtues of Federalism in Canadian Labour Law." In *The Direction of Labour Policy in Canada,* ed. F. Bairstow, 58-72. Montreal: McGill University Industrial Relations Committee.

–. 1980. *Reconcilable Differences: New Directions in Canadian Labour Law.* Toronto: Carswell.

Workplace Health and Safety Agency (WHSA). 1994. *The Impact of Joint Health and Safety Committees on Health and Safety Trends in Ontario.* Toronto: WHSA.

–. 1995. *Accomplishments of the Workplace Health and Safety Agency (WHSA) (January 1991-June 1995).* Toronto: WHSA.

Part 4: Rehabilitation and Return to Work

Given the dramatic rise in soft tissue injury and work-related musculo-skeletal conditions, Hogg-Johnson et al. take on the task of defining effective treatment interventions for the broad categories of lower back and upper extremity problems in a review of the most recent evidence. Their analysis compels us to think about the recovery stage from soft tissue injuries as a three-phase process: acute, sub-acute, and chronic. Limited interventions in the acute phase appear to yield dramatic response with respect to health outcomes, functional improvements, and return to work. In the sub-acute phase, a number of intervention factors that are associated with reducing disability from major soft tissue injury are reviewed. It may well be that what we understand now from careful outcome study is more about what does not work. Nevertheless, this may help to avoid some of the issues associated with doctor-induced disability (iatrogenesis). Hogg-Johnson et al.'s review promotes the notion of getting all of the key actors onside: the employer, the employee, the insurer, and the clinician.

Picking up on this third phase of recovery from soft tissue injury, that is, the phase beyond about twelve weeks when conditions begin taking on a more chronic nature, Tunks, Crook, and Crook review the natural history and the effectiveness of specific treatment remedies for chronic pain. This area has taken on topical significance in Canada, with the development of a number of regulatory attempts to limit entitlement for treatment and benefits associated with chronic musculoskeletal pain. Tunks, Crook, and Crook carefully review what is known about the natural history of these chronic conditions, including a range of risk factors and prognostic factors that may be important points for primary and secondary interventions.

Brooker et al. take on the definition of effective disability management and return-to-work practices for work-related musculoskeletal injury conditions. They highlight what is known from studies of low back pain and the relative contribution of clinical and workplace interventions in promoting early and safe return to work. In particular, they focus on the importance of supportive workplace policies; constructive cooperation among the worker, the health care professional, and the worker representative in the workplace; offers of modified work; and overall evaluation of return-to-work programs. Brooker et al. also highlight the challenge of return-to-work programs for the smaller firms that represent a large part of the workforce. Drawing from recent empirical work, Brooker et al. note that fewer than one-third of small firms typically had arrangements designed to help injured workers return to work, whereas almost half of those with 1,000 or more employees had some form of assistance available to encourage safe and early return to work. Like many others, Brooker et al. conclude by calling for a dual-tier approach, with special programs for smaller firms (including management education) to get across the real financial and workforce benefits of modified work and early return-to-work programs.

9
Staging Treatment Interventions following Soft Tissue Injuries

Sheilah Hogg-Johnson, Donald Cole, Pierre Côté, and John Frank

Low back, neck, and arm pain are among the most common causes of disability and handicap in industrialized countries. Taken together, they represent the majority of compensable injuries in Canada and the largest burden of cost and suffering (NWISP 1997). Although they are poorly understood, they are most often changes in soft tissues (i.e., muscles, tendons, ligaments, joints, and nerves in contrast to fractures or other bony disorders). When linked to work, they are often termed work-related musculoskeletal disorders (WMSDs), although application of this term is often limited to non-traumatic neck and arm disorders. In the last two decades, we have witnessed remarkable changes in the suggested approaches to treatment and work rehabilitation of those with soft tissue disorders, based on slowly accumulating evidence that issues of timing, site, and type of interventions are crucial.

This chapter aims to describe these approaches. We start with clarification of the nature and burden to society of these disorders followed by a description of their usual course over time, both clinically and administratively. We support the staged approach to assessment and treatment, sharing the best, most relevant evidence available. Finally, we set out several important ongoing issues and suggest some avenues for responding to them.

Nature and Burden of Soft Tissue Injuries

Evidence suggests that between 50 and 80 percent of the population in industrialized countries will experience back pain during their lifetime (Frank et al. 1996a). *Occupational* back pain is low back pain either "caused" by work or exacerbated by work (Frank et al. 1996b). It may result from a traumatic incident such as a fall or a blow, or from repetitive or continuous exposure to physically heavy work, whole-body vibration, bending and twisting, or static sedentary posture (NIOSH 1997; Punnett et al. 1991; Kerr 1997). As Kerr notes in this volume, there is growing evidence that psychosocial stressors at work also play a role (Houtman et al. 1994; Bongers et al. 1993; NIOSH 1997; Frank et al. 1996a; Kerr 1997) in both the development and the recovery from back pain. Cases of back pain typically constitute the largest single category of time loss claims to workers' compensation boards in North America. Approximately 30 percent of all time loss claims are for back injuries (NCCI 1993; AWCBC 1997) and the majority of back claims are for sprains and strains.

WMSDs of the upper extremity are a multifaceted group of disorders affecting soft tissue structures extending from the neck to the hand that are "caused" by or aggravated by work. This group of disorders includes the conditions commonly referred to as "repetitive strain injuries" (RSI) or "cumulative trauma disorders." They can be non-specific in nature and present as pain, swelling, and discomfort, or be specific pathologies such as carpal tunnel syndrome and epicondylitis. Statistics on the overall incidence of WMSDs of the upper extremity vary greatly from source to source, due to large variations in how these types of injuries are labelled, classified, and identified (Beaton 1995). But regardless of how WMSDs of the upper extremity are identified, most sources agree that the incidence rate is increasing (Jolley 1995; Bonzani et al. 1997). High incidence and prevalence of WMSDs of the upper limb has been found in particular occupational groups and associated with highly repetitive work involving continuous movements and forceful exertion of the arm or hand. In addition, psychosocial factors such as workplace stress (NIOSH 1997) are associated with WMSDs.

Occupational neck pain is common in the working-age population (Côté and Cassidy 1997). As for WMSDs of the upper extremity, these probably result from a combination of work-related physical and psychosocial factors. Because little is known about the rehabilitation of occupational neck pain, we borrow information from another type of commonly compensated neck pain: whiplash-associated disorders (WADs). Although WADs typically result from traffic collisions, they share common characteristics with work-related soft tissue injuries, and so they will be discussed here.

Course of WMSD Disorders
Clinical course refers to the course of a disorder from diagnosis to recovery (Cole and Beaton 1997) as observed by a clinician. However, when claims for disability are the primary focus of interest, we are concerned with the "administrative course," often represented by the length of time one receives wage-replacement benefits from an insurer. For injuries associated with workers' compensation, the starting point refers to the reported accident date. There are striking similarities in the administrative course of back pain claims, upper extremity WMSD claims, and WAD claims. Figure 9.1 shows the percentage of claimants still receiving benefits at particular points in time post-accident date for low back sprain/strain claimants to the Ontario Workplace Safety Insurance Board[1] (WSIB), upper extremity WMSD

claimants to the Ontario WSIB (1992), and WAD claimants to the Société d'assurance automobile du Québec (SAAQ).[2] All three curves are characterized by a very steep descent at the beginning of the coverage period, suggesting that for many people prognosis is good and the injury resolves quickly. Typically, the majority of claims costs for soft tissue injury claims are incurred by the small proportion of the claimants with prolonged disability, that is, those who do not recover in the first few weeks (Hashemi et al. 1997; Spitzer et al. 1995; Abenhaim and Suissa 1987). Variations in the curve may be found in different jurisdictions. For example, the whiplash data presented in Figure 9.1 come from a province with no-fault, single payer auto insurance, and we suspect that a tort system or a no-fault system with different administrative rules and benefits would lead to different curves. Also, particular subsets of injuries such as carpal tunnel syndrome (Cheadle et al. 1994) may lead to differences also – although the basic shape generally remains similar.

Figure 9.1

Time on benefits: Comparing low back, whiplash, and upper extremity WMSD claimants

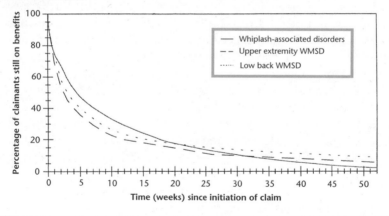

Sources: Hogg-Johnson et al. (1994); Spitzer et al. (1995); Beaton (1995).

When appraising the administrative course of a condition, it is important to remember that the accident date may have different meanings for different claimants. For those experiencing a traumatic event, such as a motor vehicle accident or a fall, the accident date represents the actual date of the incident. However, for repetitive strain injuries to the back, neck, or upper limb, the accident date does not necessarily correspond to the appearance of symptoms, but rather to the date when the worker was no longer able to cope with work as a result of the injury. For instance, a study of RSI claimants to the Manitoba WCB showed that claims were filed on average eight months after symptom onset (Yassi et al. 1996). And in a study of primary care shoulder complaints in the Netherlands, 49 percent of participants had been experiencing symptoms for over one month prior to their first doctor visit (van der Windt 1997). Also, in a recent Institute for Work and Health study of newspaper workers, only a small subset of workers with pain and symptoms reported those symptoms to the workplace or filed a claim (Polanyi et al. 1997). Therefore, the onset of the administrative course may occur at different points in the clinical course of the disorder, which implies that therapeutic interventions may be more appropriately based on clinical course rather than administrative course of a condition.

Phasing and Staging

It is useful to consider three stages of recovery, using time since onset as depicted in Figure 9.2. These stages were introduced for occupational low back pain (for which most of the research on soft tissue injuries has been carried out) by Frank et al. (1996b) who were building upon the work of the Quebec Task Force on Spinal Disorders (Spitzer et al. 1987). Stage 1, the acute stage, extends from symptom onset up to three or four weeks later. Importantly, it is during this stage that the steepest decline in the duration curve occurs. The percentage of cases recovering during this stage depends on the setting of interest. In a primary care setting (where cases include a range of symptom severity and claimant status), approximately 90 percent of cases will recover in the first four weeks (Coste et al. 1994; Bigos et al. 1994). In a workers' compensation setting, however, approximately 50 to 60 percent of claimants will be on wage replacement benefits for four weeks or less. These differences may be explained by differences in severity of symptoms or in duration of symptoms. Evidence suggests back pain sufferers who file time loss claims and miss time from work are experiencing more severe symptoms (Hogg-Johnson et al. 1997; Smith et al. 1997) than non-claimants. Therefore, they may take longer to recover than someone visiting the doctor for the first time, with milder symptoms. Furthermore, they may be more reticent to return to an injury-provoking job. Regardless of setting, the course of these conditions is favourable, with the majority recovering in Stage 1. The second stage – the sub-acute stage – lasts from about three or four weeks up to about twelve weeks after symptom onset. During Stage 2, the likelihood of recovery goes down considerably. After twelve weeks, many experts suggest that early chronic pain syndrome has set in (Frank et al. 1996b). In this third stage, the recovery curve is very flat indicating that for those with unresolved problems, very few recover. The percentage of claimants remaining on benefits at one year post-accident varies from 5 to 10 percent depending on the jurisdiction of interest (Hogg-Johnson et al. 1994; Cheadle et al. 1994; Abenhaim and Suissa 1987).

For whiplash-associated disorders, the Quebec task force (Spitzer et al.

Figure 9.2

Three stages of soft tissue injury: Low back pain

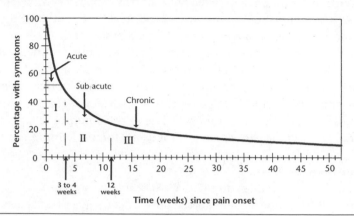

Source: Frank et al. (1996b).

1995) provided a grading system based on initial clinical findings (pain, symptoms, range of motion, point tenderness, neurological signs, X-ray findings) rather than staging alone. Grade I WAD applies to a case where there is pain, stiffness, or tenderness but no physical signs. If there are musculoskeletal signs (decreased range of motion and point tenderness), then the WAD is grade II. Grade III WAD is appropriate when neurological signs and symptoms are present. Grade IV WAD, where the injury involves a fracture or dislocation, is not considered further here. The task force's guidelines for care are based on both WAD grade and key time points since onset (i.e., stage). Here again, the interval between three and twelve weeks post-onset represents the critical time to prevent chronicity.

As for back pain and WAD, the course of many upper extremity conditions is often acute and self-limiting (Kaplan et al. 1990; van der Windt 1997; Beaton 1995; Himmelstein et al. 1995). The relevant stages for upper extremity disorders are more difficult to ascertain, partly due to the wide variation in duration of symptoms at the time of clinical presentation (Kaplan et al. 1990; van der Windt 1997; Himmelstein et al. 1995). Staging initially proposed in Australia for RSI (Browne et al. 1984) has not been widely adopted. Different disorders have varying relevant time courses: two and six weeks for wrist tendinitis (AAOS 1998) to weeks to months for lateral epicondylitis (Gerberich and Priest 1985). For shoulder disorders treated by Dutch primary care practitioners, rates of recovery by one and three months varied from a high of 38 percent and 67 percent for acute bursitis, through 20 percent and 38 percent for rotator cuff tendinitis, to a low of 8 percent and 32 percent for chronic bursitis (van der Windt 1997).

Such reports of clinical studies use similar time points as in low back pain and neck studies. In a case series of neck and arm pain in office workers, Patkin (1991) found that the majority (75 percent) of those with less than one month of symptoms recovered but that this dropped considerably for those with symptoms of two months duration (50 percent) and three to twelve months of symptoms (29 percent). In a case series of patients presenting to a clinic specializing in work-related upper extremity disorders, rates of return to work for those with symptoms of less than six months' duration (70 percent) were substantially higher than those with symptoms of greater than six months' duration (41 percent) (Himmelstein et al. 1995). Hence, current evidence suggests that for broad descriptive purposes, one-month and three-month time periods may also be useful for the definition of stages.

Interventions by Stage

Because of the favourable course of WMSDs, it is important to review the scientific evidence on treatment based on the stages described above. Here we focus on the stage (when?), the site (where?), and the nature of the intervention (what?). Based on the typical administrative history, a sensible case-management objective for soft tissue claims could be to prevent long-term disability by providing appropriate care and interventions while avoiding overtreatment of those cases most likely to recover quickly. Overtreatment in the early stages of WMSDs can lead to iatrogenesis, that is, further problems and complications caused by a physician's treatment (Frank et al. 1996b, 1997). There are still many gaps in the current scientific evidence so our summary includes evidence available to date. Various efforts have been undertaken to produce systematic algorithms for managed care (AAOS 1998; Wiesel et al. 1994). But the relationship between these decision rules and the scientific evidence is not always transparent. Note that "insufficient evidence" does not mean there is evidence against a particular intervention; it does mean there have been insufficient studies of high quality to determine whether a particular intervention is useful or not. Unfortunately, this is true for the majority of health care interventions (Goldberg and McGough 1991).

Back Sprains/Strains: The Acute Stage

An extensive review of the available evidence for medically prescribed treatment for acute low back pain was released by the Agency for Health Care Policy Research (AHCPR) in December 1994 (Bigos et al. 1994). The panel focused on studies with patient-oriented clinical outcome measures (i.e., symptom relief and improved functioning). Despite an extensive literature search that yielded approximately 4,000 articles for critical review, the panel found very few studies meeting high scientific standards. However, the panel did provide recommendations for the clinical care of acute low back pain, based on scientific evidence available and the panel's clinical experience. The AHCPR guidelines suggested that in the absence of red flags for serious underlying conditions, diagnostic tests are rarely necessary (e.g., X-ray, MRI) and that the best approach in the first four weeks is reassurance, promotion of activity (such as return to regular activities including work as soon as possible), use of over-the-counter medication, and spinal manipulation for pain relief. Although early return to work is recommended, the AHCPR guidelines acknowledge that "specific activities known to increase mechanical stress on the spine, especially prolonged unsupported sitting, heavy lifting, and bending or twisting the back while lifting" (Bigos et al. 1994: 50) should be avoided initially and that modified work may be appropriate. Also, for employed patients, health care providers need to "consider the patient's age and general health, and the physical demands of required job tasks" (ibid.: 50).

Since the release of the guidelines, a number of scientific studies on interventions for back pain have been published. The studies underwent critical appraisal (WCB 1997) with attention given to methodological quality, applicability to Canadian compensation settings, effect of treatment on return-to-work outcomes, and the nature and timing of the intervention. The evidence to date is reviewed below for four types of intervention in the acute stage of low back pain. These four categories represent the more common treatments that are paid for by workers' compensation boards and have an existing body of useful evidence concerning their effectiveness.

With regard to physiotherapy and exercise, the AHCPR panel did not evaluate the evidence on physiotherapy as a whole, but summarized evidence regarding therapeutic modalities used by physiotherapists such as physical agents and modalities (ice, heat, massage, ultrasound, electrical stimulation), transcutaneous electrical nerve stimulation (TENS), exercise, and manipulation. The panel concluded there was insufficient evidence to support the use of physical agents and modalities or TENS in a clinical setting. Nevertheless, the panel acknowledged that some patients with acute low back pain obtain symptom relief with physical agents and modalities and therefore they recommended application of heat and cold at home.

Since the release of the guidelines, several high-quality studies (Sinclair et al. 1997; Malmivaara et al. 1995; Faas 1996; Faas et al. 1995) of physiotherapy and supervised exercise programs in the acute stage of injury showed no benefit in terms of time until return to work, pain levels, or functional status.

In the domain of spinal manipulation and chiropractic care, the AHCPR panel concluded that the evidence supports the use of spinal manipulation to reduce pain and improve functioning within the first month of symptoms. Spinal manipulation is performed by chiropractors, physiotherapists, and some primary care physicians. Since the release of the guidelines, further evidence suggests spinal manipulation relieves pain and symptoms during the acute stage of low back pain (Shekelle et al. 1992; Koes et al. 1996). However, as far as returning workers more rapidly to work, the evidence is mixed. A systematic review (van der Weide et al. 1997) suggests there is moderate evidence of a short-term positive effect on vocational outcomes of spinal manipulation over other conservative treatments such as activation physiotherapy.

Chiropractors are the main providers of spinal manipulation in North America. However, chiropractic care can entail other elements such as physical modalities and exercise programs. Some recent studies have investigated chiropractic care as a whole rather than spinal manipulation as a single element of care. One recent study (Carey et al. 1995), which included both claimants and non-claimants, suggests that chiropractic care does not lead to more rapid functional recovery but costs more than care provided by primary care physicians and orthopaedic surgeons. However, the patients receiving chiropractic care tended to be more satisfied with their care than patients receiving other types of care (Carey et al. 1995). On the other hand, another recent study of workers' compensation claimants in California showed shorter durations of work absence for those claimants receiving chiropractic care as opposed to physician care (Johnson and Baldwin, forthcoming). However, the reduced costs for wage-replacement benefits were "more than offset by higher health care costs" (ibid.) associated with chiropractic care.

Educational interventions were the subject of two structured reviews (van der Weide et al. 1997; Cohen et al. 1994). An examination of back schools or group education interventions found mixed results and insufficient details on the content of the programs to allow meaningful comparisons of results. Both reviews concluded there is insufficient evidence to determine the efficacy of these interventions within three months of pain and symptom onset with respect to time away from work. (A slightly different perspective on educational studies is presented in the chapter by Norman and Wells in this volume.)

The AHCPR panel (Bigos et al. 1994) concluded that "relief of discomfort can be accomplished most safely with nonprescription medication (nonsteroidal anti-inflammatory drugs (NSAIDs) or acetaminophen) and/or spinal manipulation." The panel also concluded that muscle relaxants and opioid analgesics could be used, but with caution since they may lead to side effects or complications. Currently, reviews comparing NSAIDs and muscle relaxants for the treatment of acute low back pain are under way.

In a recent study, a multidisciplinary workplace early intervention program for nurses with compensable back injuries was evaluated at a Manitoba teaching hospital (Cooper et al. 1996; Yassi et al. 1995). The intervention started immediately after injury and included assessment and treatment by a physiotherapist under the guidance of a physiatrist, occupational therapy for those still off work after four days of lost time, and modified work for up to seven weeks. Compared to a control group of nurses, the intervention resulted in a decrease of compensable time loss back claims in the study group and a decrease in amount of time lost and WCB costs. It also led to reductions in pain and functional disability (Cooper et al. 1996).

Back Sprains/Strains: The Sub-Acute Stage

We can expand upon the AHCPR work (Bigos et al. 1994), not only by adding more recent studies (Frank et al. 1997), but also by considering interventions provided in the sub-acute stage, and interventions offered outside of a clinical setting (WCB 1997). Two recent studies of high quality show promising results.

A graded activity program at a Swedish automobile manufacturer, provided to blue-collar workers who had been on sick-leave for eight weeks due to low back pain, was evaluated using rigorous methods (Lindstrom et al. 1992). The program did not involve any ergonomic changes to the workplace but did include an evaluation of functional capacity, a workplace visit to assess workplace demands, back school for education about back problems, and a graduated exercise program geared to the work demands of the individual workers. Workers who received the graded activity program had at least 30 percent less sick-leave in both the first and second year of the study.

A second study, conducted in Quebec (Loisel et al. 1997; Loisel, Durand, Abenhaim, et al. 1994), involved thirty-one workplaces in one city. The intervention was targeted at workers who were absent from work due to low back pain for six weeks. There were two components to the intervention. One component, the "occupational" intervention consisted of a visit to an occupational physician for direction to appropriate care and a participatory ergonomics evaluation involving an ergonomist, the worker, the supervisor, and both management and union representatives. From the ergonomics evaluation, "precise solutions to improve the worksite were submitted to the employer," that is, permanent solutions to change the work situation. The "clinical" component started after eight weeks of work absence. It involved a visit to a back pain specialist, back school, and for workers still off work at twelve weeks, a multidisciplinary work rehabilitation intervention. The intervention led to a 50 percent reduction in duration of absence, and most of the reduction was attributed to the occupational component of the intervention (although the sample size in the study was probably insufficient to allow a proper evaluation of the clinical component).

Although the nature of the interventions in these "sub-acute" studies was quite different, their approaches to the management of low back pain, emphasizing contact and cooperation with the workplace, both demonstrated positive effects on return-to-work rates.

Whiplash-Associated Disorders: Acute and Sub-Acute Stages

The Quebec Task Force on Whiplash-Associated Disorders (Spitzer et al. 1995) summarized the evidence available on the effectiveness of interventions for WAD. As for the AHCPR panel on acute low back pain, the Quebec task force found very few studies that met basic scientific criteria for quality. It concluded there was a lack of evidence available for many of the therapeutic interventions commonly used to treat WAD, including cervical pillows, acupuncture, TENS, electrical stimulation, heat, ice, and massage. Also, there was evidence to suggest that some therapies are not helpful, including soft cervical collars, rest, corticosteroid injections, and pulsed electromagnetic treatment. On the other hand, there was evidence that the promotion of activity, mobilization, manipulation, and exercises in conjunction with analgesics or non-steroidal anti-inflammatory medications are effective in the short term. Studies published since the release of the Quebec task force report largely support these findings (Hurwitz et al. 1996; Borchgrevink et al. 1998; Shekelle and Coulter 1997).

In the end, the Quebec task force recommended an immediate return to usual activities for patients with grade I WAD and return to usual activities as soon as possible for grades II and III WAD. They suggested that arrangements for modified work may be appropriate for grade II and III WAD, but they should be used only on a short-term basis. Symptoms persistent beyond seven days for grade I WAD and three weeks for grades II and III WAD call for reassessment. A specialist referral is warranted if a patient has not recovered after three weeks for grade I and six weeks for grades II and III. Finally, a multidisciplinary team evaluation is recommended after six weeks for grade 1 and twelve weeks for grades II and III.

Upper Extremity Acute and Sub-Acute Stages

Guideline development on the care and management of WMSDs of the upper extremity has been less systematic than for other conditions. Several guidelines are not published (e.g., Oregon state guidelines for carpal tunnel syndrome [Ross 1995]) and some are in languages other than English (e.g., guidelines issued by the Dutch College of General Practitioners as described by van der Windt [1997]). The reasons for the lack of guidelines to date, as suggested by Cole and Beaton (1997), are the multiplicity of conditions included in "upper extremity WMSD," and the even greater dearth of rigorous scientific evidence on the management of these conditions.

However, some guidelines for primary care physicians are currently being developed by the American Academy of Orthopaedic Surgeons (AAOS) Task Force on Clinical Algorithms (AAOS 1998). At the 1998 annual meeting of the AAOS, drafts of the management algorithms covering the first twelve weeks of symptoms (corresponding to the acute and sub-acute stages from Figure 9.2) were circulated for wrist pain and shoulder pain. The algorithms were formulated using a combination of scientific evidence and consensus opinion among clinical experts.

In the acute stage of wrist pain, the AAOS task force recommends ruling out serious underlying conditions (e.g., fracture, dislocation, infection, tumour). They recommend a two- to six-week course of therapy involving activity modification (including no repetitive tasks, limited exposure to vibration, avoiding extreme wrist positions), splinting, and NSAIDs. If there is little or no response after the initial course of therapy, the algorithm recommends further activity modification, rest, injection, aspiration, or possible referral to a specialist.

For shoulder pain, after ruling out serious underlying conditions (possibly using imaging), the AAOS algorithms recommend activity modification, NSAIDs, and range-of-motion exercises. No timelines for the length of this course of treatment have been provided. A similar message is provided by guidelines issued by the Dutch College of General Practitioners, as summarized by van der Windt (1997). They suggest NSAIDs and rest for some shoulder conditions, and NSAIDs and mobilization, exercise therapy, or physiotherapy for other shoulder conditions.

Sheon and colleagues provided a practical strategy to physicians for the management of repetitive strain injuries (Sheon 1997). The suggested approach has many parallels with the messages of the AHCPR guidelines for acute low back pain, the recommendations of the Quebec Task Force on Whiplash-Associated Disorders and the algorithms set out by the AAOS Task Force on Clinical Algorithms. The authors recommend: ensuring there is no serious underlying condition; identifying and eliminating aggravating factors; reassuring the patient about the essentially benign cause and course of the disorder; instructing the patient in self-help strategies such as heat, massage, and exercises; providing pain relief, preferably with simple measures.

However, some evidence exists that claimants with RSI often delay filing a claim for their pain and symptoms (Yassi et al. 1996), and so they may be farther along in the clinical course of the condition at the start of a time loss claim (i.e., they may already be sub-acute or chronic cases). Given that RSI claimants are less likely than non-RSI claimants to return to the same job (Yassi et al. 1996), Yassi (1997) argues that reduction or elimination of ergonomic hazards through workplace interventions is an important means of reducing aggravating factors. Such approaches are echoed by Sheon (1997), the AAOS task force (AAOS 1998), and the National Institute for Occupational Safety and Health (NIOSH 1997). Formal evaluation of the effectiveness of such approaches remains to be carried out.

Chronic Stage
For most musculoskeletal conditions, early chronic pain syndrome is thought to set in at around twelve weeks post-onset (Frank et al. 1996b).

Programs to deal with chronic pain are on the policy agenda for WCBs across Canada. Nova Scotia introduced a new approach for claims management of chronic pain in 1996 and is currently evaluating its impact. The Ontario Workplace Safety Insurance Board identified chronic pain research as a research priority at a recent conference[3] and an expert panel is now considering the issue with a view to making recommendations to the Ontario WSIB. This expert panel has initiated a comprehensive review of the scientific literature on chronic pain, focusing on etiology, prognosis, treatment, and disability management, and the recommendations made will be based on the available evidence.

Sufficient evidence on the effectiveness of some interventions for chronic pain is available for systematic critical reviews to be performed. The Institute for Work and Health (IWH) is at the time of publication completing two systematic reviews for chronic low back pain; one on multidisciplinary team programs and the other on all non-surgical approaches for the management of low back pain (e.g., antidepressants, exercise, manipulation, education, behavioural therapy, multidisciplinary pain clinics, functional restoration, surgery). A multidisciplinary team program is one that addresses the physical, psychological, and social/occupational aspects of chronic pain. Such programs typically incorporate physical treatment (i.e., fitness, work conditioning, progressively increased exercises, etc.), cognitive and behavioural interventions (dealing with pain, coping skills, problem-solving techniques, etc.), and a vocational component (including job circumstances, accommodation, communication with the workplace, vocational counselling, etc.). Four published reviews of multidisciplinary programs for chronic low back have been consulted for this IWH work (Guzman et al. 1997; Bendix et al. 1996; Cutler et al. 1994; Flor et al. 1992). Generally, the poorer quality studies demonstrate substantial improvements in return-to-work rates attributable to the multidisciplinary programs. The higher quality studies demonstrate a more modest effect on return to work. More extensive results from new systematic reviews for chronic low back pain are forthcoming. Tunks, Crook, and Crook provide an overview of the natural history of chronic musculoskeletal pain and treatment efficacy in this volume.

Conclusion

In the early stage of most uncomplicated musculoskeletal disorders (i.e., in the absence of serious underlying conditions), the evidence supports an approach emphasizing reassurance and education leading toward resuming activities of daily living in a timely manner, since many conditions are self-limiting and will resolve regardless of the clinical treatments provided. This message was consistent for all the types of soft tissue injury considered here. There are iatrogenic risks from over-investigation, overtreatment, and inadvertent encouragement of a sick role in mild cases during the acute stage of soft tissue injury (Frank et al. 1996b, 1997). However, patients/claimants need to be reassured about their condition, and the likelihood of a favourable outcome in time. It is important that the reassurance be offered in a meaningful and sincere manner leading to a feeling of validation (Tarasuk and Eakin 1995, 1994), rather than distrust.

But current practices (clinical and case management) do not consistently conform to the suggested approach. Releasing guidelines alone, delivering them in the mail, or providing the messages in a lecture do not change behaviour (Davis and Taylor-Vaisey 1997). Many factors influence practitioners' integration of evidence-based guidelines into their practices including patient expectations, ethics, rewards and incentives, regulations, and social norms (Davis and Taylor-Vaisey 1997). To change behaviours of health care practitioners, a concerted effort involving collaboration with policy makers, insurers, recipients, and the targeted practitioners in a change process is recommended – and such efforts require an outlay of resources. Efforts are now under way in various locations across North America to integrate the messages of the AHCPR guidelines into clinical practice. An Institute for Work and Health effort in Ontario is targeted at health care practitioners at the community level. It has involved identifying opinion leaders within the community and collaboratively developing tools to educate both the practitioners and the patients. An evaluation of effectiveness will be conducted after the study is complete.

The approach suggested above is intended for uncomplicated cases. However, health practitioners and case managers face many cases that are complicated or don't match the targeted patient scenarios, and the guidelines do not address what to do when this is the case. Patients are not "standardized." There is wide variation across individuals in symptoms at presentation, duration of symptoms when filing a claim, past history, complicating factors like other health problems, job demands, and so on. Some patients/claimants may well fall within the large grey zones of clinical practice (Lomas and Lavis 1996; Lomas 1993; Naylor 1995) or claims management, and in those situations, evidence alone cannot guide clinical practice (Naylor 1995).

It is also important in a claimant population to consider the stage of symptoms, and not just the stage of claim, since most of our knowledge about interventions and the guidelines for clinical care are geared toward stage of symptoms. Indeed, some of the guidelines for care may no longer be relevant if the claimant has passed beyond the time lines covered by the guidelines.

At the administrative end, it may prove beneficial to develop a tiered, rationally structured care system based on stage of symptoms. Such a system would include mechanisms for tracking people. Furthermore, it would provide a structure of support for the health care practitioners and claimants to work through the cases together.

The evidence reviewed here strongly points to the importance of the workplace reaction to injury. The chapter in this volume by Brooker et al. summarizes the available evidence on effective disability management and return-to-work practices. It is often necessary to fix the workplace as well as the worker. If a job is clearly leading to musculoskeletal disorders through continuous or repetitive exposure to risky working conditions, it is most beneficial to acknowledge this and change the job. The successful intervention reported by Loisel and colleagues (Loisel et al. 1997, 1994) included an evaluation of and suggested changes to the work environment. Similarly, the study by Lindstrom et al. (1992) involved an integrated effort between health care practitioners and the workplace, in conjunction with the worker. Therefore, evidence suggests an interactive process between health care practitioners, workplace representatives, the worker, and WCB representatives will be the most fruitful for return to work and for staying at work (Sinclair et al. 1998). However, there is no evidence for the acceptability or feasibility of workplace changes in other jurisdictions. Furthermore, interchanges between these parties have sometimes been difficult. But it appears "getting all the players onside" (Frank et al. 1997) may prove to be the most successful approach for all parties.

Last, there is a need for further evidence that is convincing to the full range of stakeholders. "Insufficient evidence" was a common summary throughout our review. There is a need for more research programs carried out in collaboration with the various stakeholders to examine this important social issue of work-related disability. Given the similarity in time on benefits and the evidence around best interventions for the various soft tissue injuries considered here, it appears more cross-condition research would be helpful. A better understanding of the factors that influence outcomes could also lead to a better understanding of the types of interventions that would prove most beneficial to all the parties involved in work-related disability. Notwithstanding all of this, there is much that can be done now to improve the treatment of soft tissue injuries. This will require synergistic efforts of the WCB as insurers, health care providers, and workplace actors.

Notes

1 The Workers' Compensation Board of Ontario was renamed the Workplace Safety Insurance Board of Ontario in January 1998.

2 Data for whiplash-associated disorders originally appeared in Spitzer et al. (1995: 16S, Table 3 and Figure 2). These data were used here with permission.

3 "Shifting the Paradigm." Toronto, February 1998.

References

Abenhaim, L., and S. Suissa. 1987. "Importance and Economic Burden of Occupational Back Pain: A Study of 2,500 Cases Representative of Quebec." *Journal of Occupational Medicine* 29 (8): 670-4.

American Academy of Orthopedic Surgeons (AAOS). 1998. "Draft clinical algorithm on wrist pain." Working Paper of the AAOS.

Association of Workers' Compensation Boards of Canada (AWCBC). 1997. *Work Injuries and Diseases Canada 1994-1996*. Mississauga: AWCBC.

Beaton, D.E. 1995. "Examining the Clinical Course of Work-Related Musculoskeletal Disorders of the Upper Extremity Using the Ontario Workers' Compensation Board Administrative Database." MSc thesis, University of Toronto.

Bendix, T., A.F. Bendix, E. Busch, and A. Jordan. 1996. "Functional Restoration in Chronic Low Back Pain." *Scandinavian Journal of Medicine and Science in Sports* 2: 88-97.

Bigos, S., O. Bowyer, G. Braen, et al. 1994. *Acute Low Back Problems in Adults: Clinical Practice Guideline No. 14*. AHCPR publication 95-0642. Rockville, MD: Agency for Health Care Policy and Research, Public Health Service, US Department of Health and Human Services.

Bongers, P.M., C.R. De Winter, M.A.J. Kompier, and V.H. Hildebrandt. 1993. "Psychosocial Factors at Work and Musculoskeletal Disease: A Review of the Literature." *Scandinavian Journal of Work, Environment, and Health* 19 (5): 297-312.

Bonzani, P.J., L. Millender, B. Keelan, and B. Mangieri. 1997. "Factors Prolonging Disability in Work-Related Cumulative Trauma Disorders." *Journal of Hand Surgery – American Volume* 22A: 30-4.

Borchgrevink, G.E., A. Kaasa, D. McDonagh, T.C. Stiles, O. Haraldseth, and I. Lereim. 1998. "Acute Treatment of Whiplash Neck Sprain Injuries: A Randomized Trial of Treatment during the First 14 Days after a Car Accident." *Spine* 23 (1): 25-31.

Browne, C.D., B.M. Nolan, and D.K. Faithful. 1984. "Occupational Repetition Strain Injuries: Guidelines for Diagnosis and Management." *Medical Journal of Australia* 140: 329-32.

Carey, T.S., J. Garrett, A. Jackman, C. McLaughlin, J. Fryer, D.R. Smucker, and North Carolina Back Pain Project. 1995. "The Outcomes and Costs of Care for Acute Low Back Pain among Patients Seen by Primary Care Practitioners, Chiropractors, and Orthopedic Surgeons." *New England Journal of Medicine* 333: 913-7.

Cheadle, A., G. Franklin, C. Wolfhagen, J. Savarino, P.Y. Liu, C. Salley, and M. Weaver. 1994. "Factors Influencing the Duration of Work-Related Disability: A Population-Based Study of Washington State Workers' Compensation." *American Journal of Public Health* 84: 190-6.

Cohen, J.E., V. Goel, J.W. Frank, C. Bombardier, and F. Guillemin. 1994. "Group Education Interventions for People with Low Back Pain." *Spine* 19 (11): 1214-22.

Cole, D.C., and D.E. Beaton. 1997. "Upper Extremity Work-Related Musculoskeletal Disorders." In *Integrated Health Management*, ed. J. Harris and R. Loeppke, 196-201. Beverly Farms, MA: Occupational and Environmental Medicine Press.

Cooper, J.E., R.B. Tate, A. Yassi, and J. Khokhar. 1996. "Effect of an Early Intervention Program on the Relationship between Subjective Pain and Disability Measures in Nurses with Low Back Injury." *Spine* 21 (21): 2329-36.

Coste, J., G. Delecoeuillerie, A. Cohen de Lara, J.M. Le Parc, and J. Paolaggi. 1994. "Clinical Course and Prognostic Factors in Acute Low Back Pain: An Inception Cohort Study in Primary Care Practice." *British Medical Journal* 308: 577-80.

Côté, P., and J.D. Cassidy. 1997. "The Epidemiology of Neck Pain." In *Advances in Chiropractic*, ed. D.J. Lawrence, J.D. Cassidy, M. McGregor, W.C. Meeker, and H.T. Vernon, 1-39. Toronto: Mosby.

Cutler, R.B., D.A. Fishbain, H.L. Rosomoff, E. Abdel-Moty, T.M. Khalil, and R.S. Rosomoff. 1994. "Does Nonsurgical Pain Center Treatment of Chronic Pain Return Patients to Work? A Review and Meta-Analysis of the Literature." *Spine* 19 (6): 643-52.

Davis, D.A., and A. Taylor-Vaisey. 1997. "Translating Guidelines into Practice: A Systematic Review." *Canadian Medical Association Journal* 157: 408-16.

Faas, A. 1996. "Exercise: Which Ones Are Worth Trying, for Which Patients, and When?" *Spine* 21 (24): 2874-9.

Faas, A., J.T.M. van Eijk, A.W. Chavannes, and J.W. Gubbels. 1995. "A Randomized Trial of Exercise Therapy in Patients with Acute Low Back Pain: Efficacy on Sickness Absence." *Spine* 20 (8): 941-7.

Flor, H., T. Fydrich, and D.C. Turk. 1992. "Efficacy of Multidisciplinary Pain Treatment Centers: A Meta-Analytic Review." *Pain* 49: 221-30.

Frank, J.W., M.S. Kerr, A.S. Brooker, S.E. Demaio, A. Maetzel, H.S. Shannon, T. Sullivan, R.W. Norman, and R.P. Wells. 1996a. "Disability Resulting from Occupational Low Back Pain, Part I: What Do We Know about Primary Prevention? A Review of the Scientific Evidence on Prevention before Disability Begins." *Spine* 21 (24): 2908-17.

Frank, J.W., A.S. Brooker, S.E. Demaio, M.S. Kerr, A. Maetzel, H.S. Shannon, T. Sullivan, R.W. Norman, and R.P. Wells. 1996b. "Disability Resulting from Occupational Low Back Pain, Part II: What Do We Know about Secondary Prevention? A Review of the Scientific Evidence on Prevention after Disability Begins." *Spine* 21 (24): 2918-29.

Frank, J., S. Sinclair, S. Hogg-Johnson, H. Shannon, C. Bombardier, D. Beaton, and D. Cole. 1997. "Preventing Disability from Low Back Pain: New Evidence Gives New Hope – If We Can Just Get All of the Players Onside." *Canadian Medical Association Journal* 158 (12): 1625-31.

Gerberich, S., and J.D. Priest. 1985. "Treatment for Lateral Epicondylitis: Variables Related to Recovery." *British Journal of Sports Medicine* 19 (4): 224-7.

Goldberg, H.I., and H. McGough. 1991. "Testing the Implementation of Clinical Guidelines." *IRB: A Review of Human Subjects Research* 13 (6): 1-7.

Guzman, J., R. Esmail, E. Irvin, and C. Bombardier. 1997. "A Systematic Review of Multidisciplinary Team Approaches for the Treatment of Chronic Low Back Pain." *Arthritis and Rheumatism* 40: S310 (abstract).

Hashemi, L., B.S. Webster, E.A. Clancy, and E. Volinn. 1997. "Length of Disability and Cost of Workers' Compensation for Low Back Pain Claims." *Journal of Occupational and Environmental Medicine* 39: 937-45.

Himmelstein, J.S., M. Feuerstein, E.J.I. Stanek, K. Koyamatsu, G.S. Pransky, W. Morgan, and K.O. Anderson. 1995. "Work-Related Upper-Extremity Disorders and Work Disability: Clinical and Psychosocial Presentation." *Journal of Occupational and Environmental Medicine* 35: 1278-86.

Hogg-Johnson, S., C. Bombardier, J. Guzman, J. Smith, M. Kerr, S. Sinclair, and S. Shields. 1997. "A Comparison of Symptoms and Disability from Acute Low Back Pain (LBP) among Three Study Settings." *Arthritis and Rheumatism* 40: S263 (abstract).

Hogg-Johnson, S., J.W. Frank, and E.G.S. Rael. 1994. "Prognostic Risk Factor Models for Low Back Pain: Why They Have Failed and a New Hypothesis." Working Paper 19. Toronto: Ontario Workers' Compensation Institute (OWCI).

Houtman, I.L.D., P.M. Bongers, P. Smulders, and M.A.J. Kompier. 1994. "Psychosocial Stressors at Work and Musculoskeletal Problems." *Scandinavian Journal of Work, Environment, and Health* 20 (2): 139-45.

Hurwitz, E.L., P.D. Aker, A.H. Adams, W.C. Meeker, and P.G. Shekelle. 1996. "Manipulation and Mobilization of the Cervical Spine: A Systematic Review of the Literature." *Spine* 21 (15): 1746-60.

Johnson, W.G., and M.L. Baldwin. Forthcoming. "The Costs and Outcomes of Chiropractic and Physician Care for Work-Related Back Pain." *Industrial and Labor Relations Review*.

Jolley, L. 1995. Presentation at Canadian Auto Workers (CAW) Health and Safety Conference, 16 June 1995, Port Elgin, ON.

Kaplan, S.J., S.Z. Glickel, and R.G. Eaton. 1990. "Predictive Factors in the Non-Surgical Treatment of Carpal Tunnel Syndrome." *Journal of Hand Surgery* 15 (1): 106-8.

Kerr, M.S. 1997. "A Case-Control Study of Biomechanical and Psychosocial Risk Factors for Low-Back Pain Reported in an Occupational Setting." PhD diss., University of Toronto.

Koes, B.W., W.J.J. Assendelft, G.J.M.G. van der Heijden, and L.M. Bouter. 1996. "Spinal

Manipulation for Low Back Pain: An Updated Systematic Review of Randomized Clinical Trials." *Spine* 21 (24): 2860-73.

Lindstrom, I., C. Ohlund, C. Eek, L. Wallin, L.E. Peterson, W.E. Fordyce, and A.L. Nachemson. 1992. "The Effect of Graded Activity on Patients with Subacute Low Back Pain: A Randomized Prospective Clinical Study with an Operant-Conditioning Behavioral Approach." *Physical Therapy* 72 (4): 279-93.

Loisel, P., L. Abenhaim, P. Durand, J.M. Esdaile, S. Suissa, L. Gosselin, R. Simard, J. Turcotte, and J. Lemaire. 1997. "A Population-Based, Randomized Clinical Trial on Back Pain Management." *Spine* 22 (24): 2911-8.

Loisel, P., P. Durand, L. Abenhaim, L. Gosselin, R. Simard, J. Turcotte, and J.M. Esdaile. 1994. "Management of Occupational Back Pain: The Sherbrooke Model. Results of a Pilot and Feasibility Study." *Occupational and Environmental Medicine* 51: 597-602.

Lomas, J. 1993. "Teaching Old (and Not So Old) Docs New Tricks: Effective Ways to Implement Research Findings." Working Paper series 93-4. Centre for Health Economics and Policy Analysis (CHEPA), McMaster University, Hamilton, ON.

Lomas, J., and J. Lavis. 1996. "Guidelines in the Mist." Working Paper series 96-34. Centre for Health Economics and Policy Analysis (CHEPA), McMaster University, Hamilton, ON.

Malmivaara, A., U. Hakkinen, T. Aro, M. Heinrichs, L. Koskenniemi, E. Kuosma, S. Lappi, R. Paloheimo, C. Servo, and V. Vaaranen. 1995. "The Treatment of Acute Low Back Pain – Bed Rest, Exercises, or Ordinary Activity?" *New England Journal of Medicine* 332 (6): 351-5.

National Council on Compensation Insurance (NCCI). 1993. *Workers' Compensation Back Claim Study*. Boca Raton: NCCI.

National Institute for Occupational Safety and Health (NIOSH). 1997. *Musculoskeletal Disorders and Workplace Factors: A Critical Review of Epidemiologic Evidence for Work-Related Musculoskeletal Disorders of the Neck, Upper Extremity, and Low Back*. Baltimore: US Department of Health and Human Services.

National Work Injuries Statistics Program (NWISP). 1997. *Work Injuries and Diseases*. Edmonton: Association of Workers' Compensation Boards of Canada (AWCBC).

Naylor, C.D. 1995. "Grey Zones of Clinical Practice: Some Limits to Evidence-Based Medicine." *Lancet* 345: 840-2.

Patkin, M. 1991. "Neck and Arm Pain in Office Workers: Causes and Management." In *Promoting Health and Productivity in the Computerized Office*, ed. S. Sauter, M.J. Dainoff, and M.J. Smith, 207-31. New York: Taylor and Francis.

Polanyi, M., D.C. Cole, D.E. Beaton, J. Chung, R. Wells, M. Abdolell, L. Beech-Hawley, S.E. Ferrier, M.V. Mondloch, S.A. Shields, J.M. Smith, and H.S. Shannon. 1997. "Upper Limb Work-Related Musculoskeletal Disorders among Newspaper Employees: Cross-Sectional Survey Results." *American Journal of Industrial Medicine* 32: 620-8.

Punnett, L., L.J. Fine, W.M. Keyserling, G.D. Herrin, and D.B. Chaffin. 1991. "Back Disorders and Nonneutral Trunk Postures of Automobile Assembly Workers." *Scandinavian Journal of Work, Environment, and Health* 17 (5): 337-46.

Ross, S.K. 1995. *Carpal Tunnel Syndrome Diagnosis and Treatment Guideline*. Salem, OR: Department of Consumer and Business Services, Workers' Compensation Division.

Shekelle, P.G., A.H. Adams, M.R. Chassin, E.L. Hurwitz, and R.H. Brook. 1992. "Spinal Manipulation for Low-Back Pain." *Annals of Internal Medicine* 117 (7): 590-8.

Shekelle, P.G., and I. Coulter. 1997. "Cervical Spine Manipulation: Summary Report of a Systematic Review of the Literature and a Multidisciplinary Expert Panel." *Journal of Spinal Disorders* 10: 223-8.

Sheon, R.P. 1997. "Repetitive Strain Injury. 1. An Overview of the Problem and the Patients." *Postgraduate Medicine* 102: 53-68.

Sinclair, S.J., S.A. Hogg-Johnson, M.V. Mondloch, and S.A. Shields. 1997. "The Effectiveness of an Early Active Intervention Program for Workers with Soft Tissue Injuries: The Early Claimant Cohort Study." *Spine* 22 (24): 2919-31.

Sinclair, S.J., T.J. Sullivan, J.A. Clarke, and J.W. Frank. 1998. "A Framework for Examining Return to Work in Workers' Compensation: A Review from One North American Jurisdiction." In *International Examinations of Medical-Legal Aspects of Work Injuries*, ed. E.H. Yates and J.F. Burton, 263-300. London: Scarecrow Press.

Smith, J.M., C. Bombardier, J.W. Frank, S. Hogg-Johnson, M.S. Kerr, H.S. Shannon, and H.A. Smythe. 1997. "Clinical Profile of Cases in Worksite of Low Back Pain According to WCB Claim and Lost-Time Status at Baseline and 26 Weeks." *Arthritis and Rheumatism* 40: S263 (abstract).

Spitzer, W.O., F.E. Leblanc, M. Dupuis, L. Abenhaim, A.Y. Belanger, R. Bloch, C. Bombardier, R.L. Cruess, G. Drouin, N. Duval-Hesler, J. Laflamme, G. Lamoureux, A.L. Nachemson, J.J. Page, M. Rossignol, L.R. Salmi, S. Salois-Arsenault, S. Suissa, and S. Wood-Dauphinee. 1987. "Scientific Approach to the Assessment and Management of Activity-Related Spinal Disorders: A Monograph for Clinicians." Report of the Quebec Task Force on Spinal Disorders. *Spine* 12 (7, supplement): S4-S55.

Spitzer, W.O., M.L. Skovron, L.R. Salmi, J.D. Cassidy, J. Durançeau, S. Suissa, and E. Zeiss. 1995. "Scientific Monograph of the Quebec Task Force on Whiplash-Associated Disorders: Redefining 'Whiplash' and Its Management." *Spine* 20 (8, supplement): 1S-73S.

Tarasuk, V., and J.M. Eakin. 1994. "'Back Problems Are for Life': Perceived Vulnerability and Its Implications for Chronic Disability." *Journal of Occupational Rehabilitation* 4 (1): 55-64.

–. (1995). "The Problem of Legitimacy in the Experience of Work-Related Back Injury." *Qualitative Health Research* 5: 204-21.

van der Weide, W.E., J.H. Verbeek, and M.W. van Tulder. 1997. "Vocational Outcome of Intervention for Low-Back Pain." *Scandinavian Journal of Work, Environment, and Health* 23 (3): 165-78.

van der Windt, D.A.W.M. 1997. "Shoulder Disorders in Primary Care." Ph.D. diss., Free University of Amsterdam.

Wiesel, S.W., S.D. Boden, and H.L. Feffer. 1994. "A Quality-Based Protocol for Management of Musculoskeletal Injuries: A Ten-Year Prospective Outcome Study." *Clinical Orthopaedics and Related Research* 301: 164-76.

Workers' Compensation Board of Ontario (WCB). 1997. *Management of Soft Tissue Injuries: An Evidence-Based Approach to Low Back Injuries.* Toronto: Worker's Compensation Board of Ontario.

Yassi, A. 1997. "Repetitive Strain Injuries." *Lancet* 349: 943-7.

Yassi, A., J. Sprout, and R. Tate. 1996. "Upper Limb Repetitive Strain Injuries in Manitoba." *American Journal of Industrial Medicine* 30: 461-72.

Yassi, A., R. Tate, J.E. Cooper, C. Snow, S. Vallentyne, and J.B. Khokhar. 1995. "Early Intervention for Back-Injured Nurses at a Large Canadian Tertiary Care Hospital: An Evaluation of the Effectiveness and Cost Benefits of a Two-Year Pilot Project." *Occupational Medicine* 45: 209-14.

10
The Natural History and Effective Treatment of Chronic Pain from Musculoskeletal Injury

Eldon Tunks, Joan Crook, and Mikaela Crook

Work injury and pain exact a heavy toll upon workers financially, psychologically, physically, and socially, and they consume considerable societal and employer resources (Spitzer 1987). Approximately three-quarters of workers who sustain a work-related back injury return to work within two to three weeks (Spengler et al. 1986; Spitzer et al. 1987). About 7 percent, however, still have not returned to work after six months; this minority of claimants accounts for 75 percent of costs to the system, such as lost hours, indemnities, and costs related to the use of health care services (Spitzer et al. 1987; Spengler et al. 1986; Snook 1988; Webster and Snook 1990; Volinn et al. 1988).

The disproportionate burden borne by this minority of chronic claimants has created considerable interest in persistent pain, its effective treatment, and its insurability, as noted by Sullivan and Frank in the introduction to this volume. This chapter offers a critical review of the current understandings of persistent pain and current treatment modalities. The objectives of this critical review are to: (1) describe and critically review the natural history and current uni-modal and multi-modal therapies used in the management of chronic musculoskeletal pain; (2) assess which approaches in the literature have been determined to be effective and efficacious through appropriate and rigorous research methods; and (3) synthesize the research findings into a concise summary of the relative efficacy and effectiveness of each treatment modality.

Meta-analysis and reviews were independently rated by the authors using the criteria of Oxman and Guyatt (1991). There was complete agreement in the ratings on a three-point scale of acceptable, borderline, and unacceptable. Randomized controlled trials (RCTs) were rated by one author using the criteria of Jadad and Haynes (1998).[1]

Natural History of Post-Traumatic Musculoskeletal Pain

The temporal course of post-traumatic musculoskeletal pain has heretofore eluded comprehensive conceptual description. The process of recovery or development of disability is understood, primarily, from two rather simplistic biomedical perspectives.

In the first biomedical perspective, illness is believed to be solely due to biological pathology (Leibowitz 1991; Turk 1991), and injury is understood as a linear sequence from casual factor, to pathology, to symptoms or manifestations (Haldeman 1990). Symptoms and disability, according to this view, are directly related and proportionate to the physical pathology (Waddell 1987). Elimination of the pathological causes, accordingly, is assumed to lead to cure or improvement. In reality, however, a pathological explanation of pain cannot be made in over 85 percent of work-related injury cases of low back pain (Spitzer et al. 1987), and, further, the explanation fails to predict disability.

Another perspective on the process of recovery and the development of disability is grounded in the assumption that wounds heal and do so according to a predictable time line. This perspective, which conforms well to the framework outlined by Hogg-Johnson et al. in this volume, holds that normal healing of damaged musculoskeletal soft tissue follows a three-stage process: inflammation, laying down of scar tissue, and remodelling of scar tissue (Caillet 1988; Fess and Philips 1987). The assumption that wounds heal in this fashion and that any pain persisting past usual wound healing time is "chronic," is convenient, but based on an assumption that complex physiological, psychological, and functional phenomena can be distinguished on a unitary time dimension. The healing process can be affected by a number of mediating factors, such as systemic disease. It is also thought that psychological reactions to injury can have physiological effects on healing (Holden Lund 1988), although "complementary healing" in a controlled trial did not apparently improve wound healing (Wirth and Barrett 1994). The downside of the wound healing model is the dismissal or suspicion of persistent pain sufferers on grounds that the injury "ought to have healed by now." Another downside is the assumption that those who will recover will be a majority and will do so within the usual bracket of simple wound healing, and those who do not conform to the proposed time frame will be a simple minority who will become chronic.

Early research seemed to offer a favourable prognosis for persistent musculoskeletal pain. Panel studies of primary-care-based samples, for example, suggested that 90 percent of patients seeking treatment for back pain will be pain free within one month (Kelsey and White 1980; Nachemson 1985; Deyo and Tsui-Wu 1987). Certain types of outcome measures, such as return to work, may reflect some but not all factors needed to evaluate outcome (Mitchell and Carmen 1990; Butler et al. 1995). Further, retrospective research designs employed in much of the research, particularly in the study of the evolution of back pain, can lead to overestimation of favourable outcome since often the populations ultimately examined do not include those for whom prognosis is poor. Prospective studies are more revealing (Wahlgren et al. 1997; Crook et al. 1998). More recent research challenges the earlier findings of favourable outcome.

Recent work by Baldwin et al. (1996) highlights the "fallacy" of favourable outcome created by use of initial return to work as the sole outcome measure. First return to work after injury marks a return to stable employment for less than 40 percent of injured workers. If, as Baldwin et al. note, initial return to work had been the sole objective in their survey of Ontario workers with permanent impairment, they would have had to assume that 85 percent of the workers recovered and returned to work. In fact, they found that 61 percent of the workers who initially returned to work incurred periods of work absence related to the original injury (Baldwin et al. 1996). Crook et al. (1998) found, in a prognostic follow-up study of injured workers, that if workers had not returned to work by three months, there was a 50 percent probability that they would still be off work at fifteen months, and a 22 percent probability that they would remain on work disability and not make any attempt to return to work. Similarly, in a population-based study of Washington State Workers' Compensation, 17.5 percent of all initial disability claims were found to involve at least six months of lost time. A further 12 percent involved one year of lost time, and 7.4 percent involved at least two years of lost time (Cheadle et al. 1994).

Current research in the area of musculoskeletal injury and pain has sought to elucidate, among other things, the natural history and trajectory of recovery, prognostic factors, and outcome measures. The research has employed a variety of designs, including epidemiological survey follow-ups, long-term prognostic examinations of specific conditions/problems, and long-term follow-ups of treatment with control groups, in the investigation of these issues. This body of research is discussed below.

Natural History and Trajectory of Recovery
At this juncture, there appear to be four critical findings on the natural history of post-traumatic musculoskeletal pain. First, there is a higher level of persistent pain and functional disability than previously assumed (Wahlgren et al. 1997; von Korff and Saunders 1996; von Korff et al. 1993). In a study of primary back pain patients, Von Korff reported that 24 percent of recent onset patients and 36 percent of non-recent onset patients experience a fair to poor outcome in the long term (i.e., at one-year follow-up). Approximately 33 percent of primary care patients with back pain experienced back pain of at least moderate intensity and 15 percent reported severe intensity back pain. Twenty to 25 percent of patients, the research suggests, will continue to report substantial activity limitation (von Korff and Saunders 1996). Wahlgren et al. (1997) conducted a cohort study of seventy-six males experiencing a first episode of back pain. Follow-ups were

made at two, six, and twelve months. At six and twelve months post-pain onset, most (78 percent and 72 percent, respectively) continued to experience pain. Twenty-six percent at six months and 14 percent at twelve months reported marked disability. Follow-up measurement revealed greater change in the cohort in the two- to six-month interval than in later assessments. By six and twelve months, there was relative stability. The authors suggest that individuals at risk for marked symptoms one year after the initial episode of back pain can be identified early. Unwarranted assumptions based on administrative data on return to work, or on health care utilization, do not provide an accurate reflection of the natural history of back pain. All acute problems do not completely dissipate within six months. Many individuals return to work or do not seek medical care but may continue to experience moderate to severe back pain (von Korff 1994; Linton and Hallden 1997).

A number of studies suggest that there is high variability in sub-acute and chronic pain conditions (Turk and Rudy 1988; von Korff et al. 1992; Klapow et al. 1993; Tunks 1990) and trajectories (Crook et al. 1989; Crook and Moldofsky 1996). The course of back pain, for example, has been found to be highly unpredictable and unstable (von Korff and Saunders 1996; Linton and Hallden 1997). It is now clear that there is a wide range of outcomes in workers whose injuries initially appear similar. A majority of injured workers will achieve full recovery; however, others will suffer recurrent episodes and a small minority will go on to chronicity and disability.

The research into pain trajectory reveals the impact of treatment upon the clinical course of post-traumatic pain. Comparing untreated to treated conditions in the long term of one or more years, untreated conditions were found to show not dissimilar trajectories of recovery of pain, disability, and return to work, although treated groups had an initial advantage (Lindstrom et al. 1992; Mitchell and Carmen 1990). An increase in other musculoskeletal morbidity with time was noted even in treated individuals, but more in those untreated (Lindstrom et al. 1992; Harkapaa et al. 1990).

A body of current research suggests that there is a "perseveration" effect in the clinical course of musculoskeletal pain (i.e., some workers will fail to get better but not get worse while others will improve) (Philips and Grant 1991a, 1991b; Philips et al. 1991). Wahlgren et al. (1997) suggest that problems associated with chronic pain may not reflect a progressive worsening of symptoms, but rather a failure of symptoms to resolve after onset (von Korff and Saunders 1996). Other research challenges this notion of "perseveration" of injured workers. Change, according to this body of research, is far more multi-dimensional than the perseveration effect would suggest. Crook and Moldofsky (1996), for example, demonstrated that some variables improved equally over time and other variables tended not to improve very much, or to improve rather unequally over time. McArthur et al. (1987) also found considerable variability in outcome measures, not the simple dichotomy of better-worse suggested by the perseveration effect. McArthur et al. (1987) conducted a five-year follow-up of treatment outcome of a cognitive behavioural program for chronic low back pain patients. They reported that 12 percent of the cases had completely favourable outcomes on six behavioural measures: return to work, not in litigation, low self-rating of pain, pain does not prevent activity, not using pain medications, and not hospitalized for pain. On average, 7 percent of the cases reported a complete lack of favourable outcome. On certain measures, such as return to work and use of medication, the results indicated a steady improvement over time for participants of the treatment program. In other areas, such as the impairment of activity, the results were not consistent over time. At the first long-term follow-up, a small but significant proportion of participants reported favourably on all six measures. At all subsequent follow-ups, the majority of these successful participants reported no change in status. In addition, a number of unsuccessful participants no longer reported any unfavourable outcomes. A few cases in later follow-ups, however, reported one or more unfavourable outcomes, and a large percentage of the sample never presented a completely successful picture at any observation. Maruta et al. (1998) followed a cohort of patients with chronic pain thirteen years after treatment in a pain management centre. As there was no control group, comparisons were not made and any inferences would be speculative; nevertheless, several observations are of interest. First, there was improvement in employment status on follow-up (from 12 percent employed pre-treatment to 25 percent). Second, there was long-term stability in reports of bodily pain (68 percent of the respondents); problems with work or other daily activities, social functioning, and physical functioning were attributed to this pain.

Risk and Prognosis

Factors associated with a higher rate of back pain have been reported to include heavy, unpleasant, and dangerous work (Frank et al. 1995; Spitzer et al. 1987), higher age and lower wage (Volinn et al. 1991), and previous pain sick-listings (Goertz 1990; Pedersen 1981).

The desire to predict injury, disability, and handicap has led to a multitude of studies, each claiming to have found a significant explanatory variable. As noted by Kerr in this volume, a distinction must be made between factors related to an increase in the risk of incurring injury or an incident of pain and those related to the clinical course of an injury already sustained (prognostic factors). The factors associated with an increased risk for injury are not necessarily the same as those associated with a worse prognosis (Crook 1994). Some factors, for example, heavy work/labour/construction, may be both a risk factor for back injury and a prognostic factor for continued work loss. Risk factors for injury are covered by Kerr and by Norman and Wells (this volume) as well as in reviews by Battié and Bigos (1991), Borenstein (1990), Hulshof and van Zantern (1987), Taylor (1989), Pope (1989), Yu et al. (1984), Frymoyer and Cats-Baril (1991), Frymoyer and Pope (1978), Frymoyer et al. (1983), Troup (1984), and Heliovaara (1989).

The probability of return to work decreases with the number of months off the job. At two months it is about 70 percent, at six months, 50 percent, at twelve months, 30 percent, and at two years, 10 percent (Waddell 1992). As noted, it is the small number of chronic claimants who accrue most of the injury costs (Spitzer et al. 1987; Spengler et al. 1986; Snook 1988; Webster and Snook 1990; Volinn et al. 1991). Little is known about those workers who are at high risk for developing a chronic problem and continued work disability. A number of studies have identified many potential factors associated with a worse prognosis in musculoskeletal pain. Unfortunately, few of the studies met accepted methodological standards for studies of prognosis. The most serious methodological shortcomings were: (1) a failure to distinguish between etiologic and prognostic factors; (2) a failure to control for the time at which subjects were enrolled; and (3) a failure to perform multivariate analysis (Crook 1994; Crook et al. 1998). Given the methodological quality of the studies, the evidence suggests that, out of the hundreds identified, only the following factors may affect recovery: socio-demographic factors, work factors, compensation factors, physical impairments, psychological impairments, functional disabilities, and social support.

Socio-Demographic Factors
Socio-demographic factors have been examined by several researchers. Increasing age has been positively associated with increased work disability (Rossignol et al. 1988; Goertz 1990; Volinn et al. 1991; Cheadle et al. 1994; Butler et al. 1995). Lower levels of education were more likely to result in lower rates of returning to work (Deyo and Diehl 1988; Butler et al. 1995). Similarly, lower socio-economic status and lower wage have been reported as important factors in work disability (Deyo and Tsui-Wu 1987; Volinn et al. 1991).

Gender also affects work disability. In worker surveys, women had fewer injuries than men, but a significantly increased risk of having a high cost injury claim (Spengler et al. 1986). However, the pattern was not noted by Rossignol et al. (1988), Coste et al. (1994), nor Cheadle et al. (1994). Females had one-third the rate of return to work of males, although they were more likely to remain at work once they had returned (Crook and Moldofsky 1994). This finding was in contrast to that of Butler et al. (1995), whose results showed that gender does not affect the probability of returning to work, but that among those who do return, women are much more likely than men to experience multiple spells of work absence and unsuccessful returns to work. Chung et al. (this volume) provide a most up-to-date review of the role of gender in disability.

Work Factors

Length of time out of work (Gallagher et al. 1989), strenuous work, the overall working environment and conditions, the interaction of job demands, and the physical limitation experienced in performing work have been associated with an increase in the duration of work disability (Yelin et al. 1986). Job dissatisfaction and adversarial relationships on the job have also been implicated (Bigos et al. 1991), although work dissatisfaction may also be a function of the inability to perform the job (Dehlin and Berg 1977) or the symptoms experienced during activity (Feuerstein et al. 1985; Sandstrom and Esbjornson 1986). Conversely, job availability (Polatin et al. 1989), ease of changing occupations (Gallagher et al. 1989; Hewson et al. 1987), use of aids, and modified job requirements to promote a fit between worker's capacity and the job requirements are important factors in decreasing work disability (Yelin et al. 1986; Crook et al. 1998). The availability of a modified job was found to be positively associated with return-to-work rates. The rate doubled in instances where a modified job was available to injured workers upon their return to the workplace. Some of the ways employers modified jobs were through a change in the physical or cognitive demands of the job, shorter hours, more or longer rest periods, modification of machinery, or a decrease in expected output (Crook et al. 1998). The number of times work re-entry is tried increases the likelihood of success in returning to work (Crook 1994). Larger firms had shorter durations of disability (Cheadle et al. 1994).

Compensation Factors

Some authors have regarded compensation as being a prognostic factor in the perpetuation of pain disability (Fordyce 1995; Battié and Bigos 1991), but this viewpoint has not been universally accepted. Dworkin et al. (1985) found that differences in pre-treatment disability were a key variable. Those who were not working had poorer outcomes than those who still worked, and when employment and compensation were used to predict outcome in a multiple regression analysis, only employment was significant. Flor et al. (1992) found, in a meta-analysis, that virtually no significant correlations were found between effect sizes of treatment, compensation and litigation, pain duration, treatment duration, or age. Some clinicians have recommended legal settlement before beginning rehabilitation (Sternbach 1987). This serves only to delay treatment and to decrease the likelihood of a favourable outcome.

Physical Impairments

The prognostic importance of pain characteristics has been examined by several researchers. The site of symptoms (Rossignol et al. 1988; Cheadle et al. 1994; Butler et al. 1995), the number of painful sites (Crook et al. 1998; von Korff et al. 1988), pain grades (a measure based on pain intensity and number of disability days) (von Korff 1991), and pain behaviour (Crook et al. 1998) were found to be prognostically important. Previous pain sick-listings have also been implicated (Goertz 1990).

Several measures of health, for example, general health and overall health status (von Korff et al. 1991), affected the probability of work loss. Fatigue was also identified as an important factor in relation to work disability (Linton et al. 1989).

Psychological Impairments

Co-morbidity of persistent pain with psychological factors, particularly depression and anxiety or dysthymic conditions, is an important clinical and prognostic factor (Dworkin et al. 1986; Valfors 1985; Crook et al. 1986; Tunks 1996). There are several studies that demonstrate almost a threefold risk of development of depression in the approximately two years from onset of chronic pain (Atkinson et al. 1988; Brown 1990; Magni et al. 1994; Breslau et al. 1994). The presence of depression is an important factor in increasing pain intensity, impairment, and behaviour (Haythornthwaite et al. 1991). For this reason, identification and treatment of depression is of high priority in persistent pain sufferers. Crook et al. (1986) demonstrated that psychosocial factors had an important influence in the selection factors that brought persistent pain sufferers to specialty clinics. These factors also importantly influenced prognosis on follow-up (Crook et al. 1986) and return to work (Crook et al. 1998).

Functional Disability

The prognostic importance of functional disability in relationship to work disability appears well established from early studies (Berkowitz 1976; Nagi 1976). Limitations in specific physical functions, namely, walking, bending, and climbing, contributed to work disability (Yelin et al. 1986). Activities of daily living (Sandstrom and Esbjornson 1986) or discomfort in activities (Turner et al. 1983) were also identified as prognostically important.

Social Support

Social support has been suggested as a buffer or modifier of the effects of injury. There is descriptive evidence that chronic pain sufferers experience continuing stressors, particularly in the areas of diminished social functioning, role changes, financial, marital, and sexual strain. These factors have not been examined in methodologically sound studies so their influence on chronicity or work disability remains suggestive only.

Changes in Prognostic Status as a Function of Time

Time-dependent covariates describe changes in workers' prognostic status as a function of time. The importance of time-dependent models lies, partly, in their ability to identify changes that occur over time. One cohort study of workers with musculoskeletal injuries who had not returned to work by three months (Crook et al. 1998) has dealt with the effects of variables that may change over the follow-up period. The variables examined were: pain, physical and psychological impairments, functional and social disability, and the resulting handicaps. These variables were entered into time-dependent models. Functional disability and handicap for physical independence were negatively associated with return-to-work rates.

While the above indicators show significant relationships to outcome, and are useful and important flags, an adjudicator who finds a report of multiple predictive factors at two months should not use this to disallow further treatment or claims, since these predictions hold for groups, and not necessarily for individuals. However, red flags can be useful in early identification of those who require special attention, more vigorous multimodal assessment or treatment, or interpretation of treatment failures.

Crook and Moldofsky (1996) developed cluster groupings of workers who had not returned to work three months after the injury based on prognostically important clinical variables: pain sites, functional limitations, and pain behaviours. Their purpose was to divide the original cohort into subgroups of injured workers who were similar in their prognostic expectations in relation to future work disability. Those considered high-level impaired (25 percent) had the highest number of painful sites, the highest number of functional limitations and greatest pain behaviour. When followed over time, the highest level impaired injured workers tended to demonstrate the greatest emotional distress and interference in occupational, social, familial, and recreational roles, and these difficulties increased over time. Pain, sleep disturbance, fatigue, and overall impairment increased over time in the high risk group. The ability of these three variables to predict return to work in injured workers who were sick-listed for three months was deemed valid.

Systematic Review of Treatments and Meta-Analyses
In order to search for relevant publications, searches were performed on Medline/Pubmed and in the Cochrane Library, searching from 1980 to the present. Searches were performed with respect to clinical disorder, publication type, and intervention type. The search categories were: "pain and chronic disease," "back pain," "neck pain," and "cumulative trauma disorders." Meta-analytic and systematic reviews were independently rated by two authors using the criteria of Oxman and Guyatt (1991).

Physical Therapies for Chronic Non-Malignant Pain
Outcome assessment in the selected meta-analyses did not reflect a uniform strategy. This was due to a wide diversity in experimental design in

the included RCTs, the plethora of subjective and objective outcome measures, differences in the study question, as well as other factors such as the uneven quality of design.

In the included meta-analyses, the data were combined across various types of outcome. Twelve of the meta-analyses used the RCTs' outcome measures – that is, whether the experimental and control/comparison treatment outcomes were significantly different – three used Odds Ratios, one used pooled p- values, ten used some form of Effect Sizes (ES), and three were primarily studies of RCT validity but included clinical outcomes.

Manipulation and Manual Therapy

Beckerman et al. (1993) and Koes et al. (1991) found that some studies of chronic back or neck pain showed manipulation to be more effective than comparison condition, on measures of function, and sometimes on pain measures. Better studies tended to not demonstrate a significant difference between the manual or manipulative therapy and comparison treatment. Hurwitz et al. (1996) found that the pooled Effect Size for the manipulation condition outcomes approached significance on measures of pain relief (ES = 0.42). Shekelle et al. (1992) found five acceptable controlled studies of manipulation therapy, four of which reported manipulation to be better than control. Van Tulder et al. (1997) found that manipulation was more effective than placebo, but the evidence was inconsistent for the efficacy of manipulation versus other conservative treatments. The evidence leans to a conclusion that manual therapies or manipulation are probably efficacious, for pain or function, in chronic neck or back pain, but not necessarily better than other conservative treatment alternatives.

Various Physical Therapy Modalities

In chronic musculoskeletal and spinal pain, there is either no evidence or inconclusive evidence for the efficacy of ultrasound (Beckerman et al. 1993), soft laser (Beckerman et al. 1993; Gam et al. 1993; Gross et al. 1997a), electromagnetic therapy (Beckerman et al. 1993; Gross et al. 1997a), traction (Gross et al. 1997a; van der Heijden et al. 1995), bed rest (Spitzer et al. 1987), corset or belt (Scheer et al. 1997), facet joint injections (Scheer et al. 1997), or electromyographic biofeedback for chronic lower back pain (CLBP) (van Tulder et al. 1997).

Beckerman et al. (1993) noted that soft laser appeared in several studies to be more effective than placebo, but efficacy was not apparently linked to dose, which diminishes the credibility of efficacy. Gam et al. (1993) concluded that the best studies showed no evidence for effect of laser on musculoskeletal pain, though some benefit was reported in poorer quality studies. Gross et al. (1997a) likewise concluded that soft laser was not effective.

Gross et al. (1997a) concluded that the electromagnetic studies they reviewed appeared to demonstrate some benefit for chronic pain at about three to four weeks, but not at six to twelve weeks. Beckerman et al. (1993) noted that of eighteen trials retrieved, nine were of better quality. Of these nine, one demonstrated the efficacy of electromagnetic therapy versus placebo. On the basis of this evidence, electromagnetic therapy is probably ineffective.

In the meta-analysis by Gross et al. (1997a), comparing studies of traction versus conservative physical therapy for chronic neck pain, no significant differences were found to support traction as treatment for musculoskeletal pain of the neck. Van der Heijden et al. (1995), in a meta-analysis comparing twenty-one studies, showed only four to have a significant effect on some measures. Studies were generally of a poor quality. Traction cannot be recommended for chronic spinal pain.

In their systematic review, Spitzer et al. (1987) reported that no more than two days' bed rest could be recommended for acute back pain without radiation to a leg (sciatica), but bed rest could not be recommended for more persistent back pain conditions. Prolonged bed rest should not be recommended for back pain.

Three meta-analyses concluded that active exercise for chronic back and neck pain is more effective than less active exercise or passive treatment (Spitzer et al. 1987; Gross et al. 1997a; van Tulder et al. 1997). Several meta-analyses concluded that there was no evidence, or there was contradictory evidence that exercise was significantly superior to other conservative treatments or physical therapy (Koes, Bouter et al. 1991; Beckerman et al. 1993; Scheer et al. 1997; van Tulder et al. 1997).

Spitzer et al. (1987) concluded that for lower back pain (LBP) of greater than seven weeks' duration, transcutaneous electrical nerve stimulation (TENS) was effective in pain relief. Gadsby and Flowerdew (1997) used Odds Ratios to compare studies of TENS and ALTENS[2] against comparison treatments. On pain measures, they found an advantage of TENS over placebo, with an Odds Ratio of 1.6. TENS/ALTENS had an advantage over placebo with an Odds Ratio of 2.11, but with no improvement of functional status as measured by Sickness Impact Profile (SIP). For ALTENS versus placebo, they found an Odds Ratio of 7.22 for pain relief, and 6.61 for improved range of motion.

Most meta-analyses concluded that TENS was no more effective than comparison or control treatment, or the evidence for effectiveness was contradictory (Malone and Strube 1988; Gross et al. 1997a; van Tulder et al. 1997). The evidence is limited because the numbers of pooled RCTs surveyed for these studies were very small – Malone and Strube, two studies; Gross et al., one study; van Tulder et al., three studies.

In the meta-analyses dealing with acupuncture, the evidence for efficacy was contradictory, but somewhat favouring acupuncture in musculoskeletal and spinal pain (Patel et al. 1989; Ter Riet et al. 1990; Gross et al. 1997a; van Tulder et al. 1997). Ter Riet et al. (1990) in comparing fifty-one studies, found that they were about equally divided between positive or negative outcomes. For musculoskeletal non-spinal pain, the ratio of positive to negative outcome studies was 5:8, while for musculoskeletal spinal pain the ratio of positive to negative outcomes was 11:8. Patel et al. (1989) found that for low back pain or head and neck pain more trials favoured acupuncture over comparison. Blinded trials were associated with a smaller significant difference between acupuncture and comparison. Van Tulder et al. (1997) concluded that evidence for efficacy was contradictory in studies of acupuncture versus other or no treatment for CLBP.

Systemic Medication

According to Spitzer et al. (1987), non-steroidal anti-inflammatory drugs (NSAIDs), analgesics, and muscle relaxants, were efficacious for LBP of less than seven days' duration. Koes et al. (1997) likewise concluded that NSAIDs were more effective than placebo for acute uncomplicated LBP, but equivocal for acute or chronic back pain when compared to other conservative treatments. Only van Tulder et al. (1997) believed that there was evidence for efficacy of NSAIDs over placebo for chronic low back pain.

There is no evidence that one NSAID is superior to another in treatment of chronic low back pain (Koes et al. 1997; van Tulder et al. 1997). Given the potential for toxicity from these medications, if an NSAID is used, lower potential for toxicity should be a determining factor in drug choice and drug dose.

Two meta-analyses evaluated the effects of antidepressants in chronic pain (Onghena and van Houdenhove 1992; Turner et al. 1993), while two further meta-analyses focused primarily on validity issues but included some evaluation of efficacy (Goodkin and Gullion 1989; Goodkin et al. 1995). Antidepressants of various types were found to be more effective for headache and probably for neuropathic pain, but the evidence for efficacy in CLBP and mixed pain syndromes or soft tissue pain was considered to be equivocal. Van Tulder et al. (1997), comparing four studies, found that antidepressants were not significantly more effective than placebo.

Onghena and van Houdenhove (1992) were able to calculate Effect Sizes in order to combine the results of thirty-nine antidepressant studies. They concluded that tricyclic antidepressants (TCAs) were more effective than comparison conditions (ES = 0.69). The Effect Size for heterocyclic antidepressants versus comparison conditions was 0.36. Antidepressants were more effective for pains in the head region (ES = 0.93) than in other body regions (ES = 0.44). The analgesic effect was unrelated to organic versus psychogenic diagnosis, or to the presence of co-morbid depression or to an apparent antidepressant effect of treatment, and unrelated to the presence or absence of sedation. It was noted that drugs with a "less selective" biogenic amine re-uptake inhibitory effect appeared to be associated with a higher Effect Size (ES = 0.73) than drugs with a more selective effect on biogenic amines (ES 0.32 to 0.40).

Epidural Cortisone (for Sciatica)

Watts and Silagy (1995), comparing six RCTs of epidural cortisone injection for LBP with sciatica, found that the Odds Ratio for short-term relief by epidural cortisone was 2.67; for near complete relief, 2.79; and for long-term relief, 1.87. Both caudal and lumbar injection routes were found to be effective. Epidural steroid for this indication is found to be better than placebo, but the evidence is contradictory when comparing epidural steroid to other injected drugs (local anaesthetic or morphine) (van Tulder et al. 1997). Benefits were more often seen in the short term.

Psychological Treatments for Chronic Pain

Uni-modal Psychological Treatment

Malone and Strube (1988) calculated Effect Sizes in order to examine the efficacy of various psychological treatments in comparison to no treatment. Effect Size for "autogenic training" was 2.74; for biofeedback, 0.95; for relaxation, 0.67; and for "placebo," 2.23. Placebo was thus more effective than no treatment and was comparable to some active psychological treatments. They also found that operant therapy had Effect Size of 0.55, which is scarcely different from the control condition. Turner (1996), comparing studies of cognitive or behavioural therapies versus control for CLBP, found that Effect Sizes favoured the cognitive or behavioural therapies on subjective measures (pain report, self-reported pain behaviour, self-reported functional disability), but not in measures of depression or of observed pain behaviour. Scheer et al. (1997) came to similar conclusions in their meta-analysis of cognitive-behavioural therapy (with or without other modalities) compared to other management or to waiting-list control. Cognitive-behavioural therapy was not found to be more effective than comparison conditions on objective measures (work hours, work absences, sick-days, percent of workers re-entering employment, or pensioned workers). Van Tulder et al. (1997), in comparing eleven studies, found that behavioural therapy was effective when compared to no treatment, but the outcomes were contradictory when comparison was made to other conservative treatments or to other forms of behavioural treatment.

Patient Education and Back or Neck School

For LBP of greater than seven days' duration, Spitzer et al. (1987) concluded that "back school," "functional training," or "ergonomic intervention" could be recommended. Cohen et al. (1994) found that studies of patient education for back and neck pain showed inconsistent outcomes. In acute LBP, education interventions reduced pain duration and initial sick-leave in one of two relevant studies. For CLBP, relevant studies were inconsistent with regard to pain and function as outcomes of the education intervention. In their review, Cohen et al. concluded that education was more effective than passive treatment or no treatment, but exercise and active treatment was as effective as or better than patient education. DiFabio (1995) found that patient education alone was not as effective as multi-modal therapy with regard to pain and functional outcomes. Gross et al. (1997b) concluded that group or individual patient education with or without associated medical or physical therapy did not significantly alter pain outcomes more than control or placebo conditions. Scheer et al. (1997) found that patient education resulted in improvement on subjective measures but no difference was demonstrated in objective measures such as duration of work absence or number of sick-leaves. Van Tulder et al. (1997) found that "back school" was significantly more effective than no treatment, but that there was limited evidence for effectiveness when compared with other conservative treatments. Koes et al. (1994) reported that patient education was associated with short-term benefits for acute, recurrent, or chronic low back pain. Improvement was more likely if the educational program was intensive and multidisciplinary in specialized settings, or in occupational settings.

Although patient education plays a useful role in therapist-patient interaction, results in subjective improvement, and is a standard part of most multi-modal therapy, by itself it is an inadequate treatment for chronic neck and back pain.

Multi-Modal Pain Management Programs

Malone and Strube (1988) found an Effect Size of 1.33 in comparing the efficacy of multi-modal programs to no treatment. Flor et al. (1992) found that multi-modal therapies in comparison to controls had Effect Sizes of 0.62 (for shorter duration pains) and 0.81 (for longer duration pains). Multi-modal techniques were more effective than uni-modal treatments. The greatest efficacy difference was seen in comparing multi-modal with placebo or no treatment, and smaller differences were seen in comparing multi-modal with physical therapy. DiFabio (1995) found that multi-modal therapy combined with "patient education" was more effective than patient education alone with respect to improving pain and function. Studies of inpatient multi-modal programs demonstrated greater Effect Sizes than comprehensive outpatient multi-modal programs, suggesting that intensity of treatment is an effective ingredient. Efficacy in return-to-work measures was found to be greater in pain centres (Cutler et al. 1994). The more intensive pain centre environment appears to result in greater efficacy for the "back school" or patient education components of treatment (DiFabio 1995; Koes et al. 1994).

It is important to realize that third-party agencies such as workers' compensation boards and disability carriers are major referring sources for multi-modal pain centres. Yet, there is not unanimity on the question of efficacy in returning patients to work. Scheer et al. (1997) found no convincing evidence that any single modality of treatment used in pain centres was significantly effective in returning injured workers to work. On the contrary, Cutler et al. (1994) concluded that multi-modal pain centres were significantly more effective in returning workers to full-time or part-time work, whether or not the workers had been employed at the outset. The scale of efficacy could be seen in the 56 percent increase in employment in multi-modal-treated patients in comparison to dropouts, and the 40 percent increase in employment when compared to groups of patients who were provisionally accepted for treatment but who were refused insurance funding. With regard to return to work as an outcome, Flor et al. (1992) found a mean Effect Size of 0.67, reflecting a combined return to work in 68 percent of multi-modal-treated patients and in only 36 percent of control patients. The approach of Scheer et al. was to look at individual treatments within pain centres, while the approaches of Cutler et al. and Flor et al. was to look at the efficacy of the multi-modal programs taken together. This difference may account for the apparent contradiction.

These results strongly indicate the efficacy of multi-modal pain management programs. Although "cognitive-behavioural" therapy is the dominant psychological school at present in the multi-modal pain management field, there is no evidence for the superiority of any particular psychological therapy "school" in the success of multi-modal programs. There is adequate demonstration that back school alone is not adequate as treatment unless it is combined with other active modalities, which usually include goal-setting, active exercise by quotas, and some form of tension control or coping skills training, vocational counselling, and usually social systems intervention. The intensity of multi-modal treatment is probably an effective ingredient for this therapy, which is indicated for patients who do not show the expected pattern of recovery from persistent pain.

Review of Injection Therapies for Chronic Pain[3]

Injections into Soft Tissue for Chronic Back and Neck Pain and Myofascial Pain

Nine studies dealt with injections into soft tissue. Of these, two were graded at 5, one at 4, five at 3, and one at 2. Ongley et al. (1987) reported a study of a rather complex treatment consisting of injection of a proliferant (sclerosing) agent plus cortisone and lidocaine, plus manipulation; this was compared to a control condition of saline, lidocaine, and minor manipulation. The experimental treatment was more effective than the control. This was one of the better studies, but it does not allow one to decipher the relative efficacy of the components of the treatment.

The three studies that compared soft tissue saline injection to comparison treatment came to contradictory results. The best of these three studies favoured saline to lidocaine injection in a period up to two weeks. The study by Sonne et al. (1985) favoured lidocaine plus cortisone over cortisone alone on self-report and pain up to two weeks. The three studies of lidocaine versus comparison injection came to contradictory results, but the best of these studies favoured saline over lidocaine up to two weeks. One of the best studies (Garvey et al. 1989) failed to show an advantage of invasive treatment (either injection or acupuncture) over non-invasive treatment (vapocoolant and acupressure). These results do not support the efficacy of injection therapies over control treatment for chronic back, neck, and myofascial pain.

Injections into Spinal Facet Joints for Low Back Pain

Of the three studies in this group, none scored high on design. The best study by Carette et al. (1991) found that at six months, but not at one and three months, patients who had the cortisone injection into facet joints fared better than those with saline injection to facet joints, on pain and function measures. However, Marks et al. (1992) found that those with facet blocks were significantly better only at one month than those who had blocks around but not in facets, but significant advantages were not found at other times up to three months follow-up. Lilius et al. (1989) found that there were no advantages of facet over non-facet injections, or of cortisone over non-cortisone injections. Facet injection for chronic back pain is not supported by these studies.

Injection of Cortisone versus Comparison for Low Back Pain

In this group, two studies were graded 5, and three were graded 3. The two best studies (Garvey et al. 1989; Carette et al. 1991) came to contradictory results. Of the five studies in the group, three came to the conclusion that cortisone injections (with or without anaesthetic) were significantly better than comparison treatment on measures of pain and self-report.

Injection of Non-Cortisone Agents versus Comparison for Back/Neck/Muscle Pain

Of the seven studies in this group, two were graded at 5, one at 4, three at 3, and one at 2. Inconsistent results were found for saline versus lidocaine (two studies), and for saline versus sterile water (two studies). Garvey et al. (1989) did not demonstrate greater efficacy for invasive treatments, while

Ongley et al. (1987) demonstrated efficacy for a complex intervention that involved both invasive and non-invasive components.

Injection Therapies for Pain in the Upper Back/Neck or the Lower Back

Three studies involved upper back and neck pain, while eight involved lower back pain. The best studies tended to involve lower back pain, but there were no studies comparing outcomes in pain relief in upper versus lower back. There did not appear to be any trend for either upper or lower back studies to reflect a greater success rate of experimental versus control condition.

Eight studies concerned patients with pain of three months or more, one concerned "acute" myofascial pain, and from three studies it was not possible to clearly determine pain durations of subjects. There did not appear to be trend for shorter or longer duration pain to reflect a greater success rate of experimental versus control condition.

Although injection therapy of anaesthetic or cortisone into chronic back or neck soft tissue or facet joints is a widespread clinical practice, the evidence for efficacy for injection of anaesthetic, saline, sterile water, or cortisone into painful soft tissues or facet joints is at best inconsistent and contradictory.

Opiate for Chronic Non-Malignant Pain

Although there is a growing literature that increasingly favours the practice of prescribing opiates for some patients with non-malignant chronic pain, to date most of the literature has depended on uncontrolled studies and extrapolations from palliative care practice (Portenoy 1994). Consensus guidelines have also been drawn up in several jurisdictions for opiate use in non-malignant pain, including the Alberta College of Physicians and Surgeons (1993); the British Columbia College of Physicians and Surgeons, adopting the Alberta guidelines; the joint guidelines of the American Academy of Pain Medicine and the American Pain Society (1997); the Medical Board of California (1994); and the American Society of Anesthesiologists (1997).

Only two good RCTs to date specifically deal with this issue. Arkinstall et al. (1995) report an RCT double-blind study of thirty patients with diagnoses mostly of a variety of musculoskeletal disorders. Although the illness duration is not given, the mean duration of opiate use was 72.6 ± 65.8 months. Moderate doses of sustained-release codeine were compared to placebo over a week, with a further nineteen weeks of unblinded use for follow-up. The outcomes significantly favoured the codeine on pain, Pain Disability Index (PDI), self-report, and use of rescue doses; efficacy was not apparently lost during the further unblinded use.

Moulin et al. (1996) conducted an RCT double-blind study on forty-six patients with a variety of musculoskeletal disorders, of duration 4.1 years. Moderate doses of sustained-release morphine were compared to active placebo (benztropine) over a study duration of nine weeks (before crossover). The morphine group did significantly better on pain, but other measures including PDI, drug liking, and a mood scale failed to show significant difference. A sequence effect was noted at the end of the first arm of the trial, influencing the results of the second arm of the trial.

The conclusion from the above is that there is some evidence that a mixed diagnostic group of chronic musculoskeletal patients will experience at least pain relief, if not self-report of functional improvement, in nine to nineteen weeks of follow-up, using sustained-release opioids in moderate doses. Whether a more liberal view toward the use of opioids in non-malignant pain leads to longer-term problems of analgesic failure, complication, or misuse in this population is still to be ascertained by further studies.

Measurement Issues in Outcomes

Flor et al. (1992) found greater differences in outcomes by using less subjective measures, and more objective and functional measures, in studies of multi-modal treatment. Malone and Strube (1988) found that reported symptoms, mood, and electromyography (EMG) recordings consistently showed improvement, and the least variation, as outcomes for psychological interventions.

Measures and Clinical Indicators

Numerous measures exist and no one measure can be generally recommended for all administrative or clinical purposes. There are no "gold-standard" measures for psychological co-morbidity, physical function, or pain distress. However, in every case where differences are demonstrated, the differences can be accounted for by these three variables (e.g., see Harkapaa et al. 1990), that is, it is good counsel to advise a validated measure in each of these three categories.

Time is also a factor that must be considered in interpreting studies. Numerous studies demonstrate that those who have not yet recovered by between two and six months are highly likely to have persistent significant problems at one year or more (e.g., Wahlgren et al. 1997).

Measures serve different purposes and must be chosen accordingly. Scientific studies depend on widely accepted objective standardized measures designed for the population under study. These same measures may be useful as flags in individual cases, though no one objective measure recommends itself for all individual cases. However, self-report measures, and those with more of a subjective quality, may be more helpful in certain clinical situations, individual case management, or decision making by clinicians (i.e., pain drawing, pain scales, disability rating, depression/ psychological distress scales, etc.).

Key Issues

In the process of individual patient care, treatment outcome research can inform sound choices of treatment based on demonstrated benefits and efficacy of treatment alternatives, but does not supersede clinicians' judgment regarding patient care. Such research can form the basis of clinical treatment guidelines, algorithms, care maps, and clinical indicators that serve as "red flags" to alert the clinician or adjudicator to irregularities in the course of illness, to treatment options that have not been considered, or to complications that need attention. However, such research-derived data cannot become the sole grounds for denying individual claims, for truncating treatment, or for invalidating clinical diagnoses or prognoses based on a proper clinical assessment.

A simplistic account of injury and recovery leaves little place for "chronic pain." As noted in the chapter by Hogg-Johnson et al. in this volume, evidence points to an early watershed of approximately three months, before which prognosis for musculoskeletal pain is favourable, and after which the prognosis rapidly declines. Given the present state of knowledge, efforts must be redoubled during the early period to restore function, and to re-evaluate if the recovery does not follow the expected trajectory. When the clinical indicators begin to point to chronicity as a possible outcome, re-evaluation is needed to define the problem more clearly, to identify possible co-morbidity, and to mobilize appropriate intensive treatment. With failure of this approach, or with evidence for significant psychological risk factors for chronicity, referral to specialized pain centres is indicated.

We no longer are in the dark regarding the nature of what we should be looking for in "pain centre" intervention. Individual treatment modalities (physical, anaesthesiological, pharmacological, or psychological), even in specialized pain centres, do not have a remarkable efficacy. It is the coordinated, intensive, and goal-oriented rehabilitation that combines active physical therapy and functional restoration with practical psychological intervention that has greatest demonstrated efficacy, and this should be the standard base of treatment.

Clinical outcomes will vary and exceptions require not suspicion and an adversarial attitude from the health care and insurance system, but rather re-evaluation of relevant complicating factors. Yet there comes a time when one must "cut bait," as it were, in recognizing that further efforts are yielding little progress and that it is not in the best interests of the patient or the health care system to perseverate with ineffective intervention. To assist in that regard, evidence of "engagement" and "informed consent" on the patient's part are important indicators of the appropriateness of sustained treatment or of ceasing these efforts.

The element of prevention within our grasp is to recognize early the patterns that are leading to persistence, especially in the first two or three months, and to mobilize more intensive treatment as soon as such risk factors are identified. It is essential to realize that there is no "typical chronic pain problem," that chronic pain involves a range of possible medical and psychological factors, but that problems that recover slowly probably are multi-factorial and require coordinated and more intensive intervention.

Conclusion

Responsible management of health care and service systems requires a commitment to evidence-based practices and to the active promotion of research in efficacy. However, the tradition in medical care has been that every patient should be treated by the doctor of the patient's choosing. A key question is whether these values can be reconciled. If one could be sure that all physicians and clinics would adhere to best evidence, there would be no conflict. Yet individual patient differences and individual clinical judgment sometimes march right off the care map. It will take creativity, leadership, and goodwill to bring together the "freedom of medical choice" with the "accountability for evidence-informed choice," and to involve both workers' compensation boards as well as grass-roots medical service providers.

There is an increasing need for a flexible system of decision making, using indicators and red flags to aid adjudication and disposition, but also taking into account clinical perspectives unique to the individual patients. One must not "treat the algorithm" – one treats the patient. One must avoid using treatment guidelines or algorithms rigidly or proscriptively, especially in regard to individual cases. The challenge is to promote a responsive agency approach that can adjust to red flags and clinical indicators on an individual basis.

If one accepts the evidence that problems that do not resolve in the first three months need a rapid re-evaluation and more intensive and coordinated rehabilitation approach, there is the risk that the sheer volume of such injured workers would create a demand for new services. These new "clinics" could well spring up without any quality control. The challenge is how to promote a controlled development of quality services that are at arm's length from the referring agency, and yet transparent with regard to quality control, outcome tracking, and the use of evidence.

There is an increasingly large literature on multi-modal specialty pain centres, but there is still no "gold standard" for the most essential elements of multi-modal treatment. Furthermore, the issues of arm's length and transparency with regard to quality control apply equally to "specialty pain centres," especially if a greater demand for multi-modal pain centre services is envisioned.

The challenges are daunting, but the knowledge is evolving. Ingenuity, creativity, leadership, and goodwill are the ingredients that will synthesize an informed and humane collaboration between service providers treating chronic pain and workers' compensation agencies.

Notes

1 In order to search for relevant publications, searches were performed on Medline/Pubmed and in the Cochrane Library. There was no specified time limit. Searches were performed with respect to clinical disorder, publication type, intervention type, and "related articles." The categories for clinical disorder were: "pain and chronic disease," "back pain," "neck pain," and "cumulative trauma disorders." The categories for publication type were: "meta-analysis," "systematic review," "randomized control trial (RCT)," "follow-up studies," "treatment outcome studies," and "practice guidelines." The categories for intervention type were: "cognitive therapy," "combined modality therapy," "multi-modal," "manipulation," "chiropractic," "patient education," "psychotherapy," and "behaviour therapy." The "related articles" option was chosen in Medline/Pubmed. Language choice was English. While the main strategy was to retrieve quality systematic reviews and meta-analyses to perform a review of reviews, the literature on injection therapies for "myofascial pains" and soft tissue pain has only a few RCTs. Hence, these RCTs were used for the section on "injection therapies." The retrieved articles were hand-searched for articles that may have been missed by the computer searches. Other experts were consulted for other articles that might have been missed. Inclusion criteria were systematic reviews or meta-analytic reviews of non-surgical treatment of non-malignant chronic musculoskeletal pain. Exclusion criteria were narrative reviews, reviews that did not include either natural or clinical course, or treatment. Some retrieved citations were rejected on the basis of published abstracts, and a few were rejected after the authors scanned the retrieved articles for inclusion criteria.

   If there were significant disagreements, a consensus meeting was arranged. An Oxman and Guyatt rating of 0 to 3 was considered "unacceptable" for inclusion, 4 was "borderline" but was included, and 5 to 7 was "acceptable." For the comparison on injection therapy for soft tissue pain, and for opioid treatment of chronic pain, RCTs were rated by one author using the criteria of Jadad and Haynes (1998). Author blinding was not used. There was complete agreement between the two independent raters on the overall quality of studies, and on those that should be included or excluded.

   The evidence summaries are available from the authors and were part of the original report to the Royal Commission on Workers' Compensation but were omitted here for reasons of length.

2 ALTENS or "acupuncture-like TENS" actually refers to low-frequency TENS, as opposed to the higher frequencies that are often used in TENS. One should not confuse ALTENS with acupuncture. The above are all forms of electrical stimulation applied superficially to the skin.

3 Additional RCTs were retrieved from Medline/Pubmed and Cochrane databases, using the search strategies already described and including the terms "injection," "anaesthetic-local," "chronic pain," and the "related citations" option. Exclusion criteria were not being RCT, not dealing with chronic soft tissue pain, or non-English publications. Bibliographies were hand-searched for additional articles. All twelve retrieved articles were graded for quality according to Jadad and Haynes (1998). No article was discarded on quality alone, since the number of RCTs was not large. Of the twelve RCTs located, three were graded at 5 on a scale of 0 to 5. One was graded at 4, seven were graded at 3, and one at 2.

References

Alberta College of Physicians and Surgeons. *Guidelines for the Management of Non-Malignant Pain*. www.cpsa.ab.ca/policy guidelines/painchronic.html.

American Pain Society. 1997. *Principles of Analgesic Use in the Treatment of Acute Pain and Cancer Pain*. Glenview, IL: American Pain Society.

American Society of Anesthesiologists. Task Force on Pain Management, Chronic Pain

Section. 1997. "Practice Guidelines for Chronic Pain Management." *Anesthesiology* 86: 995-1004.

Arkinstall, W., A. Sandler, B. Goughnour, et al. 1995. "Efficacy of Controlled-Release Codeine in Chronic Non-Malignant Pain: A Randomised, Placebo-Controlled Clinical Trial." *Pain* 62: 169-78.

Atkinson, J.H., M.A. Slater, I. Grant, et al. 1988. "Depressed Mood in Chronic Low Back Pain: Relationship with Stressful Life Events." *Pain* 35: 47-55.

Baldwin, M.L., W.G. Johnson, and R.J. Butler. 1996. "The Error of Using Returns-to-Work to Measure the Outcomes of Health Care." *American Journal of Industrial Medicine* 29: 632-41.

Battié, M.C., and S.J. Bigos. 1991. "Industrial Back Pain Complaints: A Broader Perspective." *Orthopedic Clinics of North America* 22 (2): 273-82.

Beckerman, H., L.M. Bouter, G.J.M.G. van der Heijden, R.A. de Bie, and B.W. Koes. 1993. "Efficacy of Physiotherapy for Musculoskeletal Disorders: What Can We Learn from Research?" *British Journal of General Practice* 43: 73-7.

Beckerman, H., R.A. de Bie, L.M. Bouter, H.J. de Cuyper, and R.A.B. Oostendorp. 1992. "The Efficacy of Laser Therapy for Musculoskeletal and Skin Disorders: A Criteria-Based Meta-Analysis of Randomized Clinical Trials." *Physical Therapy* 72 (7): 483-91.

Berkowitz, M. 1976. *Public Policy toward Disability*. New York: Praeger.

Bigos, S.I., M.C. Battié, D.M. Spengler, et al. 1991. "A Prospective Study of Work Perceptions and Psychosocial Factors Affecting the Report of Back Injury." *Spine* 16 (1): 1-6.

Borenstein, D. 1990. "Low Back Pain: Current Opinion." *Rheumatism* 2 (2): 233-41.

Breslau, N., et al. 1994. "Migraine and Major Depression: A Longitudinal Study." *Headache* 34: 387-93.

Brown, G.K. 1990. "A Causal Analysis of Chronic Pain and Depression." *Journal of Abnormal Psychology* 99: 127-37.

Butler, R.J., W.C. Johnson, and M.I. Baldwin. 1995. "Management of Work Disability: Why First Return to Work Is Not a Measure of Success." *Industrial Labor Relations Review* 48 (3): 452-69.

Caillet, R. 1988. *Soft Tissue Pain and Disability*. 2nd ed. Philadelphia: F.A. Davis.

Carette, S., S. Marcoux, R. Truchon, et al. 1991. "A Controlled Trial of Corticosteroid Injections into Facet Joints for Chronic Low Back Pain." *New England Journal of Medicine* 325: 1002-7.

Cheadle, A., G. Franklin, C. Wolfhagen, J. Savarino, P.Y. Liu, C. Salley, and M. Weaver. 1994. "Factors Influencing the Duration of Work-Related Disability: A Population-Based Study of Washington State Workers' Compensation." *American Journal of Public Health* 84: 190-6.

Cohen, J.E., V. Goel, J.W. Frank, C. Bombardier, P. Peloso, and F. Guillemin. 1994. "Group Education Interventions for People with Low Back Pain: An Overview of the Literature." *Spine* 19 (13): 1214-22.

Coste, J., G. Delecoeuillerie, A. Cohen de Lara, J.M. Le Parc, and J. Paolaggi. 1994. "Clinical Course and Prognostic Factors in Acute Low Back Pain: An Inception Cohort Study in Primary Care Practice." *British Medical Journal* 308: 577-80.

Crook, J.M. 1994. *A Longitudinal Epidemiological Study of Injured Workers: Prognostic Indicators of Work Disability*. Toronto: University of Toronto Press.

Crook, J.M., and H. Moldofsky. 1994. "The Probability of Recovery and Return to Work from Work Disability as a Function of Time." *Quality of Life Research* 3: S97-S109.

–. 1996. "The Clinical Course of Musculoskeletal Pain in Empirically Derived Groupings of Injured Workers." *Pain* 67: 427-33.

Crook, J.M., H. Moldofsky, and H. Shannon. 1998. "Determinants of Disability after a Work-Related Musculoskeletal Injury." *Journal of Rheumatology* 25 (8): 1570-7.

Crook, J.M., E. Tunks, E. Rideout, et al. 1986. "Epidemiologic Comparison of Persistent Pain Sufferers in a Specialty Pain Clinic and in the Community." *Archives of Physical Medicine and Rehabilitation* 67: 451-5.

Crook, J.M., R. Weir, and E. Tunks. 1989. "An Epidemiological Follow-Up Survey of Persistent Pain Sufferers in a Group Family Practice and Specialty Pain Clinic." *Pain* 36: 49.

Cutler, R.B., D.A. Fishbain, H.L. Rosomoff, E. Abdel-Moty, T.M. Khalil, and R.S. Rosomoff. 1994. "Does Nonsurgical Pain Center Treatment of Chronic Pain Return Patients to Work? A Review and Meta-Analysis of the Literature." *Spine* 19 (6): 643-52.

Dehlin, O., and S. Berg. 1977. "Back Symptoms and Psychological Perceptions of Work: A Study among Nursing Aides in a Geriatric Hospital." *Scandinavian Journal of Rehabilitation Medicine* 9: 61-5.

Deyo, R.A., and A.K. Diehl. 1988. "Psychosocial Predictors of Disability in Patients with Low Back Pain." *Journal of Rheumatology* 15 (10): 1557-64.

Deyo, R.A., and Y.J. Tsui-Wu. 1987. "Descriptive Epidemiology of Low-Back Pain and Its Related Medical Care in the United States." *Spine* 12 (3): 264-8.

DiFabio, R.P. 1995. "Efficacy of Comprehensive Rehabilitation Programs and Back School for Patients with Low Back Pain: A Meta-Analysis." *Physical Therapy* 75: 865-78.

Dworkin, R.H., D.S. Handlin, D.M. Richlin, et al. 1985. "Unravelling the Effects of Compensation Litigation, and Employment on Treatment Response in Chronic Pain." *Pain* 23: 49-59.

Dworkin, R.H., D.M. Richlin, D.S. Handlin, et al. 1986. "Predicting Treatment Response in Depressed and Nondepressed Chronic Pain Patients." *Pain* 24: 343.

Fess, E., and C.A. Philips. 1987. *Hand Splinting: Principles and Methods.* 2nd ed. Toronto: Mosby.

Feuerstein, M., S. Sult, and M. Houle. 1985. "Environmental Stressors and Chronic Low Back Pain: Life Events, Family, and Work Environment." *Pain* 22: 295-307.

Flor, H., T. Fydrich, and D.C. Turk. 1992. "Efficacy of Multidisciplinary Pain Treatment Centers: A Meta-Analytic Review." *Pain* 49: 221-30.

Fordyce, W.E. 1995. *Back Pain in the Workplace: Management of Disability in Nonspecific Conditions.* Seattle: IASP Press.

Frymoyer, J.W., and W.I. Cats-Baril. 1991. "An Overview of the Incidence and Costs of Low Back Pain." *Orthopedic Clinics of North America* 22 (2): 263-71.

Frymoyer, J.W., and M.H. Pope. 1978. "The Role of Trauma in Low Back Pain: A Review." *Journal of Trauma* 18: 628-34.

Frymoyer, J.W., M.H. Pope, J.H. Clements, D.S. Wilder, B. MacPherson, and T. Ashikaga. 1983. "Risk Factors in Low-Back Pain: An Epidemiological Survey." *Journal of Bone and Joint Surgery* 65 (A): 213-8.

Gadsby, J.G., and M.W. Flowerdew. 1997. "The Effectiveness of Transcutaneous Electrical Nerve Stimulation (TENS) and Acupuncture-Like Transcutaneous Electrical Nerve Stimulation (ALTENS) in the Treatment of Patients with Chronic Low Back Pain." In *Back Review Module of the Cochrane Database of Systematic Reviews,* ed. C. Bombardier, A. Nachemson, R. Deyo, R. de Bie, L. Bouter, P. Shekelle, G. Waddell, M. Roland, and F. Guillemin (updated 1 September). http://www.iwh.on.ca/cochrane/brget.htm.

Gallagher, R.M., V. Rauh, L.D. Haugh, et al. 1989. "Determinants of Return to Work among Low Back Pain Patients." *Pain* 39: 55-67.

Gam, A.N., H. Thorsen, and F. Lønnberg. 1993. "The Effect of Low-Level Laser Therapy on Musculoskeletal Pain: A Meta-Analysis." *Pain* 52: 63-6.

Garvey, T.A., M.R. Marks, and S.W. Wiesel. 1989. "A Prospective Randomized Double Blind Evaluation of Trigger-Point Injection Therapy for Low Back Pain." *Spine* 14 (9): 962-4.

Goertz, M.N. 1990. "Prognostic Indicators for Acute Low Back Pain." *Spine* 15 (12): 1307-10.

Goldberg, R.T., and R. Maciewicz. 1994. "Prediction of Pain Rehabilitation Outcomes by Motivation Measures." *Disability and Rehabilitation* 16 (1): 21-5.

Goodkin, K., and C.M. Gullion. 1989. "Antidepressants for the Relief of Chronic Pain: Do They Work?" *Annals of Behavioral Medicine* 11: 83-101.

Goodkin, K., M.A.E. Vrancken, and D. Feaster. 1995. "On the Putative Efficacy of the Antidepressants in Chronic, Benign Pain Syndromes: An Update." *Pain Forum* 4: 237-47.

Gross, A.R., P.D. Aker, C.H. Goldsmith, and P. Peloso. 1997a. "Physical Medicine Modalities for Neck Pain: Conservation Management of Mechanical Neck Disorders. Part Two: Physical Medicine Modalities." In *Back Review Group for Spinal Module of the Cochrane Database of Systematic Reviews,* ed. C. Bombardier, A. Nachemson, R. Deyo, R.

de Bie, L. Bouter, P. Shekelle, G. Waddell, M. Roland, and F. Guillemin (updated 2 December). http://www.iwh.on.ca/cochrane/brget.htm.

–. 1997b. "Patient Education for Neck Pain: Conservative Management of Mechanical Neck Disorders. Part Four: Patient Education." In *Back Review Group for Spinal Module of the Cochrane Database of Systematic Reviews*, ed. C. Bombardier, A. Nachemson, R. Deyo, R. de Bie, L. Bouter, P. Shekelle, G. Waddell, M. Roland, and F. Guillemin (updated 2 December). http://www.iwh.on.ca/cochrane/brget.htm.

Haldeman, S. 1990. "Failure of the Pathology Model to Predict Back Pain." *Spine* 15 (7): 718-24.

Harkapaa, K., G. Mellin, A. Jarvikoski, et al. 1990. "A Controlled Study on the Outcome of Inpatient and Outpatient Treatment of Low Back Pain." *Scandinavian Journal of Rehabilitation Medicine* 22: 181-8.

Haythornthwaite, ~~J.A., W.J. Sieber, and R.D. Kerns. 1991. "Depression and the Chronic Pain Experience." *Pain* 46: 177-84.

Heliovaara M. 1989. "Risk Factors for Low Back Pain and Sciatica." *Annals of Medicine* 21 (4): 257-64.

Hewson, D., J. Halcrow, and C.S. Brown. 1987. "Compensable Back Pain and Migrants." *Medical Journal of Australia* 147: 280-4.

Holden Lund, C. 1988. "Effects of Relaxation with Guided Imagery on Surgical Stress and Wound Healing." *Research in Nursing and Health* 11: 235-44.

Hulshof, C., and B.V. van Zantern. 1987. "Whole-Body Vibration and Low-Back Pain. A Review of Epidemiologic Studies." *International Archives of Occupational and Environmental Health* 59 (3): 205-20.

Hurwitz, E.L., P.D. Aker, A.H. Adams, W.C. Meeker, and P.G. Shekelle. 1996. "Manipulation and Mobilization of the Cervical Spine: A Systematic Review of the Literature." *Spine* 21 (15): 1746-60.

Jadad, A.R., and R.B. Haynes. 1998. "The Cochrane Collaboration – Advances and Challenges in Improving Evidence-Based Decision Making." *Medical Decision Making* 18 (1): 2-9, 16-8.

Kelsey, J.L., and A.A. White, III. 1980. "Epidemiology and Impact of Low-Back Pain." *Spine* 5 (2): 133-42.

Klapow, J.C., M.A. Slater, T.L. Patterson, J.N. Doctor, J.H. Atkinson, and S.R. Garfin. 1993. "An Empirical Evaluation of Multidimensional Clinical Outcome in Chronic Low Back Pain Patients." *Pain* 55: 107-18.

Koes, B.W., W.J.J. Assendelft, G.J.M.G. van der Heijden, L.M. Bouter, and P.G. Knipschild. 1991. "Spinal Manipulation and Mobilisation for Back and Neck Pain: A Blinded Review." *British Medical Journal* 303: 1298-1303.

Koes, B.W., L.M. Bouter, H. Beckerman, G.J.M.G. van der Heijden, and P.G. Knipschild. 1991. "Physiotherapy Exercises and Back Pain: A Blinded Review." *British Medical Journal* 302: 1572-6.

Koes, B.W., R.J.P.M. Scholten, J.M.A. Mens, and L.M. Bouter. 1997. "Efficacy of Non-Steroidal Anti-Inflammatory Drugs for Low Back Pain: As Systemic Review of Randomised Clinical Trials." *Annals of the Rheumatic Diseases* 56: 214-23.

Koes, B.W., M.W. van Tulder, D.A.W.M. van der Windt, and L.M. Bouter. 1994. "The Efficacy of Back Schools: A Review of Randomized Clinical Trials." *Journal of Clinical Epidemiology* 47: 851-62.

Leibowitz, G. 1991. "Organic and Biophysical Theories of Behavior." *Journal of Developmental and Physical Disabilities* 3 (3): 201-43.

Lilius, G., F.M. Laasonen, P. Myllynen, et al. 1989. "Lumbar Facet Joint Syndrome." *Journal of Bone and Joint Surgery* 71 (8): 681-84.

Lindstrom, I., C. Ohlund, C. Eek, et al. 1992. "The Effect of Graded Activity on Patients with Subacute Low Back Pain: A Randomized Prospective Clinical Study with an Operant-Conditioning Behavioral Approach." *Physical Therapy* 72: 279-93.

Linton, S.J., L.A. Bradley, J. Jensen, E. Spranfort, and L. Sundell. 1989. "The Secondary Prevention of Low Back Pain: A Controlled Study with Follow-Up." *Pain* 36: 197-207.

Linton, S.J., and K. Hallden. 1997. "Risk Factors and the Natural Course of Acute and

Recurrent Musculoskeletal Pain: Developing a Screening Instrument." Proceeding of the 8th World Congress on Pain. *Progress in Pain Research and Management,* ed. T.S. Jensen, J.A. Turner, and Z. Wiesenfeld-Hallin, 8: 527-35. Seattle: IASP Press.

McArthur. D.L., M.J. Cohen, H.J. Gottlieb, B.D. Naliboff, and S.L. Schandler. 1987. "Treating Chronic Low Back Pain. II. Long-Term Follow-Up." *Pain* 29: 23-38.

Magni, C., C. Moreschi, S. Rigatti-Luchini, et al. 1994. "Prospective Study on the Relationship between Depressive Symptoms and Chronic Musculoskeletal Pain." *Pain* 56: 289-97.

Malone, M.D., and M.J. Strube. 1988. "Meta-Analysis of Non-Medical Treatments for Chronic Pain." *Pain* 34: 231-44.

Marks, R.C., T. Houston, and T. Thulbourne. 1992. "Facet Joint Injection and Facet Nerve Block: A Randomised Comparison in 86 Patients with Chronic Low Back Pain." *Pain* 49: 325-8.

Maruta, T., M. Malinchoc, K.P. Offord, and R.C. Colligan. 1998. "Status of Patients with Chronic Pain 13 Years after Treatment in a Pain Management Center." *Pain* 74: 199-204.

Medical Board of California. 1994. "New, Easy Guidelines on Prescribing: Action Report." Sacramento, CA: Medical Board of California.

Mitchell, R.I., and G.M. Carmen. 1990. "Results of a Multicenter Trial Using an Intensive Active Exercise Program for the Treatment of Acute Soft Tissue and Back Injuries." *Spine* 15 (6): 514-21.

Moulin, D.E., A. Iezzi, R. Amireh, et al. 1996. "Randomised Trial of Oral Morphine for Chronic Non-Cancer Pain." *Lancet* 347: 143-7.

Nachemson, A.L. 1985. "Advances in Low Back Pain." *Clinical Orthopaedics and Related Research* 200: 266-73.

Nagi, S. 1976. "An Epidemiology of Disability among Adults in the United States." *Millbank Memorial Fund Quarterly Health and Society* 54: 439-68.

Onghena, P., and B. van Houdenhove. 1992. "Antidepressant-Induced Analgesia in Chronic Non-Malignant Pain: A Meta-Analysis of 39 Placebo-Controlled Studies." *Pain* 49: 205-19.

Ongley, M.J., R.G. Klein, T.A. Dorman, et al. 1987. "A New Approach to the Treatment of Chronic Low Back Pain." *Lancet* 18: 143-6.

Oxman, A.D., and G.H. Guyatt. 1991. "Validation of an Index of the Quality of Review Articles." *Journal of Clinical Epidemiology* 44: 1271-8.

Patel, M., F. Gutzwiller, F. Paccaud, and A. Marazzi. 1989. "A Meta-Analysis of Acupuncture for Chronic Pain." *International Journal of Epidemiology* 18: 900-6.

Philips, H.C., and L. Grant. 1991a. "Acute Back Pain: A Psychological Analysis." *Behaviour Research and Therapy* 29: 429-34.

–. 1991b. "The Evolution of Chronic Back Pain Problems: A Longitudinal Study." *Behaviour Research and Therapy* 29: 431-41.

Philips, H.C., L. Grant, and I. Berkowitz. 1991. "The Prevention of Chronic Pain and Disability: A Preliminary Investigation." *Behaviour Research and Therapy* 29: 443-50.

Polatin, P.B., R.I. Gatchel, D. Barnes, et al. 1989. "A Psychosociomedical Prediction Model of Response to Treatment by Chronically Disabled Workers with Low Back Pain." *Spine* 14 (9): 956-61.

Pope, M.H. 1989. "Risk Indicators in Low Back Pain." *Annals of Medicine* 21 (5): 387-92.

Portenoy, R.K. 1994. "Opioid Therapy for Chronic Nonmalignant Pain: Current Status." In *Progress in Pain Research and Management,* ed. H.L. Fields and J.C. Liebeskind, 1: 247-87. Seattle: IASP Press.

Roland, M., and M. Dixon. 1989. "Randomized Controlled Trial of an Educational Booklet for Patients Presenting with Back Pain in General Practice." *Journal of Royal College of General Practitioners* 39: 244-6.

Rossignol, M., S. Suissa, and L. Abenhaim. 1988. "Working Disability Due to Occupational Back Pain: Three-Year Follow-Up of 2300 Compensated Workers in Quebec." *Journal of Occupational Medicine* 30 (6): 502-5.

Sandstrom, J., and E. Esbjornson. 1986. Return to Work after Rehabilitation: The Significance of the Patient's Own Prediction. *Scandinavian Journal of Rehabilitation Medicine* 18: 29-33.

Scheer, S.J., T.K. Watanabe, and K.L. Radack. 1997. "Randomized Controlled Trials in Industrial Low Back Pain. Part 3. Subacute/Chronic Pain Interventions." *Archives of Physical Medicine and Rehabilitation* 78: 414-23.

Shekelle, P.G., A.H. Adams, M.R. Chassin, E.L. Hurwitz, and R.H. Brook. 1992. "Spinal Manipulation for Low-Back Pain." *Annals of Internal Medicine* 117: 590-8.

Snook, S.H. 1988. "The Costs of Back Pain in Industry." *Occupational Medicine* 3 (1): 1-5.

Sonne, M., K. Christensen, S.F. Hansen, et al. 1985. "Injection of Steroids and Local Anaesthetics as Therapy for Low-Back Pain." *Scandinavian Journal of Rheumatology* 14: 343-5.

Spengler, D.M., S.J. Bigos, N.A. Martin, et al. 1986. "Back Injuries in Industry, a Retrospective Study, I: Overview and Cost Analysis." *Spine* 11 (3): 241.

Spitzer, W. 1987. "Report of the Quebec Task Force on Spinal Disorders." *Spine* 12 (7, supplement).

Sternbach, R.A. 1987. *Mastering Pain: A Twelve Step Program for Coping with Chronic Pain.* New York: Ballantyne Books 1987.

Taylor, M.E. 1989. "Return to Work following Back Surgery: A Review." *American Journal of Industrial Medicine* 16 (1): 79-88.

Ter Riet, G., J. Kleijnen, and P. Knipschild. 1990. "Acupuncture and Chronic Pain: A Criteria-Based Meta-Analysis." *Journal of Clinical Epidemiology* 43: 1191-9.

Troup, J.D.G. 1984. "Causes, Prediction and Prevention of Back Pain at Work." *Scandinavian Journal of Work, Environment, and Health* 10: 419-28.

Tunks, E. 1990. "Is There a Chronic Pain Syndrome?" In *Advances in Pain Research and Therapy,* ed. S. Lipton, E, Tunks, and M. Zoppi, 13: 257-66. New York: Raven Press.

–. 1996. "Comorbidity of Psychiatric Disorder and Chronic Pain." In *Pain 1996 – an Updated Review,* ed. J.N. Campbell, 287-96. Seattle: IASP Press.

Turk, D.C. 1991. "Evaluation of Pain and Dysfunction." *Journal of Disabilities* 2 (1): 24-43.

Turk, D.C., and T.E. Rudy. 1988. "Toward an Empirically Derived Taxonomy of Chronic Pain Patients: Integration of Psychological Assessment Data." *Journal of Consulting Clinical Psychology* 56: 233-8.

Turner, J.A. 1996. "Educational and Behavioral Interventions for Back Pain in Primary Care." *Spine* 21: 2851-9.

Turner, J.A., and M.C. Denny. 1993. "Do Antidepressant Medications Relieve Chronic Low Back Pain?" *Journal of Family Practice* 37: 545-53.

Turner, J.A., J. Robinson, and C. McCreary. 1983. "Chronic Low-Back Pain: Predicting Response to Nonsurgical Treatment." *Archives of Physical Medicine and Rehabilitation* 64 (11): 560-3.

van der Heijden, G.J.M.G., A.J.H.M. Beurskens, B.W. Koes, W.J.J. Assendelft, H.C.W. de Vet, and L.J. Bouter. 1995. "The Efficacy of Traction for Back and Neck Pain: A Systematic, Blinded Review of Randomized Clinical Trial Methods." *Physical Therapy* 75: 93-104.

van Tulder, M.W., P.W. Koes, and L.M. Bouter. 1997. "Conservative Treatment of Acute and Chronic Nonspecific Low Back Pain." *Spine* 22: 2128-56.

Volinn, E., D. Lai, S. McKinney, and J.D. Loeser. 1988. "When Back Pain Becomes Disabling: A Regional Analysis." *Pain* 33: 33-9.

Volinn, F., D. Vonkoevering, and J.D. Loeser. 1991. "Back Sprain in Industry: The Role of Socioeconomic Factors in Chronicity." *Spine* 16: 542-8.

von Korff, M. 1994. "Studying the Natural History of Back Pain." *Spine* 19 (18, supplement): 2041S-6S.

von Korff, M., R.A. Deyo, D. Cherkin, and W. Barlow. 1993. "Back Pain in Primary Care." *Spine* 18: 855-62.

von Korff, M., S.F. Dworkin, L. Leresche, and A. Kruger. 1988. "An Epidemiologic Comparison of Pain Complaints." *Pain* 32: 173-83.

von Korff, M., J. Ormel, F.J. Keefe, and S.F. Dworkin. 1992. "Grading the Severity of Chronic Pain." *Pain* 50 (2): 133-49.

von Korff, M., and K. Saunders. 1996. "The Course of Back Pain in Primary Care." *Spine* 21 (24): 2833-7.

von Korff, M., E.H. Wagner, S.F. Dworkin, and K.W. Saunders. 1991. "Chronic Pain and Use of Ambulatory Health Care." *Psychosomatic Medicine* 53: 1-19.

Waddell, G. 1987. "A New Clinical Model for the Treatment of Low-Back Pain." *Spine* 12 (7): 632-45.

–. 1992."Biopsychosocial Analysis of Low Back Pain." *Ballieres Clinical Rheumatology* 6: 523-57.

Wahlgren, D.R., J.H. Atkinson, J.E. Epping-Jordan, R.A. Williams, S.D. Pruitt, J.C. Klapow, T.L. Patterson, I. Grant, J.S. Webster, and M.A. Slater. 1997. "One-Year Follow-Up of First Onset Low Back Pain." *Pain* 73: 213-21.

Watts, R.W., and C.A. Silagy 1995. "A Meta-Analysis on the Efficacy of Epidural Cortico-steriods in the Treatment of Sciatica." *Anaesthesia and Intensive Care* 23: 564-69.

Webster, B.S., and S.H. Snook. 1990. "The Cost of Compensable Low Back Pain." *Journal of Occupational Medicine* 32 (1): 13-15.

Wirth, D.P., and M.J. Barrett. 1994. "Complementary Healing Therapies." *International Journal of Psychosomatics* 41: 61-7.

Yelin, E.H., C.J. Henke, and W.V. Epstein. 1986. "Work Disability among Persons with Musculoskeletal Conditions." *Arthritis and Rheumatology* 29: 1322-33.

Yu, T.S., L.H. Roht, R.A. Wise, J. Kilian, and F.W. Weir. 1984. "Low Back Pain in Industry." *Journal of Occupational Medicine* 26 (7): 517-24.

11
Effective Disability Management and Return-to-Work Practices

Ann-Sylvia Brooker, Judy Clarke, Sandra Sinclair, Victoria Pennick, and Sheilah Hogg-Johnson

Work-related disability has a negative effect on both employees and employers. Across Canada, one worker in fifteen is injured on the job each year. In Ontario alone, 500 time loss injuries occur each day and seventy of these lead to permanent impairment (Watson Wyatt Worldwide 1997). For the injured workers and their families, these events cause pain, suffering, and anxiety. For the employers, these disabilities increase business costs through disability insurance premiums, workers' compensation premiums (frequently based on a company's safety record), and worker replacement costs.

Disability management programs (also called return-to-work programs), which provide effective and safe return to work for employees, can potentially benefit employees, employers, and insurers. However, it is critical that these programs are planned and implemented in a way that ensures their success.

The primary purpose of this chapter is to describe the principles and components of optimal disability management programs based on recent research evidence. A secondary purpose is to describe the extent to which these principles have been implemented in Canadian workplaces.

We first describe the economic and legislative context of work-related disability in Canada. Next, drawing on up-to-date research evidence, the effectiveness of disability management programs (clinical interventions as well as workplace-based interventions) for workers with back pain will be discussed. Finally, the availability and quality of workplace-based disability management programs in Canada will be presented, along with suggestions for their improvement at the societal level.

This chapter will focus on the disability management of workers with work-related back pain. Despite this focus, it is important to recognize that many of the workplace-specific principles concerning return to work are generic and will be applicable when addressing the re-employment of individuals with other types of disability.

Economic and Legislative Context

Disability and associated lost productivity have a significant impact on costs for employers. In Canada, an average of 9.5 days per employee per year are lost due to disability (Watson Wyatt Worldwide 1997). Employers typically provide benefits coverage under short-term and long-term disability as well as workers' compensation plans. A recent survey of 305 Canadian employers (Watson Wyatt Worldwide 1997) showed that the average cost of these programs equals 5.6 percent of payroll. Indirect costs such as recruiting and training replacement workers, reduced productivity due to inexperience, overtime pay for other employees, and reduced quality in product or service may reach twice the direct costs. As a result, it is estimated that Canadian employers pay between $10 and $20 billion each year in disability-associated expenses (Hillier 1997).

Workers' compensation claims generally account for over 40 percent of the direct disability costs. In 1996, there were 380,000 eligible workers' compensation claims in Canada requiring time off work (NWISP 1997). While the absolute number of claims and the workplace accident frequency rate has been declining over the past ten years, costs per claim have increased. At the same time, compensation premiums have been more directly pegged to employers' safety records, so that many more companies are beginning to pay rates that reflect their own accident experience.

Apart from humanitarian concerns and financial incentives, employers also have legal responsibilities related to the return to work of an injured worker. In Canada, labour and human rights statutes protect injured workers from dismissal based on disability and some provinces – notably New Brunswick, Quebec, and Ontario – have specific provisions to inhibit employers from dismissing employees who become disabled. In Ontario, larger employers are required to re-employ injured workers who attempt to return to work within two years of work-related injury. Re-employment must be provided to the worker's former (or a comparable) job if the worker is medically capable, or to the first suitable job available, if the worker is not so capable.

There are still other compelling reasons for employers to implement effective disability management and return-to-work programs. The presence of such programs can contribute to a safer work environment, thus reducing the incidence of other injuries involving time lost from the job (Yassi et al. 1995) and at the same time reducing employer costs. Employers and employees both gain from maintaining the employment of a skilled workforce (MFL 1995).

From the perspective of employees, successful programs can assist with re-employment; help with financial needs; and reduce the negative personal, family, and social consequences of being absent from work. Workers have more commitment and a greater sense of security in a workplace that provides help and support in the event of disability (MFL 1995).

Currently, however, employers and the injured worker are confronted with an increasingly confusing array of service providers offering assistance with rehabilitation and return-to-work issues. Questions about the effectiveness of both clinical and workplace interventions abound. The role of research evidence in decision making thus becomes increasingly important as the range of options proliferate and the costs rise.

Disability Management and Return-to-Work Practices: Low Back Pain Studies

Musculoskeletal disorders, an umbrella term encompassing sprains, strains, or inflammation of the muscles, tendons, or ligaments of the back, neck, or arms constitute more than 60 percent of work-related disability claims (NWISP 1997). In this category, back sprains and strains are the largest single diagnostic group. In addition to the high rate of incidence, there is evidence that workers with musculoskeletal problems such as low back pain have lower return-to-work rates than workers with other conditions (Butler et al. 1995; Yelin et al. 1986). It is therefore not surprising that research to date concerning disability management programs has tended to concentrate on individuals with back pain. In this chapter, work-related back pain is the focus of our discussion because of its high rates of disability and the availability of research findings. Nonetheless, many of the workplace-specific principles will be applicable when addressing the re-employment of workers with other types of disability.

The central goal of managing disability is to return the individual to work as early as is safely possible. Researchers generally agree that employee disability caused by work-related events is the result of a complex interaction of a number of factors including: the worker's condition and how it is managed clinically and at the workplace; ergonomic workplace demands; the worker's physical capabilities; a wide range of psychosocial factors; and the broader socio-economic and legislative environment (Sinclair et al. 1998).

The effectiveness of two of these factors – clinical interventions and workplace-based interventions – is discussed below, with reference to relevant research.

Clinical Interventions and Facilitating Return to Work

The vast majority of injured workers experiencing time off work due to a musculoskeletal disorder will consult with a health care provider – a physician, chiropractor, physiotherapist, occupational therapist, or some combination thereof – during the course of their recovery. The health care provider (clinician) can play a significant role in helping injured workers recover from back pain. Further, through their cooperation with workplace parties in matters such as determining appropriate modified work, clinicians can facilitate the safe and timely return to work of their patients. Nonetheless, the evidence presented below will demonstrate that clinical interventions on their own – without a tie-in to the workplace – do not reduce back-pain-related absence from work.

There is a significant and evolving body of evidence from around the world about the impact of clinical interventions on recovery from musculoskeletal disorders, particularly low back pain (Clinical Standards Advisory Group 1994; Frank et al. 1996; Spitzer et al. 1987; Bigos et al. 1994). Research about the appropriate clinical interventions and their effectiveness on pain and function seem to suggest that different types of interventions may be pertinent for different stages of recovery (Chapter 9; Frank et al. 1998). A more detailed discussion of the precise nature and timing of interventions is presented in chapters 9 and 10.

Clinical interventions without a tie-in to the workplace have not been shown to be effective at accelerating the return to work of injured workers. A Dutch review (van der Weide et al. 1997) showed that a variety of clinical treatment modalities – including drug therapy, spinal manipulation, back schools, exercise programs, case management methods, or behavioural therapy – had essentially no beneficial effect on the return to work of patients with back pain when administered at either the acute or the chronic stage. (A minor exception was spinal manipulation at the acute stage given to patients without moderating pain.)

However, workplace-based interventions that include access to health care providers have demonstrated a favourable effect on return to regular work. In a Manitoba study (Yassi et al. 1995), nurses with acute stage back pain and who worked on heavy care wards were provided with very flexible modified work in supernumerary positions, as well as worksite access to symptom relief strategies from a health care provider (e.g., heat, cold, reassurance). This intervention resulted in a significant reduction in time loss from work. In a Quebec study (Loisel et al. 1997), participatory ergonomic intervention involving the injured worker's job (see Offering Modified Work below for a more detailed description) and a visit to an occupational physician was associated with a much faster return to regular work compared to the control arm and the clinical intervention arm of the trial.

The importance of communication between health care providers and workplace participants involved in organizing the return to work of injured workers was highlighted in qualitative research in several Ontario workplaces (Clarke et al. 1999). This study indicated that health care providers who are inaccessible and incommunicative to various workplace parties (e.g., employer, union representative), can be a barrier to successful return to work for their patients. By contrast, involved and helpful health care providers can facilitate the return-to-work process by defining the worker's physical limitations and by helping to determine whether various work (or modified work) options are suitable for their patient.

The effectiveness of work hardening programs has been mixed. A Swedish trial – which included intensive work conditioning by a physical therapist for workers with sub-acute back pain after eight weeks of absence from work, targeted specifically to the physical demands of each worker's job – was associated with reduced duration of sick-leave compared to the control group (Lindstrom et al. 1992). However, the Quebec trial (Loisel et al. 1997) mentioned above did not find that clinical intervention, which included work hardening after twelve weeks, was associated with faster return to regular work compared to usual care (see Offering Modified Work below for a more detailed description of the intervention).

These studies involving workers with back pain demonstrate the futility of relying solely on clinical interventions to facilitate the return-to-work process: a workplace-based component of the intervention is essential to help reduce the duration of work-related disability due to back pain. The following section will describe in more depth the specific components of optimal workplace-based interventions and the role of various workplace parties in implementing them.

Workplace-Based Interventions and the Role of Workplace Parties
This section will describe key principles and components that are beneficial in the development of optimal return-to-work programs. These principles and components were culled from a broad range of studies. In clinical research, randomized controlled trials (RCTs) are considered to be the optimal type of research design. However, for program research, though quantitative research is useful for determining the effectiveness of a program in terms of outcome, often qualitative research is required to understand why a program fails, or to determine what elements of a program are necessary to ensure its success (Baum 1995). From a review of the relevant qualitative and quantitative literature to date, as well as ongoing qualitative research at the Institute for Work and Health (Clarke et al. 1999),[1] the following characteristics appear to be particularly important for the safe and timely return to work of workers with back pain:

- supportive workplace policies and climate
- joint labour-management cooperation
- communication and cooperation among the worker, the worker's health care professional, union or worker representative, and the workplace
- offers of modified work (preferably of the original job)
- ongoing evaluation of the program.

Development and Implementation of Return-to-Work Policies
The development of explicit policies regarding the reintegration of disabled workers can help ensure that a return-to-work program runs successfully.

Policies can cover such issues as salary replacement, job accommodation, transitional employment, and budgetary responsibility (Akabas et al. 1990). Such policies have a number of helpful functions. When they are in place, workers are more likely to feel confident to approach their employer to help them return to work. Furthermore, supervisors, who would authorize return-to-work accommodation, are also more likely to believe that it is within their power to change work requirements. When successful implementation of the policy is tied to the performance appraisal of the supervisors, the positive results are even more significant. Problems can arise when supervisors know that top management support disability management, but are concerned about how the productivity of their own department may be jeopardized by reintegrating workers (ibid.). Therefore, reintegration practices must avoid the unnecessary disruption of production schedules or make adjustments or accommodations for worker reintegration within such schedules (Clarke et al. 1999). It is also desirable to achieve joint management-labour collaboration in the development and implementation of disability management policies and procedures (Clarke et al. 1999; Bruyère and Shrey 1991; Akabas et al. 1990), a topic to which we will address ourselves shortly.

The Workplace Climate Is Key

It is important that the workplace develop a helpful and supportive environment for injured workers who return to work. An employer may appear to have comprehensive return-to-work procedures in place, but if the program operates in an adversarial or demeaning context, these efforts are unlikely to fulfil their main aim of getting injured workers back on the job in a safe and timely manner. Examples of such adverse circumstances include situations in which injured workers are treated with suspicion as to the legitimacy of their claims, or when workers believe that the priority of management is merely to maximize profits with little regard for worker well-being (Clarke et al. 1999). Institute for Work and Health (IWH) studies found that when workers' injuries were viewed suspiciously in the workplace, workplace relations could be damaged, the emotional stress of the worker was often exacerbated, and these factors in turn often delayed a worker's return to work (Smith et al. 1996; Tarasuk and Eakin 1995).

Creating a healthy workplace culture is a major challenge for workplace parties. Battié (1992) notes the importance of creating an empathetic response to injury and a supportive environment for the return to work of workers with back pain and suggests educational programs for managers and front line supervisors as a means for achieving these objectives. However, educational programs are probably not sufficient to change behaviour unless they are supported by other features of the work environment. Additional possibilities include changing incentive structures that reward behaviour, allowing workers some recourse if they are treated poorly (i.e., ombudsmen, worker representative), and developing appropriate worker-friendly policies. An added complication is that "workplace culture" may not be monolithic in nature but may vary across the organization (e.g., it may vary according to one's status). Tarasuk and Eakin (1995) found that for workers with back pain, those with lower employment status and less seniority experienced particularly negative reactions from their workplace concerning their injury.

Joint Labour-Management Cooperation

The literature on disability management programs show the importance of the joint commitment, support, and active participation of both labour and management. Cooperation between labour and management is critical to avoid the development of adversarial relationships between worker and employer (Clarke et al. 1999; Getzie 1997; Bruyère and Shrey 1991). Together, labour and management can develop appropriate policies and procedures to address the work environment issues that contribute to workplace injury and disability. When unions agree to the philosophy of safe and early return to work as a benefit that any worker may require in the future, workers are more likely to be accepting of these policies in their work environment. In non-union settings, worker representatives (perhaps the worker representatives for the joint health and safety committees) can be used in lieu of union representatives (Margaret Friesen, personal communication, 1998). Companies that are sincere about enhancing employee well-being will probably earn employee trust. The trust and buy-in of employees, and of their supervisors, union representatives, and co-workers helps create a successful return-to-work program.

Communication

A critical component of successful return-to-work programming is open communication between the worker, the worker's health care provider, the union representative, and the person within the company responsible for the return-to-work process. If the worker feels needed in the workplace and is motivated to return to work, this crucial communication link is more likely to be established. Several unionized companies have found that using a union representative as a contact for the health care provider was fruitful in promoting communication (Guest and Drummond 1992; Clarke et al. 1999). In addition, for larger firms, effective communication between departments within the firm is important for efficient return to work (Akabas et al. 1990).

Offering Modified Work

It is important that disability management programs provide modified work for their injured workers. Modified work can involve either a modification of the original job to reduce physical demands or hours worked, or the transfer of the recovering worker to a less demanding job. Offering modified work reduces disability-related costs and can be favourable to the worker's effective recovery from back pain. Such policies will also ensure that the company is in compliance with workers' compensation and human rights legislation. An IWH study found that injured workers who were offered reduced hours, a flexible schedule, a lighter job, or equipment or ergonomic changes to help them return to work had markedly reduced time on benefits compared to workers with similar injuries who were not offered these options (Brooker et al. 1998). The Manitoba nurses study found that employees themselves were the best resource to help identify the work modifications required to help them return to work most expeditiously (Yassi et al. 1995).

A recent study of 175 employees in different workplaces in Sherbrooke, Quebec, is an example that shows very promising results for participatory ergonomic interventions involving permanent workplace modification (Loisel et al. 1997). The ergonomic intervention consisted of a work-site evaluation for workers still absent from work six weeks after injury (as well as a visit to an occupational physician). The evaluation involved the ergonomist and union and employer representatives to determine the need for job modifications. Then this group, plus the injured worker and the worker's supervisor, met to discuss the situation and submit a precise solution to the employer. Workers with back injuries who received on-site ergonomic interventions were absent from regular work only half as long (sixty days, on average) as those workers who received "usual care" – essentially, whatever test, treatment, or referral to a specialist that their family physician thought necessary (120 days, on average) – or as those who received the clinical intervention (131 days). The clinical care intervention included, after eight weeks' absence from work, a visit to a back pain specialist and a school for back care education ("back school"), and after twelve weeks' absence, a multidisciplinary work rehabilitation intervention, including fitness development, work hardening, and progressive return to work on alternate days. Workers receiving the ergonomic intervention also reported less pain on a subsequent interview conducted one year after their injury.

Although Loisel et al.'s study is not a direct permanent-versus-temporary comparison and could be confounded due to the interventions having been provided at different periods post-injury, their results do suggest that permanent modifications are preferable to temporary measures (such as described in the clinical intervention). Furthermore, it is fairly reasonable to assume that an alteration of the injury-precipitating job is likely to reduce the incidence of recurrent soft tissue pain, or new incidences of soft tissue injuries in the future (although that has yet to be confirmed empirically). Unlike temporary measures such as reduced work hours or a temporary job change, a permanent job modification is less likely to require temporary replacement workers or to increase the workload of the other employees (Akabas et al. 1990). Scientific reviews that summarize the evidence concerning the etiology of work-related back pain usually distinguish between two types of work-related causes. One type of cause is physical workplace factors such as work-related lifting and forceful movements, whole-body vibration, heavy physical work, and awkward postures (NIOSH 1997). The other is workplace-related psychosocial factors such as intensified workloads or poor job control (NIOSH 1997). Thus, one might assume that either of these two types of factors could be addressed to modify the job. In practice, however, as the two types of factors are interrelated it is likely that they would have to be modified simultaneously.

Ongoing Evaluation of the Program

Like most programs, disability management initiatives require ongoing evaluation to ensure that the program operates effectively and to identify and correct weaknesses in its design or operation (MFL 1995). It is important, however, that the outcomes of the program not be measured too narrowly. Merely returning workers to modified work (or even to their regular job) and producing short-term cost savings does not necessarily make a disability management program successful. In order to ensure safe return to work, outcomes need to include worker-based outcomes such as pain and functional status. Recently, an international group of back pain researchers, who sought consistency in the outcome assessment of patients with back pain, agreed on a set of six standardized questions that included these types of outcomes (Deyo et al. 1998).

The issue of recurrences adds another layer of complexity to outcome assessment. Workers with back injuries are more likely to have recurrences than those with other types of injuries (Butler et al. 1995) and experience greater difficulty reintegrating into the workforce, partly due to the interaction of the physical limitations of their illness and the requirements of their jobs (Butler et al. 1995; Yelin et al. 1986). A one-year study of 1,546 injured workers, who filed for workers' compensation benefits with soft tissue injuries (Manno and Hogg-Johnson 1999), found that 5 percent of the sample were still on compensation after one year, 81 percent had one episode of time on benefits and were off by the end of the year, 12.3 percent had two episodes of time on benefits, and 2 percent had three or more episodes of time on benefits. Interestingly, the recurrent episodes had very similar distribution patterns to the initial episode on compensation. The distributions appear to be log-normal with a mean of about eighty days, and a median of about fifty-five days (Manno and Hogg-Johnson 1999). A study with a six-year follow-up of 5,346 workers with soft tissue injuries found that 78.2 percent of the sample had one episode of time on benefits, 14.2 percent had two episodes, and 7.6 percent had three or more episodes (Wang 1999). These two studies, based on routinely collected administrative (workers' compensation board) data, unfortunately cannot tell us to what extent the claimants in the studies were successfully reintegrated into the workforce after their periods of compensation. A study of workers with permanent partial impairments (the "permanent" indicating a more seriously injured group of workers than the two studies described above), with all types of injuries, found that after three years, only 39 percent had a single absence from work followed by a successful return to work. The rest of the sample had more complex employment patterns: 29 percent single absence, unsuccessful return to work; 21 percent multiple absences, successful return to work; and 10 percent multiple absences, unsuccessful return to work (Butler et al. 1995).

The chronic nature of soft tissue injuries probably contributes to the frequency of the recurrences. However, another possible explanation is that many workers kept returning to a job that reignited their injury. A successful disability management program tries to minimize recurrent episodes of pain and thus recurrent episodes of time off work.

Return-to-Work Programs in Smaller-Sized Firms

Drury (1991) suggested that smaller-sized firms face particular challenges when it comes to implementing sound disability management practices. First, smaller firms lack the economies of scale found in larger firms, thus hiring specialized personnel is more problematic. Second, Drury noted that smaller-sized firms appear to have much less information about disability management practices than do large firms. Furthermore, they are often not bound by legislation or experience rating incentives.

Presumably it was these assumptions concerning lack of education and economies of scale for smaller-sized firms that led to the development of the employer consortium approaches that have been piloted in the United States (Drury 1991). The consortium seeks to provide economies of scale in disability management services by bringing together a group of employers, usually under the auspices of a non-profit "lead organization." Among other things, employer consortia can provide (1) employer education services or (2) direct case management.

Yet qualitative research by Eakin and MacEachen (1998) suggests that smaller workplaces have unique social relations that present distinct challenges for occupational health and safety. As they did not investigate disability management issues, we can only speculate on the implications of their research findings for this topic. It is possible that the more personalized nature of employee-employer relations in many small workplaces and the lack of a worker's advocate may result in an underrepresentation of workers' interests. On the other hand, perhaps the more fluid, flexible, and informal management style with a shorter hierarchy may be quite adaptable to providing modified work for workers – a possible scenario put forth by Drury. The state of modified work programs in smaller-sized firms deserves further investigation.

A US study (Hester and Decelle 1990) found that small- and medium-sized firms (fewer than 250 employees) are not more resistant to having a policy for early return to work compared to larger firms. Larger firms do have more specialized staff and a greater diversity of jobs, and thus finding transitional jobs may be easier for them. However, providing part-time work, light duties, or a modification of the original pre-injury job should be as possible in medium-sized firms as it is in larger ones. These suppositions are indeed supported by the evidence in Hester and Decelle's study. Medium-sized employers may, however, require external specialized personnel to help implement and facilitate these processes. Nonetheless, it is important to recognize the distinction between medium-sized employers who have marginally fewer than 250 employees, and very small employers, that is, those with fewer than five employees. The latter may face additional difficulties, and are unlikely to be aware of the existence or importance of optimal return-to-work programs. Statistics Canada data for Ontario give the following breakdown of the Ontario workforce in terms of employer size: fewer than five employees (7 percent), five to nineteen (12 percent), twenty to forty-nine (9 percent), fifty to ninety-nine (6.9 percent), 100-499 (14.8 percent), and 500 or more (49.7 percent) (Statistics Canada 1993).

An IWH study (Brooker et al. 1998) conducted in Ontario found that smaller firms were reported to provide arrangements to help an injured worker back to work less frequently than larger firms. The study sample consisted of about 1,500 workers who had suffered work-related soft tissue injuries. In the sample, 34 percent of those who had worked in firms of fewer than five employees reported that they were offered arrangements to help them return to work at some point in the year following their injury. For larger firms, the percentages are as follows: 31 percent (firms with five to nineteen employees); 41 percent (firms with twenty to ninety-nine employees); 47 percent (firms with 100-999 employees); and 48 percent (1,000 or more employees) (Brooker et al. 1998).

Availability and Quality of Return-to-Work Programs in Canada

There are currently few reliable data on the prevalence of return-to-work employment policies, their adequacy, or effectiveness in Canada. With some exceptions, evaluations have been done in-house and are concerned primarily with financial savings for the company. However, we examined several available sources.

In one study of 305 Canadian employers (Watson Wyatt Worldwide

1997), 80 percent of respondents reported having transitional or modified return-to-work programs for employees with occupational injuries. By contrast, 74 percent offered modified work to workers who had non-occupational injuries. In a representative sample of approximately 1,500 Ontario workers with a variety of work-related soft tissue injuries (Brooker et al. 1998), an IWH study found only 44.6 percent of workers reported that they had been offered any type of arrangement to help them return to work at one year post-injury. Beyond the difference in respondent groups one possible reason for this discrepancy is that companies may have return-to-work policies in place, but may not be actively arranging modified work for every one of their injured employees.

Other researchers (Shoemaker et al. 1992) studied the characteristics of companies in the United States in which early return-to-work programs existed and found that acceptance of such programs hinged on several factors, but was most directly linked to the beliefs of key corporate executives.

With regard to the quality of return-to-work programs, again, there is limited documented evidence on those currently offered in Canada. However, one important element of success appears to be increased communication and understanding among the various players: the worker, the health care provider, and the workplace. From the Watson Wyatt Worldwide survey (1997) mentioned above, 43 percent of employers reported that educating medical providers about the workplace was a component of their disability management program. Other key components of an optimal program include educational initiatives (these were offered to supervisors and managers by 31 percent of employers), and ongoing evaluation of the disability management program by tracking return-to-work results (this was a feature of 54 percent of existing programs).

A permanent modification of the pre-injury job is the most advantageous form of modified work. Yet in the IWH study of 1,500 Ontario workers (Brooker et al. 1998) mentioned above, only 3.5 percent of workers reported that they were offered layout or equipment changes to their work station. Temporary modifications such as reduced hours, a flexible schedule, and lighter jobs were reportedly offered to 15 percent, 13 percent, and 28 percent of workers, respectively (ibid. 1998). Neglecting to alter the pre-injury job leaves open the possibility for recurrent future episodes of back pain.

Union workplace representatives have suggested that in settings where less-than-optimal return-to-work programs are in place (where direct cost savings are the focus), recurrences in injury may be more frequent, income support for subsequent time loss lower, and termination of employment more likely.

The evidence indicates that there are still numerous companies that do not have any return-to-work programs in place. Furthermore, for those companies that do have programs, the program quality can differ tremendously from one company to another. These findings were epitomized at a recent National Roundtable on Employee Health hosted by the Institute for Work and Health. At one extreme, a company was so progressive that their on-site ergonomists were an intrinsic part of the job design team, and workstation changes were made only if they satisfied ergonomic specifications and accommodated the requirements of the individuals who worked there. Further, new health and safety concerns were addressed daily by the plant manager. At the other end of the spectrum, a union representative had dealings with a firm whose modified work program was so thoughtlessly executed that it was probably exacerbating the injuries of the recently injured workers (Andy King, personal communication, 1998).

Given the range in both the prevalence and quality of return-to-work programs offered by employers, attention should focus on the factors (both internal to the firm and external) that could influence more companies to implement high-quality and safe return-to-work programs. These could include:

- special programs targeted to help smaller firms
- more stringent legislation
- additional financial incentives
- collective bargaining
- programs geared at educating corporate executives.

It is important to note that our current economic and legislative incentive system is geared toward the implementation of programs that reduce disability costs. This was noted by a number of respondents in the Work-Ready study (Clarke et al. 1999). The challenge for the future will be to create incentive systems that will also target worker-centred outcomes such as pain and functional status.

Conclusion

Research has begun to clarify the factors that affect safe and timely return to work. For workers with back pain, clinical interventions have had some success in alleviating pain. However, workplace-based interventions are key in order to facilitate the safe and timely return to work of injured workers. From evidence to date, optimal workplace-based programs include the following elements: supportive return-to-work policies and supportive responses to injury throughout the management structure including the very top levels; cooperation and communication among all parties (injured workers, employer, labour, and health care providers); an underlying philosophy of injury and disability prevention; and ongoing program evaluation.

Effective disability management programs can help maintain a healthy and involved workforce, but many workplaces in Canada have not yet adopted the type of multifaceted approach that is required for optimal efficacy. The internal and external factors that could contribute to the widespread adoption and implementation of high-quality workplace-based return-to-work programs in Canada will require further investigation and more thoughtful attention in the future.

Note

1 This qualitative research work is part of a larger study conducted by the Institute for Work and Health (IWH) along with researchers from Manitoba and Quebec and partially funded by one of the Canadian Network of Centres of Excellence initiatives (HEALNet).

References

Akabas, S.H., and L.B. Gates. 1990. "Organizational Commitment: The Key to Successful Implementation of Disability Management." *American Rehabilitation* 16 (3): 9-13, 32.

Battié, M.C. 1992. "Minimizing the Impact of Back Pain: Workplace Strategies." *Seminars in Spine Surgery* 4 (1): 20-8.

Baum, F. 1995. "Researching Public Health: Behind the Qualitative-Quantitative Methodological Debate." *Social Science and Medicine* 40 (4): 459-68.

Bigos, S., O. Bowyer, G. Braen, et al. 1994. *Acute Low Back Problems in Adults: Clinical Practice Guideline No. 14*. AHCPR publication 95-0642. Rockville, MD: Agency for Health Care Policy and Research, Public Health Service, US Department of Health and Human Services.

Brooker, A., J.M. Smith, D.C. Cole, and S.A. Hogg-Johnson. 1998. "Workplace Arrangements to Return Injured Workers to Work: Evidence from a Prospective Cohort of Workers with Soft Tissue Injuries." Unpublished paper, Institute for Work and Health (IWH), Toronto.

Bruyère, S.M., and D.E. Shrey. 1991. "Disability Management in Industry: A Joint Labor-Management Process." *Rehabilitation Counselling Bulletin* 34 (3): 227-42.

Butler, R.J., W.G. Johnson, and M. Baldwin. 1995. "Managing Work Disability: Why First Return to Work Is Not a Measure of Success." *Industrial and Labor Relations Review* 48 (3): 452-69.

Clarke, J.A., D.C. Cole, and S.E. Ferrier. 1999. "Work-Ready I: Report of Qualitative Component from Ontario." Unpublished research report for Heal Net, available from Institute for Work and Health (IWH), Toronto.

Clinical Standards Advisory Group. 1994. *Epidemiology Review: The Epidemiology and Cost of Back Pain*. London: HMSO.

Deyo, R.A., M.C. Battié, A.J.H.M. Beurskens, C. Bombardier, P. Croft, B.W. Koes, A. Malmivaara, M. Roland, M. von Korff, and G. Waddell. 1998. "Outcome Measures for Low Back Pain Research: A Proposal for Standardized Use." *Spine* 23 (18): 2003-13.

Drury, D. 1991. "Disability Management in Small Firms." *Rehabilitation Counselling Bulletin* 34 (3): 243-56.

Eakin, J. M., and E. MacEachen. 1998. "Health and the Social Relations of Work: A Study of the Health-Related Experiences of Employees in Small Workplaces." *Sociology of Health and Illness* 20 (6): 896-914.

Frank, J.W., A.S. Brooker, S.E. DeMaio, M.S. Kerr, A. Maetzel, H.S. Shannon, T. Sullivan, R.W. Norman, and R.P. Wells. 1996. "Disability Resulting from Occupational Low Back Pain, Part II: What Do We Know about Secondary Prevention? A Review of the Scientific Evidence on Prevention after Disability Begins." *Spine* 21 (24): 2918-29.

Frank, J., S. Sinclair, S. Hogg-Johnson, H. Shannon, C. Bombardier, D. Beaton, and D. Cole. 1998. "Preventing Disability from Work-Related Low-Back Pain: New Evidence Gives New Hope – If We Can Just Get All the Players Onside." *Canadian Medical Association Journal* 158 (12): 1625-31.

Getzie, T.J. 1997. "The Importance of Labour-Management Collaboration." In *Strategies for Success: Disability Management in the Workplace*, 96-105. Port Alberni, BC: National Institute of Disability Management and Research.

Guest, G.H., and P.D. Drummond. 1992. "Effect of Compensation on Emotional State and Disability in Chronic Back Pain." *Pain* 48: 125-30.

Hester, E.J., and P.G. Decelles. 1990. *The Effect of Employer Size on Disability Benefits and Cost-Containment Practices*. Topeka, KS: Menninger Foundation.

Hillier, K. "The Disability Management Journey." 1997. Disability Management Seminar: Emerging Trends in the Effective Management of Disability. Visions Claims Management Inc., Toronto.

Lindstrom, I., C. Ohlund, C. Eek, L. Wallin, L.E. Peterson, W.E. Fordyce., and A.L. Nachemson. 1992. "The Effect of Graded Activity on Patients with Subacute Low Back Pain: A Randomized Prospective Clinical Study with an Operant-Conditioning Behavioral Approach." *Physical Therapy* 72 (4): 279-93.

Loisel, P., L. Abenhaim, P. Durand, J.M. Esdaile, S. Suissa, L. Gosselin, R. Simard, J. Turcotte, and J. Lemaire. 1997. "A Population-Based, Randomized Clinical Trial on Back Pain Management." *Spine* 22 (24): 2911-8.

Manitoba Federation of Labour (MFL). 1995. *Workers with Disabilities Project: Workplace Disability Programs*. Winnipeg: Manitoba Federation of Labour.

Manno, M., and S.A. Hogg-Johnson. 1999. "Multi-State Hazard Models for Analyzing Recurrence of Soft Tissue Injury." Presented to Workers' Compensation Research Group. Cambridge, MA. 5-6 March.

National Institute for Occupational Safety and Health (NIOSH). 1997. *Musculoskeletal Disorders and Workplace Factors: A Critical Review of Epidemiologic Evidence for Work-Related Musculoskeletal Disorders of the Neck, Upper Extremity, and Low Back*. Baltimore: US Department of Health and Human Services.

National Work Injuries Statistics Program (NWISP). 1997. *Work Injuries and Diseases*. Edmonton: Association of Workers' Compensation Boards of Canada (AWCBC).

Shoemaker, R.J., S.S. Robin, and H.S. Robin. 1992. "Reaction to Disability through Organization Policy: Early Return to Work Policy." *Journal of Rehabilitation* 58 (3): 18-24.

Sinclair, S.J., T.J. Sullivan, J.A. Clarke, and J.W. Frank. 1998. "A Framework for Examining Return to Work in Workers' Compensation: A Review from One North American Jurisdiction." In *International Examinations of Medical-Legal Aspects of Work Injuries*, ed. E.H. Yates and J.F. Burton, 263-300. London: Scarecrow Press.

Smith, J., V. Tarasuk, S. Ferrier, and H. Shannon. 1996. "Relationship between Workers' Reports of Problems of Legitimacy and Vulnerability in the Workplace and Duration of Benefits for Lost-Time Musculoskeletal Injuries." *American Journal of Epidemiology* 143: S17 (abstract).

Spitzer, W.O., F.E. LeBlanc, M. Dupuis, L. Abenhaim, A.Y. Belanger, R. Bloch, C. Bombardier, R.L. Cruess, G. Drouin, N. Duval-Hesler, J. Laflamme, G. Lamoureux, A.L. Nachemson, J.J. Pagé, M. Rossignol, L.R. Salmi, S. Salois-Arsenault, S. Suissa, and S. Wood-Dauphinée. 1987. "Scientific Approach to the Assessment and Management of Activity-Related Spinal Disorders: A Monograph for Clinicians." Report of the Quebec Task Force on Spinal Disorders. *Spine* 12 (7, supplement): S4-S55.

Statistics Canada. Small Business and Special Surveys Division. 1993. Special Data Request Report. Ottawa: Statistics Canada.

Tarasuk, V., and J.M. Eakin. 1995. "The Problem of Legitimacy in the Experience of Work-Related Back Injury." *Qualitative Health Research* 5 (2): 204-21.

van der Weide, W.E., J.H. Verbeek, and M.W. van Tulder. 1997. "Vocational Outcome of Intervention for Low-Back Pain." *Scandinavian Journal of Work, Environment, and Health* 23 (3): 165-78.

Wang, H. 1999. "A Follow-Up Study of Workers with Soft Tissue Injuries Using the Databases of the Ontario Workplace Safety and Insurance Board (WSIB)." PhD diss. University of Toronto.

Watson Wyatt Worldwide. 1997. *Staying at Work: Value Creation through Integration: Results of a Canadian Survey on Disability Management*. Toronto: Watson Wyatt Worldwide.

Yassi, A., R. Tate, J.E. Cooper, C. Snow, S. Vallentyne, and J.B. Khokhar. 1995. "Early Intervention for Back-Injured Nurses at a Large Canadian Tertiary Care Hospital: An Evaluation of the Effectiveness and Cost Benefits of a Two-Year Pilot Project." *Occupational Medicine* 45 (4): 209-14.

Yelin, E., C.J. Henke, and W.V. Epstein. 1986. "Work Disability among Persons with Musculoskeletal Conditions." *Arthritis and Rheumatology* 29 (11): 1322-33.

Part 5: Entitlement, Fairness, and Sustainability

John Frank and Andreas Maetzel sketch out the significant sleeping giant on the horizon of occupational health problems. The growth of disease knowledge has identified unequivocal work-related attribution for a number of conditions not currently considered to be compensable as work-related injuries. Using the examples of low back pain, osteoarthritis of the knee and hip, and cardiovascular disease, Frank and Maetzel carefully review and summarize the so-called Bradford Hill criteria of epidemiological causation, the extent to which a given condition X can be attributable to a given cause Y. They make the compelling argument that the standard of proof present for insuring many soft tissue injury conditions is no stronger than the standard of proof available for a number of conditions that are not routinely insured as work-related injuries. Using thumbnail estimates of the total burden of osteoarthritis of the knee and hip that can be attributed to work-related causes, Frank and Maetzel sketch out the problem of sustaining workers' compensation entitlements under an arrangement where osteoarthritis of the knee and hip would be recognized broadly as a work-related injury given certain exposure thresholds. They highlight the "trilemma" of reconciling fairness, sustainability, and entitlement with this growing knowledge about multi-causality in the attribution of work-related injury and disease. Frank and Maetzel call for some rethinking of the scope of coverage of accident insurance and consider the merits and risks of competing coverage arrangements.

Terry Thomason identifies how fatality benefits should be developed and determined, using the arguments from the economic literature and the history of common law in the area of fatality benefits. Thomason argues for a more straightforward economic underpinning for fatality benefits based on treating the incomes of deceased workers as total disability wage replacement. He highlights, on a comparative basis, the range of arrangements for fatality benefits and fatality benefit levels across jurisdictions in North America. He concludes that any system based on real-wage replacement is arguably fairer and superior to one based exclusively on the relatively indeterminate dimensions of need.

In the final chapter, William Gnam explores the nature and determination of mental disability in the field of workers' compensation. He reviews the administrative categories that have developed in the common law related to acute and chronic mental injury associated with either physical or mental events. He also reviews some of the literature touched on by Kerr in his chapter related to the nature of job stress and the manner in which job stress acts as a mediating process between work exposures and a range of physical and mental health outcomes. Gnam also provides reassurance that carefully delimited approaches to chronic and mental stress can actually result in some limited entitlements that seem consistent with the criteria of fairness without foregoing sustainability. Mental stress and strain will continue to dominate entitlement issues and workers' compensation for the foreseeable future and we are challenged to develop new methods of entitlement to deal with mental health outcomes in the area of workers' compensation.

12
Determining Occupational Disorder: Can This Camel Carry More Straw?
John Frank and Andreas Maetzel

Historically, workers' compensation plans have been designed to provide health care and wage loss indemnity coverage for workers with injuries and illnesses for which there has been little question of the "cause" being directly work-related. For example, acute trauma occurring at the workplace, and clear-cut effects of toxic exposures, especially where these health effects are quite specific to the toxicant in question, fit this historically simple model of "occupational" health problems. But today's pattern of workers' compensation claims in North America is very different, and rapidly becoming more so, in that a majority of claims are for soft tissue strains, sprains, and related conditions, often of gradual onset with no history of acute trauma. For these conditions, science is beginning to paint a much more complex picture of causation, a multi-factorial one, in which workplace exposures play an important but only partial role. In addition, there is mounting epidemiological evidence that a number of equally multi-factorial degenerative conditions of later life, such as osteoarthritis and coronary heart disease, are substantially accelerated and made more severe in their onset as the result of various physical and psychosocial aspects of previous lifelong work.

This chapter does three things. It reviews the current epidemiological evidence of work-relatedness for low back pain, osteoarthritis of the knee and hip, and coronary heart disease, which are either already important in workers' compensation statistics or likely to become so should the accumulating scientific evidence of occupational causation be used to argue successfully for compensation coverage. Second, it summarizes the key scientific issues in determining the extent to which workers' compensation for these sorts of conditions should be paid, and under exactly which circumstances. Third, it suggests and briefly analyzes a range of broad policy options for dealing with this looming crisis, before workers' compensation programs face the unsavoury options of financial unsustainability, or arbitrary exclusion of certain "occupational" conditions from entitlement.

Scientific Criteria for Assessing Evidence of Causation

Criteria by which to assess scientific evidence on causation, for any health condition, have been most fully developed by epidemiologists, the best known of which is Sir Austin Bradford Hill (1897-1991). Bradford Hill put forward, in a now-famous paper (Bradford Hill 1965), nine criteria for causation that could be applied to the scientific evidence available on any given question of the form: "Does exposure to X cause health outcome Y?" These criteria are: strength of association, dose-response relationship, consistency across studies, temporality, biological plausibility, coherence, specificity, analogy, and experimental risk reversal. They are described in Appendix C in an order slightly different from the one Bradford Hill used (for clarity). There they are explained in non-technical language, with examples of exposure/disease combinations to clarify how the criteria are applied in practice. Hill himself suggested that none of these criteria, excepting perhaps "temporality," *must* be met for an exposure to be causal. Rather, they are considered collectively in relation to the whole body of evidence pertaining to a given causation question. Although some criteria provide more solid indications of causation than others, the more criteria are met, the stronger the evidence for causation.

While more recent revisions of these criteria exist (Susser 1977), they have not replaced Bradford Hill's original formulation. Thus, the present chapter will utilize these classic criteria to determine whether sufficient evidence now exists to consider various work-related exposures to be causal for two ubiquitous conditions of later life – coronary heart disease (CHD) and osteoarthritis (OA), for which workers' compensation payments are not routinely made in North America – and one exceedingly common condition of midlife – mechanical low back pain, for which compensation appears to be almost always awarded on this continent.

Three Examples: Low Back Pain, Osteoarthritis, and Coronary Heart Disease

Utilizing the standard epidemiological criteria for causation described above, we will now review accumulating epidemiological and biological evidence that suggests that these three very common conditions are at least in substantial part caused by conditions of and exposures at work, acting over a number of years of adult life. We choose these conditions because they represent major burdens of the general population burden of illness and disability on which a great deal of new etiologic evidence has been generated in recent years, which would seem to argue for credible, if partial, occupational attribution. Furthermore, they represent an instructive mix of one multi-factorial condition – low back pain – where there is currently almost universal compensability in North America, despite, or perhaps because of, virtually no meaningful capability to validly discern with current medical methods which cases actually are work-related (Deyo et al. 1991; Frank, forthcoming; Frank et al. 1996), and two equally multi-factorial conditions, eventually affecting the majority of all elderly, for which workers' compensation payments are only ever paid in North America under exceptional circumstances.

Low Back Pain

Arguably the commonest cause of disability in adults under age 45 in modern societies, low back pain (LBP) has defied all efforts to define its exact pathophysiology, that is, the nature of the underlying lesion (Bigos et al. 1994; Deyo et al. 1991; Frank et al. 1995, 1996; Frank, forthcoming; Nachemson 1992, 1994). Despite the advent of very sophisticated laboratory and imaging techniques, over 95 percent of LBP cases in the working-age population have no consistent pathological abnormalities demonstrated on any testing that physicians can currently order. Of course, such patients do have abnormal functional capacity tests, but these only attempt to quantify the degree of impairment and disability associated with LBP, rather than illuminate its cause. Indeed, the absence of any such objective findings is the criteria for labelling such patients as having "mechanical" or "idiopathic" (unknown-cause) LBP, a diagnosis of exclusion (AHCPR 1994). Although the presumed underlying pathology is soft tissue (i.e., muscle, tendon, and ligament) strain or sprain, this has never been clearly demonstrated with the scientific techniques currently available.

On the other hand, despite this failure to fully meet the "biological plausibility" criterion for causation by exposures at work, low back pain does meet a number of other Bradford Hill criteria for causation, as exhaustively reviewed by NIOSH (1997): strength of association, dose-response relationship, consistency of association, temporal relationship, and coherence of evidence. These findings are briefly summarized in Table 12.1.

As the methodologically sophisticated and comprehensive NIOSH review pointed out – and is clear from Table 12.1 – the LBP causation evidence is, overall, much more convincing for biomechanical exposures at work (e.g., heavy lifting or forceful movements, prolonged non-neutral postures, and whole-body vibration, as in prolonged driving) than it is for psychosocial exposures such as perceived time pressure, low job control, a negative social milieu in the workplace, and job dissatisfaction. However, this apparent difference in the currently available level of evidence should not be over-interpreted: biomechanical exposures have been studied much longer, and with better measurement methods, than psychosocial exposures. Thus, the rate of accumulation of new, high-quality evidence on the latter may well surpass that on the former in coming years. As an example, a new case-control study, conducted by the Institute for Work and Health (IWH), shows that perceptions of a poor-quality social environment at work (e.g., frequent

Table 12.1

Summary of current causation evidence: LBP and work-related biomechanical and psychosocial exposures

Causation criterion	Status of LBP and work psychosocial/biomechanical exposures evidence[a]
Strength of association	RRs[a] of 1.5-2.8, in a few good studies each, for perceived: • Time pressure/workload • Low job control • Negative work milieu • Job dissatisfaction RRs of 2-5 or more in many good studies for: • Forces involved in (or observed levels of) heavy lifting/forceful movements and awkward postures (out of neutral position) • Whole-body vibration/driving
Dose-response relationship	Convincingly demonstrated for most of the biomechanical exposures listed above. Not yet clear for the psychosocial exposures.
Consistency across studies	Excellent for the biomechanical exposures, much less for the psychosocial ones, but far fewer good studies have been done.
Temporality	Established for most biomechanical exposures and some psychosocial exposures.
Biological plausibility	Pathological lesion unclear, but ample laboratory evidence of several possible tissue-damage mechanisms for biomechanical exposures. For psychosocial exposures less clear, but consistent with recent psycho-neuro-endocrinologic and other biological research.
Coherence	General pattern of LBP across occupations suggests causal role for heavy physical loads at work but is difficult to assess for psychosocial factors, due to absence of routinely collected data on these exposures.
Specificity	Unclear, though traumatic effects of acute physical loads in back tissues may mirror the effects of chronic/repetitive lower loads.
Analogy	Criterion not met and unlikely to be met.
Experimental risk reversal	No convincing studies yet available.

a RR = magnitude of relative risk.

conflicts and unhelpful relationships), inadequate matching of worker skills and job tasks in the mind of the worker, and low job control all contributed independently (interquartile RRs[1] 2.6, 2.2, and 2.0, respectively) to the risk of reporting LBP to a workplace nursing station in a large car-assembly plant in Ontario in the mid-1990s (Kerr et al. 1998). Furthermore, these risk contributions were estimated after controlling for equally large risk contributions from three different, objectively measured biomechanical forces on the spine while working, and worker perceptions of job "heaviness" (Kerr et al. 1998; Norman et al., forthcoming). This is the first study to so clearly show the independent effect of both occupational biomechanical and psychosocial risk factors on LBP, indicating how young this field of research still is.

A special note is warranted on the question of "biological plausibility" evidence for LBP and occupational psychosocial factors. While it may be entirely intuitive to see a relation between LBP and biomechanical loads on the spine related to the physical tasks of work, it is more difficult to appreciate how the mental and emotional state of the worker, as affected by the workplace social environment, could also affect the risk of back injury, leading to LBP. The NIOSH review (1997) does point out a number of possible mechanisms for the latter effect, based on our rapidly growing knowledge of the body's myriad connections between the brain, the endocrine system, and the locomotor system (Sauter and Swanson 1996; Bongers et al. 1993; Bernard et al. 1994).

First, psychosocial demands may produce muscle tension and exacerbate task-related biomechanical strain. Second, psychosocial demands may affect awareness and reporting of musculoskeletal symptoms and/or perceptions of their cause. Third, initial episodes of pain based on physical insult may trigger a chronic nervous system dysfunction, physiological as well as psychological, which perpetuates a chronic pain process. Finally, in some work situations, changes in psychosocial demands may be associated with changes in physical demands and biomechanical stresses, and thus associations between psychosocial demands and musculoskeletal disorders occur through either a causal or effect-modifying relationship (NIOSH 1997: 7:3).

Some may question the entry in the last row of Table 12.1, concerning the current dearth of high-quality scientific evidence that LBP at work can be effectively prevented by intervening on the putative causal factors listed in the first row of the table, particularly the ergonomic spinal loads of jobs. As carefully explained in our 1996 comprehensive review of this subject (Frank et al. 1996), it is so difficult to design and execute controlled studies of any workplace intervention that the lack of good intervention studies of this kind may simply reflect this difficulty. A lack of high-quality evidence on prevention effectiveness is not the same as high-quality evidence (e.g., from "negative" controlled trials) that a condition cannot be prevented by an intervention. Indeed, our conclusion in that review was that there are ample basic-science and epidemiological grounds for believing that well-designed ergonomic changes should reduce rates of LBP disability in high-exposure jobs, but that proof of this may remain elusive. All such interventions consequently deserve careful evaluation of their health effects.

Coronary Heart Disease

A number of biomedical risk factors for coronary heart disease (CHD) have been known for over thirty years, and these all now meet several of the causation criteria described above. For example, smoking, high blood pressure, and high blood levels of total low-density-lipoprotein (LDL) cholesterol all

- carry interquartile relative risks of approximately 2-3 for CHD in most studies
- show dose-response relationships (which are also consistent and temporally appropriate across studies)
- have credible biological mechanisms by which they speed up the process of arteriosclerotic plaque formation in arteries
- demonstrate patterns of occurrence in space and time related to CHD rates that are consistent with causation
- have convincingly been (albeit only within the last decade, in the case of high blood pressure and elevated cholesterol) experimentally reversed so as to actually reduce CHD risks, either in smoking cessation cohort studies, or randomized control trials of drug or dietary treatment.

Family history, and a variety of new genetic markers of CHD risk, while long recognized as clinically important in CHD causation, now have met all but the last of Bradford Hill's criteria, and experimental reversal of risk may soon be within reach as a result of promising new gene therapies. Thus, all these risk factors (i.e., smoking, high blood pressure, and high blood levels of total [LDL] cholesterol) are widely recognized as causal. Indeed, many other more recently discovered CHD risk factors, such as elevated blood levels of iron and homocystine (the latter thought to be correctable by increased dietary intake of folic acid) and low levels of selenium and Vitamin E, are well on the way to meeting these same causal criteria. However new research on various psychosocial aspects of work, as risk factors for CHD, is just beginning to meet the Bradford Hill criteria and many epidemiologists, let alone practising physicians, are therefore unfamiliar with it.

By far the most solidly implicated of these psychosocial aspects of work is the degree of control or decision latitude felt by workers concerning their jobs, based on their responses to a standardized questionnaire created by Robert Karasek and Tores Theorell (Kasl 1996; Johnson and Hall 1995; Karasek 1979; Karasek and Theorell 1990; Theorell and Karasek 1996).

Typically, studies record workers' responses to these questions and follow them for some years, with periodic examinations to detect new cases of CHD, or at least record linkage to detect deaths from CHD. However, a "prospective cohort" study of this kind needs to meet a number of specific epidemiological quality standards in order to provide valid and precise estimates of the relative risk of CHD in workers with "low job control" as compared to those with "high control," while taking into account other, independent, risk factors for CHD, utilizing multivariable risk regression analyses. These standards, reviewed in detail elsewhere (Rothman 1986; MacMahon and Pugh 1970), have been taken into consideration in the selection of the studies discussed below.

Perhaps the most convincing set of publications come from the Whitehall II UK Civil Service cohort of Michael Marmot and colleagues in London. In a series of papers published in the last few years, they have documented an approximate doubling of the risk of new CHD cases in both male and female office workers with low job control (Bosma et al. 1998; Syme and Balfour 1997; Marmot et al. 1997; Bosma et al. 1997). Furthermore, comparative analyses in this same cohort reveal that there is just as strong an independent relationship (RR 2.15) between CHD and subjects' earlier responses to a recently developed questionnaire measuring the imbalance between a worker's perceived "rewards from his/her job and the effort required to do it" (Peter and Siegrist 1997; Siegrist 1996; Siegrist et al. 1990; Bosma et al. 1998). A possible shortcoming of the new Whitehall II studies is that not all of the CHD cases analyzed were medically confirmed. However, they are at least compatible with CHD, as judged by standardized questionnaire responses concerning chest pain. The cohort is still rather young for CHD, and future analyses based on the additional cases rapidly accruing should remedy this deficiency.

While such modest relative risks are clearly not in themselves strong evidence of causation, Marmot et al. have statistically controlled for such a large variety of other CHD risk factors and worker characteristics that even sceptical cardiovascular epidemiologists are paying serious attention to these studies (Davey Smith 1997). Furthermore, there is consistency between the RR estimates in these studies and those of many others – see, for example, the review by Schnall et al. (1994) – including a large and well-designed case control study of Swedish middle-aged males (Johnson et al. 1996). While there are some respectable studies that show smaller RRs (Steenland et al. 1997; Alterman et al. 1994), there tend to be technical reasons for these discrepancies, such as differences in the amount of job control for which the RR is calculated, or probable exposure misclassification due to the use of national-survey-based estimates of job control for each subject's occupational title, obtained from other times and populations.

These studies, taken together, also demonstrate a dose-response relationship for CHD risk across degrees of job control, in that workers with jobs that carry an intermediate level of control show an intermediate level of CHD risk. In the Swedish study, there is also a suggestion that worker perceptions of low social support at work, when combined with low job control, carry a stronger (RR 2.6) risk of CHD over twenty-five years of followup. This is comparable to the strength of association demonstrated for CHD and smoking, high blood pressure, or high cholesterol levels. Thus, it is possible to fill out a summary evidence table for CHD and low job control, demonstrating the fulfillment of over half of the nine Bradford Hill criteria, based on only an embryonic literature that is growing exponentially each year (Table 12.2). This again compares favourably with the performance of classic CHD "causal" risk factors, such as smoking, in such summaries of evidence for causation.

Table 12.2

Summary of current causation evidence: CHD and work-related psychosocial exposures

Causation criterion	Status of CHD and work psychosocial exposures evidence
Strength of association	RRs of about 2 in many good studies, and 2.6 for "low control" combined with "poor support" in one excellent study.
Dose-response relationship	Present in some good studies, e.g., Whitehall II.
Consistency across studies	Moderate, but higher in high-quality studies.
Temporality	Well established by prospective studies.
Biological plausibility	Rapidly becoming convincing.
Coherence	Unclear: no exposure data routinely collected.
Specificity	Not obvious at present.
Analogy	No likelihood of meeting this criterion.
Experimental risk reversal	No high-quality studies yet available.

What of the biological plausibility of the relationship between job control and CHD? New research is beginning to suggest that each individual's characteristic pattern of physiological and biochemical responses to such psychosocial stressors begins early in life (Boyce et al. 1995; Evans et al. 1994; Jemerin and Boyce 1990). Furthermore, such responses probably involve not only the classically studied neuroendocrine "fright or flight" (adrenal-gland-medulla/catecholamine-mediated) or generic "stress" (adrenal-gland-cortex-glucocorticoid-mediated) pathways, but also a host of newly discovered other connections between the brain and our immune systems, as well as our blood-clotting apparatus (Evans et al. 1994; McEwen 1998). Taken together with new evidence that the decades-long development of arterial plaques in CHD may be influenced by immune processes (Gupta et al. 1997; Gupta and Camm 1997) and that critically narrow arteries may then be closed off in a heart attack or stroke by acute tendencies to clot more easily, which may in turn build on lifelong thrombotic predispositions (Bosma et al. 1997), these new studies allow us to complete our causation evidence table for CHD and low job control as showing a high degree of biological plausibility (Table 12.2).

Unfortunately, evidence meeting the very useful last criterion in the table, experimental reversal of risk, is not yet available. Again, as with workplace ergonomic intervention studies, there are immense logistic, scientific, and ethical hurdles involved in demonstrating in a controlled experiment that workplace reforms to improve job control actually reduce CHD risks in workers over subsequent decades. A recent review of all types of workplace intervention studies found very few that did a good job of measuring even the short-term health effects of such changes (Polanyi et al. 1997).

Osteoarthritis

Osteoarthritis (OA) is usually a slowly developing degenerative condition of later life, characterized by joint pain and limited joint function, that can affect any joint of the body. It predominately affects the hands, hips, and knees, the joints that are most subjected to mechanical loading. The etiology of OA is multifactorial in that its pathologic correlate is an injured cartilage, most often resulting from chronic mechanical stress, acting in concert with a slow, age-related degradation and thinning of the joint cartilage. High levels of physical activity and obesity have been the main foci of epidemiological investigations into factors contributing to the development of OA. However, other factors, such as acutely traumatic joint injuries, smoking, and educational attainment have also been investigated. Two systematic overviews were published in 1996 and 1997, summarizing the relationship between occupational risk factors and knee disorders including OA (Jensen and Eenberg 1996), and radiologically defined knee and hip OA (Maetzel et al. 1997). Both reviews concluded that the evidence in favour of mechanical occupational exposure as a risk factor for OA is strong and consistent.

OA has been subject to many definitions depending on whether the focus is on clinical symptoms and functional deterioration, or on pathological manifestations independent of clinical status. Further confusing matters, the public tends to label all pain and malfunction in and around the joints as "arthritis and rheumatism." A safeguard used in epidemiological studies against the inclusion of inadequately defined cases has therefore been to rely on clinical diagnosis by a health professional, or radiological diagnosis according to agreed-upon criteria. A variety of definitions have therefore been used in epidemiological studies, which make direct comparisons of their results difficult.

In the published etiologic overview by Maetzel et al. (1997) all studies to date dealing with mechanical occupational exposure and the development of radiologically documented osteoarthritis of hip or knee were rated for their quality and strength of evidence according to the Bradford Hill criteria for causation (Table 12.3). The association between mechanical occupational exposure and knee OA is moderately strong, with Odds Ratios (estimates of relative risk) around 2.5, and dose-response relationships documented in several, high-quality epidemiological studies (Kivimäki et al. 1992; Anderson and Felson 1988; Felson et al. 1991). One of these studies was able to follow up the Framingham cohort over decades, as is required to investigate causation in such a slowly developing condition. It is therefore the only prospective evidence currently available of an appropriate temporal relationship between mechanical occupational exposure and the subsequent development of knee OA (Felson et al. 1991). It was found that individuals exposed to frequent knee bending at work, or to generally heavy labour, have a 2.5 times higher risk of developing knee OA. The association between mechanical occupational exposure and hip OA is less well studied than that for knee OA. Although studies examining hip OA show consistently positive results, very few of them are free of major scientific flaws (Roach et al. 1994; Vingard et al. 1991; Croft et al. 1992).

The "biological plausibility" evidence is convincing in the limited sense that we know OA to be accelerated by mechanical exposures that damage the cartilage of a joint, which acts much like a shock absorber (Bullough 1998). However, little direct human biological evidence is available on the exact mechanisms of joint damage due to prolonged low-level mechanical stress, such as that occurring in lifelong exposure to heavy work. As for the causation criterion "analogy," clinicians have known for centuries that some individuals, presumably with an unknown genetic or other basis for their susceptibility, develop rapid-onset OA, termed "post-traumatic degenerative arthritis," within less than a decade after acute joint injury. This condition would seem to represent a naturally occurring human analog of more slowly developing, garden-variety OA that afflicts the majority of the elderly at some point in their lives.

The Policy Challenge

The point of these three condition-specific summaries of causation is that there is already, even on the basis of still-incomplete evidence of occupational causation, a problematic inconsistency in the legislated compensability and practical adjudication of the three medical conditions discussed above. On the basis of the epidemiological and human biological evidence of causation tabulated above, one could argue that there are comparable grounds for considering that a substantial fraction of cases of all three conditions, arising in former or current workers with a history of the relevant

Table 12.3

Summary of current causation evidence: Knee and hip osteoarthritis and mechanical occupational exposure

Causation criterion	Strength of evidence[a]	Comments
Strength of association	A (knee) A (hip)	Odds Ratio of ~ 2.5 for jobs involving frequent knee bending or heavy labour.
Dose-response relationship	A (knee) B (hip)	Studies for both knee and hip OA generally find Odds Ratios increase with severity of exposure.
Consistency across studies	A (knee) A (hip)	Consistent relative risk estimates were found for knee OA in good quality studies. RRs higher and consistent, but studies of lower quality, in hip OA.
Temporality	B (knee) D (hip)	Framingham study is the only prospective study showing a clear temporal relationship.
Biological plausibility	B	Reasonably convincing.
Coherence	D	Data on mechanical exposures not routinely collected, but archaeological evidence consistent with heavy work/OA link.
Specificity	D	Criterion not likely to be met.
Analogy	B	Post-traumatic degenerative arthritis.
Experimental risk reversal	D	Criterion not likely to be met for ethical and logistic reasons.

a Strength of evidence is rated as follows:

A = Strong research-based evidence (multiple relevant and high-quality scientific studies).

B = Moderate research-based evidence (one relevant, high-quality scientific study or multiple adequate scientific studies).

C = Limited research-based evidence (at least one adequate scientific study).

D = No research-based evidence.

specific biomechanical or psychosocial exposures at work, could be considered to have had their clinical onset accelerated, and partially caused, by those work exposures. One rather simplistic measure (see below) of the extent to which a given cause contributes to an overall burden of multifactorial illness, often used by epidemiologists, is the "etiologic fraction in the exposed," which is equal to (RR – 1/RR) (Rockhill et al. 1998). This takes a value between one-half and two-thirds for these three conditions, in that all three have RRs between 2 and 3 for the work exposures described in Tables 12.1 to 12.3. In turn, this implies that one-half to two-thirds of cases of all three conditions, in adequately exposed workers, would not have occurred unless there had been exposures. Thus, previously "exposed" workers with these conditions, whose jobs can be shown to have had the attributes in question during their working lives, could reasonably claim a substantial proportionate compensation award for their pain and suffering from workers' compensation insurance. Yet, paradoxically, only cases of low back pain[2] are likely to have such claims taken seriously by current compensation adjudication processes in North America. Indeed, as has been pointed out (Deyo et al. 1991; Frank, forthcoming; Frank et al. 1996), virtually all LBP cases presenting as compensation claims in most North American jurisdictions are automatically awarded benefits, without any consideration of the specific degree of exposure in the individual worker's case, largely on the grounds that it is currently medically impossible to determine which of these cases are in fact caused by work. Sometime soon, one would think, a thoughtful lawyer and his client will convince a court that this is fundamentally unfair to victims of early severe osteoarthritis or heart disease who have experienced apparently causal work exposures over many years. This decision will, in turn, predictably have very challenging implications for the whole current workers' compensation model when such claims for these and other ubiquitous conditions of later life, increasingly linked to work exposures, become widespread.

How Large a Compensation Bill Might We See for CHD and OA?

We have performed some preliminary conservative calculations of what the current total burden of illness, and associated compensation claim costs, might look like, should osteoarthritis become widely compensable in Canada. We have attempted to estimate the current prevalence of work-related OA using four different scenarios, based on information from Canadian census data, national and provincial population health surveys, and other epidemiological data from international sources. The prevalence estimates were conservatively calculated only for the working age-group between thirty-five and sixty-four, based on a variety of possible case definitions for work-related OA:

- *Scenario 1:* "arthritis and rheumatism" reported by the Canadian National Population Health/Ontario Health Survey respondents as having been diagnosed by a health professional and linked by that professional to the respondents' work.
- *Scenario 2:* the work-related excess prevalence (defined as in Scenario 1) of OA in Canada, obtained from the etiologic fraction ([RR −1/RR] = 0.6, based on the relative risk of 2.5 reported in Table 12.3) applied to the population exposed to "heavy work," based on Canadian surveys.
- *Scenario 3:* "disability," in the sense of inability to carry on with normal activities of daily living, associated with "arthritis and rheumatism," reported in the Canadian National Population Health Survey as being diagnosed by a health professional, and attributed by that practitioner to the respondent's work.
- *Scenario 4:* "knee or hip OA" based on radiological population X-ray surveys in the United States or Finland, multiplied by the same etiologic fraction used in Scenario 2, for the Canadian population exposed to heavy work according to survey responses.

The overall result is that anywhere between 33,000 and 165,000 Canadians between thirty-five and sixty-five years of age in 1997 could be expected to have work-related osteoarthritis, according to these various case definitions. And this, again, excludes the elderly, in whom the condition is much more prevalent, with some OA-related disability affecting perhaps the majority of those who have been retired for a decade or more, a proportion of which is very credibly due to previous lifelong physical work exposures.

Because these prevalence estimates don't provide any sense of the potential annual compensation claims volumes or costs for work-related OA, as a reason for time taken off work, we have looked for and found data from the German statutory health insurance system showing that 1.01 percent of actively employed women ages thirty-five to sixty-five, and 1.11 percent of employed men of the same age take time off work for OA-related reasons each year, with a mean duration of disability of forty-five days (AOK-Bundesverband 1994, 1996). We may take as the mean cost per episode/claim a very conservative C$5,000, which is a reasonable mid-point estimate for the relatively few workers' compensation claims for OA and related conditions (mostly thought to be post-traumatic degenerative arthritis) that were paid out in Ontario in the mid-1990s. The result is a potential total annual compensation bill in Canada for OA of $1,255,844,159.00. Because the German absences for OA are not only for work-related OA but also all other OA cases, we could prorate by the population-attributable risk estimating the proportion of all OA due to heavy work in Canada.[3] The resultant figure, still over $320 million annually, is substantial, and probably too low, for two reasons: (1) forty-five days of lost time alone, not including medical costs, often leads to more than $5,000 in payments, on average, at current wage-replacement rates in several provinces, (2) there is a great deal of public-sector-subsidized early retirement for health-related reasons in Germany, so that employees severely affected by OA, and other disabling conditions, are much more often given attractive early retirement packages than in Canada, implying in turn that there are fewer such disabled people left in the workforce requiring sick-leave annually.

Challenges in Determining Partial Causation and Proportionate Attribution

To further complicate matters, the scientific methods currently available to calculate the proportion of a multifactorial burden of disability that is attributable to a given occupational (or other) exposure are simply not up to the task of determining the exact compensation to be appropriately given to a particular workers' compensation case. In fact, there are currently no identifiable scientific tools for validly and feasibly making this determination in the individual case, so that legislation (as in the case of low back pain versus osteoarthritis and heart disease) has generally been compelled to make each diagnosis either fully compensable or not at all compensable.

Some public health professionals and clinicians have presumed that individual compensation awards for multi-factorial conditions can be fairly decided using the sort of "etiologic fraction" calculated above (one-half to two-thirds) for the proportions of LBP, CHD, and OA in occupationally exposed populations that are "attributable to" specific work exposures, with relative risks of 2 to 3. However, as is clearly argued in a recent review of this subject, these fractions lack an essential logical quality for their use in such legal settings: the fractions can and often do add up to more than 100 percent of the whole case burden being "explained" by all the known risk factors for the condition in question (Rockhill et al. 1998). The explanation of why this is so has been provided more than once by epidemiologists (Rothman 1986; Greenland and Robins 1988; Walter 1976) but that has not stopped the publication of articles that inappropriately attempt, for example, to add up the etiologic fractions for several risk factors for a multifactorial disease, and then naïvely and artificially constrain that total to never exceed 100 percent (see Rockhill et al. 1998 for examples). Suffice it to say here that there is no appropriate way to utilize these epidemiological population-based tools for assigning an exact proportionate cost to workplace exposures in the individual workers' compensation case, especially when, as for CHD or OA, there are other non-workplace exposures (often poorly measured) also known to have credible causal links to the same outcome. In short, epidemiologists have no simple answer to the problem of assigning proportionate "blame" to one of several causes in a given case of multi-factorial disease. This does not mean that work exposures on the population level as a whole are unimportant in causing an increased burden of illness and injury for these conditions. It just means that more usual and therefore legal means, such as judicial or jury judgment, must be used in such individual cases to decide what proportion of a given claimant's "costs" should be borne by the workplace or its insurer.

Conclusion

In this final section, we briefly consider three possible policy solutions, some of which have already been informally tried, in some jurisdictions, to deal with the problem outlined above: namely, how to adjudicate the "work-caused" proportion of multifactorial health problems that should be paid for, to cover both medical and wage-loss costs, by workers' compensation insurance.

One approach involves giving up on adjudication entirely and fully compensating all claims, independent of a case's specific exposures. As previously implied in this chapter, this is in essence what we have now for LBP in most of North America. This hardly seems a viable long-term solution. Indeed, one international commentator has referred to compensable LBP as the "end of the welfare state" (Nachemson 1994). This is especially a concern given the strong likelihood of ever increasing claims in future for other common chronic diseases such as CHD or OA, now being scientifically linked to one aspect of work or another. On the grounds of fairness alone, this approach would seem unlikely to stand up in court as defensible for use with one set of multi-factorial conditions influenced in part, but only in part, by work (e.g., LBP), but not another (e.g., CHD or OA).

The second approach suggests the tightening up of eligibility criteria so as to fit the monies available for compensation (e.g., by limiting compensability to low back pain due to clear-cut acute trauma "witnessed" at work, or to acute heart attacks suffered at work). In going this route, essentially we would be attempting to mimic current LBP coverage policy in Japan, Switzerland, and a few other wealthy countries (Hadler 1995). However, one cannot judge these alternative national policies fairly unless one knows a great deal about the rest of the local social welfare net of payments available to the disabled, which "backstop" workers' compensation per se. For example, such apparently hard-nosed policies, such as requiring clear evidence of acute trauma (a fall or blow) for LBP cases to qualify for workers' compensation, may result in little absolute hardship if there is generous "no-fault" sickness pay widely available as well. This would obviously be unlike the situation in North America, where the backstop when workers' compensation fails may often be nothing but general welfare, especially for blue-collar workers without collectively negotiated short- and long-term disability benefits. While such tough policies may appear to provide improved natural justice for employers who now complain that they pay workers' compensation premiums to cover some LBP claims that are not purely work-related, these policies would inadequately penalize employers with truly adverse, and preventable, ergonomic exposures in their jobs that only gradually overload the spine in the longer term, which may soon have as strong a body of evidence linking them to LBP as any known causal factor (see Table 12.1.) Finally, it is patently ridiculous to limit coverage for chronic diseases such as CHD or OA to those cases that manifest symptom onset when the patient happens to be at work, when the underlying pathological process, now thought to be accelerated by work exposures, is known to have been developing for decades.

The third approach would involve biting the bullet and accepting the fact that many aspects of work, and life outside of work, are inextricably entwined as causal factors for a wide range of chronic diseases and conditions, as modern epidemiology is now beginning to show, and that the long-term solution is a fairer, affordable, and responsive system of "no-fault" sickness and disability insurance coverage for all citizens, whether their health problem is partly attributable to past or present work conditions or not. We suggest that the increasing list of common diseases that recent research has shown to have at least partial attribution to work constitutes a looming crisis in workers' compensation as we know it. There is no easy way out if we persist with the current simplistic "adjudication" of these conditions as either "caused" or "not caused" by work. The problem is simply not soluble without committing to a longer-term plan for generic (both occupationally and non-occupationally related) disability insurance coverage, which meets the basic needs of the whole population. Fortunately examples exist of such programs elsewhere (Mashaw et al. 1996). This is especially true for dealing with disability in the elderly, in whom most of the delayed health effects of adverse lifelong work – and other – exposures inevitably become manifest. We cannot feasibly hold past or present commerce fully responsible for all the adverse physical and psychosocial conditions of work decades ago that have, for example, contributed to their former employees' elevated rates of heart disease and osteoarthritis now.

This is not to argue that there is no place for employer liability for clearly hazardous working conditions, especially those that obviously threaten safety, or involve unacceptable exposures to known toxicants. But, when it comes to largely chronic and recurrent multi-factorial conditions of delayed onset, such as those discussed in this chapter, it would seem more appropriate to use our new-found knowledge of causation to proactively prevent ill health by improving sub-optimal job design and working conditions. This approach is certainly bound to be superior to the hope that punitive workers' compensation premiums levied decades later, when the caused cases present, will act as a deterrent. In the end, we all can expect some of our health problems of later life to be attributable to our earlier work life. The issue is how to provide adequately for our care and livelihood when that occurs. Workers' compensation in its current formation would not seem to be up to this task.

Notes

1 RR = magnitude of the *relative risk*.
2 Some jurisdictions compensate OA cases that have been clearly "aggravated" by heavy work, but this is not the same as causation in the first place. Coronary heart disease cases tend to be compensated only when occurring due to an acutely disturbing incident at work, and sometimes only if they occurred *at* work!
3 The figure would be 25.6 percent, given an RR of 2.5 and the prevalence of "heavy work," reported by 23 percent of the employed respondents in the 1990 Ontario Health Survey, and defined as "bending and lifting more than fifty times a day."

References

Alterman, T., R. Shekelle, S.W. Vernon, and K.D. Burau. 1994. "Decision Latitude, Psychologic Demand, Job Strain and Coronary Heart Disease in the Western Electric Study." *American Journal of Epidemiology* 139: 620-7.

Anderson, J.J., and D.T. Felson. 1988. "Factors Associated with Osteoarthritis of the Knee in the First National Health and Nutrition Examination Survey (HANES I). Evidence for an Association with Overweight, Race, and Physical Demands of Work." *American Journal of Epidemiology* 128: 179-89.

AOK-Bundesverband. 1996. Krankheitsartenstatistik 1994. AOK West-Tabellen A1-A3: Arbeitsunfähigkeitsfälle und -tage.

Bernard, B., S. Sauter, L. Fine, M. Petersen, and T. Hales. 1994. "Job Task and Psychosocial Risk Factors for Work-Related Musculoskeletal Disorders among Newspaper Employees." *Scandinavian Journal of Work, Environment, and Health* 20: 417-26.

Bigos, S., O. Bowyer, G. Braen, et al. 1994. *Acute Low Back Problems in Adults: Clinical Practice Guideline No. 14.* AHCPR publication 95-0642. Rockville, MD: Agency for Health Care Policy and Research, Public Health Service, US Department of Health and Human Services.

Bongers, P.M., C.R. de Winter, M.A. Kompier, and V.H. Hildebrandt. 1993. "Psychosocial Factors at Work and Musculoskeletal Disease." *Scandinavian Journal of Work, Environment, and Health* 19: 297-312.

Bosma, H., M.G. Marmot, H. Hemingway, A.C. Nicholson, E. Brunner, and S.A. Stansfeld. 1997. "Low Job Control and Risk of Coronary Heart Disease in Whitehall II (Prospective Cohort) Study." *British Medical Journal* 314: 558-65.

Bosma, H., R. Peter, J. Siegrist, and M.G. Marmot. 1998. "Two Alternative Job Stress Models and the Risk of Coronary Heart Disease." *American Journal of Public Health* 88: 68-74.

Boyce, W.T., M. Chesney, A. Alkon, J.M. Tschann, S. Adams, B. Chesterman, F. Cohen, P. Kaiser, S. Folkman, and D. Wara. 1995. "Psychobiologic Reactivity to Stress and Childhood Respiratory Illnesses: Results of Two Prospective Studies." *Psychosomatic Medicine* 57: 411-22.

Bradford Hill, A. 1965. "The Environment and Disease: Association or Causation?" *Proceedings of the Royal Society of Medicine* 58: 295-300.

Bullough, P.G. 1998. "Osteoarthritis and Related Disorders Pathology." In *Rheumatology,* ed. J.H. Klippel and P.A. Dieppe, 8.1-8. London: Mosby.

Croft, P., C. Cooper, C. Wickham, and D. Coggon. 1992. "Osteoarthritis of the Hip and Occupational Activity." *Scandinavian Journal of Work, Environment, and Health* 18: 59-63.

Davey Smith, G. 1997. "Is Control at Work the Key to Socioeconomic Gradients in Mortality?" *Lancet* 350: 1369-70.

Deyo, R.A., C. Cherkin, D. Conrad, and E. Volinn. 1991. "Cost, Controversy, Crisis: Low Back Pain and the Health of the Public." *Annual Review of Public Health* 12: 141-56.

Evans, R.G., M.L. Barrer, and T.R. Marmor, eds. 1994. *Why Are Some People Healthy and Others Not? The Determinants of Health of Populations.* New York: De Gruyter.

Felson, D.T., M.T. Hannan, A. Naimark, J. Berkeley, G. Gordon, P.W. Wilson, and J. Anderson. 1991. "Occupational Physical Demands, Knee Bending, and Knee Osteo-arthritis: Results from the Framingham Study." *Journal of Rheumatology* 18: 1587-92.

Frank, J.W. Forthcoming. "Paradoxical Aspects of Low Back Pain in Workers' Compensation Systems." In *Issues in Workers' Compensation: Foundations for Reform*, ed. M. Gunderson and D. Hyatt. Toronto: University of Toronto Press.

Frank, J.W., M.S. Kerr, A.S. Brooker, S.E. DeMaio, A. Maetzel, H.S. Shannon, T. Sullivan, R.W. Norman, and R.P. Wells. 1996. "Disability Resulting from Occupational Low Back Pain, Part I: What Do We Know About Primary Prevention? A Review of the Scientific Evidence on Prevention before Disability Begins." *Spine* 21 (24): 2908-17.

Frank, J.W., I.R. Pulcins, M.S. Kerr, H.S. Shannon, and S.A. Stansfeld. 1995. "Occupational Back Pain – An Unhelpful Polemic." *Scandinavian Journal of Work, Environment, and Health* 21: 3-14.

Greenland, S., and J.M. Robins. 1988. "Conceptual Problems in the Definition and Interpretation of Attributable Fractions." *American Journal of Epidemiology* 128: 1185-97.

Gupta, S., and A.J. Camm. 1997. "Chlamydia Pneumoniae and Coronary Heart Disease." (editorial). *British Medical Journal* 314: 1778-9.

Gupta, S., E.W. Leatham, D. Carrington, M.A. Mendall, J.C. Kaski, and A.J. Camm. 1997. "Elevated Chlamydia Pneumoniae Antibodies, Cardiovascular Events, and Azithromycin in Male Survivors of Myocardial Infarction." *Circulation* 96: 404-7.

Hadler, N.M. 1995. "The Disabling Backache. An International Perspective." *Spine* 20: 640-9.

Jemerin, J.M., and W.T. Boyce. 1990. "Psychobiological Differences in Childhood Stress Response. II. Cardiovascular Markers of Vulnerability." *Journal of Development Behaviour and Pediatrics* 11: 140-50.

Jensen, L.K., and W. Eenberg. 1996. "Occupation as a Risk Factor for Knee Disorders." *Scandinavian Journal of Work, Environment, and Health* 22: 165-75.

Johnson, J.V., and E.M. Hall. 1995. *Society and Health.* New York/London: Oxford University Press.

Johnson, J.V., W. Stewart, E.M. Hall, P. Fredlund, and T. Theorell. 1996. "Long-Term Psychosocial Work Environment and Cardiovascular Mortality among Swedish Men." *American Journal of Public Health* 86: 324-31.

Karasek, R.A. 1979. "Job Demands, Job Decision Latitude, and Mental Strain: Implications for Job Redesign." *Administrative Sciences Quarterly* 24: 285-308.

Karasek, R.A., and T. Theorell. 1990. *Healthy Work: Stress, Productivity and the Reconstruction of Working Life.* New York: Basic Books.

Kasl, S.V. 1996. "The Influence of the Work Environment on Cardiovascular Health: A Historical, Conceptual, and Methodological Perspective." *Journal of Occupational Health and Psychology* 1: 42-56.

Kerr, M.S., J.W. Frank, H.S. Shannon et al. 1998. *The Importance of Biomechanical and Psychosocial Risk Factors in Occupational Low Back Pain: A Case Control Study.* Working paper no. 61. Institute for Work and Health, Toronto.

Kivimäki J., H. Riihimäki, and K. Hanninen. 1992. "Knee Disorders in Carpet and Floor Layers and Painters." *Scandinavian Journal of Work, Environment and Health* 18: 310-16.

McEwen, B.S. 1998. "Protecting and Damage Effects of Stress Mediators." *New England Journal of Medicine* 338: 179.

MacMahon, B., and T.F. Pugh. 1970. *Epidemiology: Principles and Methods.* Boston: Little Brown.

Maetzel, A., M. Makela, G. Hawker, and C. Bombardier. 1997. "Osteoarthritis of the Hip and Knee and Mechanical Occupational Exposure – A Systematic Overview of the Evidence." *Journal of Rheumatology* 24: 1599-1607.

Marmot, M.G., H. Bosma, H. Hemingway, E. Brunner, and S. Stansfeld. 1997.

"Contribution of Job Control and Other Risk Factors to Social Variations in Coronary Heart Disease Incidence." *Lancet* 350: 235-9.

Mashaw, J.L., V. Reno, R.V. Burkhauser, M. Berkodtz, eds. 1996. *Disability Work and Cash Benefits.* Kalamazoo, MI: Upjohn Institute for Employment Research.

Nachemson, A. 1992. "Newest Knowledge of Low Back Pain. A Critical Look." *Clinical Orthopaedics and Related Research* 279: 8-20.

–. 1994. "Chronic Pain – The End of the Welfare State?" *Quality of Life Research* 3 (S1): S11-S7.

National Institute for Occupational Safety and Health (NIOSH). 1997. *Musculoskeletal Disorders and Workplace Factors: A Critical Review of Epidemiologic Evidence for Work-Related Musculoskeletal Disorders of the Neck, Upper Extremity, and Low Back.* Baltimore: US Department of Health and Human Services.

Norman, R., R. Wells, P. Neumann, J. Frank, H. Shannon, M. Kerr, and the Ontario Universities Back Pain Study (OUBPS) Group. 1998. "A Comparison of Peak vs Cumulative Physical Work Exposure Risk Factors for the Reporting of Low Back Pain in the Automotive Industry." *Clinical Biomechanics* 13 (8): 561-73.

Peter, R., and J. Siegrist. 1997. "Chronic Work Stress, Sickness Absence, and Hypertension in Middle Managers: General or Specific Sociological Explanations?" *Social Science and Medicine* 45: 1111-20.

Polanyi, M.F., J. Eakin, J.W. Frank, H.S. Shannon, and T.J. Sullivan. 1997. "Creating Healthy Work Environments: A Critical Review of the Health Impacts of Workplace Change." In *Health in Canada: Settings and Issues,* 89-143. Ottawa: National Forum on Health/Editions Multimondes.

Roach, K.E., V. Persky, T. Miles, and E. Budiman-Mak. 1994. "Biomechanical Aspects of Occupation and Osteoarthritis of the Hip: A Case-Control Study." *Journal of Rheumatology* 21: 2334-40.

Rockhill, B., B. Newman, and C. Weinberg. 1998. "Use and Misuse of Population Attributable Fractions." *American Journal of Public Health* 88: 15-9.

Rothman, K.J. 1986. *Modern Epidemiology.* Boston: Little Brown.

Sauter, S.L., and N.G. Swanson. 1996. "Psychological Aspects of Musculoskeletal Disorders in Office Workers." In *Psychosocial Factors in Musculoskeletal Disorders,* ed. S. Moon and S.L. Sauter. London: Taylor Francis.

Schnall, P.L., P.A. Landsbergis, and D. Baker. 1994. "Job Strain and Cardiovascular Disease." *Annual Review of Public Health* 15: 381-411.

Siegrist, J. 1996. "Adverse Health Effects of High-Effort/Low-Reward Conditions." *Journal of Occupational Health and Psychology* 1: 27-41.

Siegrist, J., R. Peter, A. Junge, P. Cremer, and D. Seidel. 1990. "Low Status Control, High Effort at Work and Ischemic Heart Disease: Prospective Evidence from Blue-Collar Men." *Social Science and Medicine* 31: 1127-34.

Steenland, K., J. Johnson, and S. Nowlin. 1997. "A Follow-Up Study of Job Strain and Heart Disease among Males in the NHANES1 Population." *American Journal of Industrial Medicine* 31: 256-60.

Susser, M. 1977. "Judgement and Causal Inference Criteria in Epidemiologic Studies." *American Journal of Epidemiology* 105: 1-5.

Syme, S.L., and J.L. Balfour. 1997. "Explaining Inequalities in Coronary Heart Disease." (comment). *Lancet* 350: 231-2.

Theorell, T., and R.A. Karasek. 1996. "Current Issues Relating to Psychosocial Job Strain and Cardiovascular Disease Research." *Journal of Occupational Health and Psychology* 1: 9-26.

Vingard, E., C. Hogstedt, L. Alfredsson, E. Fellenius, I. Goldie, and M. Koster. 1991. "Coxarthrosis and Physical Work Load." *Scandinavian Journal of Work, Environment, and Health* 17: 104-9.

Walter, S.D. 1976. "The Estimation and Interpretation of Attributable Fraction in Health Research." *Biometrics* 323: 829-49.

13
Fatality Benefits: Rationale and Practice

Terry Thomason

A fundamental purpose of workers' compensation programs is to compensate individuals who have suffered a loss as the result of a workplace illness or injury. However, fatal injury compensation raises two issues not presented by non-fatal claims. First, the individual who most immediately suffers the loss and who is ostensibly covered by workers' compensation – that is, the decedent worker – is no longer available to receive benefits. This raises questions as to whether anyone suffered a compensable loss, and, if so, who? Second, once the program has identified the person or persons who are entitled to compensation, the workers' compensation board must then determine the extent of their loss. While this is often a complicated exercise in non-fatal accidents involving disability, it is even more difficult for fatal injury claims, raising profound philosophical questions about the value of human life.

The purpose of this chapter is to examine the underlying rationale for the compensation of occupational fatalities by workers' compensation programs, to review current practice in North America, to discuss available policy options, and to suggest recommendations for the future direction of fatal compensation benefits.

This chapter has three parts. The first examines relevant economic considerations providing a basis for the evaluation of fatal injury compensation issues addressed later in the chapter. This includes a discussion of the impact of fatal benefits on workplace safety and administrative costs. This section also reviews the "value of life" methodology used by economists to determine the loss associated with fatal injury compensation. The second part of the chapter reviews the law relating to the compensation of fatal injuries, including work- and non-work-related injuries. Finally, the third part analyzes the problem of fatal injury compensation in light of extant law – and its underlying rationale.

Economists typically evaluate public policy using two criteria: equity and efficiency. Efficiency refers to the relative costs and benefits of a proposed policy option. An efficient policy is one that maximizes benefits net of costs.

Equity, on the other hand, refers to the distribution of those costs and benefits. While a precise and universally accepted definition is elusive, many believe that, in the context of workers' compensation, equity requires that similarly situated claimants be treated similarly. This means that claimants who suffer identical losses should receive identical compensation. Of course, the definition of terms such as "similarly situated" or "identical losses" is subject to considerable debate. For these reasons, economic analysis tends to focus on the efficiency criterion, while acknowledging that an inefficient, equitable policy may be preferred to an inequitable, efficient one.

Economic Considerations: Fatal Injury Compensation

Evaluation of the economic efficiency of fatal injury compensation requires an analysis of the impact of fatality benefits on the behaviour of workers and employers. Two effects deserve consideration. First, the existence of compensation benefits affects the pre-injury behaviour of employers and workers in ways that would, in turn, affect injury rates. Second, the process of determining the extent of loss for the purpose of compensation entails administrative or, in economics parlance, transaction costs that may not be insignificant.

Occupational injuries and illnesses are necessary by-products of the production process that impose costs on both employers and workers. The costs of accidents incurred by workers include lost wages and lost wage-earning capacity, medical and rehabilitation expenses, and non-pecuniary loss, such as pain and suffering and loss of enjoyment of leisure activities. Employers also incur costs, which include the damage to plant and equipment as well as losses due to the interruption of production processes, and these costs can be expected to increase production costs directly. Worker costs may be shifted to employers through the mechanism of the compensating wage differential or risk premium. That is, since, everything else being equal, workers would prefer safe jobs to risky ones, hazardous employers will be forced to pay higher wages to workers than safe employers in order to attract labour in a competitive market. (However, as noted below, there are reasons to suspect whether compensating wage differentials actually exist.)

By raising production costs, work injuries have two effects on economic activity. First, as injury rates and production costs rise, so do product prices, which cause product demand to decline. As a result, workplaces will become safer, since some hazardous jobs will be driven out of the market. Second, higher production costs provide employers with incentives to invest in workplace safety. The incidence and, to some extent, the severity of work injuries are at least partially affected by the behaviour of employers and workers. Employers can lower injury rates in a variety of ways – for example, by providing safety training to supervisors and employees, by modifying plant and machinery, or by providing workers with personal protective equipment, such as hard hats and safety shoes. Benefits paid to injured workers or to the families of fatally injured workers are another cost of workplace accidents for employers. If premiums are experience rated, benefits provide another incentive for employer safety investment. And there is substantial evidence indicating that experience rating is, in fact, associated with a decline in the occupational injury rate and, in particular, the fatal injury rate (Durbin and Butler 1998; Hyatt and Thomason 1998).[1]

Work injury deterrence is optimal when the joint costs of both accidents and accident prevention are minimized. Joint costs are minimized at the point where the additional dollar spent to reduce the frequency or severity of accidents is exactly equal to an additional dollar of savings in the form of reduced accident costs. This implies that when employer incentives are considered alone, compensation benefits should fully compensate the worker. If benefits are fully compensating, the expected reduction in employer accident costs is exactly equal to the reduction in total accident costs – that is, the social costs of accidents – so that employers will make socially optimal choices concerning accident prevention.

However, benefit levels that fully compensate workers for the cost of occupational injuries may lead to inefficient behaviour on the part of workers, who take less care on the job and report non-occupational injuries as work-related. There is a substantial literature suggesting that worker moral hazard is a problem. Almost every study examining the issue has found that benefits are positively related to the injury or compensation claims rate (see Thomason and Burton 1993). These results indicate that worker moral hazard dominates any incentive effect that higher benefits have on employer behaviour. While the problems of disentangling the two are formidable, Butler and Worrall (1991) have adduced evidence suggesting that this relationship is due to "reporting" as opposed to "risk bearing" moral hazard. That is, more generous compensation benefits are more likely to cause workers to report injuries that would have gone unreported, than they are to reduce the workers' level of care on the job.

On the other hand, there are good reasons to believe that the level of fatality benefits is unlikely to result in moral hazard problems. While it is possible that extravagant fatality benefits could elicit suicidal behaviour on the part of workers or homicidal behaviour on the part of their dependent survivors, these would appear to be improbable events. It seems unlikely that higher benefit levels will increase fatality reporting. Unlike non-fatal injuries, it is difficult – with the exception of occupational disease claims – to portray a non-occupational fatality as work-related. The empirical evidence indicates that, unlike compensation claims or work injuries more generally, the fatal injury rate is negatively related to benefit levels (see, for example, Moore and Viscusi 1989; and Ruser 1993). These results imply that fatal injury rates are unaffected by worker moral hazard.

For these reasons, we may conclude, that unlike income-replacement benefits paid to disabled workers, moral hazard is unlikely to be a problem with respect to fatality compensation. Taken together with the earlier observation concerning benefit levels required to induce optimal firm behaviour, we may conclude that, from the perspective of achieving an optimal level of workplace safety within the context of an experience-rated workers' compensation program, fatality benefits should be fully compensating.

The analysis thus far has failed to consider the administrative or transaction costs necessarily attendant on a legal process that transfers assets from one person to another, in this case from the employer to surviving dependants. Transaction costs include the opportunity costs of the parties involved in the determination of eligibility and the extent of the benefits. These parties potentially include the claimant, the employer, adjudicators, and associated personnel. Obviously, transaction costs are greater when one or more issues are in dispute, so that efficient rules will minimize dispute probability.

Importantly, existing research indicates that dispute probability increases as uncertainty with respect to benefit entitlement increases (Thomason et al. 1998). Other research shows that fairness perceptions are also an important determinant of dispute probability. A process that is perceived to be fair is much less likely to result in a dispute than one perceived to be unfair. Together, these observations suggest that the principles that determine fatal injury compensation should be simple, generally acceptable to the public, and incorporate relatively objective and easily understood criteria.

Historically, advocates of workers' compensation have argued that one of its advantages, relative to the tort regime that preceded it, was that compensation programs minimized transaction costs. In part, this was because, unlike the tort system, workers' compensation paid statutorily defined benefits that were largely formulaic. Benefits were mechanically determined by a statutory formula that could easily be applied to any worker. Determination of fully compensating benefits necessarily implies an individual loss assessment. The compensation program would be required to make a separate determination for each claimant. This process, particularly in the case of non-economic losses, is likely to be both expensive and litigious when compared with the current system of limited, statutorily defined benefits.

Determining Loss
The analysis presented in the previous section suggests that, under certain conditions, the payment of fatal compensation benefits results in improved levels of workplace safety.[2] As a corollary, benefits should be related to the extent of the worker's loss. As previously noted, determination of the extent of loss resulting from a fatal accident is complex, raising questions concerning the value of human life. The approach traditionally

used by the legal system, which is described in the next section, involves an accounting exercise, whereby the tribunal responsible for determining the extent of liability is required to identify each separate element of loss, and then assign a monetary value to each element. This exercise uses market measures to evaluate pecuniary loss, such as the value of lost wage income or the value of lost household services.

While this method is a relatively straightforward, accurate, and reliable way to determine the extent of a claimant's pecuniary loss, it is much more problematic when it comes to evaluating non-pecuniary damages for which there are no intuitive market measures. In recent years, economists have developed an alternative approach to the determination of fatality benefits that permits the evaluation of the total loss associated with a fatal injury, including pecuniary and non-pecuniary loss.

The economic "value of life" approach relies on the hypothesis that the operation of a competitive labour market will result in compensating differentials for hazardous jobs. If we assume that wages fully compensate workers for their expected costs of injury, then it is possible to use estimates of the wage differential between safe and hazardous jobs in conjunction with estimates of the risk of injury in these jobs to determine the value that workers attach to their own life. This approach is based on the proposition that workers choose to work at risky jobs when they are paid higher wages and that the workers' value of life is measured by the additional wage that they are willing to accept to face the additional risk.

For example, suppose that there are two jobs, one in which the annual risk of fatal injury is 0.001 and another in which the risk is 0.002. The jobs are identical in every other respect. An estimate that the risky job pays $50 per week more than the safer job implies that the worker in the risky job is willing to accept this additional risk of 0.001 for $2,600 ($50 x 52 weeks). Extrapolating, we may conclude that if the worker is willing to accept an additional risk of fatality of 0.001 for $2,600, then the worker should accept an additional risk of 0.002 for $5,200 (2 x $2,600), and an additional risk of 0.003 for $7,800, etc. Further extrapolation – to the point at which the probability of fatal injury is 1 – leads to the conclusion that the value of the worker's life, in this instance, is $2.6 million.

While this approach is appealing, it presents a number of theoretical and methodological difficulties. First, it assumes that the compensating wage differential for risk is fully compensating. As noted by Dorman and Hagstrom, "if workers have utility functions in which the expected likelihood and cost of occupational hazards enter as arguments, if they are fully informed of risks, if firms possess sufficient information on worker expectations and preferences (directly or through revealed preferences), if safety is costly to provide and not a public good, and if risk is fully transacted in anonymous, perfectly competitive labor markets, then workers will receive wage premia that exactly offset the disutility of assuming greater risk of injury or death" (Dorman and Hagstrom 1998: 116).

For example, there is credible evidence suggesting that, in general, workers' estimates of differences in the probability of injury between safe and hazardous jobs are downwardly biased, so that we can expect that workers will underestimate risk differences among jobs. As a result, a value-of-life calculation based on the risk premium will underestimate the true value that the worker places on his or her life.

Estimation of the risk premium is also problematic.[3] It involves using survey data sets that have a large number of observations on workers' wages and other job characteristics. A multiple regression equation predicting wages is then estimated, controlling for variables representing various demographic and job characteristics as well as a measure of job risk. The coefficient on the job risk variable provides the estimate of the risk premium.

Value-of-life estimates using this methodology are necessarily *average* estimates. To the extent that individuals differ in their valuation, these estimates are unlikely to be accurate for the individual worker. Of course, this limits the usefulness of the procedure as a tool for determining the appropriate level of fatality benefits for individual claims.

In addition, these estimates are critically dependent on the assumption that the investigator adequately controls for other differences in job and person characteristics correlated with wages and the risk of injury. If the investigator fails to do so, then estimates may be biased. For example, the degree of physical effort required by the job is likely to be highly correlated with the risk of fatal injury. This variable is also likely to be a working condition that affects wages; other things being equal, workers will demand higher wages for jobs that require greater physical effort. If the extent of physical effort required by the job is unobserved by the investigator, then the fatal risk measure will capture some of the variation in wages that compensates the worker for additional physical effort. As a result, the risk premium variable is likely to be biased upward; that is, the investigator will overestimate the worker's value-of-life.[4] In this connection, it is important to note that most available data sets lack good measures of working conditions.[5]

Unobserved personal characteristics are also likely to affect the risk-wage trade-off. For example, since safety is a normal good,[6] we should expect that the risk-wage trade-off will be greater for wealthier individuals. We may also expect that the wage-risk trade-off depends on the quantity and quality of the remainder of the worker's life, so that older workers or workers who are ill or infirm may require a lower risk premium than younger or healthy ones. While most data sets include an age variable, health status is generally unobserved.

Many of these variables, including the fatal risk variable and wages, are potentially measured with error, which could also affect estimates of the wage-risk trade-off. Typically, only gross wage measures are available, although after-tax wages are the appropriate metric for value-of-life calculations. This is particularly important when workers' compensation benefits are included as a control variable in the regression equation. Since compensation benefits are non-taxable income, the dependent wage variable should be expressed in comparable after-tax terms.[7]

Risk measures are problematic since they are necessarily aggregate measures, representing the risk of fatal injury for either the worker's occupation or industry. Typically, these measures are based on two-digit standard industry classification (SIC) or standard occupational classification (SOC) categories, which are quite broad and include jobs that are very different from one another with respect to risk. As such, we can expect that actual fatality risk for particular jobs is measured with error and that estimates of the fatal risk premium are downwardly biased.

This examination of the "value-of-life" methodology indicates that estimates based on the methodology should be interpreted cautiously. Nonetheless, there is a substantial literature that can provide benchmarks by which to evaluate fatal injury compensation. Viscusi (1993) reviewed twenty-four studies from which estimates of the value-of-life were or could be derived. These estimates, which were taken from studies using a variety of data sets – although primarily US data – and methodologies, ranged from a low of $600 thousand (Kneisner and Leeth 1991) to a high of $16.2 million (Moore and Viscusi 1990).[8] Most are in the $3 to $7 million range and the median estimate appears to be about $4.9 million. Viscusi (1993) puts greatest faith in his own estimate of $4.1 million (Viscusi 1978) and that of Moore and Viscusi (1988), who estimated a value-of-life of $7.3 million for workers with an average income of $19,444.[9]

The Law of Fatal Injury Compensation

Thus far, the discussion has been limited to a theoretical analysis of fatal injury compensation and its implications for social welfare. In this section, I turn my attention to actual practice, both within and outside the context of workers' compensation, beginning with a brief history of fatal injury compensation. This is followed by discussion of damages paid in negligence actions involving non-work-related fatalities. Finally, I examine fatality benefits provided by North American workers' compensation programs.

Prior to the enactment of workers' compensation statutes, the law failed to distinguish between work and non-work injuries. For both, at common law there was no right of action where the injured party died, leading to the odd result that it was cheaper for a tortfeasor to kill rather than merely maim or cripple his or her victim. This changed in 1846 with the enactment of Lord Campbell's Act, an English statute that provided certain survivors with a cause of action in the event of a death caused by negligence or some wrongful act by another. The principles embodied in this act now form the basis for similar legislation, typically entitled Fatal Accidents Act, in all common-law provinces.[10]

Workers' Compensation Acts extinguished the dependent survivors' right of action under Fatal Accidents Acts, as they did for tort actions for personal injuries more generally. This development was the product of what has been described as a "historic compromise." The essence of this compromise was that Canadian workers gave up the right of action in tort against negligent employers, in which compensation was potentially substantial but uncertain, for a guarantee of more limited compensation. In the context of non-fatal accidents, a tort suit could result in full compensation for economic loss, including the loss of earnings as well as reimbursement for medical, rehabilitation, and housekeeping expenses; non-pecuniary damages, such as those for pain and suffering; and potentially, non-compensatory, punitive, and exemplary damages. On the other hand, under workers' compensation, the injured worker is only entitled to a portion of lost earnings and no non-pecuniary compensation or non-compensatory damages.[11]

As indicated, a survivor's right to compensation prior to the enactment of workers' compensation legislation has a different statutory origin and is, consequently, somewhat different from the common-law rights of injured workers. As a result, the nature of the compromise is somewhat different. To explore this issue further, it is necessary to examine the law with respect to the compensation of non-work-related fatalities.

Dependent Compensation for Non-Work Injuries
The law embodied in provincial Fatal Accident Acts established the right to compensation for a certain class of survivors in the event of a wrongful death. These survivors are typically limited to the widow and minor children of the deceased, but in some provinces the right of action has been extended to certain other persons, including stepchildren, grandparents, grandchildren, and siblings. Damages are typically limited to economic or pecuniary loss, although some provinces have broadened the definition of pecuniary loss to include items such as a loss of guidance, care, and companionship, which can include compensation for grief.

Calculations of pecuniary loss are guided by the principle of *restitutio in integrum*. That is, the purpose of compensation is to restore the survivor to the position that he or she would have occupied had the injury not occurred. Damages are awarded in a lump sum and include both special damages for specific losses, such as the cost of the decedent's funeral, as well as general damages. General damages are calculated by determining (1) the level of benefits the claimant would have received if it were not for the claimant's death and (2) the period during which the claimant would have received those benefits.[12]

Benefit levels are based on two factors: lost income and the value of lost household services.[13] Income loss is equal to that proportion of the decedent's net income (gross income after deductions for taxes, etc.) that would have been available to the survivor if the decedent had lived. While calculation of net income is relatively straightforward, determination of the survivor's share – also known as the dependency rate – is not. This rate is based on actuarial evidence and varies depending on the decedent's circumstances. For example, it is typically assumed that a working adult male who is the sole support for his family will spend 70 percent of his income on his spouse and an additional 4 percent for each child. This rate is often reduced for two-earner families. Household services are determined by estimating the amount of time that the decedent would spend performing these services and multiplying this amount by the going market rate for each service.

In calculating the period of the loss, courts attempt to determine the length of time that the dependent survivor could have reasonably expected to enjoy these benefits. Calculation of this period is based on actuarial tables, although the parties may adduce evidence showing that the survivor departs from the norm. For the surviving spouse the period is generally deemed to be equal to the joint life expectancy of the decedent and spouse, while for the child, it is typically the period between death and the age of majority. Courts also take into account contingencies that can affect the period of loss. These contingencies include events that would have ended the period of dependency had the decedent lived, such as the probability of divorce, or events that affect the claimant's dependency after the fact, such as the probability that the spouse will remarry or the probability that surrogates will care for the decedent's dependent children.

There are a number of similarities with and differences between the compensation of fatal workplace injuries through workers' compensation and compensation of fatal non-work injuries under fatal accidents legislation. Both types of legislation provide compensation to specific classes of beneficiaries, and benefits are, for the most part, based on pecuniary loss. However, as will be seen, workers' compensation programs typically compensate survivors for only a portion of their pecuniary loss. In addition, similar to non-fatal injuries, there is no requirement that the compensation claimant demonstrate employer fault, merely that the accident arose out of and in the course of employment.[14]

Compensation of Fatal Work Injuries

Two basic issues are presented by an analysis of fatality benefits provided by workers' compensation programs: *eligibility* and *benefits levels*. This section will discuss each in turn.

In general, *eligibility* for workers' compensation survivor benefits is conditioned on two criteria: a relationship to the decedent worker that meets statutory requirements and dependency on the decedent worker.

In most jurisdictions the statute defines certain classes of relationship – typically the spouse and minor children, but often others as well – that are eligible for benefits.[15] Claimants must first satisfy the compensation agency or court that they fall into one of those classes, which are defined by specific relationships, although sometimes the statute will include a general class, such as "member of the family," either in addition to or instead of more specific ones.

Most Canadian provinces indicate that the "wife, husband, father, mother, grandfather, grandmother, stepfather, stepmother, son, daughter, grandson, granddaughter, stepson, stepdaughter, brother, sister, half-brother, half-sister, and a person who stood in loco parentis to the worker or to whom the worker stood in loco parentis" are members of the worker's family and thereby "dependants" for the purpose of fatal injury compensation. Some US states have a more extensive list, including in-laws, aunts, uncles, nieces, or nephews. Others limit compensation to the surviving spouse, children, and parents, while in still others, dependency is the sole criterion for benefit eligibility.

Where the statute defines specific classes and does not mention a more general one, determination of whether the claimant is eligible by virtue of his or her relationship to the decedent is not difficult. In general, the courts and workers' compensation agencies responsible for administering the law have applied common-law definition and ordinary domestic law.

Problems sometimes arise where the claimant's relationship is through common-law marriage or where the marriage is otherwise deemed to be invalid, for example, because the decedent had failed to obtain a divorce from a previous marriage. Common-law relationships are also problematic. Compensation is payable in US states where common-law relationships are legally recognized. Most Canadian jurisdictions provide benefits to a common-law spouse, although they frequently require a minimum period of cohabitation.[16] In some jurisdictions, benefits are not payable to a common-law spouse where the worker also left a spouse who was living apart from the decedent worker. However, in some provinces, benefits are apportioned between the spouse and common-law spouse when the spouse is only partially dependent on the decedent worker.

Problems have also arisen with respect to the status of posthumous or illegitimate children. At one time, courts routinely held that an illegitimate child was not a "child" for the purpose of workers' compensation legislation, under the common-law doctrine of *filius nullius*, that is, that the illegitimate child is "nobody's child." However, Ison (1994) notes that the tendency in Canada has been to extend the right to compensation to illegitimate children, and, since 1973, differential treatment of illegitimate and legitimate children has been considered a violation of the Equal Protection Clause of the Fourteenth Amendment of the US Constitution.

In many jurisdictions, there is a conclusive statutory presumption that the surviving spouse and children were dependent on the deceased worker if they were living with the decedent at the time of his or her death. In some jurisdictions, there is no requirement of living together.[17] Questions of dependency arise, however, where there is no such presumption or where the claimant is someone other than the parent or child.

Dependency does not generally require a showing that the decedent provided the claimant with the necessities of life or that the claimant would have been destitute without the decedent's support. All that is required is that the claimant relied on the decedent's support to maintain an accustomed standard of living. While there is typically no need for the claimant to show that the decedent had a legal obligation to support the claimant, in some jurisdictions the mere existence of a legal obligation is insufficient to substantiate a claim of dependency.

Often statutes distinguish between total and partial dependency, paying less generous compensation to persons in the latter category. Partial dependency is found where claimant has other sources of support. However, if that support is insubstantial or sporadic, the claimant may be considered to be totally rather than partially dependent.

Benefits

While there is substantial variation among jurisdictions with respect to benefits paid to compensation claimants, there are some common features found in most jurisdictions. First, benefits are typically limited to two items: (1) payment of funeral and other expenses related to the disposal of the decedent worker's remains and (2) replacement of the lost earnings of the decedent worker. Second, earnings-replacement benefits typically vary, depending on the nature of the claimant's relationship to the decedent spouse. Greatest benefits are paid to the surviving spouse. Other claimants are typically entitled to less generous benefits.

This section will discuss benefits paid to these different claimant categories separately. Since the surviving spouse and his or her dependent children are the sole or primary beneficiaries in the overwhelming majority of fatal injury claims, this section will provide a detailed review of spousal benefits.[18] A briefer discussion of benefits paid to other claimant categories follows.

Workers' compensation legislation customarily prioritizes beneficiaries where there is more than one category of claimants dependent on the survivor. Typically, only one category is entitled to benefits at any one time, although if that category loses its entitlement – for example, through death or remarriage – the category that is next in line would then become eligible. Claimants deemed to be totally dependent have priority over partial dependants, and a spouse and children typically have priority over dependent parents who, in turn, normally have priority over other dependants. Total benefits are usually limited, so that where more than one beneficiary is eligible for benefits at any one time, this total amount will be shared. If both claimants were totally dependent, then the rule is typically "share and share alike." Where there are multiple partial dependants, they will share according to the extent of their dependency.[19]

The tables in Appendix D report the statutory parameters of benefits paid to the surviving spouse and children by workers' compensation programs in North America.[20] Table D1 presents information on the statutory parameters that define the periodic benefit payment, while Table D2 displays statutory parameters that limit benefit duration as well as other aspects of fatal injury compensation. In all cases, the tables report data in effect on 1 January 1997. Together, they show that there is substantial variability in fatal compensation benefits paid to the decedent's spouse and children.

In those jurisdictions that pay periodic (weekly or monthly) benefits to dependants, the amount of the weekly benefit is typically equal to a proportion of the deceased worker's pre-injury earnings – called the replacement rate – subject to a minimum and a maximum. Since the replacement rate may vary by the number of dependants (dependent children), Table D1 reports replacement rates for a variety of dependency situations, from claims in which the surviving spouse has no minor children to claims in which the surviving spouse has five or more minor children. The minimum and maximum may also vary by number of dependants. To simplify presentation, Table D1 only reports the applicable maximum and minimum for spouses without children. (Where the maximum and minimum vary by number of dependants, these data are reported in footnotes.) Finally, in some jurisdictions, an additional flat amount is paid for each child. This is reported in the right-hand-most column of Table D1.

In all but three US states – Idaho, Oregon, and Wyoming – and the two Canadian territories, benefits are equal to a proportion of the worker's pre-injury wage. In those five jurisdictions, benefits are equal to a flat amount that is increased as the number of dependent children increases. As can be seen, the replacement rate varies with the number of dependants in seventeen US states and three Canadian provinces. Additionally, several states pay a flat amount per child, while in several other states, the minimum or the maximum varies with the number of dependent children. All together, in over one-half of US and in all Canadian jurisdictions, compensation benefits are related to the number of dependent children.

In three Canadian provinces, benefits depend on the employment of the surviving spouse. In Alberta, a spouse with no dependent children (or whose eldest child is over eighteen years old) who is employed or who refuses to seek gainful employment will receive a five-year pension that is reduced by 20 percent per year. If the spouse is capable of employment, then the spouse will receive up to five years of benefits while actively engaged in a vocational rehabilitation program; upon completion of this program, the spouse will receive the five-year reducing pension described earlier. However, if incapable of employment, there is no limitation on benefits. Similarly, Manitoba will pay a monthly pension equal to 90 percent of the decedent worker's wages in lieu of the lump sum award for invalid spouses or spouses aged forty-nine or older.

The statutory formula for fatality benefits in British Columbia is somewhat unusual. While it is common to pay benefits that increase with the number of dependants, and while several provinces pay a lump sum that varies with the claimant's age, Ontario is the only other jurisdiction to use both factors to determine spousal benefits.

In most North American jurisdictions, benefits for the surviving spouse are paid for the period of dependency, which is usually defined as until death or remarriage. Compensation paid to or for non-invalid children is typically limited to the age of majority, although this period may be extended for children enrolled in an educational institution. These limits are indicated in the two right-hand-most columns in Table D2. Some states and most Canadian jurisdictions further limit the duration of periodic payment to the surviving spouse by establishing a maximum period during which the spouse may collect benefits, a maximum dollar amount of benefits that may be received, or a maximum age at which benefits may be paid. These limits are shown under the rubric "Limits on the duration of spousal benefits."

Proportionately, Canadian programs are more likely to limit the duration of pension benefits paid to the surviving spouse – although US programs are more likely to terminate benefits upon remarriage. On the other hand, Canadian programs, particularly those that limit the duration of pension benefits, are much more likely to pay a generous lump sum payment in addition to a pension.

In most Canadian provinces, spousal benefits remain unaffected by the claimant's remarriage. However, in all US states and in three Canadian jurisdictions, benefits terminate upon remarriage if there are no dependent children. In most US states where periodic benefits terminate on remarriage and in all such Canadian jurisdictions, the spouse receives a lump sum payment. As can be seen, the typical US payment is the equivalent of 104 weeks of benefits at the periodic rate, while it is the equivalent of 52 weeks for all Canadian programs. In most US programs and all Canadian ones, benefits may continue after the spouse has remarried if there are dependent children. In a few programs, full spousal benefits continue until the youngest child has reached the age of majority.

Two factors not depicted in Tables D1 and D2 also affect compensation benefits. First, in eleven US states and five Canadian provinces, benefits are reduced by payments made to surviving claimants by the Social Security, CPP, or QPP programs. The precise formula used to determine the amount of the offset varies substantially across jurisdictions. For example, in some states the offset is equal to 50 percent of the Social Security benefit, while in others, the combined benefit is equal to 80 percent of the decedent worker's wage. Second, nine Canadian jurisdictions and eight US states adjust compensation benefits annually, based on changes in the cost of living as measured by the CPI or the average wage in the jurisdiction. Some jurisdictions put a cap on the amount of the adjustment or otherwise reduce it. While the first factor results in a relatively small reduction in the value of the award, the second can substantially increase the commuted value of compensation benefits.

As can be seen, the complexity of factors determining fatal injury compensation prevents an easy comparison of the relative generosity of benefits across jurisdictions. To enable such a comparison, two measures of benefit generosity are computed for all North American jurisdictions and reported in Table D4. The first of these are the expected benefits that will be paid to the spouse of a worker who has suffered a fatal injury as the result of an occupational accident. These benefits are calculated using a uniform distribution of beneficiaries, which varies by age and number of dependent children. Calculations were also based on a standard wage distribution and the jurisdiction's average weekly wage in 1996.[21]

The second measure, reported in Table D4, is an index of the ratio of expected benefits – as described in the previous paragraph – to a standard. This standard is equal to the benefits that would have been paid if the jurisdiction had adopted the statutory parameters prescribed by the Model Act that was promulgated by the Council of State Governments (US) in the mid-1970s. The advantage of this second measure is that it accounts for differences in average wages across jurisdictions and, therefore, differences in national currency.[22]

Where there is no spouse, the primary beneficiaries are the decedent worker's dependent children. The benefit entitlement of orphan children in most jurisdictions is similar, if not identical, to spousal benefits. Those jurisdictions that vary the overall level of benefits paid to a spouse according to the number of dependent children do the same when only orphan children are entitled to compensation, although the amounts may vary. For example, in British Columbia, a single orphan child is entitled to 40 percent of the amount paid to a dependent spouse with two or more children, while two orphan children are entitled to 50 percent of that amount, and three orphans receive 60 percent. An additional $209.40 is paid monthly for each child above three in number.

Compensation for other claimants is based on the extent of the claimants' dependency. In some jurisdictions, the periodic amount due to a total dependant is identical to that which would be paid to a dependent spouse. In most it is a lesser amount, reflecting a more remote relationship with the decedent worker. For example, in Arizona a single dependent parent receives 25 percent of the claimant's pre-injury wage, two dependent parents receive 40 percent, one sibling receives 25 percent, while two or more siblings receive 35 percent share and share alike.

In most North American jurisdictions, partial dependants receive awards that are proportional to those paid to a total dependant based on the average contribution of the decedent worker to the claimant dependant. In some jurisdictions, this proportion is equal to the ratio of this average contribution to the decedent worker's total income, while in others it is equal to the ratio of this average contribution to the dependent claimant's total income. In some US states, the amount for partial dependants is a fixed proportion of the worker's pre-injury income and therefore does not vary with degree of dependency. In still some other states, the amount paid to partial dependants is at the discretion of the agency administering the compensation program.

For the most part, the duration limitations that apply to dependent children where there is a surviving spouse are identical to the limitations applicable to orphans. In some US states, these same limitations apply to siblings and grandchildren. Many states have a fixed statutory limitation on the number of weeks during which benefits may be paid or on the total amount of benefits paid to these other dependent classes. In addition to or instead of these limitations, the statute may prescribe that the claimant is only entitled to compensation for "as long as he can have reasonably expected" to receive support from the decedent worker.

Most American states – but no Canadian provinces or territories – provide for the payment of some amount, in addition to funeral expenses, in the event that the claimant dies without eligible dependants. These monies are most often paid to the state's Second Injury Fund or to some other fund maintained by the state for a purpose related to the functioning of the workers' compensation program. However, in some states, an award is made to either the claimant's estate, the claimant's parents, or the claimant's next-of-kin. The total value of awards is reported in Table D4.

Conclusion

The examination of the law of fatal accident compensation suggests that there are two general sets of issues that need to be addressed by workers' compensation programs. The first comprises issues related to eligibility for compensation: How should we determine who is eligible for fatality benefits and who is not? Under what circumstances should the workers' compensation program pay fatal compensation benefits? The second set involves issues relating to benefit levels: How much compensation is appropriate for a fatal accident claim? Should benefit levels vary among surviving claimants or should the same level be paid in every claim? What is (are) the appropriate basis (bases) for compensation benefits?

Eligibility

As indicated, in most North American jurisdictions, receipt of compensation benefits is conditioned on two criteria: (1) a family relationship and (2) dependency, although the latter requirement is often waived in the case of a spouse or child. Importantly, where no person meets these eligibility criteria, in many jurisdictions no compensation is paid.

The economic analysis presented earlier suggests that the payment of fatal compensation benefits in the context of an experience-rated workers' compensation system results in a more efficient level of workplace safety. By increasing workers' compensation costs, higher benefits induce experience-rated employers to invest in safety. A logical inference is that compensation should be paid in every fatal injury claim, even those where there are no dependants. Equity considerations seem to demand an identical result – employer compensation costs should be related to the number of fatal injuries experienced by the employer, not simply those in which there was an eligible dependant. This would seem an important consideration when one recalls that fatal injury claims are rare, but costly, and that US data show that for a substantial proportion of claims, there are no eligible dependants.

If benefits are paid in every fatal injury claim, how do we determine who is eligible and who is not? This question is largely beyond the scope of economic analysis, involving questions regarding the nature of family obligations. In many jurisdictions, current law – which prescribes a list of eligible dependants – reflects a somewhat anachronistic paternalism compared with privately provided life insurance where the worker is permitted to choose his or her beneficiary. Since workers' compensation confers no-fault liability on employers, the insurance analogy would seem to be particularly appropriate.

In addition, economic analysis suggests that policy makers, particularly in the context of a no-fault program, should minimize transaction or administrative costs associated with the determination of eligibility. In particular, this would suggest a policy that minimizes dispute probability. Coupled with the previous observation that benefits should be paid in every fatal claim, this implies that a conclusive presumption of dependency for the decedent's spouse or minor children is warranted.[23] If there is no spouse or minor children, the decedent worker should be allowed the opportunity to name his or her own beneficiary(ies). This could be done upon initial employment using a form supplied by the workers' compensation board, with a provision for allowing the worker to change beneficiaries at any later time. Where there is no named beneficiary, benefits would be paid to a family member who could demonstrate dependency. If no person could demonstrate dependency, benefits would be paid to the next-of-kin.

Permitting workers to select their own beneficiaries, where there is no spouse or children, should have the happy twofold result of eliminating some of the paternalism inherent in the present system and avoiding at least some disputes that would otherwise occur. In addition, by allowing the worker some choice of beneficiaries, the program would confer a benefit upon the fatally injured worker that he or she does not currently enjoy. The exception accorded the spouse and child recognizes a widely accepted social norm regarding family obligations as well as the fact that the decedent's death is likely to have the greatest economic impact on a spouse and minor children.[24] To the extent that other persons, such as parents or siblings, are dependent on the injured worker, we could reasonably expect that those individuals, whom the worker cared for while alive, would be named as beneficiaries in the event of his or her death. Importantly, the payment of benefits to named beneficiaries should resolve many of the questions that currently could arise with respect to the determination of dependency and thereby substantially reduce transaction costs. In this context, it is important to recall that many features of workers' compensation were designed to reduce litigiousness.

In the absence of a named beneficiary and other dependants, the WCB should pay benefits to the decedent's estate. This alternative is to be preferred to one that calls for no contribution or a contribution to be made to, for example, the Enhancement Reserve fund, since such a contribution would reduce costs associated with work accidents in the industry.

Benefit Levels

The economic analysis presented earlier suggests that benefits should be related to the workers' loss and that compensation equivalent to the worker's loss is likely to result in optimal accident prevention. Estimates produced by Viscusi and others suggest that this requires fatal awards in the range of $4 to $5 million. However, it is important to recall that workers' compensation was a quid pro quo arrangement whereby workers agreed to accept limited benefits in exchange for no-fault employer liability. Payment of full-compensation benefits would be tantamount to reneging on this social contract, an act with adverse political and – perhaps – economic consequences. For these reasons, it would be prudent to maintain the current limited compensation scheme, which would require that benefits be something less than the compensation awarded to the victims of non-work-related accidents. In the context of the fatal accident legislation that applies to non-work-related fatalities, this would imply a system of benefits intended to compensate survivors for a portion of lost wage income with no additional compensation for non-pecuniary loss.

As previously noted, the rules determining compensation benefits vary substantially across jurisdictions. There are two general conclusions that can be drawn from an examination of these rules. First, in many jurisdictions the rules are complex, and – perhaps – difficult for surviving dependants to understand. Why should a forty-year-old surviving spouse without children receive a pension that has a present value that is nearly seven times greater than the lump sum paid to a thirty-nine-year-old spouse without children? Disregarding the very real equity problems raised by these rules, because it is difficult to discern an underlying rationale, the perception of unfairness could arise, which will increase dispute probability.

Second, many of these rules – for example, replacement ratios that vary with the number of dependent children or the termination of spousal benefits upon remarriage – appear to base compensation on the survivor's needs rather than the worker's loss. To the extent that this is the case, the rule is contrary to the principle that the survivor should be compensated for lost wage income. As indicated, a jurisdiction is more likely to achieve optimal workplace safety where benefits are related to the loss suffered by the injured worker.

This suggests that the principle determining fatal injury compensation should be simple and easily understood. The analysis also suggests that compensation be based on the decedent worker's loss and not the survivor's needs. Taken together, these observations imply that dependent compensation should not vary by type of beneficiary or even by the extent of dependency. Based on the notion that the fatally injured worker's loss is at least as great as that experienced by the totally disabled worker, fatal injury compensation should be equivalent to that paid to a permanently and totally disabled worker. Since the loss is a permanent one, benefits should be paid for the period for which the decedent worker would have been paid wages, that is, until age sixty-five.

Notes

1 There are dissenting voices. In a recent review of the literature, Boden (1995: 287) submits: "We cannot conclude that workers' compensation premiums provide effective incentives to reduce workplace hazards. Moreover, where workers' compensation costs are high, employers may engage in loss prevention activities that limit the availability of compensation for injured workers, distort employment policies, and lead to socially inefficient expenditures to identify 'accident-prone' workers and fraudulent claims."

2 The conditions are that the worker is unable to accurately judge the risk of workplace injury; the worker is mobile, that is, can move freely into and out of labour markets; and that workers' compensation is experience-rated.

3 See Viscusi (1993) for a review of this literature.

4 Dorman and Hagstrom (1998) recently found that inclusion in wage regressions of industry

dummy variables or other variables measuring industry characteristics that affect wages substantially reduces the measured wage differential, to the point that it is no longer statistically different from zero.

5 The risk of non-fatal injury is highly correlated with the fatal risk measure and, at least theoretically, can be expected to influence wages. Many "value-of-life" studies have included a measure of the risk of non-fatal injury as a regressor in the wage equation. However, this variable is problematic for two reasons. Typically, the occupation or industry non-fatal injury rate is used as a proxy for non-fatal risk. Unfortunately, due to risk-bearing and reporting moral hazard, we may expect that this variable measures risk with substantial error. In addition, this variable is highly correlated with the fatal risk measure, resulting in substantial multi-collinearity problems.

6 A normal good is one where consumption is positively related to income. In other words, as income rises, consumers will increase their consumption of a normal good.

7 As indicated, the risk premium should be reduced by workers' compensation benefits, since these benefits reduce the worker's expected costs of accidents. Omission of this variable from the regression equation will bias the risk coefficient downward, leading the investigator to underestimate the risk premium.

8 The average annual income (in 1990 dollars) in the Kneisner and Leeth study was $26,226, while it was $19,194 in the Moore and Viscusi study.

9 Average income in the Moore in the Viscusi studies was $24,834 (in 1990 dollars).

10 Other statutory law, typically entitled Survival of Actions Acts, permits an independent cause of action by the decedent's estate. The right to sue is the decedent's; entitlement to damages, with some limitations, is identical to that which the decedent would have enjoyed but for his or her death. In many provinces, damages are limited to the pecuniary loss suffered by the estate, including the cost of medical services. There is variation across provinces as to whether the estate may claim damages for the loss of future earnings. Some provinces allow the estate to collect damages for non-pecuniary loss, or even non-compensatory damages.

11 In recent years, several provincial compensation programs have begun to award permanently disabled claimants a lump sum amount that is independent of the award for earnings loss. For example, since 1985 Ontario, has paid two awards for permanent disability: an award based on the claimant's actual (or deemed) wage loss, called a FEL (future economic loss) award and an award based on the extent of the claimant's functional impairment, called a NEL (non-economic loss) award. As the name implies, the NEL, and like awards in other provinces, represent compensation for non-pecuniary loss.

12 Since awards are paid in a lump sum, it is necessary to commute the stream of lost wages into a present value, which requires estimating a discount rate. In many provinces, the discount rate is established by statute.

13 This ignores claims for loss of accumulated wealth, that is, claims that were it not for the decedent's premature death, he or she would have accumulated a more substantial estate that would eventually have devolved to the dependent survivor. These claims are frequently countered by the argument that survivors received their portion of the estate earlier than otherwise due to the untimely death. As a result, they received a benefit from the "acceleration of inheritance." These claims are often offsetting so that there is no net benefit to the survivor.

14 In fact, many jurisdictions do not even require a showing that the injury "arose out of" employment if the death occurred on the employer's premises (or in the course of employment).

15 Typically, invalid children or children who are mentally or physically incapacitated from earning wages, who have reached the age of majority, are also eligible for benefits. In addition, most North American jurisdictions extend eligibility to adult children who are currently enrolled in an accredited educational institution for a few years beyond the age of majority. In British Columbia, "a child under the age of 21 years who is regularly attending an academic, technical or vocational place of education" is eligible for compensation benefits (Section 17[1] [c] of the Workers' Compensation Act).

16 In British Columbia, the minimum period is three years.

17 In several states, a legal obligation to provide support is sufficient for demonstrating dependency. In others, dependency is presumed unless the spouse had voluntarily abandoned the decedent worker without justifiable cause. No other Canadian province makes a statutory presumption of dependency.

18 National fatal injury data from the United States indicate that for over 78 percent of all such claims, the primary beneficiary was a spouse. Since in over 14 percent of these claims, there was no eligible dependant, only slightly more than 7 percent of all fatal injuries led to claims where the primary beneficiary was someone other than the spouse.

19 Where the beneficiaries are a spouse and children, compensation is most often paid to the spouse and the children do not have a separate entitlement.

20 In most US states, benefits are paid weekly, while in all Canadian provinces survivor benefits are paid monthly. In these tables, I have converted monthly amounts to their weekly counterparts to facilitate comparison between jurisdictions.

21 The wage distribution and the distribution of dependent beneficiaries were both obtained from the National Council of Compensation Insurers (NCCI), Boca Raton, Florida.

22 Importantly, the Model Act prescribes maximum and minimum benefits as a percentage of the state's average weekly wage, that is, the maximum is equal to 200 percent of the average wage, while the minimum is set at 50 percent. While the Model Act prescribes that the maximum and minimum are based on the average wage from two years previous, for simplicity, the calculations use 1996 wages to compute 1997 benefits.

23 These categories should be defined broadly in accordance with recent trends. Dependent children includes illegitimate as well as legitimate children, adopted as well as natural, stepchildren, and posthumous children. The definition of "spouse" should include common-law spouses as well as divorced or separated spouses for whom there is a legal obligation of support.

24 In addition, priority to the spouse and children will be in accordance with the decedent's wishes in the overwhelming majority of cases.

References

Boden, L. 1995. "Creating Economic Incentives: Lessons from Workers' Compensation Systems." *Proceedings of the Forty-Seventh Annual Meeting of the Industrial Relations Research Association,* Madison, WI: Industrial Relations Research Association (IRRA).

Butler, R., and J. Worrall. 1991. "Claims Reporting and Risk-Bearing Moral Hazard in Workers' Compensation." *Journal of Risk and Insurance* 53: 191-204.

Dorman, P., and P. Hagstrom. 1998. "Wage Compensation for Dangerous Work Revisited." *Industrial and Labor Relations Review* 52 (1): 116-35.

Durbin, D., and R.J. Butler. 1998. "Prevention of Disability from Work Related Sources: The Roles of Risk Management, Government Intervention, and Insurance." In *New Approaches to Disability in the Workplace,* ed. Terry Thomason, John F. Burton, Jr., and Douglas Hyatt, 63-86. Madison, WI: Industrial Relations Research Association (IRRA).

Hyatt, D., and T. Thomason. 1998. *Evidence on the Efficacy of Experience Rating in British Columbia.* Report to the Royal Commission on Workers' Compensation in British Columbia. Available from author.

Ison, T.G. 1994. *Compensation Systems for Injury and Disease: The Policy Choices.* Toronto and Vancouver: Butterworths.

Kneisner, T., and J. Leeth. 1991. "Compensating Wage Differentials for Fatal Injury Risk in Australia, Japan, and the United States." *Journal of Risk and Uncertainty* 4: 75-90.

Moore, M., and W. Kip Viscusi. 1988. "Doubling the Estimated Value of Life: Results Using New Occupational Fatality Data." *Journal of Policy Analysis and Management* 7: 476-90.

–. 1989. "Promoting Safety through Workers' Compensation: The Efficacy and Net Wage Costs of Injury Insurance." *Rand Journal of Economics* 20: 499-515.

–. 1990. "Discounting Environmental Health Risks: New Evidence and Policy Implications." *Journal of Environmental and Economic Management* 18: S51-S62.

Ruser, J. 1993. "Workers' Compensation and the Distribution of Occupational Injuries." *Journal of Human Resources* 28: 594-617.

Thomason, T., and J. Burton. 1993. "The Economics of Workers' Compensation in the

United States: Private Insurance and the Administration of Compensation Claims." *Journal of Labor Economics* 11: S1-S37.

Thomason, T., D. Hyatt, and K. Roberts. 1998. "Disputes and Dispute Resolution." In *New Approaches to Disability in the Workplace,* ed. Terry Thomason, John F. Burton, Jr., and Douglas Hyatt, 269-98. Madison, WI: Industrial Relations Research Association (IRRA).

Viscusi, W. Kip. 1978. "Wealth Effects and Earnings Premiums for Job Hazards." *Review of Economics and Statistics* 60: 408-16.

–. 1993. "The Value of Risks to Life and Health." *Journal of Economic Literature* 31: 1912-46.

14
Psychiatric Disability and Workers' Compensation
William Gnam

Over the last three decades, awareness of the potential mental effects of the work environment has grown among both academic health researchers (Karasek and Theorell 1990) and the lay public. Workers' compensation claims for mental disabilities have proliferated since 1980 (deCarteret 1994), compelling most jurisdictions in Canada and the United States to consider broad issues involving the psychological and emotional aspects of work. The results of these deliberations are a patchwork of different compensation policies enacted by boards across North America. These policies pertain to a variety of claims related to mental conditions: "chronic mental stress," "occupational stress," "cumulative psychiatric injury," and various mental disorders that are allegedly work-related.

Mental stress claims represented 2.8 percent of all occupational disease claims in Alberta and British Columbia in 1993 (AWCBC 1996). At their peak in 1990, mental stress claims comprised 9 percent of all new claims in California, but by 1994 the figure had fallen to less than 4 percent (Elisburg 1994). Mental claims have never represented more than a small percentage of the overall claims submitted to North American compensation boards, but they consistently have generated attention and controversy. In the United States, the number of mental stress claims more than doubled between 1980 and 1987 (deCataret 1994), and prominent jurisdictions such as California experienced even faster growth rates. Insurers, employers, and policy makers feared that an "epidemic" of mental-health-related compensation claims would lead to soaring insurance costs (deCataret 1994; Boustedt 1990). These fears were never realized, perhaps because in the early 1990s, many jurisdictions passed legislative measures to severely restrict compensability.

Several salient facts suggest that compensation policies for mental stress and mental disability deserve closer scrutiny than they have often received. First, mental disability claims in workers' compensation are costly: in British Columbia, the costs associated with mental stress claims in 1992 averaged

$12,645 per claim (AWCBC 1996). A recent study performed by the US National Council of Compensation Insurance (NCCI) reported that charges for compensated "mental injury" claims were 52 percent higher than those for an average traumatic bodily injury. Mental stress claims also lasted longer, an average of thirty-nine weeks, while the average physical injury claim lasted twenty-four weeks, and the average occupational illness claim lasted thirty-six weeks (Elisburg 1994). Second, mental disability claims in workers' compensation are frequently appealed and contested, pitting workers against employers, often in a highly confrontational atmosphere. For example, debate in Ontario over the compensability of chronic mental stress claims led to acrimonious exchanges between workers' advocates and employer groups (Stritch 1995). In the United States, the counterpart to appeal has been litigation. The NCCI reports that 53 percent of mental stress claims in the United States involve attorneys, compared to 8 percent of physical injury claims and 36 percent of occupational disease claims (Yorker 1994). Third, the experience of jurisdictions such as California suggests that ill-considered compensation policies for mental conditions may result in a dramatic escalation of insurance costs. Following several key court rulings, the costs of mental stress claims in California grew by 700 percent from 1979 to 1984, and temporarily became the most pressing concern for employers and insurers regarding workers' compensation (Elisburg 1994). Finally, mental conditions and their relation to the workplace are poignant examples of the difficulties boards face in assigning causation when the illnesses or conditions are believed to be multi-causal in nature (Shainblum et al., forthcoming). In this respect the compensation issues raised by mental conditions are germane to a growing list of occupational diseases.

From a critical perspective, this chapter summarizes the scientific and clinical understanding of mental disability and occupational stress, and evaluates the evidence implicating workplace factors in the causation of these conditions. The general analytical approach is to extract the key implications for compensation policy from scientific health research. The chapter also surveys and critiques the myriad policies adopted for mental stress claims across North America. Finally, the chapter considers the ongoing policy dilemmas with chronic stress claims.

Frequent reference is made to policy experiences of the United States, largely because the forerunners of Canadian mental claims occurred in several key US states. American workers who have access to lawyers and courts, traditionally have considered creative legal claims, and the incentives for American workers and lawyers to bring forth such claims have often been compelling. It hardly surprising that many state compensation boards have considerably more policy experience with mental stress claims than their Canadian provincial counterparts.

This chapter is organized into five sections as follows. The first section describes the categorization of mental claims commonly used in workers' compensation systems, and relates these categories to the terminology used by academic health researchers and mental health clinicians. These relationships are important to clarify because most of the relevant scientific evidence on mental disorders, mental stress, and disability does not adopt the categorization of compensation boards. In the first section I also itemize the controversies common to most mental disability claims in workers' compensation systems. The second section identifies the types of mental disorder most plausibly related to the workplace, and summarizes the evidence that relates these mental disorders to adverse labour market outcomes such as work disability. This section concludes that mental disorders and other mental conditions cause significant disability that may result in absenteeism and other adverse labour market outcomes. The pivotal issue for workers' compensation policy is whether mental conditions can be shown to occur "in the course of and arising out of employment." The third section addresses the complicated issues of work-related causation. The fourth section then reviews the policies adopted by British Columbia and other Canadian provinces, and finally, the fifth section considers policy options.

The Terminology of Mental Claims and Mental Disorders
Workers' compensation claims involving mental aspects fall into three categories: "physical-mental," "mental-physical," and "mental-mental." These categories arose from the landmark treatise by Arthur Larson (1992) and have been adopted almost universally by boards across Canada and the United States. The term "mental" is generally understood to include both psychological and emotional aspects. A "physical-mental" claim arises when a work-related physical injury or stimulus gives rise to a mental condition that causes or increases disability. A limb amputation that precipitates a disabling clinical depressive disorder would be an example. "Mental-physical" claims arise when a work-related mental stimulus results in a disabling physical illness or condition. The most commonly cited examples are a myocardial infarction precipitated by a traumatic job event, or specific job characteristics that increase the risk for cardiovascular disease. Other examples are gastrointestinal illnesses or traffic accidents related to job stress (Alfredsson et al. 1985). "Mental-mental" claims arise when a mental stimulus or repeated mental stimuli result in a mental disorder or other mental condition. Examples include witnessing an industrial accident at work, which precipitates a post-traumatic stress disorder (PTSD), or repeatedly stressful work conditions resulting in emotional exhaustion. For each of the three categories note that the stimulus leading to the disabling condition could be singular, or consist of repeated stimuli over time.

Subject to certain restrictions, physical-mental and mental-physical claims are generally held to be compensable, although for practical reasons workers may find it difficult to convince boards of the merits of these claims (Elisburg 1994). Mental-mental claims provoke far more controversy than the other two categories, and the subgroup of claims arising from repeated stressful work-related stimuli (the so-called chronic stress or cumulative psychiatric injury conditions) are the most controversial of all. Chronic stress claims have posed vexing issues for boards, and British Columbia is no exception (Munro 1993).

The controversies surrounding mental-mental claims arise from several factors. Definitions of mental stress lack standardization, which creates confusion for policy makers and variability in the manner by which such claims are evaluated clinically. Causal models of occupational stress and mental disorders typically posit the importance of multiple factors, including factors beyond the work environment. This framework complicates the legal evaluation of work-related causation for any claimant with a mental disability. Compensating work disability arising from mental stress is widely predicted to result in skyrocketing costs (Elisburg 1994). Moreover, the subjective nature of medical and psychiatric evaluation in mental-mental claims may create incentives for fraudulent claims, or claims for genuine mental disability that are unrelated to work. These controversies have many dimensions, but a clear scientific understanding of mental stress and its relations to disability, mental disorder, and the workplace could assist boards in formulating rational and equitable policy.

Larson's categorization serves a useful descriptive function for boards and legal analysis, but it only loosely corresponds to the terminology used by most psychologists and psychiatrists. The terms "stress," "occupational stress," and "chronic mental stress" are not recognized by mental health clinicians as distinct clinical conditions. Only a minority of clinicians recognizes proposed industrial mental conditions such as "job burnout." The term "stress" itself has multiple meanings, and can be used to denote either the nature of the stimulus ("stressors") or the individual's response ("stress reaction"). Some authors have recommended discarding the term "stress" because of this ambiguity (Wessely 1996). Nonetheless, research psychologists have proposed many models of stress and its relation to health (Beehr 1995); relatively few of these models have been validated by extensive empirical studies. Models of occupational stress have also been developed, the most important of which is the *job strain* model of Karasek and Theorell (1990), which has greatly enhanced our understanding of the health consequences of the work environment.

When mental claims are clinically evaluated, the most commonly used classification system is the *Diagnostic and Statistical Manual of Mental Disorders (DSM-IV)*, fourth edition, published by the American Psychiatric Association (APA 1994). Some jurisdictions (such as California since 1994) have made the presence of a DSM-IV mental disorder a necessary condition for compensating mental claims. DSM-IV mental disorders are also called "psychiatric disorders," and this chapter uses these terms synonymously. A "mental condition" for the purposes of this chapter refers to a psychological or emotional state that a clinician evaluates as "clinically significant," but does not meet the criteria for the diagnosis of a mental disorder. In practice, this group of conditions may be small. This is because the DSM-IV includes a "not otherwise specified" (NOS) category for most groups of mental disorders, which is intended to capture individuals who have clinically significant distress or impairment, but do not qualify for the other formal definitions of mental disorder (APA 1994). For example, persons experiencing significant distress or impairment with some features of a clinical depression (but failing to meet the threshold for a DSM-IV major depressive disorder) could be classified as having a "mood disorder not otherwise specified" under the DSM system (ibid.).

Two limitations of the DSM-IV classification should be stated at the outset. Most mental disorders in the manual are not defined by operationalized disability criteria. Consequently, the presence of a DSM-IV diagnosis does not automatically imply disability. This limitation is noted explicitly in the preamble to the manual (ibid.). The second limitation closely relates to the first; mental conditions failing to meet the diagnostic criteria for a DSM-IV mental disorder may nonetheless be associated with disability. The policy relevance of these limitations is considered later in this chapter (see "Policy Options").

Despite these limitations, it is important to understand the types and frequencies of DSM-IV mental disorders suffered by mental-mental claimants in workers' compensation. Surprisingly, only one published study addresses this issue. The California Workers' Compensation Institute (CWCI) reported the frequencies of mental disorders arising from 390 claimants chosen randomly from all claims for "cumulative psychiatric injury" (chronic stress) filed in 1990 in California (CWCI 1995). Based upon the opinions of the workers' treating psychologists and psychiatrists, in 36 percent of cases claimants were suffering from a diagnosable mood (i.e., depressive) disorder, in 27 percent from an anxiety disorder, and in 29 percent from an adjustment disorder. The remainder (8 percent) of claimants also had DSM-IV mental disorders, but details are unavailable. The fact that claimants had high rates of mental disorder does not establish work-related causation. Moreover, one study may not generalize to other jurisdictions. Reviewing our knowledge of these mental disorders and their consequences will have some relevance to workers' compensation systems, and it is this review that constitutes the next two sections.

Mental Disorders and Adverse Outcomes in the Labour Market
This section reviews the evidence linking mental disorders to adverse labour market outcomes and disability. In the context of workers' compensation

this review serves several purposes. It establishes a list of those mental disorders for which work causation has at least prima facie plausibility, and rules out other mental disorders without plausibility. It evaluates the general credibility of the claim that certain mental disorders cause significant impairment and work disability. Finally, the review offers some estimates of the magnitude of these phenomena, from both a societal and workplace perspective, which can be helpful in anticipating the consequences of policy decisions in this area.

The disability and social consequences of some mental disorders have only been rigorously established in the last decade, and until very recently, much of this evidence was not available to boards across North America. Large population surveys have become the vital scientific instrument for establishing the general credibility of the association between psychiatric disorders, disability, and other adverse labour market consequences. An important innovation of these surveys has been the development of structured diagnostic psychiatric interviews delivered by trained interviewers, which closely reproduce the diagnoses that experienced clinicians would make on the basis of face-to-face interviews (Wittchen 1994). These surveys are highly confidential, implying that respondents have no incentives to misrepresent their mental status or personal circumstances. The confidentiality represents an important advantage over clinical evaluation in the workers' compensation setting, where the self-report of injured workers has potential consequences for compensation judgments. Table 14.1 provides a list of DSM-IV mental disorders for which work causation has prima facie validity. The table also includes a list of mental disorders with possible but more speculative work causation.

Several exclusions from the table should be briefly justified. Chronic and debilitating mental disorders such as schizophrenia or severe bipolar disorder (manic-depression) are not listed. Persons with these mental disorders have minimal relevance to workers' compensation because the probability

Table 14.1

DSM-IV mental disorders that plausibly or possibly have work-related causation

Plausible work causation	Possible work causation
Major depressive disorder	Specific phobias (certain subtypes)
Mood disorder NOS (minor depression)	Panic disorder with agoraphobia
Acute stress disorder	Panic disorder without agoraphobia
Post-traumatic stress disorder (PTSD)	Social phobia
Anxiety disorder NOS ("partial" PTSD)	Pain disorder
Adjustment disorders	

Note: Entries in bold have highest plausibility and greatest relevance to the workers' compensation setting. NOS = not otherwise specified.

that they would obtain the kind of regular employment covered by workers' compensation is low (Ettner et al. 1997; Friedland and Evans 1996). Moreover, evidence from genetics and twin studies strongly implicates genetic and biological factors in the causation of these disorders, although certain life events may trigger relapses or specific episodes (APA 1994). DSM-IV eating disorders (such as bulimia nervosa or anorexia nervosa) are also excluded. Certain occupations (such as modelling or ballet dancing) encourage women to adopt extremely slim body shapes, and in some cases this might be viewed clinically as a precipitating or perpetuating causal factor in these disorders. However, these occupations are not frequently covered by workers' compensation insurance. Personality disorders are also excluded. These diagnoses are based upon certain enduring dysfunctional personality characteristics that become manifest by adolescence (APA 1994). They are obviously not caused by work. Note, however, that the presence of a personality disorder may complicate the adjudication of work causation when other mental disorders are simultaneously present, because some evidence suggests that personality disorders may act as "pre-existing" conditions, and independently elevate the risk of developing other mental disorders such as post-traumatic stress disorder (Deering et al. 1996).

The entries under the "possible work causation" heading of the table deserve brief mention. The first four entries are anxiety disorders that feature episodic symptoms that in some cases will be triggered by ordinary non-traumatic workplace stimuli. While these disorders might satisfy a "but for" legal standard of work-related causation (but for the workplace stimulus, the anxiety episode would not have occurred), they probably would not satisfy more substantial concepts of causation. An example may clarify this point. A specific phobia is a marked and persistent fear of a discernible, circumscribed object or situation, exposure to which almost always provokes immediate severe fear and anxiety (APA 1994). The most illustrative example in a work setting is the blood/injection/injury subtype, where afflicted persons often have severe involuntary anxiety and fainting when confronted by blood or injury. This phobia could cause disability among health workers and certain other occupations, and obviously a work-related stimulus serves as a trigger for a particular episode. From a scientific perspective, however, there is strong evidence that blood/injection/injury anxiety follows a clear familial pattern, suggesting that genetic or other biological factors play a pivotal role in causation (ibid.). Similar considerations pertain to panic disorder with or without agoraphobia, and to social phobia. The frequency with which these disorders result in prolonged work disability is unknown. Pain disorder describes a chronic pain condition initiated by physical factors but perpetuated by mental factors (ibid.). While this might represent a form of physical-mental injury, almost no evidence to date relates this disorder to the workplace setting (ibid.). Note, however, that considerable evidence suggests that coexisting psychiatric disorders do play a role in perpetuating chronic pain conditions (see Tunks et al. in this volume).

The entrants highlighted in bold in the lefthand list have both the highest plausibility of work-related causation and the greatest relevance to the workers' compensation setting. The diagnosis of acute stress disorder is made when an individual suffers from the typical symptoms constituting post-traumatic stress disorder, but the duration of the disorder does not exceed one month (ibid.). Acute stress disorder is jointly considered with PTSD for the purposes of this chapter. Adjustment disorders are not reviewed here. They represent controversial DSM categories because many experts believe that they do not constitute distinct categories. Moreover, the scientific evidence describing the disability consequences of these disorders is sparse (ibid.).

Psychiatric disorders in general are associated with high levels of disability and significant adverse labour market outcomes. The most recent large epidemiological survey of psychiatric disorders in the United States found that employed respondents with a psychiatric disorder reported three times as many short-term work-loss days across all occupations, compared to those without a psychiatric disorder (six days per 100 workers per month, compared with two days per 100 workers per month) (Kessler and Frank 1997). Respondents with a psychiatric disorder also reported three times as many work cutback days compared to those without a disorder. Respondents diagnosed with more than one psychiatric disorder simultaneously reported twenty-five times the number of work-loss days and work cutback days compared to respondents with no psychiatric disorder. The Medical Outcomes Study found that patients with depressive disorders or prolonged depressive symptoms had impaired physical, social, and role functioning comparable to or worse than the impairment associated with most chronic medical conditions (Wells et al. 1989). Analysis from an earlier major survey (the Epidemiological Catchment Area study) indicated that respondents with a depressive disorder experienced almost five times the rate of work-loss days attributable to the depression, compared to respondents without depression (Broadhead et al. 1990). A separate analysis from the same survey found that clinically depressed respondents were four times as likely to lose a week of work compared to healthy respondents (Johnson et al. 1992).

The last three studies confirmed that even those respondents with prolonged depressive symptoms (but not sufficient to qualify for the diagnosis of depressive disorder) reported significantly higher work absence rates. This finding reiterates what was suggested above: relying exclusively on the presence of a DSM diagnosis would fail to identify some persons who experience significant work disability.

There is also some research that examines more carefully the duration of work disability associated with mental disorders. The first study to examine the economic impact of depression in a white-collar workforce found that depressive disorders had the longest average length of disability compared to all other conditions, including low back pain and heart disease (Conti and Burton 1994). Depressive disorders were also associated with the highest recurrence of short-term disability within the twelve months of return to work, and were associated with medical costs comparable to those of heart disease. In the longitudinal Whitehall II study of English civil servants, mental disorder was the fifth most common reason for temporary work absence, but as the duration of work absence increased, mental disorders became the most common reason (Stansfeld et al. 1997).

The long-term consequences of mental disorders for workers are not well understood (Tweed 1993), but an excellent recent study suggests that the deleterious effects of mental disorders probably persist beyond the time of recovery from symptoms. This study found that any past or current history of a mental disorder resulted in large decreases in permanent income, suggesting that mental disorders may have prolonged adverse effects on productivity and labour market success (Ettner et al. 1997). The implications of this finding for workers' compensation systems are tentative, but potentially huge. If a work-caused mental disorder leads to long-term impairment of productivity and earning capacity, this may have to be factored into the compensation awards in jurisdictions where such reductions in productive capacity are compensable.

Among anxiety disorders, post-traumatic stress disorder has been most studied in relation to the workplace. Some cases of PTSD arising from workplace trauma represent the most unequivocal examples of work-caused mental disability, from both a scientific and legal perspective. PTSD and other post-traumatic mental conditions are important to British Columbia, since almost all of the 261 mental stress claims paid in 1994 by the BC WCB involved post-traumatic stress (AWCBC 1996).

One criterion for the diagnosis of PTSD stipulates that a person must have experienced a traumatic event that is outside the range of usual human experience, and that would be markedly distressing to almost anyone (APA 1994). This criterion has assisted boards in evaluating these claims, since unusually traumatic workplace stimuli are rare and often objectively verifiable. Some of the disabling symptoms of PTSD include intrusive psychological re-experiencing of the trauma, persistent avoidance of stimuli associated with the trauma, profound emotional detachment, and a prolonged over-aroused mental state that interferes with such functions as sleep and concentration. These symptoms may be experienced short term (less than one month), but as many as one-third of those with PTSD have chronic symptoms and disability (McFarlane 1988a).

Convincing survey evidence demonstrates that some traumatized persons not meeting all of the diagnostic criteria for PTSD nonetheless have chronic and disabling post-traumatic symptoms (Stein et al. 1997; Weisaeth 1986). Thus, the diagnosis of PTSD implies a high probability of disability, yet some traumatized individuals with post-traumatic symptoms but no full-blown disorder are also disabled. (This finding has implications for jurisdictions that demand the presence of a diagnosable DSM-IV disorder as a prerequisite to compensation [California 1993].)

PTSD has an extremely high prevalence among soldiers and Vietnam veterans, but several meticulous case studies of industrial disasters or high-risk occupations demonstrate that PTSD may be precipitated by workplace trauma. Weisaeth (1986) studied PTSD in workers exposed to a devastating industrial disaster. Of thirty-four workers who developed PTSD, only two were free of symptoms after three years of treatment, and for ten workers the symptoms and disability remained marked or severe. McFarlane examined the post-traumatic morbidity of a group of 469 firefighters exposed to a brushfire disaster (McFarlane 1988b). PTSD and other post-traumatic stress conditions were common. The design of this study is especially appealing because the firefighters were volunteers and not covered by any form of employment insurance. Thus, the self-reports of their symptoms were not prejudiced by the possibility of monetary compensation. Another significant finding of this study was that previous similar traumatic experiences increased the probability of developing PTSD, and worsened the course of the disorder. A study of Canadian firefighters also reported high rates of post-traumatic symptoms (Corneil 1993), and a significant adverse cumulative effect of earlier traumas. Similar results were obtained in a study of US firefighters and paramedics (Beaton et al. 1995). These results have implications for workers' compensation systems because they demonstrate, at least in the case of extreme trauma, that repeated stressful stimuli lead to higher levels of worker impairment from a mental disorder, compared to a single traumatic stimulus.

Workers' compensation systems are also concerned with physical injuries, industrial diseases, and how these conditions might affect the risk of developing a mental disorder. This has particular relevance to physical-mental claims, but there may also be broader implications for the design of rehabilitation and treatment systems. For example, at least one thoughtful observer of workers' compensation systems in Canada has complained that psychiatric assessment is often considered too late in the case of workers who have failed rehabilitation, or who have not recovered from a physical injury as rapidly as expected (Ison 1994). The most important research finding here is that the presence of a chronic medical condition (such as chronic pain or physical disability) increases the risk of developing a mental disorder, especially a depressive or anxiety disorder (Wells et al. 1988). The magnitude of increased risk is approximately 50 percent for a major depressive disorder, and 35 percent for an anxiety disorder. This finding was originally made on a population sample from five cities in the United States, but was recently replicated in a large survey of physical and mental health conducted in Ontario (Gnam et al. forthcoming). The Ontario study also suggested that the risk of developing a mental disorder increases with the severity of the chronic medical condition. Depressive disorders that coexist with industrial physical injuries generally exacerbate the disability associated with physical injury, and are associated with longer work absences (Wells et al. 1989). Mental disorders have been associated with delayed return to work among workers with various soft tissue injuries, although these studies are based on small numbers of compensation claimants (Ash and Goldstein 1995; Frymoyer 1992; Leavitt 1990).

In summary, several robust lines of evidence indicate that psychiatric disorders cause work absenteeism and disability. The evidence implicating depressive disorders and post-traumatic conditions is particularly convincing, and these disorders are precisely the ones most commonly associated with workers' compensation claims. Depressive and anxiety disorders occur more frequently in workers with chronic medical conditions or disabilities, providing general scientific support for the credibility of physical-mental claims. PTSD studies have established that a purely mental work stimulus of sufficient severity may produce chronic disability.

How important are these problems in aggregate, when considered from a broad perspective? To answer this, it is important to consider the prevalence of these mental disorders in the whole population and in the working population. Major depression has a lifetime prevalence in males as high as 12 percent, and in females a lifetime prevalence of between 20 and 25 percent (Kessler et al. 1994). The lifetime prevalence of anxiety disorders in the general population is even higher. Among the working population, the short-term prevalence of a psychiatric disorder (i.e., having a disorder within the thirty days preceding the diagnostic interview survey) has recently been estimated (Kessler and Frank 1997). In a recent large diagnostic survey of Americans, major depression occurred in 4.4 percent, any anxiety disorder occurred in 11.6 percent, and PTSD occurred in 2.2 percent of employed respondents. These prevalence figures suggest that mental disorders represent significant public health problems, and have important adverse labour market consequences. Economic estimates of lost work productivity attributable to depressive disorders run into the billions of dollars in the United States (Greenberg et al. 1993) and Canada (Gnam 1997). With this background, it is appropriate to now consider the pivotal issue of work-related causation.

Work-Related Causation

Several quite distinct lines of scientific evidence support the view that certain enduring characteristics of individual jobs are causal factors in mental conditions and physical illness. The substantial but not definitive evidence also suggests that general organizational aspects of the work environment are causal factors in mental conditions and physical illness. The most convincing evidence supporting the first contention comes from the job strain model of Karasek and Theorell (1990). According to the model, the most stressful jobs are characterized by the combination of high psychological workload and low decision latitude. A job with high workload is one that requires workers to work fast and hard to accomplish an excessive amount of work in too short a time. A job with low decision latitude is one that does not allow workers to make decisions on their own, does not involve learning new skills or developing special skills, but does involve a lot of repetitive work. A recent comprehensive review of research on job strain and cardiovascular disease noted that almost all of the thirty-seven studies published between 1981 and 1993 found a strong association between high levels of job strain and increased risk of cardiovascular disease, mortality, and important cardiac disease risk factors such as hypertension (ibid.). Frank and Maetzel (this volume) appraise the strength of evidence of causation for a subset of these studies and conclude that many studies meet standard epidemiological criteria used to adjudicate causation. Estimates of the increased risk fall between 2.0 and 2.5 times the population baseline risk (i.e., the Odds Ratios are between 2.0 and 2.5) (ibid.). This evidence provides a credible scientific basis for some mental-physical claims, at least as they relate to cardiac disease. The evidence relating job strain to other medical conditions is less voluminous, but consistent with the cardiac disease findings (ibid.).

Job strain has also been studied as a risk factor for the development of mental disorders (and the disability induced by mental disorders). Using nationally representative samples of the male workforce in Sweden and the United States (Karasek 1979), and large samples of male and female workers in Germany and Finland (Braun and Hollander 1988; Kauppinen-Toropainen and Hanninen 1981), mental disorders such as depression were reported to occur much more frequently in jobs with high strain. These three studies share some results and design features that suggest a causal relationship between job strain and mental disorder. They all reported a strong association (relative risk [RR] of 1.5 or greater) between job strain and mental disorder and some evidence of gradient (higher reported job strain was associated with higher rates of mental disorder). Moreover, the psychiatric diagnostic instruments used were adequate to define mental disorders using non-professional interviewers. However, these studies also share one critical limitation in establishing causation. None of them adequately controlled for selection bias – the process whereby workers more susceptible to mental disorder either chose or were assigned to jobs with higher strain. Multivariate regression analyses are inadequate controls for bias when selection occurs on the basis of respondent characteristics that were unobserved by the study. In studies involving psychiatric disorders, selection on the basis of unobserved characteristics appears very plausible.

Job strain predicted short-term absence due to mental disorder in the Whitehall II study of English civil servants (Stansfeld et al. 1997; Fletcher 1988). This study also found that lower decision authority, lower work skill discretion, higher work demands, and lower levels of job social support were all associated with higher levels of mental disorder. Conflicting work demands, and the threats of job loss or position change were also associated with higher levels of mental disorder. The Whitehall II study shares the favourable design features noted in the three studies above. A further desirable feature is longitudinal follow-up, which allows the temporal sequence of job strain and mental disorder to be determined. A plausible temporal sequence is supportive of causal relation (and in the Whitehall II study "exposure" to various job characteristics clearly preceded the occurrence of mental disorder), but the Whitehall II study did not address the problem of selection bias described above.

These studies are mutually consistent and add some scientific credibility to the hypothesis that chronic non-traumatic workplace stress causes mental disorders. The strength of the evidence is not completely conclusive, mainly because these studies fail to account for selection bias in their analyses.

Subjective experiences of workplace stress have been associated with low work satisfaction and high rates of minor psychological symptoms, but these findings do not establish causation nor demonstrate significant worker disability (Fletcher 1998). A large literature in organizational psychology attempts to associate complex dimensions of workplace organization to individual worker health outcomes (Beehr 1995). Studies in this area have generally failed to find consistent links between serious mental morbidity and workplace organization, although they have important implications for worker morale and productivity.

Chevalier et al.'s study (1996) of employees of the French National Electricity and Gas Company is the only research that explicitly examines mental disorders in relation to work organizational factors. They reported that rates of DSM anxiety disorders and depressive disorders were elevated among those who faced major changes in work content or work organization. While this study did not measure disability, from the evidence presented above, it would be reasonable to assume that those employees with anxiety and depressive disorders also had higher rates of work disability. The study's low response rates and failure to consider selection bias limit any causal conclusions. A six-year follow-up study of 15,348 Finnish employees (Appelberg et al. 1996) found that interpersonal conflict at work predicted disability only among women who simultaneously reported marital conflict (RR of 2.54.). Potential selection bias again precludes definitive causal inference, but this study does suggest that subtle interactions may occur between the organizational aspects of the workplace and other risk factors for mental disorder. These interactions would considerably complicate the scientific and legal task of determining causation.

In summary, scientific research from several sources strongly supports the view that certain mental aspects of the workplace may lead to medical illness, mental disorders, and other disabling mental conditions. Collectively, the studies cited above provide as strong or stronger evidence of workplace causation than exists for several industrial diseases. However this evidence is often based on epidemiological measurement techniques, and does not necessarily assist boards in their evaluation of work-related causation for any individual mental disability claim. Because psychiatric assessment does not use "objective" assessment tools (such as laboratory or radiological examinations), the assessment of work causation must rely on careful assessment of family, psychological, and interpersonal factors that may also contribute to the mental condition (Sperry et al. 1994; Brodsky 1990). Research to validate these clinical assessment techniques is difficult in the absence of a "gold standard" to which comparisons can be made. Nonetheless, detailed clinical assessment techniques have been published (Brodsky 1992; Bisbing 1992), and consistent standards for clinical assessment of all mental claims have been adopted in many jurisdictions, including British Columbia (WCBBC 1996).

Policy Practices

There has been little resistance to authorizing the compensability of mental conditions arising from physical injury (Elisburg 1994; AWCBC 1996). Payment for this kind of injury is well established in case law and compensation statutes (Elisburg 1994). Physical-mental claims policy thus conforms broadly to the scientific evidence presented earlier, which established that workers with physical injuries or chronic industrial diseases face an elevated risk of developing a mental disorder. Physical-mental claims are often subject to extensive evaluation by a clinical psychologist or psychiatrist. However, once the relationship between the physical injury and the mental condition has been established, these mental conditions are usually compensable.

Subject to restrictions, most boards have also decided that mental-physical claims are compensable, so long as the work-relation test can be satisfied. Across Canada, one major restriction applies: if the physical disability arises from chronic rather than acute workplace stresses, it is not compensable (AWCBC 1996). The partially subjective nature of clinical assessment means that there are practical difficulties in establishing the authenticity of mental-physical claims. These difficulties are contentious in practice but in principle are not barriers to compensability. These practical difficulties are also shared by several compensable physical conditions such as low back strain and chronic pain (Pryor 1997).

Mental-mental claims (and chronic stress claims in particular) have historically evoked the widest variation in policy response. The five types of policy enacted by jurisdictions are summarized in Table 14.2. We will describe each type briefly (Elisburg 1994).

Table 14.2

Policy variations in managing WCB mental-mental claims

Mental-mental claim policy	Jurisdiction example
Compensable even if stimulus gradual and not unusual compared to ordinary life or workplace employment	California 1985-90
Compensable if stimulus gradual, but must be unusual or clearly related to the illness and disability	Saskatchewan[a]
Compensable only if stimulus sudden, traumatic, unusual	British Columbia and most provinces
Never compensated	Washington, West Virginia
No written policy	Yukon Territory

a   Since 1996, the work stress must also be the predominant cause of the injury to be compensated.

The most inclusive jurisdictions have compensated mental injury even if the stimulus is gradual and not unusual compared to ordinary life or workplace employment. No Canadian province has explicitly adopted such a position (or had such policy suggested through tribunal decisions) (AWCBC 1996). Historically, the most important jurisdiction to adopt this policy was California in the mid-1980s and early 1990s. California's experience has had widespread influence, and is considered further in the next section (see "Policy Options").

The second category of jurisdiction finds that mental injury is compensable even if the stimulus is gradual, but only if the work stress is unusual or clearly related to the illness and disability. At the time of this publication, Saskatchewan was the only Canadian example of this category, and its policy has evolved over the last several years. Saskatchewan recognizes that certain occupations (such as teaching and air-traffic control) are inherently stressful, but is willing to consider (chronic) work stress claims from any occupation (AWCBC 1996). In 1993, the Saskatchewan WCB received 142 chronic stress claims, and 36 percent were compensated at a total cost (for lost work, medical, and rehabilitation) of $736,791 (WCBS 1998). By 1995, the number of chronic stress claims had grown to 218. In response to both stress claim proliferation and overall fiscal pressures, Saskatchewan tightened its compensation policy in 1996. The amended policy stated that to be compensable chronic stress claims must satisfy two criteria. There must be "clear and convincing evidence that work stress was excessive and unusual" in comparison to usual working conditions, and work stress must be the predominant cause (WCBS 1996). These amendments are probably responsible for the proportional reduction in compensated chronic stress claims in 1995, when of 218 claims filed only 24 percent were allowed (E. Hinck, Client Services, WCBS, personal communication, 1998).

The third category of jurisdiction compensates mental-mental claims, but only if the stimulus was sudden and of a traumatic and unusual nature. British Columbia fits this category, although the board may provide survivor benefits if the worker commits suicide as a result of cumulative workplace trauma or stress (WCBBC 1995). In 1991, the Appeal Division of British Columbia overturned earlier WCB decisions involving an ambulance driver with post-traumatic stress symptoms. The Appeal Division accepted that repeated cumulative stressful work experiences exacerbated his condition, thereby overtly including the effects of repeated traumatic stimuli in their judgment (WCBBC 1991). Most Canadian provinces have adopted policy positions similar to British Columbia, although court decisions in Nova Scotia and Prince Edward Island have recently held that board policy may not restrict the definition of "accident" to sudden or traumatic events (and in doing so reject any consideration of claims where the alleged work stresses were chronic) unless the legislation itself imposes the restriction (AWCBC 1996).

A fourth category of jurisdiction has explicitly ruled never to compensate mental-mental claims (the states of Washington and West Virginia are examples), and a fifth category of jurisdiction does not have explicit policies on mental stress claims (the Yukon Territory falls into this last group). No Canadian *province* currently falls into these latter two groups.

Policy Options

Mental claims pose difficult policy questions for compensation boards, but they also exemplify a more fundamental challenge to traditional workers' compensation systems. As evolving scientific evidence causally implicates workplace factors in more and more diseases and mental conditions, boards must grapple with claims for which the straightforward adjudication of work-relation is not possible (Shainblum et al. forthcoming). The multicausal models for mental conditions are examples of a general paradigm shift in the way causation is viewed for many medical conditions. Ultimately, workers' compensation systems cannot ignore this emerging scientific consensus without violating the historical compromise that led to the advent of workers' compensation systems in the first place: the avoidance of destructive and wasteful tort liability by employees against employers, in return for a no-fault insurance system that covers all medical and mental conditions arising out of and in the course of employment (Pryor 1997). Verifying the authenticity of mental disability claims and their work-relation may be difficult, but jurisdictions where all mental-mental claims have been prohibited now face the possibility of tort liability. For cultural and socio-economic reasons, Canadian workers have infrequently resorted to the courts, especially when compared to US workers. However, as one Canadian legal scholar has argued (Lippel 1990), no one should assume that this passivity will be maintained. Jurisdictions in the United States that refuse all mental-mental claims (by requiring, for instance that some physical injury be present) may be diverging sharply from the implications of an extensive corpus of scientific studies.

Current policies for mental-physical claims and post-traumatic stress claims are considered first, before moving on to more general issues and the dilemmas posed by chronic mental-mental ("chronic stress") claims. The current practice of restricting mental-physical claims to medical conditions that arise from a single traumatic event may ultimately not be sustainable. The section on "Work-Related Causation" above indicated that robust scientific evidence causally implicates long-term workplace factors (job strain) to medical disease and poor health outcomes. Although all Canadian jurisdictions (including British Columbia) restrict these claims to acute traumatic events (AWCBC 1996), the weight of scientific evidence may eventually influence court decisions, which in turn will force boards to revise this policy. Relaxing these restrictions would certainly increase the volume of mental-physical claims, but beyond this the impact is difficult to predict. Boards in the United States accepting mental-physical claims on the basis of chronic workplace stresses have typically demanded evidence that the workplace was unusually stressful, or that the workplace factors are responsible for a minimum percentage threshold of causation, before granting compensation. In practice these standards substantially restrict the numbers of compensated claims (Elisburg 1994).

A second specific policy implication follows from the PTSD studies. The cumulative effects of trauma are causally significant in PTSD and post-traumatic stress conditions, particularly for police, firefighters, and ambulance workers, where the probability of repeated exposure to traumatic stimuli is high. The lifetime risk of PTSD has been estimated at 2.7 percent for women and 1.2 percent for men, and the lifetime risk of less severe post-traumatic stress conditions is higher (Stein et al. 1997). Only a small minority of these conditions are precipitated by traumatic work experiences, and an even smaller percentage of these traumatic work experiences involve repeated trauma. Post-traumatic conditions already comprise the bulk of accepted mental-mental claims in British Columbia, and there is no reason to expect a substantial increase in claim volume by allowing for repeated trauma so long as the policy states that the traumatic events must be unusual.

The most difficult policy choices fall under chronic stress claims. Most Canadian boards have ruled that chronic stress claims are not compensable (AWCBC 1996). These restrictions demonstrate how legal standards for proof of causation may diverge from scientific standards. Current policy restrictions cannot be justified by the scientific evidence reviewed earlier, but may be justifiable when considering the absence of valid and reliable clinical standards by which to adjudicate individual claims (Brodsky 1990). This issue is considered further below.

Another frequently cited justification for restricting chronic stress claims is that the clinical adjudication of chronic stress will inevitably leave uncertainty, which creates incentives for fraudulent claims (Pryor 1997). While this concern is almost universal, no statistical evidence has been published indicating the frequency of such claims.

A related concern states that dramatic cost escalation will occur if chronic stress claims are found compensable (Elisburg 1994). There are compelling historical precedents to suggest that cost escalation could occur. In the mid-1980s, six US states experienced a dramatic rise in chronic stress claims, after court decisions created liberal definitions of what could be considered compensable stress. In California, psychiatric disability was recognized in case law dating back to the first few years following the enactment of the state's workers' compensation statute. The California State Supreme Court ruled in 1986 that workplace causation need be only "more than infinitesimal or inconsequential" for a mental injury to be entirely the employer's responsibility. This judgment fuelled an extraordinary growth in mental disability claims – particularly in the "mental-mental" category (CWCI 1990, 1995). By 1990, mental stress had become the most common cumulative injury claim in California. These claims were more expensive than other claims, and 98 percent of them were litigated, adding significantly to the costs for employers and workers (CWCI 1995). Before successive legislative restrictions were invoked in the 1990s, California boards compensated claims that in retrospect appear extreme. As examples, numerous claims were paid where the stressful stimuli included dismissal or lay-off, or even being criticized by bosses at work (Dertouzos 1988). The volume of chronic stress claims grew by 700 percent between 1985 and 1989.

The experience of California in the late 1980s strongly fortified the perception that mental stress claims were expanding "out of control" in all jurisdictions, and it has influenced subsequent policy deliberations in Canadian jurisdictions. Care should be exercised in extrapolating California's experience to other places, however. California workers faced compelling incentives to bring forward mental stress claims; winning compensation was often the only method to retain access to medical services. The excessively high rates of litigation also furnished strong financial incentives for lawyers and mental health providers to encourage such claims. The incentives for workers, lawyers, and mental health providers in British Columbia are clearly quite different. The recent experience of Saskatchewan suggests, however, that Canadian jurisdictions are not immune to a proliferation of chronic stress claims if a broader definition is adopted.

None of the evidence presented earlier suggests that there is anything inherent in the nature of mental conditions to warrant treating them differently than physical conditions. Most jurisdictions in Canada (with Saskatchewan and in special circumstances Quebec excepted) have deemed that the mental stimulus causing the mental disability be singular and acute rather than repeated over time, and yet we have not restricted physical injuries such as back pain to only those injuries that occurred from a single physical stimulus (Pryor 1997).

Why then treat mental conditions differently? One policy option would process mental-mental claims no differently than physical injury claims. For physical impairment scenarios, the claimant must show that the employment caused the impairment in a "but for" sense: that is, but for the employment, the impairment would not have occurred. In the case where the claimant has a pre-existing or predisposing condition, the general rule is that the employer "takes the employee as she finds her," and the worker still receives compensation. To apply the same principles to mental conditions might well result in blanket coverage of all mental conditions, work-related or not (Pryor 1997). The evidence suggests that employment to some degree probably does aggravate many mental impairments in ways the employer cannot prevent, or cannot be expected to prevent given the current limitations in knowledge. When employment has not contributed to mental impairment, policy makers have legitimate concerns that the uncertainties regarding cause and the degree of impairments could lead to many false positives if a trivial causal threshold were established.

Why would the high positive rate under the minimal causation rule be undesirable? This approach would place upon employers the costs of some impairments that they could not act in good faith to prevent. This would contradict a compelling economic rationale for workers' compensation, which states that optimal incentives for employers to create a healthy work environment occur when employers bear the costs of preventable work-related injury. If, as seems likely, some mental impairments are not preventable by anyone, then the minimal work causation rule would in effect become an employer mandate to provide disability insurance to all mental impairments suffered by workers (Pryor 1997). Such a mandate runs contrary to the historical aim of workers' compensation. Workers' compensation systems were never intended to insure losses that were not primarily attributable to the workplace. Creating such a mandate would also immediately raise equity issues with other classes of disability: why fund a mandatory disability system for mental disabilities, and not for other types?

Another policy option for chronic stress claims is to fortify the minimum causal test by requiring that employment cause some specified degree of the resulting impairment, such as a "substantial" degree. (Recently amended California legislation now requires that the workplace be responsible for at least 51 percent of the impairment [California 1993].) California has added further restrictions, by eliminating mental claims based solely on lay-offs or work dismissal. Due to limitations in measurement, asking clinicians to specify a percentage of causation would not produce valid and reliable numerical estimates. However, it is far more reasonable to expect that clinicians can offer reasoned opinions about whether the workplace made a "substantial" contribution to the mental condition (Brodsky 1992). Lamentably, there are no studies that validate the clinical assessment methods currently used to evaluate claims. The new standards in California have been accepted widely by employers, and psychiatric disabilities no longer rank among their most pressing concerns (Pryor 1997). The California policy does not solve the limitations inherent in clinical assessment techniques, and therefore beyond containing compensation costs we cannot judge whether the current policy represents any improvement in comparison to its predecessor.

Several other practical policy issues should be mentioned in passing. California's most recent chronic stress legislation now requires that claimants have a mental disorder defined by the DSM system as a prerequisite to compensability. It is suggested above (see "Mental Disorders and Adverse Outcomes in the Labour Market" and "Work-Related Causation") that this approach may be too restrictive. Having a DSM-IV diagnosis does not necessarily imply disability. More significantly, some workers have disabling mental conditions arising from work that do not fit the DSM diagnoses. The DSM system should not be discarded entirely for workers' compensation purposes – DSM-IV diagnoses often assist treatment decisions, and the presence of certain diagnoses (such as depressive disorders or PTSD) increases the expectation that the worker is truly disabled.

Another practical issue involves the need for extensive psychological or psychiatric evaluation. Meeting the standards established by the British Columbia clinical guidelines for psychological assessment in the WCB setting (WCBBC 1996) necessarily involves an extensive inquiry into the claimant's personal background. Without such inquiries, mental health clinicians cannot generally achieve a reasoned opinion regarding work-related causation, because they are unable to rule out personal, familial, or other factors that may have contributed to the mental condition. The personal and intrusive nature of psychological assessment may be resisted by workers, and may become part of the antagonism between workers' groups and employers. In Ontario, unions have opposed such assessments in chronic stress claims (Stritch 1995). The argument for retaining these assessments, however, is strong. If workers making compensated mental claims could refuse such assessments, the ability of clinicians to achieve reasoned opinions on work causation would be severely curtailed.

Finally, the role of prevention should be briefly mentioned. It is beyond the scope of this chapter to review the evaluations of interventions to reduce workplace stress (Elkin and Rosch 1990), both Kerr et al. and Wells et al. (this volume) explore this issue. However, in the context of workers' compensation one observation is particularly relevant: no studies have convincingly demonstrated that workplace interventions significantly reduce the kind of mental disability that would probably be claimed under workers' compensation (Briner 1997). This research deficit has been noted (Hotopf and Wessely 1997), and intervention trials in this area have started.

Conclusion

This chapter illustrates both the promise and limitations of current mental health research in the context of workers' compensation. Scientific evidence provides a rational basis for asserting that physical-mental and mental-physical conditions are associated with significant impairment and that (in some instances) they can legitimately be considered as caused by work-related factors. The evidence provides similar support for mental-mental claims involving PTSD. Unfortunately, scientific research has not validated clinical assessment techniques to the point where they provide a sound basis for establishing legal standards of proof. This clinical deficit is most apparent in evaluation of chronic mental stress claims, particularly where the mental stress is non-traumatic. Even with these deficits, boards across North America would benefit from better evaluation of the outcomes of various mental claims policies. Unfortunately, with the possible exception of California, few jurisdictions are pursuing such evaluations.

The difficulties posed by mental conditions and mental-mental claims will prompt boards across North America to periodically revisit the issues raised in this chapter. Compared to twenty years ago, our comprehension of mental disorders and the adverse labour market consequences of mental disorders has advanced considerably. In the areas of physical-mental and mental-physical claims, this understanding yields useful policy implications. Unfortunately, state-of-the-art knowledge regarding chronic stress claims offers no convenient policy prescription. Credible scientific evidence suggests that disabling mental conditions may arise from workplace factors, but the practical uncertainties of clinical adjudication for individual claims imply that restrictions on compensability of chronic stress claims may well persist. These policies will require periodic scrutiny and re-evaluation so long as our knowledge continues to evolve.

References

Alfredsson, L., C-L, Spetz, and T. Theorell. 1985. "Type of Occupation and Near-Future Hospitalization for Myocardial Infarction and Some Other Diagnoses." *International Journal of Epidemiology* 14: 378-88.

American Psychiatric Association (APA). 1994. *Diagnostic and Statistical Manual of Mental Disorders, Fourth edition (DSM-IV)*. Washington, DC: American Psychiatric Association Press.

Appelberg, K., K. Romanov, K. Heikkila, M-L Honkasalo, and M. Koskenvuo. 1996. "Interpersonal Conflict as a Predictor of Work Disability: A Follow-Up of 15,348 Finnish Employees." *Journal of Psychosomatic Research* 40: 157-65.

Ash, P., and S.I. Goldstein. 1995. "Predictors of Returning to Work." *Bulletin of the Academy of Psychiatry Law* 23 (2): 205-10.

Association of Workers' Compensation Boards of Canada (AWCBC). 1996. *Occupational Stress: How Canadian Workers' Compensation Boards Handle Stress Claims*. AWCBC report.

Beaton, R., S. Murphy, K. Pike, and M. Jarrett. 1995. "Stress-Symptom Factors in Firefighters and Paramedics." In *Organizational Risk Factors for Job Stress*, ed. S.L. Sauter and L.R. Murphy. Washington, DC: American Psychological Association.

Beehr, T.A. 1995. *Psychological Stress in the Workplace*. London and New York: Routledge.

Bisbing, S.B. 1992. "The Psychological Injury Claim in Workers' Compensation: Unravelling One of the Industry's Most Vexing Challenges." Paper presented at the Second APA and NIOSH Conference on Occupational Stress, Washington, DC.

Boustedt, A. 1990. "Job-Related Stress Claims Expected to Pass All Others in the '90s." *Psychiatry Times* 7: 78.

Braun, S., and R.B. Hollander. 1988. "Work and Depression among Women in the Federal Republic of Germany." *Women and Health* 14: 5-24.

Briner, R.B. 1997. "Improving Stress Assessment: Toward an Evidence-Based Approach to Organizational Stress Interventions." *Journal of Psychosomatic Research* 43: 61-71.

Broadhead, W.E., D.G. Blazer, L.K. George, and C.K. Tse. 1990. "Depression, Disability Days, and Days Lost from Work in a Prospective Epidemiologic Survey." *Journal of the American Medical Association* 264 (19): 2524-8.

Brodsky, C.M. 1990. "A Psychiatrist's Reflection on the Workers' Compensation System." *Behavioral Sciences and the Law* 8: 331-48.

–. 1992. "The Psychiatric Evaluation in Workers' Compensation." In *Psychiatric Disability*, ed. A.T. Myerson and T. Fine. Washington, DC: American Psychiatric Association Press.

California. State Legislature. 1993. *Legislative Counsel's Digest: Amendments to the Labor Code Relating to Workers' Compensation*. Sacramento, CA.

California Workers' Compensation Institute (CWCI). 1990. "Mental Stress Claims in California Workers' Compensation – Incidence, Costs and Trends." *CWCI Research Notes*. San Francisco: California Workers' Compensation Institute (CWCI).

–. 1995. *Cumulative Psychiatric Injuries in the California Workers' Compensation System (Research Abstract)*. San Francisco: California Workers' Compensation Institute (CWCI).

Chevalier, A., S. Bonenfant, M.-C. Picot, J.-F., Chastang, and D. Luce. 1996. "Occupational Factors in Anxiety and Depressive Disorders in the French National Electricity and Gas Company." *Journal of Environmental and Occupational Medicine* 38: 1098-1107.

Conti, D.J., and W.N. Burton. 1994. "The Economic Impact of Depression in the Workplace." *Journal of Occupational Medicine* 36: 983-8.

Corneil, W. 1993. "Prevalence of Post-Traumatic Stress Disorders in a Metropolitan Fire Department." PhD diss., Johns Hopkins University.

deCarteret, J.C. 1994. "Occupational Stress Claims: Effects on Workers' Compensation." *American Association of Occupational Health Nursing Journal* 4: 494-8.

Deering, C.G., S.G. Lover, D. Ready, H.C. Eddleman, and R.D. Alarcon. 1996. "Unique Patterns of Comorbidity in Post-traumatic Stress Disorder from Different Sources of Trauma." *Comprehensive Psychiatry* 37: 336-46.

Dertouzos, J.N. 1988. "Wrongful Termination: Legal and Economic Costs." In *Liability for Employee Grievances: Mental Stress and Wrongful Termination,* ed. R.B. Victor. Cambridge, Mass.: Workers Compensation Research Institute.

Elisburg, D. 1994. "Workplace Stress: Legal Developments, Economic Pressures, and Violence." John Burton's *Workers' Compensation Monitor* 6: 12-9.

Elkin, A.J., and P.J. Rosch. 1990. "Promoting Mental Health at the Workplace: The Prevention Side of Stress Management." *Occupational Medicine State of the Art Review* 5: 739-54.

Ettner, S.L., R.G. Frank, and R.C. Kessler. 1997. "The Impact of Psychiatric Disorders on Labor Market Outcomes." *Industrial and Labor Relations Review* 51 (1): 64-81.

Fletcher, B. 1988. "The Epidemiology of Occupational Stress." In *Causes, Coping and Consequences of Stress at Work,* eds. C.L. Cooper and R. Payne. Toronto and New York: Wiley.

Friedland, R.B., and A. Evans. 1996. "People with Disabilities: Access to Health Care and Related Benefits." In *Disability, Work, and Cash Benefits,* ed. J.L. Mashaw, V. Reno, R.V. Burkhauer, and M. Berkowitz. Kalamazoo, MI: Upjohn Institute for Employment Research.

Frymoyer, J.W. 1992. "Predicting Disability from Low Back Pain." *Clinical Orthopaedics and Related Research* 279: 101-9.

Gnam, W. 1997. "The Economic Costs of Depressive Disorders in Ontario 1990." MSc thesis, University of Toronto.

Gnam, W.H., J.I. William, and M. Agha. Forthcoming. "The Coexistence of Psychiatric Disorder with Chronic Medical Conditions in a Population-based Sample." *Psychological Medicine.*

Greenberg, P.E., L.E. Stiglin, S.N. Finkelstein, and E.R. Berndt. 1993. "The Economic Burden of Depression in 1990." *Journal of Clinical Psychiatry* 54: 405-18.

Hotopf, M., and S. Wessely. 1997. "Stress in the Workplace: Unfinished Business." (editorial). *Journal of Psychosomatic Research* 43: 1-6.

Ison, T.G. 1994. *Compensation Systems for Injury and Disease: The Policy Choices.* Toronto and Vancouver: Butterworths.

Johnson, J., M.M. Weissman, and G.L. Klerman. 1992. "Service Utilization and Social Morbidity Associated with Depressive Symptoms in the Community." *Journal of the American Medical Association* 267 (11): 1478-83.

Karasek, R. 1979. "Job Demands, Job Decision Latitude, and Mental Strain: Implications for Job Redesign." *Administrative Science Quarterly* 24: 285-307.

Karasek, R., and T. Theorell. 1990. *Healthy Work: Stress, Productivity, and the Reconstruction of Working Life.* New York: Basic Books.

Kauppinen-Toropainen, K., and V. Hanninen. 1981. "Job Demands and Job Content: Effects on Job Dissatisfaction and Stress." Department of Psychology, Institute of Occupational Health, Helsinki. Mimeograph.

Kessler, R.C., and R.G. Frank. 1997. "The Impact of Psychiatric Disorders on Work Loss Days." *Psychological Medicine* 27: 861-73.

Kessler, R.C., K.A. McGonagle, S. Zhao, C.B. Nelson, and M. Hughes, et al. 1994. "Lifetime and 12-Month Prevalence of DSM-III-R Psychiatric Disorders in the United States." Results from the National Comorbidity Survey. *Archives of General Psychiatry* 51: 8-19.

Larson, A. 1992. *Workmen's Compensation for Occupational Injuries and Death.* Desk edition. Section 42: 23-25. New York: M. Bender.

Leavitt, F. 1990. "The Role of Psychological Disturbance in Extending Disability Time among Compensable Back Injured Industrial Workers." *Journal of Psychosomatic Research* 34: 447-53.

Lippel, K. 1990. "Compensation for Mental-Mental Claims under Canadian Law." *Behavioral Sciences and the Law* 8: 375-98.

McFarlane, A. 1988a. "The Longitudinal Course of Post-Traumatic Morbidity: The Range of Outcomes and Their Predictors." *Journal of Nervous and Mental Disease* 176: 30-9.

–. 1988b. "The Phenomenology of Post-Traumatic Stress Disorders following a Natural Disaster." *Journal of Nervous and Mental Disease* 176: 22-9.

Munro, C. 1993. *Psychological Disabilities and Workplace Stress.* Vancouver: Workers' Compensation Board of British Columbia (WCBBC).

Pryor, E.S. 1997. "Mental Disabilities and the Disability Fabric." In *Mental Disorder, Work Disability, and the Law,* ed. R.J. Bonnie and J. Monahan. Chicago and London: University of Chicago Press.

Shainblum, E., T.J. Sullivan, and J.W. Frank. Forthcoming. "Multicausality, Non-Traditional Injury and the Future of Workers' Compensation." In *Issues in Workers' Compensation: Foundations for Reform,* ed. M. Gunderson and D. Hyatt. Toronto: University of Toronto Press.

Sperry, L., J.P. Kahn, and S.H. Heidel. 1994. "Workplace Mental Health Consultation: a Primer of Organizational and Occupational Psychiatry." *General Hospital Psychiatry* 16: 103-11.

Stansfeld, S.A., R. Fuhrer, J. Head, J. Ferrie, and M. Shipley. 1997. "Work and Psychiatric Disorder in the Whitehall II Study." *Journal of Psychosomatic Research* 43: 73-81.

Stein, M.B., J.R. Walker, A.L. Hazen, and D.R. Forde. 1997. "Full and Partial Post-Traumatic Stress Disorder: Findings from a Community Survey." *American Journal of Psychiatry* 154: 1114-9.

Stritch, A. 1995. "Homage to Catatonia: Bipartite Governance and Workers' Compensation in Ontario." In *Chronic Stress: Workers' Compensation in the 1990s: Social Policy Challenge,* ed. T. Thomason, G. Vaillancourt, T. Bogyo, and P. Stritch. Toronto: C.D. Howe Institute.

Tweed, D.L. 1993. "Depression-Related Impairment: Estimating the Concurrent and Lingering Effects." *Psychological Medicine* 23: 373-86.

Weisaeth, L. 1986. "Post-Traumatic Stress Disorders after an Industrial Disaster: Point Prevalences, Etiological and Prognostic Factors." In *Social, Epidemiologic, and Legal Psychiatry,* ed. G.L. Klerman et al. New York: Basic Books.

Wells, K.B., J.M. Golding, and M.A. Burman. 1988. "Psychiatric Disorder in a Sample of the General Population with and without Chronic Medical Conditions." *American Journal of Psychiatry* 145: 976-88.

Wells, K.B., A. Stewart, R.D. Hays, M.A. Burman, and W. Rogers, et al. 1989. "The Functioning and Well-Being of Depressed Patients: Results from the Medical Outcomes Study." *Journal of the American Medical Association* 262: 914-9.

Wessely, S. 1996. "The Meaning of Stress." *Journal of the Royal Society of Medicine* 302: 19-92.

Wittchen, H.U. 1994. "Reliability and Validity Studies of the WHO-Composite International Diagnostic Interview (CIDI): a Critical Review." *Journal of Psychiatric Research* 28: 57-84.

Workers' Compensation Board of British Columbia (WCBBC). 1991. *Workers' Compensation Reporter* Decision 92-1516.

–. 1995. *Rehabilitation and Claims Policy Manual* Section 22.33.

–. Psychology Department. 1996. *Guidelines for Medico-Legal Assessment in Psychological Practice in the WCB Setting.*

Workers' Compensation Board of Saskatchewan (WCBS). 1996. *Policy Manual.*

Yorker, B. 1994. "Workers' Compensation Law: An Overview." *American Association of Occupational Health Nursing Journal* 42: 420-4.

Appendix A: Categories of Injury and Disease

Table A1

Major categories for classifying injuries, 1952-96

Strain	Impact	Miscellaneous
Back strain	Caught in or between	Electricity and temperature
Overexertion	Falls from one level	Explosions
Strains and sprains	Falls on the level	Harmful substances
	Strike against or step on	Rubbed and abraded
	Struck by objects	Vehicles and transport
	Slips	Miscellaneous
		Uncoded

Table A2

Major categories for classifying industrial disease and new conditions added, 1959-96

Respiratory	RSI[a]	Dermatitis	Radiation	Other
Asbestosis	Bursitis	Conjunctivitis	Cold	Chemical
Silicosis	Carpal	Dermatitis	Heat	burns
Respiratory	tunnel	Infected	Ultraviolet (UV)	Infectious
irritation	syndrome	blisters	Welding	disease
Tuberculosis	Tenosynovitis		Other radiation'	Poisoning
	Other			Miscellaneous
	inflammation			Uncoded
				Allergic
				reaction[b]
				Cancer[b]
				Stress[b]
				Vibration
				White Finger
				Disease

Note: The category of hearing loss remained unchanged in the period and therefore does not appear in the table.
a Category introduced in 1978; until 1978, stress claims were categorized as either "bursitis" or "tenosynovitis."
b Claims first awarded in 1992.

Appendix B: Gender Differences in Work Exposure and Injury

Figure B1

Women's and men's proportion of accepted time loss claims in Canada, 1982-96

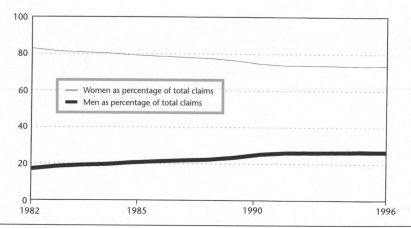

Note: These percentages exclude "unknown" and "not coded" claims.
Source: AWCBC (1999).

Figure B2

Distribution of accepted time loss claims by industrial sector in Canada, 1996

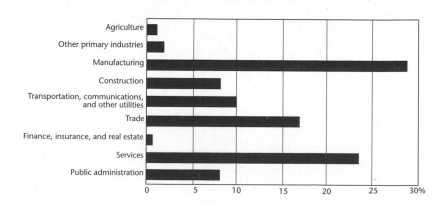

Note: These percentages exclude "unknown" and "not coded" claims.
Source: AWCBC (1999).

Figure B3

Women's proportion in employment and in accepted time loss claims by industrial sector in Canada, 1995

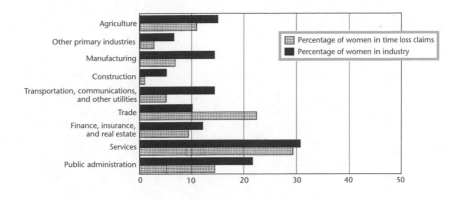

Sources: Claims data: AWCBC (1999); employment data: Statistics Canada (1995).

Figure B4

Perceived exposure to workplace health hazards by gender, 1991

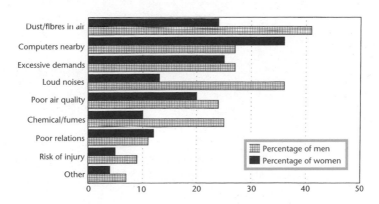

Sources: Statistics Canada, catalogue 11-612E, no. 8, reprinted in Statistics Canada (1994).

Appendix C: Bradford Hill's Criteria for Assessing Evidence of Causation

Strength of Association

By this is meant the magnitude of the relative risk (RR) that describes how much more often the disease, or other health outcome in question, occurs after the exposure of interest, as compared to its frequency without that exposure. For example, lung cancer was shown in the 1950s to occur about ten times more frequently in persons who smoke about a pack of cigarettes a day than in non-smokers. This is considered a high relative risk, indicating a strong association. Most exposures thought to play causal roles in the more common diseases of our time, such as coronary heart disease (CHD) and cancer, have much smaller relative risks, indicating associations of more moderate strength. For example, both smoking and high blood pressure carry approximately two- to threefold risks of CHD, depending on just how much one smokes or how high one's blood pressure is. Although relative risks below 2, and especially below 1.5, indicate that the risk of the outcome in question is 50 to 100 percent higher in those exposed (an RR of 1.0 indicates no association at all), they describe what epidemiologists refer to as "weak associations," and the quality of study required to estimate such small RRs accurately is much higher. (Detailed discussion of how to judge epidemiological study quality is beyond the scope of this paper. A number of standard epidemiological texts describe how the quality of the evidence can be assessed from any causation study that estimates relative risk – the reader is referred to these [Rothman 1986; MacMahon and Pugh 1970]). Thus strong associations, with RRs above 5, while not frequently found, constitute firm prima facie evidence of causation even if several of the other criteria listed below are not met. On the other hand, a weak association, while not ruling out a causal role for an exposure, requires a great deal more evidence to be adduced for causation to be established.

"Biological Gradient" (Dose-Response Relationship)

Closely related to the first criteria ("Strength of Association") is the notion that causal exposures should increase the risk of a health outcome more if they are intense, or "high-dose," than if they are "low-dose." Thus the fact that smokers of two or more packs a day are known to suffer up to twenty times as much lung cancer as non-smokers, compared to the tenfold increase in risk for smokers of a pack a day, constitutes additional evidence of causation. Note, however, that some exposures are inherently rather "all or nothing," such as having a "Type A personality," so that there is no possibility of fulfilling this criterion, and it is therefore unhelpful in assessing causation in these situations. Additionally, there may be "saturation effects" in nature, whereby additional exposure beyond a cer-tain "threshold" simply cannot elevate the risk of the adverse health outcome any further, and studies of exposures above this threshold will therefore not demonstrate such a gradient.

Consistency across Studies and Settings

Whether a given scientific literature on a specific causation question consistently shows the same strength of association, and dose-response relationship, is very important, where enough high-quality studies have been done. For many situations, however, such as that described in this volume for the causes of occupational low back pain, only a handful of high-quality studies exist, making this criterion unhelpful.

Temporality

This almost self-evident criterion refers to the logical necessity that causes must precede their effects in time. This is not in question in longitudinal cohort studies, where subjects without the outcome are followed over time to find out who succumbs to the outcome, after measures of the exposure are taken at baseline. However, epidemiologists frequently use other study designs, such as case-control, where questions about exposures may be asked of subjects after some have experienced the outcome in question. In these circumstances, it is sometimes not so straightforward to be sure that the disease has not influenced the assessment of exposure. For example, a study comparing the personality types of persons who have recently had a heart attack, due to CHD, to "controls" without CHD would obviously need to ensure that the personality type measurement instrument used (usually a questionnaire) does not give different results in the same person before and after a heart attack, a profound event in one's life with known psychological effects. Otherwise, one is studying the personality-related effects rather then causes of CHD, leading to a "chicken and egg" problem in interpreting study results.

(Biological) Plausibility

This refers to the degree to which the biological laboratory in vitro and in vivo evidence on the exposure's effects in living systems is compatible with the human health effects observed in epidemiological studies. For example, we now know that cigarette smoke contains many chemical compounds capable of carcinogenesis – the causing of cancers by cigarette smoke constituents has been observed in a wide range of lab animal models and tissue samples under controlled exposure conditions. Thus it is not surprising to basic biologists that smoking leads to a ten- to twenty-fold increase in lung cancer risk. However, it is important to note here that the epidemiological evidence of the risk elevation was obtained many years before firm laboratory evidence on the specific biological effects of the smoke components. This was partly because technical methods of demonstrating carcinogenesis in the lab lagged behind our ability to do epidemiological studies. Thus there arise situations, especially with new exposures, for example, to newly synthesized chemicals, wherein no such laboratory evidence of causal mechanisms is yet available. However, this lack of evidence is not to be interpreted as evidence against causation; it can simply be a statement of our biological ignorance at a point in time.

Coherence

The term 'coherence' refers to whether a factor is coherent with descriptive epidemiological and other knowledge. If an observed association between an exposure and a health outcome is causal, then there should be observable situations where the initial occurrence (or an increase in the frequency/intensity) of the exposure is later followed by an increased incidence of the outcome. More generally, settings in time and space without the exposure should have less of the outcome in their populations than those with the exposure, other things being equal. For example, sharp increases in lung cancer were seen in the Western world about twenty-five to thirty-five years after major increases in population smoking rates. This modern epidemic of lung cancer occurred first for men, and is now past its peak, but is still peaking for women, since they began serious smoking decades later. Note however that this association in time would have been missed by an epidemiologist looking at lung cancer time-trends in, say 1950 – simply because the lag required for lung cancers to develop after smoking is decades long. Furthermore, simple comparisons of lung cancer rates in global settings with and without much smoking are confused (epidemiologists would say "confounded") by differences in other exposures between settings, such as occupational and environmental pollutants (e.g., radon, etc.) that are known to cause lung cancer, but may be hard to measure well and thereby "control for" in the comparisons. Thus there are many reasons why existing knowledge of an exposure's and an outcome's occurrence may not obviously suggest a causal relationship between the two, even though other criteria listed here are met.

Specificity of a Given Exposure-Effect Pair

It is truly strong evidence of causation if one finds that a given exposure leads only to one specific health effect, and there are some known examples, such the occurrence of angiosarcoma of the liver after vinyl chloride exposure, and specific clinical infections after adequate exposure to particular pathogens. However, as already suggested above, most human diseases have more than one cause, and most harmful exposures have more than one sort of health effect. For example, many sorts of cancer, CHD, stroke, peripheral vascular disease, emphysema/ chronic bronchitis, to name only a few medical conditions, are now known to be at least partly caused by smoking, and yet each of these also has numerous other contributory causes, both genetic and environmental. Indeed, CHD, as explored in Chapter 12, now has well over twenty "independent risk factors" associated with its occurrence, most of which meet a number of the causal criteria listed here. Generally, only very uncommon exposures and outcomes meet this criterion, which is therefore rarely useful.

Analogy with a Known Causal Disease Process

Again, where available, the known causal occurrence of a similar health outcome in humans or animals, after exposure to the same or a similar hazard, is usually considered strong evidence of causation. There are many infectious disease examples of this, such as the similarities between various animal models of viral hepatitis and specific forms of human hepatitis. Unfortunately, good analogies are uncommon for the main health outcomes of importance in our work insurance schemes today.

Experiment

This criterion refers to availability of evidence – from well-designed and -conducted experimental studies such as randomized control trials (RCTs) – that removal of the exposure reduces the risk of the outcome in question. While undoubtedly the most powerfully convincing criterion of those listed here, this sort of evidence is often simply unethical to obtain (i.e., for exposures already strongly suspected as being harmful, even if all their specific health effects are not fully known) or else infeasible (e.g., the randomization of humans to chronic unpleasant or demanding exposures thought to possibly have very delayed health effects). Thus, while always desirable in principle, meeting this criterion is often not practicable. As a second-best and often very illuminating alternative, "quasi-experimental" analyses of "natural experiments," such as tracking the long-term health effects of the introduction of mass-smoking in whole populations, can often approximate this ideal, provided that competing alternative explanations for the resultant observations can be ruled out.

Appendix D: Fatality Benefit Comparisons

Table D1

Weekly fatality benefit parameters

Jurisdiction	Replacement rates for surviving spouse[a]						Maximum and minimum for spouse alone[b]		
	Spouse only	One child	Two children	Three children	Four children	Five or more children	Weekly minimum benefit[c]	Weekly maximum benefit	Added for child[d]
Canada									
Alberta	0.9[e]	0.9[e]	0.9[e]	0.9[e]	0.9[e]	0.9[e]	$231.98	$553.88	$0
British Columbia (age>50)	0.45	0.6375	0.75	0.75	0.75	0.75	$277.10	$802.60	$55.41
British Columbia (age<40)	—[f]	0.6375	0.75	0.75	0.75	0.75	$277.10	$802.60	$55.41
Manitoba[g]	0.9[e]	0.9[e]	0.9[e]	0.9[e]	0.9[e]	0.9[e]	$0	$503.08	$0
New Brunswick	0.8[e,h]	0.8[e,g]	0.8[e,g]	0.8[e,g]	0.8[e,g]	0.8[e,g]	$0	$503.82	n/a
Newfoundland	0.8[e]	0.8[e]	0.8[e]	0.8[e]	0.8[e]	0.8[e]	$200	$458.23	n/a
Northwest Territories	n/a	n/a	n/a	n/a	n/a	n/a	$310.96	$310.96	$70.67
Nova Scotia	0.85[e]	0.85[e]	0.85[e]	0.85[e]	0.85[e]	0.85[e]	$0	$494.35	$45.23
Ontario	0.4[e]	0.9[e]	0.9[e]	0.9[e]	0.9[e]	0.9[e]	$294.47	$691.44	n/a
Prince Edward Island	0.63	0.7	0.77	0.84	0.84	0.84	$0	$273.57	n/a
Quebec	0.495[e]	0.495[e]	0.495[e]	0.495[e]	0.495[e]	0.495[e]	$0	$339.12	$85.15
Saskatchewan	0.9[e]	0.9[e]	0.9[e]	0.9[e]	0.9[e]	0.9[e]	$258.29	$620.20	n/a
Yukon	n/a	n/a	n/a	n/a	n/a	n/a	$390.87	$390.87	$156.35

United States

Alabama	0.5	0.667	0.667	0.667	0.667	0.667	$125[j]	$456	n/a
Alaska	0.8[e]	0.8[e]	0.8[e]	0.8[e]	0.8[e]	0.8[e]	$75[j,k]	$700	n/a
Arizona	0.35	0.5	0.65	0.667	0.667	0.567	$0	$484.62[l]	n/a
Arkansas	0.35	0.5	0.65	0.667	0.667	0.667	$20	$348	n/a
California	0.667	0.667	0.667	0.667	0.667	0.667	$224	$490	n/a
Colorado	0.667	0.667	0.667	0.667	0.667	0.667	$120.88	$483.52	n/a
Connecticut	0.75[e]	0.75[e]	0.75[e]	0.75[e]	0.75[e]	0.75[e]	$20	$678	n/a
Delaware	0.667	0.7	0.75	0.8	0.8	0.8	$130.82	$392.46	n/a
District of Columbia	0.5	0.667	0.667	0.667	0.667	0.667	$188.33	$753.33[k]	n/a
Florida	0.5	0.667	0.667	0.667	0.667	0.667	$20[l]	$479	n/a
Georgia	0.667	0.667	0.667	0.667	0.667	0.667	$25[j]	$300	n/a
Hawaii	0.5	0.667	0.667	0.667	0.667	0.667	$191.20[m]	$764.80[k]	n/a
Idaho	n/a	n/a	n/a	n/a	n/a	n/a	$195.30[k]	$195.30[k]	n/a
Illinois	0.667	0.667	0.667	0.667	0.667	0.667	$287.89	$767.71	n/a
Indiana	0.667	0.667	0.667	0.667	0.667	0.667	$75[l]	$642	n/a
Iowa	0.85	0.85	0.85	0.85	0.85	0.85	$152.71[l]	$873	n/a
Kansas	0.667	0.667	0.667	0.667	0.667	0.667	$25	$338	n/a
Kentucky	0.5	0.6	0.75	0.75	0.75	0.75	$89.40	$447[k]	n/a
Louisiana	0.325	0.4625	0.65	0.65	0.65	0.65	$0	$349	n/a
Maine	0.85	0.85	0.85	0.85	0.85	0.85	$0	$441	n/a
Maryland	0.667	0.667	0.667	0.667	0.667	0.667	$25[j]	$550.33	n/a
Massachusetts	0.667	0.667	0.667	0.667	0.667	0.667	$110	$631.03	$6
Michigan	0.8[e]	0.8[e]	0.8[e]	0.8[e]	0.8[e]	0.8[e]	$297.78	$536	n/a
Minnesota	0.5	0.6	0.667	0.667	0.667	0.667	$0	$615	n/a
Mississippi	0.35	0.45	0.55	0.65	0.667	0.667	$25	$269.67	n/a
Missouri	0.667	0.667	0.667	0.667	0.667	0.667	$40	$513.01	n/a
Montana	0.667	0.667	0.667	0.667	0.667	0.667	$193.50[l]	$387	n/a

▲ *Table D1*

| | Replacement rates for surviving spouse[a] | | | | | | Maximum and minimum for spouse alone[b] | | |
Jurisdiction	Spouse only	One child	Two children	Three children	Four children	Five or more children	Weekly minimum benefit[c]	Weekly maximum benefit	Added for child[d]
Nebraska	0.667	0.75	0.75	0.75	0.75	0.75	$49[j]	$441.22	n/a
Nevada	0.667	0.667	0.667	0.667	0.667	0.667	$0	$473.69	n/a
New Hampshire	0.6	0.6	0.6	0.6	0.6	0.6	$151[j]	$756	n/a
New Jersey	0.5	0.55	0.6	0.65	0.7	0.7	$128	$480	n/a
New Mexico	0.667	0.667	0.667	0.667	0.667	0.667	$0	$363.60	n/a
New York	0.667	0.667	0.667	0.667	0.667	0.667	$45	$600	n/a
North Carolina	0.667	0.667	0.667	0.667	0.667	0.667	$30	$512	n/a
North Dakota	0.667	0.667	0.667	0.667	0.667	0.667	$105	$210	$10
Ohio	0.667	0.667	0.667	0.667	0.667	0.667	$255.50	$511	
Oklahoma	0.5	0.65	0.75	0.75	0.75	0.75	$0	$426	n/a
Oregon	n/a	n/a	n/a	n/a	n/a	n/a	$330.68	$330.68	$34.62
Pennsylvania	0.51	0.6	0.667	0.667	0.667	0.667	$254.50[k]	$509	n/a
Rhode Island	0.75[e]	0.75[e]	0.75[e]	0.75[e]	0.75[e]	0.75[e]	$20	$503	$20
South Carolina	0.667	0.667	0.667	0.667	0.667	0.667	$75j	$450.62	n/a
South Dakota	0.667	0.667	0.667	0.667	0.667	0.667	$186[j]	$371	$11.54
Tennessee	0.5	0.667	0.667	0.667	0.667	0.667	$71.78	$457.46	n/a
Texas	0.75	0.75	0.75	0.75	0.75	0.75	$74	$491	n/a
Utah	0.667	0.667	0.667	0.667	0.667	0.667	$45[k]	$379	$5
Vermont	0.667	0.717	0.767	0.767	0.767	0.767	$231	$691	n/a
Virginia	0.667	0.667	0.667	0.667	0.667	0.667	$124[j]	$496	n/a

Washington	0.6	0.62	0.64	0.66	0.68	0.7	$44.05^k	$580.75	n/a
West Virginia	0.7	0.7	0.7	0.7	0.7	0.7	$144.70	$434.09	n/a
Wisconsin	0.667	0.667	0.667	0.667	0.667	0.667	$30^l	$494	n/a
Wyoming	n/a	n/a	n/a	n/a	n/a	n/a	$286	$286	$23.08

a Replacement rates as a proportion of gross pre-injury wages unless otherwise stated. "n/a" indicates that claimants are paid a flat rate.

b Maximum and minimum benefits are expressed in each country's currency.

c Unless otherwise stated, the weekly minimum is absolute.

d Additional weekly amount per child. Unless otherwise specified, this amount is paid for each child. "n/a" indicates that the jurisdiction does not pay an allowance for children.

e Pendable earnings.

f See Table D3 for details.

g Less payments to other dependents (to a limit of $1,090).

h Compensation is reduced by surviving spouse's earnings.

i Replacement rate for spouse aged 40 years. Subtract 0.01 for each year under 40 — to a minimum of 0.20 — and add 0.01 for each year above 40 — to a maximum of 0.60.

j Actual wages are paid if below the minimum.

k Varies by number of dependent children.

l Maximum wage. Maximum benefits are equal to $484.62 multiplied by the replacement rate.

m Varies by dependant. Actual wages paid if less than the minimum, except benefit can not be less than $38 per week.

Table D2

Statutory parameters: Lump sum payments and limitations on benefit duration

Jurisdiction	Lump sum	Limits on the duration of spousal benefits[a]			Remarriage payment[b]	Limits on the duration of benefits to children[c]	
		Maximum weeks	Maximum award	Maximum age		Minor	Student
Canada							
Alberta	$1,300	520[d]	n/a	n/a	n/a	18	n/a
British Columbia[e]	$1,847[f]	n/a	n/a	n/a	n/a	18	21
Manitoba	$29,930[g]	260[h]	n/a	65[i]	n/a	18	n/a
New Brunswick	0	n/a	n/a	65[j]	52 weeks	18	22
Newfoundland	$15,000[k]	n/a	n/a	65[l]	n/a	18	25
Northwest Territories	$1,900	n/a	n/a	n/a	52 weeks	16	n/a
Nova Scotia	$15,000	n/a	n/a	65[m]	n/a	18	25
Ontario	$27,778[n]	n/a	n/a	n/a	n/a	19	None
Prince Edward Island	$10,000	n/a	n/a	65[o]	52 weeks	18	22
Quebec	$73,641[p]	156[q]	n/a	n/a	n/a	18	25
Saskatchewan	0	256	n/a	n/a	n/a	18	25
Yukon	0	n/a	n/a	n/a	n/a	19	21
United States							
Alabama	0	500	n/a	n/a	No	18	n/a
Alaska	0	n/a	n/a	n/a	104 weeks	19	n/a
Arizona	0	n/a	n/a	n/a	104 weeks	18	22
Arkansas	0	n/a	n/a	n/a	104 weeks	18	25
California	0	n/a	$135,000[r]	n/a	No	18	n/a

State							
Colorado	0	n/a	n/a	n/a	104 weeks	18	21
Connecticut	0	n/a	n/a	n/a	No	18	22
Delaware	0	n/a	n/a	n/a	104 weeks	18	25
District of Columbia	0	n/a	n/a	n/a	104 weeks	18	23
Florida	0	n/a	$100,000	n/a	26 weeks[s]	18	22
Georgia	0	400[t]	$100,000[u]	65	No	18	22
Hawaii	0	n/a	$238,617[v]	n/a	104 weeks[w]	18	22
Idaho	0	500	n/a	n/a	104 weeks	18	n/a
Illinois	0	1040	$250,000[x]	n/a	104 weeks	18	25
Indiana	0	500	$214,000	n/a	104 weeks[y]	21[z]	21
Iowa	0	n/a	n/a	n/a	104 weeks	18	25
Kansas	0	n/a	$200,000	n/a	100 weeks[aa]	18	23
Kentucky	$25,000[bb]	n/a	n/a	65[cc]	104 weeks	18	22
Louisiana	0	n/a	n/a	n/a	104 weeks	18	23
Maine	$3,000	500	n/a	n/a	$500	18	n/a
Maryland	0	n/a	n/a	n/a	104 weeks	18	23
Massachusetts	0	n/a	$157,758[dd]	n/a	No	18	—[ee]
Michigan	0	500	n/a	n/a	$500	21	n/a
Minnesota	0	520	n/a	n/a	No	18	25
Mississippi	$550	450	n/a	n/a	No	18	23
Missouri	0	n/a	n/a	n/a	104 weeks	18	22
Montana	0	500	n/a	n/a	No	18	22
Nebraska	0	n/a	n/a	n/a	104 weeks	18	25
Nevada	0	n/a	n/a	n/a	104 weeks	18	22
New Hampshire	0	n/a	n/a	n/a	No	18	25
New Jersey	0	n/a	n/a	n/a	100 weeks	18	23
New Mexico	0	700	n/a	n/a	104 weeks	18	23
New York	0	n/a	n/a	n/a	104 weeks	18	23

▲ *Table D2*

Jurisdiction	Limits on the duration of spousal benefits[a]				Remarriage payment[b]	Limits on the duration of benefits to children[c]	
	Lump sum	Maximum weeks	Maximum award	Maximum age		Minor	Student
North Carolina	0	400	n/a	n/a	No	18	n/a
North Dakota	$300[ff]	n/a	$197,000	n/a	104 weeks	18	22
Ohio	0	n/a	n/a	n/a	104 weeks	18	25
Oklahoma	$20,000[gg]	n/a	n/a	n/a	104 weeks	18	23
Oregon	0	n/a	n/a	n/a	104 weeks	18	23
Pennsylvania	0	n/a	n/a	n/a	104 weeks	18	23
Rhode Island	0	n/a	n/a	n/a	104 weeks	18	23
South Carolina	0	500	n/a	n/a	No	18	23
South Dakota	0	n/a	n/a	n/a	104 weeks	18	22
Tennessee	0	n/a	$182,984[hh]	n/a	No	18	n/a
Texas	0	n/a	n/a	n/a	No	18	25
Utah	0	n/a	n/a	n/a	52 weeks[ii]	18	n/a
Vermont	0	n/a	n/a	62[jj]	No	18	n/a
Virginia	0	500	n/a	n/a	No	18	n/a
Washington	0[kk]	n/a	n/a	n/a	104 weeks	18	23
West Virginia	0	n/a	n/a	n/a	No	18	25
Wisconsin	0	n/a	—[ll]	n/a	No	18	n/a
Wyoming	0	23[1]	n/a	n/a	No	21	n/a

a Limits apply to spousal benefits only.
b "n/a" signifies that benefits do not terminate upon remarriage. "No" signifies that there is no remarriage payment.
c Limits apply to non-disabled children only.

d Spouses without children: Working spouses or spouses who refuse to seek employment are paid a pension that is reduced by 20 percent of the initial benefit each year. Spouses who are unemployed but capable of working are entitled to up to five years of benefits while enrolled in a vocational rehabilitation program; upon termination of rehabilitation, a reducing pension is paid, which terminates after five years. Spouses with children receive benefits until the youngest child reaches age 18. At that time, the spouse is eligible for benefits identical to those paid to spouses without children. There is no limit on benefit payments to a spouse incapable of working.

e See Table D3 for further details.

f Spouse aged less than 40 years without children is entitled to an additional lump sum payment in lieu of a pension.

g Minimum lump sum payment. Spouse aged 45 receives a lump sum equal to $49,530. This amount is reduced by 2 percent for each year older or younger than age 45.

h Applies to spouses without children. For spouses with children, time limit begins to toll once the youngest child reaches age 18 or the spouse reaches age 71, whichever comes first.

i Applies to spouses aged 60 to 63. Spouses 63 and older receive benefits for two years.

j At age 65, spouse entitled to a annuity that as funded by 8 percent of all benefits paid up to age 65.

k Or twenty-six times the workers' average weekly net earnings, whichever is greater.

l Or until youngest child reaches age 18.

m Replaced by an annuity equal to the cumulative total of a 5 percent monthly reserve.

n Minimum payment. Spouse aged 40 years receives $55,555.55. This amount is reduced by $1,388.88 for every year younger than age 40 and increased by that same amount for every year older than age 40, up to a maximum of $83,333.30.

o Or until the worker would have reached age 65, whichever is greater.

p Minimum payment. Lump sum is equal to the workers' gross annual income multiplied by a factor that varies with the surviving spouse's age. This factor increases from 2 for those spouses age 20 and younger up to 3 for spouses aged between 40 and 45, and then declines to 1 for spouses aged 65 or older. The maximum benefit is $147,000.

q Limits apply to spousal benefits only. Benefits for children are paid until age 18 (22 for students). Duration limit varies from one year for spouses age 34 and less, up to three years for spouses aged 45 to 54, to two years for spouses aged 55 or over.

r Varies with the number of dependants. Where there is one or more totally dependent minor children, weekly payments continue after the maximum aggregate benefit is exhausted until the youngest child reaches age 18.

s Or balance of award, whichever is less.

t Or age 65, whichever provides greater benefits.

u Applies to spouse alone.

v 312 times maximum weekly benefit for total disability.

w Or balance of the award, whichever is less.

x Or 20 years of benefits, whichever is greater.

y Or balance of award, whichever is less.

z Lesser of 500 weeks or until age 21.

▲ *Table D2*

aa Or balance of award, whichever is less.

bb Includes cost of burial.

cc Benefits terminate when decedent employee would have qualified for Social Security benefits, which is presumed to be age 65.

dd 250 multiplied by the state average weekly wage. Applies only to spouses who are self-sufficient.

ee Qualified for exemption as a dependant under the Internal Revenue Code.

ff An additional $100 is paid for each dependent child.

gg Minimum payment. Varies with number of dependent children. Includes burial expense.

hh 400 multiplied by maximum benefit.

ii First 312 weeks of benefits, payment is equal to the remaining payments from time of remarriage to 312 weeks, limited to 312 weeks. After 312 weeks, no remarriage award.

jj Except for benefit termination due to the death of the surviving spouse, the minimum aggregate payable is $228,030. This includes a spouse who is older than 62 years.

kk Payment equal to monthly wage of decedent worker.

ll Maximum aggregate award is equal to four times the average annual earnings of the decedent worker.

Table D3

Spousal benefits in British Columbia

Claimant age	No children	One child	More than one child
		Number of dependent children	
Younger than 40	Lump sum of $36,948.28. No periodic benefits.	85 percent of compensation paid to spouse with more than one child.	Equivalent to compensation paid to worker with permanent total disability plus $240.09 per month for each child beyond two.
40 to 50	$775.79 per month plus one-eleventh of the difference between $775.79 and the amount that 50-year-old claimant would receive, for each year between 40 and 49.	85 percent of compensation paid to spouse with more than one child.	Equivalent to compensation paid to worker with permanent total disability plus $240.09 per month for each child beyond two.
50 and older	60 percent of compensation paid to spouse with more than one child, but not less than $775.79 per month.	85 percent of compensation paid to spouse with more than one child.	Equivalent to compensation paid to worker with permanent total disability plus $240.09 per month for each child beyond two.

Table D4

Expected fatal injury compensation

Jurisdiction	Expected benefits ($)	Index (%)
Canada		
Alberta	186,052	59.84
British Columbia	497,907	152.27
Manitoba	150,808	54.31
New Brunswick	269,363	97.81
Newfoundland	324,391	113.18
Nova Scotia	161,901	60.83
Ontario	901,132	267.58
Prince Edward Island	141,259	53.45
Quebec	106,585	35.72
Saskatchewan	119,472	43.62
Northwest Territories	479,976	123.69
Yukon	1,021,132	273.07
United States		
Alabama	98,219	38.99
Alaska	177,433	54.76
Arizona	127,943	48.27
Arkansas	132,045	58.91
California	113,275	35.32
Colorado	267,545	93.90
Connecticut	1,555,182	414.68
Delaware	245,293	78.78
District of Columbia	827,097	204.41
Florida	65,191	25.44
Georgia	139,761	49.72
Hawaii	157,801	57.78
Idaho	80,891	33.70
Illinois	252,005	78.58
Indiana	121,956	44.79
Iowa	233,958	94.78
Kansas	95,792	38.60
Kentucky	184,213	74.62
Louisiana	139,171	54.43
Maine	102,218	43.00
Maryland	276,588	93.31
Massachusetts	144,247	41.80
Michigan	138,381	42.12
Minnesota	133,704	46.06
Mississippi	53,025	24.19
Missouri	246,398	90.69
Montana	99,288	47.20
Nebraska	222,719	95.75

▶

◄ *Table D4*

Jurisdiction	Expected benefits ($)	Index (%)
Nevada	248,683	90.42
New Hampshire	250,598	88.47
New Jersey	259,503	71.41
New Mexico	100,083	43.12
New York	335,616	89.13
North Carolina	95,922	37.47
North Dakota	130,937	61.25
Ohio	276,420	97.04
Oklahoma	172,077	73.11
Oregon	277,775	103.16
Pennsylvania	229,612	78.81
Rhode Island	427,651	160.39
South Carolina	110,320	45.15
South Dakota	203,482	100.55
Tennessee	108,242	41.17
Texas	278,206	96.19
Utah	219,577	89.74
Vermont	499,756	204.74
Virginia	125,363	45.13
Washington	251,217	88.54
West Virginia	228,690	93.94
Wisconsin	83,638	31.91
Wyoming	81,640	35.13

Contributors

Ann-Sylvia Brooker is a doctoral candidate in Public Health Sciences at the University of Toronto. She is a Research Associate with the Institute for Work and Health.

Jinjoo Chung is a sociologist and was the first Mustard Fellow in Work Environment in Health at the Institute for Work and Health.

Judy Clarke is an anthropologist with special interest in disability issues and return to work. She is a Research Associate at the Institute for Work and Health.

Donald Cole is an occupational health physician and epidemiologist, Associate Professor in the Department of Clinical Epidemiology and Biostatistics at McMaster University, and Senior Scientist at the Institute for Work and Health.

Pierre Côté is an award-winning chiropractic researcher completing his doctorate in epidemiology at the University of Toronto. He is a Research Associate at the Institute for Work and Health.

Joan Crook is Professor of Nursing at McMaster University and has studied extensively the problems of chronic musculoskeletal pain in injured worker populations.

Mikaela Crook is an employee relations analyst with the Hamilton Health Sciences Corporation.

John Frank is a physician, epidemiologist, and Professor of Public Health Sciences at the University of Toronto, currently on leave at the School of Public Health, University of California at Berkeley. Former Research Director at the Institute for Work and Health, John is Fellow of the Population Health Program, Canadian Institute for Advanced Research and Senior Scientist at the Institute for Work and Health.

William Gnam is a psychiatrist and health economics researcher in the Department of Health Policy at Harvard University.

Morley Gunderson is the CIBC of Youth Employment at the University of Toronto and Professor at the Centre for Industrial Relations and the Department of Economics. He is a Research Associate of the Institute for Policy Analysis, the Centre for International Studies, and the Institute for Human Development, Life Course and Ageing, and a Senior Adjunct Scientist at the Institute for Work and Health.

Sheilah Hogg-Johnson is Senior biostatistician and Scientist at the Institute for Work and Health. She is Assistant Professor of Public Health Sciences at the University of Toronto.

Douglas Hyatt is an Associate Professor at the Scarborough Campus, the Faculty of Management and the Centre for Industrial Relations, and a Research Associate of the Institute for Policy Analysis at the University of Toronto. He is also a Senior Scientist at the Institute for Work and Health.

Michael Kerr is an epidemiologist and Manager of Workplace Studies and Scientist at the Institute for Work and Health. He is a lecturer in Public Health Sciences at the University of Toronto.

Andreas Maetzel is a clinical epidemiologist and Research Fellow at the Arthritis and Immune Disorder Research Centre, The Toronto Hospital.

Robert Norman is an occupational biomechanist and former Dean of Applied Health Sciences at the University of Waterloo. He is also Chair of the Workplace Safety and Insurance Board's Research Advisory Council in Ontario, a Senior Adjunct Scientist at the Institute for Work and Health, and member of the Research Advisory Committee of the Institute for Work and Health.

John O'Grady is a labour market economist and former research director of the Ontario Federation of Labour. He is an independent consultant on a range of workplace issues and he is a member of the Board of Directors of the Institute for Work and Health.

Aleck Ostry is an epidemiologist in the Department of Health Care and Epidemiology at the University of British Columbia. His interests are in occupational health issues and psychosocial factors in work-related health problems.

Victoria Pennick is a nurse and Manager of Health Services and Evaluation Research at the Institute for Work and Health.

Harry Shannon is Professor of Clinical Epidemiology and Biostatistics and Director of the Program in Occupational Health and Environmental Medicine at McMaster University, Senior Scientist responsible for Workplace Studies at the Institute for Work and Health, and a statistician by training.

Sandra Sinclair is Director of Research Programs at the Institute for Work and Health. She is a physiotherapist, occupational therapist, and epidemiologist. She is an Assistant Professor in the Department of Rehabilitation Sciences at McMaster University.

Terrence Sullivan is President of the Institute for Work and Health and Leader of the Workplace Laboratory for HEALNet, a Network of Centres of Excellence in health research. A sociologist, Terry has played senior health policy roles for the Ontario government and holds external appointments at York University and University of Toronto.

Terry Thomason is Director of the Charles T. Schmidt Research Centre and Associate Professor of Industrial Relations at University of Rhode Island. He has published widely in the area of economics of workers' compensation.

Eldon Tunks is a Professor of Psychiatry at McMaster University, Hamilton Health Sciences Corporation. He also runs an innovative chronic pain program at the Chedoke McMaster Hospital.

Richard Wells is a biomechanical engineer and Member of the Faculty of Applied Health Sciences at the University of Waterloo. He is also a Senior Adjunct Scientist at the Institute for Work and Health.

Index

JHSC = Joint health and safety
 committee
LBP = Low back pain
OHS = Occupational health and
 safety
RSI = Repetitive strain injury
WCB = Workers' Compensation Board
WMSD = Work-related musculoskeletal
 disorder
(f) = figure
(t) = table

ACOHOS (Ontario Advisory Council on
 Health and Occupational Safety), 184-5
Acupuncture, for chronic pain, 229-30
Adversarialism (employer-employee),
 164-6, 166-7
Age of workers: and increased disability,
 224; and number of claims, 61; work-
 force participation, by gender, 69-70
Agency for Health Care Policy Research
 (AHCPR), 206-7, 208, 213
Agricultural sector, employment/compen-
 sation costs, 49(t), 50, 57(t)
AHCPR. *See* Agency for Health Care Policy
 Research
Alberta. *See* Provinces and territories
Australia, impact of JHSCs, 187
Automobile industry, factors influencing
 OHS, 144-6

Bargaining, for OHS, 167, 173-4
Beaudry Report, and internal responsi-
 bility system, 164
Bradford Hill criteria, for causation, 263,
 266, 332-4
British Columbia, industrial restructuring.
 See Industrial restructuring

British Columbia, JHSCs and OHS, 153-4,
 168(t)-169(t), 170-4, 184. *See also*
 Provinces and territories
Burkett Report, view of adversarialism,
 165-6, 167
Bursitis, claims, 41, 42-3
Business cycles, and employment/claims,
 28, 29, 33-4, 34-6, 43

Cardiovascular disease. *See* Heart disease
Carpal tunnel syndrome, 42-3, 76, 78,
 117
Causation. *See* Entitlement to
 compensation
Chiropractic care, for LBP, 207-8
Chronic pain: low back pain (*see* Low
 back pain); natural course of musculoskeletal pain, 219-21; nature of,
 221-3; "perseveration" effect, 222-3;
 recovery stages, 199, 204, 205(f), 211-2;
 return to work (*see* Return to work;
 Return-to-work programs); and risk of
 mental disability, 314-5
Chronic pain, treatment: effectiveness,
 12-3, 222-3, 249; effectiveness, clinical
 indicators, 236; injection therapies,
 233-5; medication, 230-1, 235-6; multi-
 modal management, 232-3; outcome
 measurements, 236-8; patient choice,
 238-9; patient education, 231-2;
 physical therapies, 227-30; prognosis,
 function of time, 224, 226-7, 236;
 psychological factors, 226, 231;
 restricting coverage, 13, 15
Chronic stress. *See* Mental
 disabilities/stress
Claims. *See* Time loss claims
Coal mines, safety study, 150-1
Compensating wage differentials, 166,
 285, 288-9